P9-CRN-718

GMAT®

2008 Edition

Comprehensive Program

Other Kaplan Books on Business School Admissions

Get Your M.B.A. Part-Time

GMAT 800

GMAT Verbal Workbook

GMAT Math Workbook

GRE & GMAT Writing Workbook

GRE & GMAT Math Workbook

GMAT 2008 Edition: Premier Program

GMAT®

2008 Edition

Comprehensive Program

The Staff of Kaplan Test Prep and Admissions

PUBLISHING

New York

GMAT® is a registered trademark of the Graduate Management Admission Council, which is not affiliated with this book.

This publication is designed to provide accurate and authoritative information in regard to the subject matter covered. It is sold with the understanding that the publisher is not engaged in rendering legal, accounting, or other professional service. If legal advice or other expert assistance is required, the services of a competent professional should be sought.

Contributing Editors: Susan Kaplan, Chris Snyder
Editorial Director: Jennifer Farthing
Editor: Monica P. Lugo
Production Editor: Fred Urfer
Cover Designer: Carly Schnur

© 2007 Kaplan, Inc.

Published by Kaplan Publishing, a division of Kaplan, Inc.
1 Liberty Plaza, 24th Floor
New York, NY 10006

All rights reserved. The text of this publication, or any part thereof, may not be reproduced in any manner whatsoever without written permission from the publisher.

Printed in the United States of America

June 2007
10 9 8 7 6 5 4 3 2

ISBN-13: 978-1-4195-5130-7

Kaplan Publishing books are available at special quantity discounts to use for sales promotions, employee premiums, or educational purposes. Please email our Special Sales Department to order or for more information at kaplanpublishing@kaplan.com, or write to Kaplan Publishing, 1 Liberty Plaza, 24th Floor, New York, NY 10006.

Table of Contents

PART THREE: FULL-LENGTH PRACTICE TEST

PART FOUR: PRACTICE TEST ANSWERS AND EXPLANATIONS

PART FIVE: GETTING INTO BUSINESS SCHOOL

GMAT RESOURCES

How to Use the GMAT Comprehensive Program

Are you ready for a totally unique test prep experience?

The GMAT team at Kaplan understands what you are going through. First, you're facing perhaps the single most important test of your career. Second, you're struggling to balance your normal activities—social life, school, or even work—with GMAT prep. And finally, you need options about when to study, where to study, and most of all—*how to study.*

That's why you need the GMAT Comprehensive Program. It's *your* program—flexible and customizable. *You* control the variety and amount of study that best suits your skills and objectives.

We know you want lots of practice, so we added that. But since you learn best by varying study and practice methods, we also made the Program interactive, with both book and online resources.

To get you started, we put a Diagnostic Quiz and several essay prompts online so you can get used to moving between book and computer—and making the most of your GMAT Comprehensive Program components. Then, to make sure you were comfortable with taking a test on computer, we added a full-length Practice Test to your online companion.

Kaplan is the world leader in test prep. In the interactive program, the main techniques and approaches from Kaplan's classroom and tutoring programs are distilled in a clear, easy-to-grasp format. Here's the plan, step-by-step.

STEP 1: REGISTER YOUR PROGRAM ONLINE

To register, you will need to have your book in front of you. You will be prompted for the serial number on the lower left corner of the inside back cover. Go to:

kaptest.com/GMATbooksonline

The web address is case sensitive, so enter it carefully.

Registration is important because:

1. It gives you access to all the GMAT Comprehensive Program components that are not included between the covers of this book. That means your Diagnostic Quiz, essay writing practice, and links to Kaplan's best GMAT information.

2. It protects your GMAT Comprehensive Program so that your practice content remains exclusive to you.

3. It gives you access to your online syllabus and important GMAT information and developments, along with any updates and additions to this book.

Once you have registered, access your online syllabus whenever you'd like. It lists all Program elements—Diagnostic Quiz, book chapters, online Practice Test, and more!

STEP 2: TAKE THE ONLINE DIAGNOSTIC QUIZ

The Diagnostic Quiz will help you to diagnose your strengths and weaknesses—information that will enable you to focus and customize your study time.

1. This half-length GMAT includes samples of each question type, allowing you to accurately gauge what you know and what you need to practice.

2. Review the explanation for each question to better understand where you went wrong and to target your practice time to specific concepts.

KAPLAN

STEP 3: TRY AN ONLINE ESSAY PROMPT

Your online syllabus includes essay prompts similar to those you will see on Test Day.

1. Choose a prompt, and allow yourself 25 minutes to write your essay.

2. When you are finished, compare it to the model essay provided and check it against the scoring rubric.

How did you do? There are additional essay prompts to try during the course of your study so you can track your improvement.

STEP 4: IDENTIFY YOUR WEAKNESSES AND REINFORCE YOUR STRENGTHS

Check your answers to the Diagnostic Quiz, noting how many questions you got right and how many you got wrong. Look for patterns. Did you ace Reading Comprehension? Did Data Sufficiency trip you up?

1. Go back to the syllabus to help you find those concepts you need to work on, so you can chart your personalized study plan.

2. Don't limit your initial review to the questions you got wrong. Read all of the explanations—even those you got right—to reinforce key concepts and sharpen your skills. As time permits, go back to the question types that you aced so you can keep that material sharp.

STEP 5: CUSTOMIZE YOUR STUDY PLAN USING THE ONLINE SYLLABUS

Based on your performance on the Diagnostic Quiz (and the amount of time you have available to study), use the online syllabus to select the lessons, practice sets, Practice Test, and other tools that will constitute your customized study plan. Then stick to it—your plan works only if you follow it!

The best study plan will adapt to your individual needs and should:

- Start with a review of content weaknesses and include quizzes on weaker topics to boost skills and understanding

- Devote time to reinforcing content strengths through lesson reviews and practice sets

- Use full-length practice tests as milestones

1. Think about the topics on which you need to focus. Read those lessons in the book, take the practice sets, and read the answer explanations. Fill in your scores for quizzes and practice tests so you can chart your improvement.

2. Plan time to go online and practice with the essay prompts, even if writing is your best subject. Understanding the essay requirements and practicing periodically will help you deliver the right paragraphs on Test Day, when it really counts.

STEP 6: REVIEW, REINFORCE, AND BUILD SKILLS

Targeted GMAT study is a sure way to perform well on the test. You will maximize your study time by focusing on those areas you need to cover most. Download the one-page study sheet of formulas, word roots, and key strategies for study on the go.

As soon as you get comfortable with the question types and Kaplan Methods, take a full-length practice test. There are 2 full-length practice tests in this Comprehensive Program, but don't save them both for the final weeks. Test yourself periodically and chart your progress on the syllabus.

ABOUT THIS PROGRAM BOOK

In addition to the online syllabus, this book has a detailed Table of Contents. This will help you to navigate the GMAT Comprehensive Program when you are away from your computer.

Throughout the book, we have added icons to highlight selected points.

Icon Key

 READ MORE – Suggestions for additional study materials

GO ONLINE – More information and practice online

KAPLAN **EXCLUSIVE** – Methods to score higher on the GMAT

KAPLAN STRATEGY – Proven strategies to master the GMAT

The material in this book is up-to-date at the time of publication. However, GMAC may institute changes in the test or in the registration process after that time. Be sure to read carefully the official GMAT materials you receive. Any important late-breaking developments—or updates for this book—can be found in your online companion.

EXCLUSIVE: "GETTING INTO BUSINESS SCHOOL" SECTION

Your GMAT performance is very important, but a host of other parts of your application can make or break your candidacy. To give you the best odds, you'll find expert advice to lead you through the application process before and beyond the GMAT: an overview of the application process and a plan to make your application as strong as it can be.

HOW DID WE DO?

After you have completed the GMAT Comprehensive Program and have taken your GMAT, go back to the online syllabus and fill out the online survey. We want to know how you did on the exam—and how we did in helping you prepare.

Good luck!

PART ONE

The GMAT

Chapter 1: **Introduction to the GMAT**

- GMAT Administrative Changes
- GMAT Format
- GMAT Scoring
- GMAT Attitude
- GMAT Checklist

Let's start with the basics: The GMAT is, among other things, an endurance test. It is a computerized test, consisting of 150 minutes of multiple-choice testing, plus two 30-minute analytical essays. Add in the administrative details, plus two 10-minute breaks, and you can count on being in the test center for about 4 hours.

It's a grueling experience, to say the least. And if you don't approach it with confidence and rigor, you'll quickly lose your composure. That's why it's so important that you take control of the test, just as you take control of the rest of your application process to business school. Here are the basics.

GMAT ADMINISTRATIVE CHANGES

As of January 2006, ACT, Inc., and Pearson VUE took over the responsibilities of developing and delivering, respectively, the GMAT exam from the Educational Testing Service (ETS) and Thomson Biometric. According to the Graduate Management Admissions Council (GMAC), the benefits of this transfer include enhanced customer service, state-of-the-art technology, and the ability to register and access test scores online.

The content, format, and scoring of the exam did not change, and scores from tests taken before 2006 are equivalent to the scores from tests taken after the transition. However, paper-based exams are no longer offered. The test is only delivered in the computer-adaptive test (CAT) format.

In addition, test-takers can only take the GMAT once every 31 days, and no more than 5 times in a year. Also, those who score an 800 on the exam cannot test again for 5 years from that test date…not that you'd really want to with a perfect score!

More information on administrative regulations and testing procedure changes that took place in 2006 are found throughout this chapter. Be sure to visit www.kaptest.com/gmat for the latest news and updates on the test.

GMAT FORMAT

The GMAT begins with the Analytical Writing Assessment (the AWA). You will be required to compose 2 different essays, typing them each into the computer using a simple word-processing program. You are given 30 minutes for each essay.

One essay is the "Analysis of an Issue" topic. You'll have to analyze a given issue or opinion and then explain your point of view on the subject. You will be required to cite relevant reasons and/or examples drawn from your own experience, observations, or reading.

The other essay is the "Analysis of an Argument" topic, where you'll have to analyze the reasoning behind a given argument and then critique that argument. Your own views on the subject are not relevant.

After the essay sections and a 10-minute break, there are two 75-minute multiple-choice sections—one Quantitative (Math) and one Verbal. The Quantitative section contains 37 questions in two formats: Problem Solving and Data Sufficiency, which are mixed together throughout the section. The Verbal section contains 41 questions in three formats: Reading Comprehension, Sentence Correction, and Critical Reasoning, which are also mixed throughout the section. Within each section, question types appear in random order, so you never know what's coming next.

This is how the sections break down:

AWA: 60 minutes, 2 essay assignments

- Analysis of an Issue Topic (30 minutes)
- Analysis of an Argument Topic (30 minutes)

> **Quantitative (Math) Section: 75 minutes, 37 questions**
>
> - Data Sufficiency questions
> - Problem Solving questions

> **Verbal Section: 75 minutes, 41 questions**
>
> - Reading Comprehension questions
> - Sentence Correction questions
> - Critical Reasoning questions

Some important things to note:

- After you have completed the second essay, you'll get a 10-minute break. Then, between the two multiple-choice sections, you will get another break.

- So-called "experimental" questions will be scattered through the test. They will look just like the other multiple-choice questions, but won't contribute to your score.

We'll talk more about each of the question types in later chapters. For now, note the following: You'll be answering roughly 78 multiple-choice questions in 2 1/2 hours. That's less than 2 minutes per question, not counting the time it takes to read the passages. Clearly, you'll have to move fast. But you can't let yourself get careless. Taking control of the GMAT means increasing the speed of your work without sacrificing accuracy!

GMAT SCORING

Despite the change in vendors, the scoring system of the GMAT exam has not changed. The only change is that an online score-reporting system is now in place.

You'll receive four scores for the GMAT:

- Overall scaled score, from 200–800

- Quantitative scaled subscore, from 0–60

- Verbal scaled subscore, from 0–60

- AWA score, from 1–6. This score is separate from your overall score for quantitative and verbal.

KAPLAN

Because the test is graded on a preset curve, the scaled score will correspond to a certain percentile, which will also be given on your score report. A 590 overall score, for instance, corresponds to the 80th percentile, meaning that 80 percent of test takers scored at or below this level. The percentile figure is important because it allows admissions officers at business schools to quickly get a sense of where you fall in the pool of applicants.

 READ MORE

To learn more about how schools use your scores, go to **mba.com** and click on "Take the GMAT."

SOME SAMPLE PERCENTILES

Percentile	Approximate Score (Range 200–800)
99th percentile	750
95th percentile	700
90th percentile	670
80th percentile	620
75th percentile	600
50th percentile	530

Though many factors play a role in admissions decisions, the GMAT score is usually an important one. And, generally speaking, being average just won't cut it. While the median GMAT score is around 500, you need a score of at least 600 to be considered competitive by the top B-schools. According to the latest Kaplan/Newsweek careers guide, the average GMAT scores at the best business schools in the country—such as Stanford, Sloan (MIT), Kellogg (Northwestern), and Wharton (Penn)—are above 670. That translates to a percentile figure of 90 and up!

Fortunately, there are strategies that can give you an advantage on the computer-adaptive GMAT. You can learn to exploit the way that the computer-adaptive test (CAT) generates a score. We'll explain how in the next section.

Score Reports

About 20 days after your test date, your official score report will be available online. You'll receive an e-mail when yours is ready. Reports will only be mailed to candidates who request that service. The official score report includes your scores for the Analytical Writing Assessment (AWA), Verbal, and Quantitative sections, as well as your total score and percentile ranking. As of January 2006, test-takers who skip the AWA do not receive score reports.

Your report also includes the results of all the exams you've taken in the 5 years before January 2006, including cancellations. Any additional reports are US$28 each. All score-report requests are final and cannot be canceled.

GMAT ATTITUDE

In the chapters that follow, we'll cover techniques for answering the GMAT questions. But you'll also need to go into the test with a certain attitude and approach. Here are some strategies:

The Art of Using Noteboards

Since January 2006, test-takers have no longer been given scrap paper to work with during the test. Instead they are given noteboards, which are spiral bound booklets of laminated paper, and a black wet-erase pen. Here are the specs, so you know what to expect on test day:

Noteboard

- 5 sheets, 10 numbered pages

- Spiral-bound at top

- Legal-sized paper (8.5″ × 14″) in U.S., Canada, and Mexico; A4 paper is likely used elsewhere

- First page has test administration and chair operation instructions, and is not suitable for scratchwork. Pages 2–10 consist of a gridded work surface.

- Pale yellow paper in U.S., Canada, and Mexico; may be a different color elsewhere

Pen

- Staedtler, black, fine-point, wet-erase pen

You will not be given an eraser, and you are not supposed to reuse the noteboard. Each time you fill up your noteboard during the test, the administrator will replace your used noteboard with a clean one. You can also request a new pen, if necessary. The noteboards cannot be removed from the test room during or after the exam, and you must return them to the administrator when your exam is complete.

We know how important it is for test-takers to be as prepared as possible for the actual testing experience. That's why we have always recommended that students use scratch material with our GMAT preparation program, including with the practice questions and tests in this book. Since the noteboards will be your only option on test day, we suggest that you use an eraser board (or anything with a similar surface) and a non-permanent marker while doing the practice tests. Although using them won't mimic the test-day experience exactly, at least you'll get the feel of working on a comparable medium. And at the very least, using the noteboard and pen on test day won't be jarring or unfamiliar, as it might have been otherwise. In fact, students who take a Kaplan classroom course receive a noteboard that mimics the writing surface that GMAT test-takers use, as well as the same type of pen.

KAPLAN

Most test-takers have not had any difficulties using the noteboards and pens on test day. Plus, practicing with the eraser board and marker will help you feel even more comfortable and in control. However, nothing is perfect, so based on all the feedback we've received from test-takers, here are two snags that you just can't prepare for...and how to tackle them:

1. **Erasable ink you're not supposed to erase:** Say you make a mistake during a calculation, or you smudge your work with your hand. The noteboard's surface probably won't lend itself to quick-and-easy erasing (not surprisingly, since you are not meant to reuse it). And you can't write on top of the smudge or error because you'll just be left with a blob of ink that you can't read. So what should you do? Just start over. Seriously. Think of it this way—you won't waste precious time that you could have spent on the question in a futile attempt to save what is essentially a sinking ship.

   Left-handed test-takers (and some right-handed ones, too) might find that their writing styles make them particularly susceptible to smudging. If this sounds like you, practicing with the eraser board will help you work out any such problems before test day.

2. **A problematic pen:** Difficulties with pens are not common at all. The test administrators are careful to provide good writing utensils so test-takers don't have any extra anxieties. Also, keep in mind that you should recap your pen when you are not using it so that it doesn't dry out.

   However, you could get a pen that's simply dry from the get-go, or dries out quickly no matter how careful you are. Don't sweat it. The best thing to do is to just get a new pen. And should you be saddled with a pen that leaves wayward blobs of ink, don't waste time with it either. Ask the administrator for a new pen as soon as it starts to act up.

More Noteboard Strategies

Using one booklet for an *entire section*, and requesting a replacement during breaks, is perhaps the most efficient method for using the noteboards. Since you are given nine pages to write on, this technique can be used without difficulty, especially with planning and practice.

However, should you need a new noteboard (or pen) during a section, hold the used one in the air to immediately clarify the nature of the request (rather than just raising your hand).

Draw a Grid

If you find crossing off answer choices on paper tests particularly helpful (as a process of elimination), consider doing the same thing here. It's an obvious challenge, however, since you're working on computer, but it can be done with your noteboard.

Your noteboard is already gridded, so reserve 5 lines at the top of one of the pages, and label them A through E before you begin the exam. Use the grid to mark off answer choices that you have eliminated, as shown below. That way, you can tell at a glance which answer choices are still in the running. If you end up using it often, it'll be worth the 10 seconds it takes to draw it up.

A	✗	✗		✗		✗			✗		✗		
B		✗	✗	✗			✗	✗	✗	✗		✗	
C					✗			✗					✗
D	✗		✗		✗		✗		✗		✗		
E	✗	✗		✗			✗			✗			

Be Systematic

Because it's so important to get to the hard questions as early as possible, work systematically. Use your noteboard to organize your thinking. If you eliminate choices, cross them off on your noteboard using the grid just described, and guess intelligently.

Make sure to leave enough time to answer every question in the section. You'll be penalized for questions you don't reach.

Pace Yourself

Of course, the last thing you want to happen is to run out of time before you've done all the questions. Pace yourself, so that this doesn't happen. We're not saying you have to spend exactly 90 seconds, for instance, on every Critical Reasoning question. But you should have a sense of how much time to spend on each question. (We'll talk about general timing guidelines later.)

Before you go in to take the exam, you must get a sense of how long is too long to spend on a question. This is something you can do only with practice, so while working on the practice questions in this book, time yourself. (If you're using your watch, take off your watch and set it on the table in front of you.)

GO ONLINE

Use a watch or clock to get in the habit of pacing yourself. Work with the Diagnostic Quiz in your Online Companion.

Stop the Clock

The timer in the corner of the GMAT screen can work to your advantage, but if you find yourself looking at it so often that it becomes a distraction, turn it off for 10 or 15 minutes and try to refocus. Even if you lose track a bit without the clock, there is no replacement for focus and accuracy.

Don't Waste Time on Questions You Can't Do

Yes, foregoing a tough question is easier said than done. It's natural to want to plow through a test and answer every question as it appears. But that doesn't pay off here. If you dig in your heels on a tough question, refusing to move on until you've cracked it, you're letting your test macho get in the way of your test score. Like life itself, a test section is too short to waste on lost causes.

Remain Calm

It's imperative that you remain calm and composed during the test. You can't let yourself get rattled by one hard question or a Reading Comp passage to the degree that it throws off your performance on the rest of the Verbal section.

When you face a tough question, remember that you're surely not the only one finding it difficult. The test is designed to challenge everyone who takes it. Having trouble with a difficult question isn't going to ruin your score, but getting upset and letting it throw you off track will. When you understand that part of the test maker's goal is to reward those who keep their composure, you'll recognize the importance of not panicking when you run into challenging material.

GMAT CHECKLIST

Before the Test

The GMAT is taken by appointment, at your convenience, almost every day of the year. But Admissions deadlines for business schools vary. Check with the schools and make your test appointment early enough to allow your scores to be reported before the schools' application deadlines. You will be required to register online before making an appointment.

Choose a Test Center

☐ Before you register to take the exam, search for a test center that's convenient for you and determine whether that site has available seats. Each test center operates on its own schedule and can accommodate varying numbers of test takers throughout the day. To locate a test center near you, go to www.mba.com/mba/TaketheGMAT/Tools/2006TestCenterList.

Register and Schedule Your Appointment

☐ Available time slots change continuously as people register for the test. You will find out what times are available at your chosen test center when you register. You may be able to schedule an appointment within a few days of your desired test date, but popular dates (especially weekends) fill up quickly.

Identify Yourself Correctly: When scheduling your test appointment, be sure that the spelling of your name matches the name on the ID you will present at the test center. If those names do not match, you will not be permitted to take the test and your test fee will be forfeited. For more important information on identification requirements, see pages 12–13.

You may register and schedule your appointment online, by phone, by mail, or by fax:

- Online: Go to www.mba.com/mba/TaketheGMAT

- Phone: Use one of the following numbers, based on your location:
  - **The Americas:** Call toll-free (within the U.S. & Canada only): 1-800-717-GMAT (4628); or call the Customer Service line: 1-952-681-3680. The lines are operational from 7:00 a.m. to 7:00 p.m. Central Time.
  - **Asia Pacific:** +61 2 9478 5430, 9:00 a.m. to 6:00 p.m. AEST; In India: +91 (0) 120 432 4628, 9:00 a.m. to 6:00 p.m. Indian Standard Time
  - **Europe/Middle East/Africa:** +44 (0) 161 855 7219, 9:00 a.m. to 6:00 p.m. BST

- Mail or Fax (slowest options): To register by mail or fax, you must first complete the GMAT Appointment Scheduling form, available at www.mba.com/mba/TaketheGMAT/Tools/2006AppointmentScheduleForm. In order to fill out the form completely, you should also download the Test Center List, as well as the Country Code List (at www.mba.com/mba/TaketheGMAT/Tools/2006CountryCodeList).

  - If you wish to fax your form, use one of the following fax numbers, based on your location:
    - **The Americas:** 1-952-681-3681
    - **Asia Pacific:** +61-2-9901-3330
    - **Europe/Middle East/Africa:** +44-0-161-855-7301

  - If you wish to mail your form, send your completed form to the address below. Keep in mind that mail from some countries can take as long as 8 weeks to arrive in the United States:

Pearson VUE Attention: GMAT Program PO Box 581907 Minneapolis, MN 55458-1907 USA	*If using a courier service, send to:* Pearson VUE Attention: GMAT Program 5601 Green Valley Drive, Suite 220 Bloomington, MN 55437 USA

KAPLAN

The fee to take the GMAT is US$250 worldwide (at the time of printing). It is payable online by credit card, or by mailing in a check. If you have questions about GMAT registration, Visit www.mba.com/mba/TaketheGMAT, contact Customer Service at GMATCandidateServicesAmericas@pearson.com, or call 1-800-717-GMAT (4628).

Rescheduling or Canceling an Appointment

☐ **If you need to reschedule the date, time, or location of your appointment,** there is a US$50 fee (at the time of printing) as long as you reschedule at least 7 days before your original appointment. If you need to reschedule less than 7 days before your original date, you have to pay the full registration amount again.

- Rescheduling can be done online at www.mba.com/mba/TaketheGMAT, or by calling one of numbers listed on page 11, based on your location.
- You cannot reschedule an appointment by mail or fax.

☐ **If you need to cancel your appointment,** you will receive a US$80 refund (at the time of printing) as long as you cancel at least 7 days before your original appointment. If you cancel less than 7 days before your original date, you forfeit the entire registration fee. For registration fees paid by credit card, the refund amount will be credited to the card. If the fee was paid by check or money order, you will receive a check in the mail.

- Cancellations can be made online at www.mba.com/mba/TaketheGMAT, or by calling one of numbers listed on page 11, based on your location.
- You cannot cancel an appointment by mail or fax.

The Day of the Test

Entrance into the Testing Center

☐ **Checking In:** You should arrive at your testing center 30 minutes *before* the time of your scheduled appointment. A late arrival (15 minutes or more) may result in you being turned away from the test center and the forfeiture of your test fee. Plus, there are a number of security measures that you must complete before you will be allowed to take the exam.

- *Presentation of proper identification:* You will be asked to present ID—no exceptions. The following are the only acceptable forms:
  - Passport
  - Government-issued driver's license
  - Government-issued national/state/province identity card (including European ID card)
  - Military ID card

The ID must be current (not expired) and legible, and should contain all 4 of the elements listed below. If you do not have one ID with all 4 of these elements, you will need to bring a second ID (also from the list above) that shows the missing elements:

- *Your name in the Roman alphabet.* It must be *exactly the same* as what you provided when you made your appointment.
- *Your date of birth.* The date of birth must also *exactly match* the date provided when you made your appointment.
- *A recent, recognizable photograph*
- *Your signature*

If these elements do not match what the test administrator has for you on file, you will not be allowed to take the GMAT and your test fee will be forfeited.

Before you schedule your test appointment, make sure you understand all the requirements that are particular to your situation, and have acquired or renewed the ID you will use. Also, note that if your ID is found to be fraudulent or invalid after you take the exam, your scores will be canceled and your test fee forfeited.

- *Further identification:* Once your government-issue ID is approved, the administrator will take your fingerprint, signature, and photograph using digital equipment. The testing rooms are also equipped with audio and video recorders that are active during the exam. If you do complete the entire check-in process, or refuse to be recorded, you will not be allowed to take the GMAT and your test fee will be forfeited.

- *Agreements:* When you arrive at the center, you will be asked to agree to the GMAT Examination Testing Rules & Agreement. Once you are seated at a workstation, you will electronically confirm that you agree to the GMAT Nondisclosure Agreement, and the General Terms of Use statement. If you do not agree, you will not be allowed to take the GMAT and your test fee will be forfeited.

Administrative Regulations and Testing Procedures

☐ **Prohibited items:** The following items cannot be brought to the testing room.

- Notes, scratch paper, books, pamphlets, dictionaries, translators, or thesauri
- Any writing utensils, such as pens or pencils, or measuring tools such as rulers
- Electronic devices, including calculators, watch calculators, stop watches, watch alarms, personal data assistants (PDAs), cell phones, beepers, pagers, cameras, stereos, radios, or any other devices that may cause distractions, provide aid during testing, or be used to remove exam content from the testing room.

It is possible that your test center has storage space available, such as lockers, where you can leave possessions that are prohibited from the testing room. However, this may not be the case at all centers. Call your test center to inquire about storage, and plan accordingly.

KAPLAN

☐ **Disruptive behavior:** You will not be allowed to smoke, eat, or drink in the testing room. You also cannot leave the testing room without the administrator's permission. Some test centers offer the use of headphones to keep noise to a minimum; if this interests you, call your test center for details. Should you have any questions or problems during the exam, raise your hand and wait for the administrator to approach you.

☐ **Noteboards:** To make notes during the exam, you will be provided with a spiral bound booklet that is comprised essentially of 5 pieces of laminated, legal-size paper, as well as a black pen. For more information on the noteboards, refer to page 7.

☐ **Breaks:** The length of your appointment is approximately four hours. There are two breaks scheduled into the exam—one, after the second essay is complete, and another in between the two multiple-choice sections. Each time you leave and return to the testing room, you will be digitally fingerprinted. If you exceed the allotted time, the excess time will be deducted from the next section of your exam.

For more information on administrative regulations and testing procedures, visit www.mba.com/mba/TaketheGMAT/TheEssentials/TestDay

Bring the Names of 5 Business Schools You Wish to Receive Your Scores

☐ You may select up to 5 schools to receive your scores before you take the test. Your registration fee will cover that cost. Before test day, decide which schools you want to get your GMAT scores and bring that list with you. You will not be able to change the list once you have made your selection.

Download Your Online Study Sheet and Bring It to the Test Center.

☐ As you travel to the test center, review the key items on your Study Sheet. It will give you a quick refresher—and will put you in the right mindset for the exam.

Chapter 2: **CAT Test Mechanics**

- The CAT Explained
- Navigating the GMAT: Computer Basics
- Pros and Cons of the Computer-Adaptive Format
- Kaplan's CAT Strategies

KAPLAN) EXCLUSIVE

There is nothing "adaptive" about the AWA, since it is in the form of a basic essay. You will type your essay into the computer using a basic word processing program.

The GMAT is a computer-adaptive test—a CAT. A CAT is designed to assess your abilities using fewer test questions than traditional paper-based tests. There are several things that make a CAT unique:

- It is a computer-based test that you take at a special test center, by yourself, at a time you schedule. You will sit at a private workstation, though there will be other test-takers around you.

- It adapts to your performance. Each person's test is unique, and the multiple-choice questions adjust to your ability level. In other words, each test taker is given different questions. The questions are weighted according to their difficulty and other statistical properties—not according to their position in the test.

- It bases your score on two things:

  1. The number of questions you answer—whether you answer them correctly or incorrectly

  2. The level of difficulty (and other statistical characteristics) of each question

THE CAT EXPLAINED

The computer-adaptive format of the GMAT takes some getting used to—in fact, it's pretty unusual at first. Here's how it works.

There's a large pool of potential questions ranging from moderately easy to very difficult. To start, you're given a question of moderate difficulty. If you get it right, the computer will give you a harder question next. But if you get it wrong, the computer will give you an easier question next. In other words, the computer scores each question and then uses that information—along with your previous responses and the requirements of the test design— to determine which question to present next. The process continues throughout, and the computer will have an accurate assessment of your ability level.

If you keep getting questions right, the test will get harder and harder; if you slip up and make some mistakes, it will adjust and start giving you easier problems. But if you begin to answer those easier problems correctly, the test will go back to the hard ones.

Ideally, you are given enough questions to ensure that scores are not based on luck. If you get one hard question right, you might just have been lucky, but if you get 10 hard questions right, then luck has little to do with it. So the test is self-adjusting and self-correcting.

You will see only one question at a time. Because the computer must score a question before providing you a new one, you'll be required to answer every question. For this reason, too, once you have confirmed your response and moved on to the next question, you will not be able to return to a question. The computer has already scored your response and has selected a new question for you.

Random guessing can significantly lower your scores. So if you don't know the answer to a question, just eliminate whatever answer choices you can and then select the answer you think best.

Another major consequence of the GMAT format is that hard questions are worth more than easy ones. It has to be this way, because the very purpose of this adaptive format is to find out at what level you reliably get about half the questions right; that's your scoring level.

GO ONLINE

Your Diagnostic Quiz will give you an idea of what it is like to take a computer-based test.

Imagine two students—one who does 10 basic questions, half of which she gets right and half of which she gets wrong, and one who does 10 very hard questions, half of which she gets right and half of which she gets wrong. The same number of questions have been answered correctly in each case, but this does not reflect an equal ability on the part of the two students.

In fact, the student who got 5 out of 10 hard questions wrong could still get a very high score on the GMAT. But in order to get to these tough questions, she first had to get medium-difficulty questions right.

So no matter how much more comfortable you might be sticking to the basic questions, you definitely want to get to the hard questions if you can, because that means your score will be higher.

🨺 KAPLAN STRATEGY

CAT in a nutshell:

When you start a section, the computer:

- Assumes you have an average score.
- Gives you a question of medium difficulty. About half the people who take the test would get this question right, and half would get it wrong.

If you answer the question correctly:

- Your score goes up.
- You are given a slightly harder question.

If you answer the question incorrectly:

- Your score goes down.
- You are given a slightly easier question.

This continues for the rest of the test. Every time you get the question right, the computer raises your score, then gives you a slightly harder question. Every time you get a question wrong, the computer lowers your score, then gives you a slightly easier question.

NAVIGATING THE GMAT: COMPUTER BASICS

Let's preview the primary computer functions that you will use to move around on the GMAT. The screen below is typical for an adaptive test.

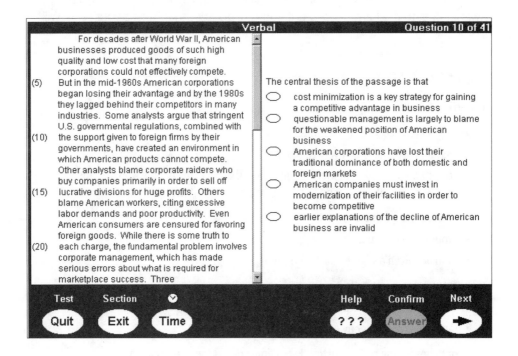

As you can see, there are empty bubbles for the answer choices—no letters (A), (B), (C), (D), (E). This is different from most multiple-choice tests.

 EXCLUSIVE

To make the questions in this book seem as test-like as possible, the 5 answer choices do not include choices (A), (B), (C), (D), or (E). You will see only blank bubbles, as you will see on the computer for the real exam. For the purposes of discussion, however, we do include letters in our answer explanations.

KAPLAN

Here's what the various buttons do.

The Time Button

Clicking on this button turns the time display at the top of the screen on and off. When you have 5 minutes left in a section, the clock flashes and the display changes from Hours/Minutes to Hours/Minutes/Seconds.

The Exit Button

This allows you to exit the section before the time is up. If you budget your time wisely you should never have to use this button—time will run out just as you are finishing the section.

The Help Button

This one leads to directions and other stuff from the tutorial. You should know all this already, and besides, the test clock won't pause just because you click on Help.

The Quit Button

Hitting this button ends the test.

The Next Button

Hit this when you want to move on to the next question. After you press Next, you must hit Confirm.

The Confirm Button

This button tells the computer you are happy with your answer and are really ready to move to the next question. You cannot proceed until you have hit this button.

The Scroll Bar

Similar to the scroll bar on a Windows-style computer display, the scroll bar is a thin, vertical column with up and down arrows at the top and bottom. Clicking on the arrows moves you up or down the page you're reading.

PROS AND CONS OF THE COMPUTER-ADAPTIVE FORMAT

There are both good and annoying things about the GMAT's computer-adaptive format. The following are a few things you should be thankful for/watch out for as you prepare to try your luck on the test.

7 Good Things about the CAT

- There's a timer at the top of the computer screen to help you pace yourself. (You can hide it if it distracts you.)

- There will be only a few other test-takers in the room with you—it won't be like taking an exam in one of those massive lecture halls with distractions everywhere.

- You get a 10-minute pause between each section. The pause is optional, but you should always use it to relax and stretch.

- You'll find the CAT much more convenient for your schedule than the pencil-and-paper exam. It's offered at hundreds of centers almost every day of the year.

- Registering to take the exam is very easy, and sometimes you can sign up just a few days before you'd like to go. However, depending upon the time of the year and the availability of testing centers in your area, you may have to register several weeks in advance for a desired test date.

- The CAT format gives you more time to spend on each question than you had on the paper-based test.

- Perhaps the CAT's best feature is that it gives you an immediate score, and your chosen schools will receive it just 10 to 15 days later.

KAPLAN)

7 Annoying Things about the CAT

- You cannot skip around. You must answer the questions one at a time in the order the computer gives them to you. There is only one question on the screen at a time.

- If you realize later that you answered a question incorrectly, you cannot go back and change your answer.

- If the person next to you is noisy or distracting, the proctor cannot move you or the person, since your test is on the computer.

- You cannot cross off an answer choice and banish it from your sight (it's on a computer screen, after all), so you have to be disciplined about not reconsidering choices you've already eliminated.

- You have to scroll through Reading Comp passages, which means you won't be able to see the whole thing on the screen at once.

- You can't write on your computer screen the way you can on the paper test (though some have tried), so you have to use noteboard they give you, which will be inconveniently located away from the computer screen.

- Lastly, many people find that computer screens tire them and cause eyestrain—especially after 4 hours.

KAPLAN'S CAT STRATEGIES

Using certain CAT-specific strategies will have a direct, positive impact on your score:

- At the start of the section, each question you get right or wrong will rapidly move the computer's estimate of your score up or down. Your goal is to get the computer's estimate of your score up to where you're handling the hard questions. That's because getting a hard question right will help your score a lot, but getting a hard question wrong will hurt your score only slightly.

In other words, it pays to spend more time on the early questions, double-checking each answer before you confirm it. Getting to the hard questions as soon as possible can only help your final score.

- As you progress through the middle part of the section, try your best not to get several questions in a row wrong, as this will sink your score on the CAT. If you know that the previous question you answered was a blind guess, spend a little extra time trying to get the next one right.

- The CAT will switch from one question type to another within a section (going from Reading Comprehension to Sentence Correction, for example) without automatically showing the directions for each new question type. Knowing the format and directions of each GMAT question type beforehand will save you a lot of time—and aggravation—during the exam.

- Because the level of difficulty of questions on the CAT is not predictable, always be on the lookout for answer-choice traps.

- Because each right or wrong answer directly affects the next question you get, the CAT does not allow you to go back to questions you've already answered. In other words, you cannot go back to double-check your work. So be sure about your answers before moving on.

KAPLAN EXCLUSIVE

Once you answer a question, it's part of your score, for better or worse. You cannot skip around within a section or do questions in the order that you like.

- The CAT does not allow you to skip questions. So if you're given a question you cannot answer, you'll have to guess. Guess intelligently and strategically by eliminating any answer choices that you know are wrong and guessing among those remaining.

- Don't get rattled if you keep seeing really tough questions. It just means you're doing very well! Keep it up!

- At the end of the section, you are penalized more heavily for not getting to a question at all than for answering it wrong. So if you have only a minute or two left and several questions remain, guess at random. Do not leave anything unanswered.

And if you're down to the very last question and have almost no time left, click on (any) response first and then think through the question. That's because you're allowed to confirm whatever answer you've picked after the time has run out—and if you need to change it, you can.

PART TWO

Strategies and Practice

Chapter 3: **Verbal Section Strategies and Practice**

- **How to Manage the Verbal Section**
- **How the Verbal Section Is Scored**

A little more than half of the multiple-choice questions on the GMAT appear in the Verbal section. You'll have 75 minutes to answer 41 Verbal questions in three formats: Reading Comprehension, Sentence Correction, and Critical Reasoning. These three types of questions are mingled throughout the Verbal section, so you never know what's coming next. Here's what you can expect to see.

Verbal Question Type	Approximate Number of Questions
Critical Reasoning	12
Reading Comprehension	13
Sentence Correction	16
Total:	**41 questions in 75 minutes**

In the next three chapters, we'll show you strategies for each of these question types. But first, let's look at some techniques for managing the whole section.

HOW TO MANAGE THE VERBAL SECTION

The best way to attack the GMAT is to exploit the way it determines your score. Since early questions are worth more than later ones, spend more time on these. If you get stuck, you will have to guess intelligently—that's because you cannot skip any questions.

KAPLAN

Spend a solid amount of time on the first 10–15 questions, double-checking your answers before you move on. These questions are crucial in determining your ability estimate, so invest the necessary time and try to answer these questions correctly.

Pace yourself, however, so that you have time to complete every question; you'll be penalized for questions you don't reach. If you don't have time to think about the answer to every question, guess if necessary during the final minutes allotted to you in order to get to the end of the section.

Guessing

Whether it is because you're running short of time or you've hit a question that totally flummoxes you, you will have to guess occasionally. But don't just guess at random. You should try to narrow down the answer choices before you guess. This will greatly improve your chances of guessing the right answer. When you guess, you should follow this plan:

1. Eliminate answer choices you know are wrong. Even if you don't know the right answer, you can often tell that some of the answer choices are wrong. For instance, on Sentence Correction questions, you can eliminate answer choices as soon as you find an error, thus reducing the number of choices to consider.

2. Avoid answer choices that make you suspicious. These are the answer choices that just "look wrong" or conform to a common wrong-answer type. For example, if an answer choice in a Reading Comprehension question mentions a term you don't remember reading, chances are it will be wrong. (The next three chapters will have more information about common wrong-answer types on the Verbal section.)

3. Choose one of the remaining answer choices.

Avoid the Penalty

If you don't complete a section, you will be penalized. In fact, every question you leave unanswered at the end of a section is twice as damaging to your score as an incorrect answer. Therefore, you must try your best to answer all the questions. If you have only a minute or two to go and have several questions remaining, guess at random to get to the end of the section.

Treat Every Question as if It Were Scored

About 25% of the questions on the test are experimental—questions that the test makers are checking out for possible use on future tests. These questions do not contribute to your score, and there is no way of identifying them. Treat every question as if it were scored.

 GO ONLINE

Complete your Diagnostic Quiz as soon as you can. That way, you can get started focusing on your weak areas. Concentrate on quality—not on the number of questions you got right.

HOW THE VERBAL SECTION IS SCORED

The Verbal section of the GMAT is quite different from the Verbal sections of most paper-and-pencil tests. The major difference that the GMAT "adapts" to your performance. Each test taker is given a different mix of questions depending on how well he is doing on the test. In other words, the questions get harder or easier depending on whether you answer them correctly or not. Your GMAT score is not directly determined by how many questions you get right, but by how hard the questions you get right are.

When you start a section, the computer:

- Assumes you have an average score (500)

- Gives you a medium-difficulty question. About half of the people who take the test will get this question right, and half will get it wrong

What happens next depends on whether you answered the question correctly.

If you answer the question correctly:

- Your score goes up

- You are given a slightly harder question

If you answer the question incorrectly:

- Your score goes down

- You are given a slightly easier question

This pattern continues for the rest of the section. Every time you get a question right, the computer raises your score, then gives you a slightly harder question. Every time you get a question wrong, the computer lowers your score, then gives you a slightly easier question. In this way, the computer tries to "home in" on your score.

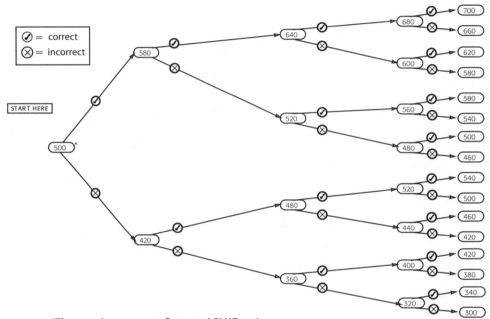

*These numbers may not reflect actual GMAT scoring.

Chapter 4: **Critical Reasoning**

- Question Format and Structure
- The 7 Basic Principles of Critical Reasoning
- Critical Reasoning Question Types
- Kaplan's 4-Step Method for Critical Reasoning

Critical Reasoning tests reasoning skills involved in making arguments, evaluating arguments, and formulating or evaluating a plan of action. These questions are based on materials from a variety of sources, though you will not need to be familiar with any subject matter beforehand.

Specifically, you are measured on your ability to reason in the areas of:

- **Argument construction**: Recognizing the basic structure of an argument, properly drawn conclusions, underlying assumptions, explanatory hypotheses, or parallels between structurally similar arguments

- **Argument evaluation**: Analyzing an argument; recognizing elements that would strengthen or weaken it; identifying reasoning errors committed in the argument; or aspects of the argument's development

- **Formulating and evaluating a plan of action**: Recognizing the relative appropriateness, effectiveness, and efficiency of different plans of action as well as factors that would strengthen or weaken a proposed plan of action

QUESTION FORMAT AND STRUCTURE

The directions for Critical Reasoning questions are short and to the point. They look like this:

Directions: Select the best of the answer choices given.

About 12 Critical Reasoning questions appear on the GMAT. Here's an example of one:

> A study of 20 overweight men revealed that each man experienced significant weight loss after adding SlimDown, an artificial food supplement, to his daily diet. For 3 months, each man consumed one SlimDown portion every morning after exercising, and then followed his normal diet for the rest of the day. Clearly, anyone who consumes one portion of SlimDown every day for at least 3 months will lose weight and will look and feel his best.
>
> Which one of the following is an assumption on which the argument depends?
>
> ○ The men in the study will gain back the weight if they discontinue the SlimDown program.
>
> ○ No other dietary supplement will have the same effect on overweight men.
>
> ○ The daily exercise regimen was not responsible for the effects noted in the study.
>
> ○ Women won't experience similar weight reductions if they adhere to the SlimDown program for 3 months.
>
> ○ Overweight men will achieve only partial weight loss if they don't remain on the SlimDown program for a full 3 months.

On the GMAT, in business school, and in your career, you'll need the ability to see and understand complex reasoning. It's not enough to sense whether an argument is strong or weak; you'll need to analyze precisely why it is so. This presumes a fundamental skill that's called on by nearly every Critical Reasoning question—the ability to isolate and identify the various components of any given argument. And that brings us to the basic principles of Critical Reasoning.

THE 7 BASIC PRINCIPLES OF CRITICAL REASONING

Here are the basic things that you need to succeed on CR questions:

1. Understand the structure of an argument.

First, you must know how arguments are structured, so that you can know how to break them down into their core components. When we use the word *argument*, we don't mean a conversation where 2 people are shouting at each other. An argument in Critical Reasoning means any piece of text where an author puts forth a set of ideas and/or a point of view, and attempts to support it.

> **KAPLAN) EXCLUSIVE**
>
> Words such as *because, since, for, as a result of*, and *due to* signal evidence. Worlds such as *consequently, hence, therefore, thus, clearly, so*, and *accordingly* signal a conclusion.

Every GMAT argument is made up of two basic parts:

- The **conclusion** (the point that the author is trying to make)
- The **evidence** (the support that the author offers for the conclusion)

Success on this section hinges on your ability to identify these parts of the argument. There is no general rule about where conclusion and evidence appear in the argument—the conclusion could be the first sentence, followed by the evidence, or it could be the last sentence, with the evidence preceding it. Consider the stimulus (in other words, a passage):

> The Brookdale Public Library will require extensive physical rehabilitation to meet the new building codes passed by the town council. For one thing, the electrical system is inadequate, causing the lights to flicker sporadically. Furthermore, there are too few emergency exits, and even those are poorly marked and sometimes locked.

Suppose that the author of this argument was allowed only one sentence to convey her meaning. Do you think she would waste her time with the following statement? Would she walk away satisfied that her main point was communicated?

> The electrical system [at the Brookdale Public Library] is inadequate, causing the lights to flicker sporadically.

Probably not. Given a single opportunity, she would have to state the first sentence to convey her real purpose:

> The Brookdale Public Library will require extensive physical rehabilitation....

That is the conclusion. If you pressed the author to state her *reasons* for making that statement, she would then cite the electrical and structural problems with the building. That is the *evidence* for her conclusion.

But does that mean that an evidence statement like, "The electrical system is inadequate" can't be a conclusion? No, we're just saying it's not the conclusion for this particular argument. Every idea, every new statement, must be evaluated in the context of the stimulus in which it appears.

For the statement above to serve as the conclusion, the stimulus would be:

> The electrical wiring at the Brookdale Public Library was installed over 40 years ago, and appears to be corroded in some places (evidence). An electrician, upon inspection of the system, found a few frayed wires as well as some blown fuses (evidence). Clearly, the electrical system at the Brookdale Public Library is inadequate (conclusion).

 READ MORE

For more detail on the anatomy of a Critical Reasoning question, turn to Kaplan's *GMAT Verbal Workbook*.

To succeed in Critical Reasoning, you have to be able to determine the precise function of every sentence in the stimulus. Use structural signals when attempting to isolate evidence and conclusion. Key words in the stimulus—such as *because, for, since*—usually indicate that *evidence* is about to follow, whereas *therefore, hence, thus,* and *consequently* usually signal a *conclusion*.

The explanations for the practice test in the back of this book discuss the structure of many of the Critical Reasoning arguments on the test, so read these carefully to shore up your understanding of this crucial aspect.

2. Preview the question.

Before you read the stimulus, look over the question. This will give you some idea about what you need to look for as you read. It gives you a jump on the question. Suppose the question with the library argument above asked the following:

> The author supports her point about the need for reha-
> bilitation at the Brookdale Library by citing which of the
> following?

If you were to preview this question stem before you read the stimulus, you would know what to look for in advance—namely, evidence, the "support" provided for the conclusion. Or if the question stem asked you to find an assumption on which the author is relying, you would know in advance that a crucial piece of the argument was missing, and you could think about that right off the bat.

Previewing the stem allows you to set the tone of your attack, and thus saves you time in the long run. As you'll soon see, this technique will come in especially handy when we discuss methods for the various question types.

3. Paraphrase the author's point.

After you read the stimulus, paraphrase the author's main argument to yourself. That is, restate the author's ideas in your own words. Frequently, the authors in Critical Reasoning say pretty simple things in complex ways. So if you mentally translate the verbiage into a simpler form, the whole thing should be more manageable.

In the library argument, for instance, you probably don't want to deal with the full complexity of the author's stated conclusion:

> The Brookdale Public Library will require extensive
> physical rehabilitation to meet the new building codes
> just passed by the town council.

Instead, you probably want to paraphrase a much simpler point:

> The library will need fixing-up to meet new codes.

Often, by the time you begin reading through the answer choices, you run the risk of losing sight of the gist of the stimulus. So restating the argument in your own words will not only help you get the author's point in the first place, it will also help you hold on to it until you've found the correct answer.

4. Judge the argument's persuasiveness.

You must read actively, not passively, on the GMAT. Active readers are always thinking critically, forming reactions as they go along. They question whether the author's argument seems valid or dubious. Especially when you are asked to find flaws in the author's reasoning, it's imperative to read with a critical eye.

How persuasive is the argument about the library, let's ask? Well, it's pretty strong, because the evidence certainly seems to indicate that certain aspects of the library's structure need repair. But without more evidence about what the new building codes are like, we can't say for sure that the conclusion of this argument is valid. So this is a strong argument but not an airtight one.

Since part of what you're called on to do here is to evaluate arguments, don't let yourself fall into the bad habits of the passive reader—reading solely for the purpose of getting through the stimulus. Those who read this way invariably find themselves having to read the stimuli twice or even three times. Then they're caught short on time. Read the stimuli right the first time—with a critical eye and an active mind.

5. Answer the question being asked.

One of the most disheartening experiences in Critical Reasoning is to understand the author's argument fully but then supply an answer to a question that wasn't asked. If you're asked for an inference supported by the argument, selecting the choice that paraphrases the author's conclusion will earn you no points. Neither will selecting a choice that looks vaguely like a summary of the author's evidence if you're asked for an assumption.

The classic example of this error occurs on "Strengthen/Weaken" questions. When you're asked to strengthen or weaken an argument, you can be sure that there will be one, two, even three answer choices that do the *opposite* of what's asked. Choosing such a wrong choice is less a matter of failing to understand the argument than of failing to remember the task at hand.

The question stem will always ask for something very specific. It's your job to follow the test makers' line of reasoning to the credited response.

Also, be on the lookout for "reversers," words such as *not* and *except*. These little words are easy to miss, but they change entirely the kind of statement you're looking for among the choices.

6. Try to "prephrase" an answer.

This principle, which is really an extension of the last one, is crucial. You must try to approach the answer choices with at least a faint idea of what the answer should look like. That is, "prephrase" the answer in your own mind before looking at the choices. This isn't to say you should ponder the question for minutes—it's still a multiple-choice test, so the right answer is on the screen. Just get in the habit of framing an answer in your head.

KAPLAN) EXCLUSIVE

For a Strengthen question, a common trap is to have a statement that nicely weakens the argument among the answer choices. Don't fall for it!

Once you have prephrased, scan the choices. Sure, the correct choice on the exam will be worded differently and will be more fleshed out than your vague idea. But if it matches your thought, you'll know it in a second. And you'll find that there's no more satisfying feeling in Critical Reasoning than prephrasing correctly, and then finding the correct answer quickly and confidently.

Continuing with the library situation, suppose you were asked:

> The author's argument depends on which of the
> following assumptions about the new building codes?

Having thought about the stimulus argument, you might immediately come up with an answer here—that the argument is based on the assumption that the new codes apply to existing buildings as well as to new buildings under construction. After all, the library will have to be rehabilitated to meet the new codes, according to the author. Clearly, the assumption is that the codes apply to existing buildings. And that's the kind of statement you would look for among the choices.

Don't be discouraged if you can't always prephrase an answer. Some questions just won't have an answer that jumps out at you. But if used correctly, prephrasing works on many questions. It will really boost your confidence and increase your speed on the section when you can come up with a glimmer of what the right answer should look like, and then have it jump right off the page at you.

7. Keep the scope of the argument in mind.

When you're at the point of selecting one of the answer choices, focus on the scope of the argument. Most of the wrong choices on this section are wrong because they are "outside the scope." In other words, the wrong answer choices contain elements that don't match the author's ideas or that go beyond the context of the stimulus.

KAPLAN EXCLUSIVE

A remarkable number of wrong answer choices in CR contain scope problems. Be wary of choices that are too extreme or that don't match the stimulus in tone or subject matter.

Some answer choices are too narrow, too broad, or have nothing to do with the author's points. Others are too extreme to match the argument's scope—they're usually signaled by such words as *all*, *always*, *never*, *none*, and so on. For arguments that are moderate in tone, correct answers are more qualified and contain such words as *usually*, *sometimes*, *probably*.

To illustrate the scope principle, let's look again at the question mentioned above:

> The author's argument depends on which of the following assumptions about the new building codes?

Let's say one of the choices read as follows:

> ⬭ The new building codes are far too stringent.

Knowing the scope of the argument would help you to eliminate this choice very quickly. You know that this argument is just a claim about what the new codes will require: that the library be rehabilitated. It's not an argument about whether the requirements of the new codes are good, or justifiable, or ridiculously strict. That kind of value judgment is outside the scope of this argument.

Recognizing scope problems is a great way to eliminate dozens of wrong answers quickly. Pay special attention to the scope issues discussed in the Practice Test explanations.

CRITICAL REASONING QUESTION TYPES

Now that you're familiar with the basic principles of Critical Reasoning, let's look at the most common types of questions. Certain question types crop up again and again on the GMAT, and it pays to understand them beforehand.

Assumption Questions

An assumption bridges the gap between an argument's evidence and conclusion. It's a piece of support that isn't explicitly stated, but that is required for the conclusion to remain valid. When a question asks you to find an author's assumption, it's asking you to find the statement without which the argument falls apart.

Denial Test

To test whether a statement is necessarily assumed by an author, we can employ the Denial Test. Here's how it works: Simply deny or negate the statement and see if the argument falls apart. If it does, that choice is a necessary assumption. If, on the other hand, the argument is unaffected, the choice is wrong. Consider this simple stimulus:

> Allyson plays volleyball for Central High School.
> Therefore, Allyson must be over 6 feet tall.

You should recognize the second sentence as the conclusion and the first sentence as the evidence for it. But is the argument complete? Obviously not. The piece that's missing—the unstated link between the evidence and conclusion—is the assumption, and you could probably prephrase this one pretty easily:

> All volleyball players for Central High School are over
> 6 feet tall.

Is this an assumption really necessary to the argument? Let's negate it using the Denial Test. What if it's not true that all volleyball players for Central High are taller than 6 feet? Can we still logically conclude that Allyson must be taller than 6 feet? No, we can't. Sure, she might be, but she also might not be. By denying the statement, then, the argument falls to pieces; it is no longer valid. And that's our conclusive proof that the statement above is a necessary assumption of this argument.

So, we can use the Denial Test to check whether a statement is an assumption, but what if we haven't a clue about what the assumption is? Is there a way to track it down? Sure enough, there is!

Compare the ideas in the evidence with those in the conclusion. If the conclusion has an idea (an important word) but the evidence does not, then you've found an assumption. A new idea cannot occur in the conclusion, so there must be an assumption about this new idea. Every idea in the conclusion needs support—that is, evidence. While it may not be quite clear what the assumption is, knowing something about it allows us to prephrase and eliminate choices.

As we've just seen, you can often prephrase the answer to an Assumption question. By previewing the question stem, you'll know what to look for. And stimuli for Assumption questions just "feel" as if they're missing something. Often, the answer will jump out at you, as it did here. but in more difficult Assumption questions, it might not be so obvious. Either way, use the Denial Test to quickly check whichever choice seems correct.

Sample Question Stems

Assumption questions are worded in some of the following ways:

- Which one of the following is assumed by the author?
- Upon which one of the following assumptions does the author rely?
- The argument depends on the assumption that…
- Which one of the following, if added to the passage, will make the conclusion logical?
- The validity of the argument depends on which one of the following?
- The argument presupposes which one of the following?

Strengthen or Weaken Questions

Determining an argument's necessary assumption, as we've just seen, is required to answer an Assumption question. But it also is required to answer another common type of question: Strengthen or Weaken the Argument.

One way to weaken an argument is to break down a central piece of evidence. Another way is to attack the validity of any assumptions the author has made. The answer to many Weaken the Argument questions is the one that reveals an author's assumption to be unreasonable; conversely, the answer to many Strengthen the Argument questions provides additional support by affirming the truth of an assumption or by presenting more persuasive evidence.

Let's use the same stimulus as before but in the context of these other question types:

> Allyson plays volleyball for Central High School.
> Therefore, Allyson must be over 6 feet tall.

Remember the assumption holding this argument together? It was that all volleyball players for Central High are over 6 feet tall. That's the assumption that makes or breaks the argument. So, if you're asked to weaken the argument, you'd want to attack that assumption:

> Which one of the following, if true, would most weaken
> the argument?

Answer: Not all volleyball players at Central High School are over 6 feet tall.

We've called into doubt the author's basic assumption, thus damaging the argument. But what about strengthening the argument? Again, the key is the necessary assumption:

> Which one of the following, if true, would most
> strengthen the argument?

Answer: All volleyball players at Central High School are over 6 feet tall.

Here, by confirming the author's assumption, we've in effect bolstered the argument.

 **KAPLAN STRATEGY**

For a Strengthen or Weaken question, keep the following in mind:

- *Weakening* an argument is not the same as disproving a conclusion—and *strengthening* is not the same as proving. A weakener tips the scale toward *doubting* the conclusion, while a strengthener tips the scale toward *believing in the validity* of the conclusion.

- The wording will always take the form of, "Which one of the following, if true, would most [weaken or strengthen] the argument?" The "if true" part means that you have to accept the validity of the choice right off the bat, no matter how unlikely it may sound.

- Wrong answer choices in these questions often have the opposite of the desired effect. So if you're asked to strengthen a stimulus argument, a wrong choice will likely contain information that actually weakens the argument. And when asked to weaken a stimulus, one answer choice is sure to strengthen the argument. Pay attention to what the question stem is asking.

 KAPLAN

Sample Stems

The stems associated with these two question types are usually self-explanatory. Here's a list of what you can expect to see on Test Day:

Weaken:

- Which one of the following, if true, would most weaken the argument above?
- Which one of the following, if true, would most seriously damage the argument above?
- Which one of the following, if true, casts the most doubt on the argument above?
- Which one of the following, if true, is the most serious criticism of the argument above?

Strengthen:

- Which one of the following, if true, would most strengthen the argument?
- Which one of the following, if true, would provide the most support for the conclusion in the argument above?
- The argument above would be more persuasive if which one of the following were found to be true?

It's also common that the question stem explicitly refers to part of the argument. You might, for example, see the following:

> Which of the following, if true, casts the most doubt on the author's conclusion that the Brookdale Public Library does not meet the requirements of the new building code?

This example illustrates another advantage of Basic Principle 2: Reading the question stem first. Here we would be told outright what the author's conclusion is, making the reading of the stimulus much easier to manage.

Inference Questions

The second most common question type in Critical Reasoning is the Inference question. The process of inferring is a matter of considering one or more statements as evidence and then drawing a conclusion from them.

Sometimes the inference is very close to the author's overall main point. Other times, it deals with a less central point. In Critical Reasoning, the difference between an inference and an assumption is that the conclusion's validity doesn't logically depend on an inference, as it does on a necessary assumption. A valid inference is merely something that must be true if the statements in the passage are true; it's an extension of the argument rather than a necessary part of it.

Let's examine a somewhat expanded version of the volleyball team argument:

> Allyson plays volleyball for Central High School, despite the team's rule against participation by non-students. Therefore, Allyson must be over 6 feet tall.

Inference: Allyson is not a student at Central High School.

Clearly, if Allyson plays volleyball despite the team's rule against participation by non-students, she must not be a student. Otherwise, she wouldn't be playing despite the rule; she'd be playing in accordance with the rule. But note that this inference is not an essential assumption of the argument because the conclusion about Allyson's height doesn't depend on it.

So be careful: Unlike an assumption, an inference need not have anything to do with the author's conclusion. It may simply be a piece of information derived from one or more pieces of evidence.

Fortunately, the Denial Test works for inferences as well as for assumptions: A valid inference always makes more sense than its opposite. If you deny or negate an answer choice, and the denial has little or no effect on the argument, then chances are that choice cannot be inferred from the passage.

Sample Stems

Inference questions probably have the most varied wording of all the Critical Reasoning question stems. Some question stems denote inference fairly obviously. Others are more subtle, and still others may even look like other question types entirely. Here's a quick rundown of the various forms that Inference questions are likely to take on your test:

- Which one of the following is inferable from the argument above?

- Which one of the following is implied by the argument above?

- The author suggests that . . .

- If all the statements above are true, which one of the following must also be true on the basis of them?

GO ONLINE

Revisit the questions in your Diagnostic Quiz. This time through, prephrase an answer for each one and see if that makes the difference in helping you answer them correctly.

- The author of the passage would most likely agree with which one of the following?

- The passage provides the most support for which of the following?

- Which one of the following is probably the conclusion toward which the author is moving?

- Which of the following, if true, would best explain . . .

KAPLAN'S 4-STEP METHOD FOR CRITICAL REASONING

Now it's time to learn how to orchestrate all of this background information into a strategy for attacking Critical Reasoning questions. We've developed a method that you can use to attack each and every CR question.

Step 1: Preview the question stem.

As we mentioned in the discussion of basic principles, previewing the stem is a great way to focus your reading of the stimulus, so that you know exactly what you're looking for.

Step 2: Read the stimulus.

With the question stem in mind, read the stimulus, paraphrasing as you go. Remember to read actively and critically, pinpointing evidence and conclusion. Also get a sense for how strong or weak the argument is.

Step 3: Try to prephrase an answer.

Sometimes, if you've read the stimulus critically enough, you'll know the answer without even looking at the choices. Other times, you'll have only a general idea of what the answer will say. Either way, it will be much easier to find the answer if you have a sense of what you're looking for among the choices.

Step 4: Choose an answer.

If you were able to prephrase an answer, skim the choices for something that sounds like what you have in mind. Take this idea to the choices, aggressively. When you find one that mirrors your idea, treat the others with disdain. If you couldn't think of anything, read and evaluate each choice, throwing out the ones that are outside the scope of the argument. After settling on an answer, you may wish to briefly double-check the question stem to make sure that you're indeed answering the question that was asked.

Now let's apply the Kaplan method on the Critical Reasoning item we saw earlier:

> A study of 20 overweight men revealed that each man experienced significant weight loss after adding SlimDown, an artificial food supplement, to his daily diet. For 3 months, each man consumed one SlimDown portion every morning after exercising, and then followed his normal diet for the rest of the day. Clearly, anyone who consumes one portion of SlimDown every day for at least 3 months will lose weight and will look and feel his best.
>
> Which one of the following is an assumption on which the argument depends?
>
> ◯ The men in the study will gain back the weight if they discontinue the SlimDown program.
>
> ◯ No other dietary supplement will have the same effect on overweight men.
>
> ◯ The daily exercise regimen was not responsible for the effects noted in the study.
>
> ◯ Women won't experience similar weight reductions if they adhere to the SlimDown program for 3 months.
>
> ◯ Overweight men will achieve only partial weight loss if they don't remain on the SlimDown program for a full 3 months.

Step 1: Preview the question stem.

We see, quite clearly, that we're dealing with an Assumption question. So we can immediately adopt an "assumption mindset," which means that before even reading the stimulus, we know that the conclusion will be lacking an important piece of supporting evidence. We now turn to the stimulus, already on the lookout for this missing link.

Step 2: Read the stimulus.

Sentence 1 introduces a study of 20 men using a food supplement product, resulting in weight loss for all 20. Sentence 2 describes how they used it: once a day, for 3 months, after morning exercise. So far so good; it feels as if we're building up to something. The key word *clearly* usually indicates that some sort of conclusion follows, and in fact it does: Sentence 3 says that anyone who has one portion of the product daily for 3 months will lose weight, too.

KAPLAN

You must read critically! The conclusion doesn't say that anyone who follows the same routine as the 20 men will have the same results; it says that anyone who *simply consumes the product* will have the same results. You should have begun to sense the inevitable lack of crucial information at this point. The evidence in sentence 2 describes a routine that includes taking the supplement after daily exercise, whereas the conclusion focuses primarily on the supplement and entirely ignores the part about the exercise. The conclusion, therefore, doesn't stem logically from the evidence in the first two sentences. This blends seamlessly into Step 3.

Step 3: Prephrase an answer.

As expected, it's beginning to look like the argument has a serious shortcoming. Of course, we expected this because we previewed the question stem before reading the stimulus.

In simplistic terms, the argument proceeds like so: "A bunch of guys did A and B for 3 months and had X result. If anyone does A for 3 months, that person will experience X result, too." Sound fishy? You bet. The author must be assuming that A (the product), not B (exercise), must be the cause that leads to the result. If not (here is the Denial Test), the conclusion makes no sense.

So, you might prephrase the answer like this: "Something about the exercise thing needs to be cleared up." That's it. Did you think your prephrasing had to be something fancy and glamorous? Well, it doesn't. So, with our vague idea of a possible assumption, we can turn to Step 4.

Step 4: Choose an answer.

Because we were able to prephrase something, it's best to skim the choices looking for it. And, lo and behold, there's our idea, stated in choice (C). (C) clears up the exercise issue. Yes, this author must assume (C) to make the conclusion that eating SlimDown alone will cause people to lose weight.

At this point, if you're stuck for time, pick (C) and move on. If you have more time, check the remaining choices quickly, to double-check that none of them fits the bill. Be ready to dismiss the other choices unless they make a strong case for themselves. Since the difficulty in Critical Reasoning is often in the choices (rather than the stimulus), you can't let them make you indecisive.

Other Types of Questions

Once you grasp the structure of the argument and have located the author's central assumption, you should be able to answer any question the test makers throw at you. This one takes the form of an Assumption question, but it could just as easily be phrased as a Weaken the Argument question:

> Which one of the following, if true, casts the most doubt
> on the argument above?

Answer: Daily exercise contributed significantly to the weight loss experienced by the men in the study.

SUMMARY

The basic principles of Critical Reasoning are:

- Understand the structure of an argument.
- Preview the question.
- Paraphrase the author's point.
- Judge the argument's persuasiveness.
- Make sure you answer the question being asked.
- Try to "prephrase" an answer.
- Keep the scope of the argument in mind.

The most common question types are:

- Assumption questions
- Strengthen or Weaken questions
- Inference questions

Kaplan's 4-Step Method for Critical Reasoning is:

Step 1: Preview the question stem.

Step 2: Read the stimulus.

Step 3: Try to prephrase an answer.

Step 4: Choose an answer.

PRACTICE QUIZ

Directions: Select the best answer for each question.

1. In Los Angeles, a political candidate who buys saturation radio advertising will get maximum name recognition.

    The statement above logically conveys which of the following?

    ○ Radio advertising is the most important factor in political campaigns in Los Angeles.

    ○ Maximum name recognition in Los Angeles will help a candidate to win a higher percentage of votes cast in the city.

    ○ Saturation radio advertising reaches every demographically distinct sector of the voting population in Los Angeles.

    ○ For maximum name recognition a candidate need not spend on media channels other than radio advertising.

    ○ A candidate's record of achievement in the Los Angeles area will do little to affect his or her name recognition there.

2. In recent years, attacks by Dobermans on small children have risen dramatically. Last year saw 35 such attacks in the continental United States alone, an increase of almost 21% over the previous year's total. Clearly, then, it is unsafe to keep dogs as pets if one has small children in the house.

    The argument above depends upon which of the following assumptions?

    ○ No reasonable justification for these attacks by Dobermans on small children has been discovered.

    ○ Other household pets, such as cats, don't display the same violent tendencies that dogs do.

    ○ The number of attacks by Dobermans on small children will continue to rise in the coming years.

    ○ A large percentage of the attacks by Dobermans on small children could have been prevented by proper training.

    ○ The behavior toward small children exhibited by Dobermans is representative of dogs in general.

3. An investigation must be launched into the operations of the private group that is training recruits to fight against the Balaland Republic. The U.S. Neutrality Act plainly forbids U.S. citizens from engaging in military campaigns against any nation with which we are not at war. Since no war has been declared between the United States and the Balaland Republic, we should bring charges against these fanatics, who are in open defiance of the law.

Which of the following, if true, would most weaken the argument above?

○ The Balaland Republic is currently engaged in a bloody and escalating civil war.

○ Diplomatic relations between the United States and the Balaland Republic were severed last year.

○ The recruits are being trained to fight only in the event the United States goes to war against the Balaland Republic.

○ The training of recruits is funded not by U.S. citizens, but rather by a consortium of individuals from abroad.

○ Charges cannot be brought against the private group that is training the recruits unless an investigation is first launched.

4. Critics of strict "promotional gates" at the grade school level point to a recent study comparing students forced to repeat a grade with those promoted despite failing scores on an unscheduled, experimental competency test. Since there was no significant difference between the two groups' scores on a second test administered after completion of the next higher grade level, these critics argue that the retention policy has failed in its expressed purpose of improving students' basic skills.

Which of the following best expresses the argument made by critics of promotional gates?

○ Anxiety over performance on standardized tests often hinders a student's ability to master challenging new material.

○ A student's true intellectual development cannot be gauged by his score on a standardized competency test.

○ The psychological damage a child suffers by repeating a grade outweighs the potential intellectual benefits of a second chance at learning.

○ Strict requirements for promotion do not lead to harder work and greater mastery of fundamentals among students fearful of being held back.

○ Socioeconomic factors as well as test scores influenced whether a given student in the study was promoted or forced to repeat a grade.

5. Statistics show that more than half of the nation's murder victims knew their assailants; in fact, 24% last year were killed by relatives. Nor was death always completely unexpected. In one study, about half the murder victims in a particular city had called for police protection at least 5 times during the 24 months before they were murdered. Nonetheless, most people are more likely to fear being killed by a stranger in an unfamiliar situation than by a friend or relative at home.

Which of the following, if true, best explains the reaction of most people to the likelihood of being murdered?

○ Statistics are likely to be discounted no matter what the source, if their implication seems to run counter to common sense.

○ In the face of such upsetting problems as murder and assault, most people are more likely to react emotionally than rationally.

○ A study taken in only one city is not likely to have an effect on attitudes until similar studies have been undertaken at the national level and have yielded similar results.

○ Most people do not consider themselves to be in the high-risk groups in which murder occurs frequently between relations, but do see themselves as at least minimally susceptible to random violence.

○ People who seek police protection from relatives and friends are often unwilling to press charges when the emotions of the moment have cooled.

6. The extent to which a society is really free can be gauged by its attitude toward artistic expression. Freedom of expression can easily be violated in even the most outwardly democratic of societies. When a government arts council withholds funding from a dance performance that its members deem "obscene," the voices of a few bureaucrats have in fact censored the work of the choreographer, thereby committing the real obscenity of repression.

Which of the following, if true, would most seriously weaken the argument above?

○ Members of government arts councils are screened to ensure that their beliefs reflect those of the majority.

○ The term *obscenity* has several different definitions that should not be used interchangeably for rhetorical effect.

○ Failing to provide financial support for a performance is not the same as actively preventing or inhibiting it.

○ The council's decision could be reversed if the performance were altered to conform to public standards of appropriateness.

○ The definition of obscenity is something on which most members of a society can agree.

KAPLAN

7. The local high school students have been clamoring for the freedom to design their own curricula. Allowing this would be as disastrous as allowing 3-year-olds to choose their own diets. These students have neither the maturity nor the experience to equal that of the professional educators now doing the job.

   Which of the following statements, if true, would most strengthen the above argument?

   ○ High school students have less formal education than those who currently design the curricula.

   ○ 3-year-olds do not, if left to their own devices, choose healthful diets.

   ○ The local high school students are less intelligent than the average teenager.

   ○ Individualized curricula are more beneficial to high school students than are the standard curricula, which are rigid and unresponsive to their particular strengths and weaknesses.

   ○ The ability to design good curricula develops only after years of familiarity with educational life.

8. The rate of violent crime in this state is up 30% from last year. The fault lies entirely in our court system: Recently our judges' sentences have been so lenient that criminals can now do almost anything without fear of a long prison term.

   The argument above would be weakened if it were true that

   ○ 85% of the other states in the nation have lower crime rates than does this state

   ○ white-collar crime in this state has also increased by over 25% in the last year

   ○ 35% of the police in this state have been laid off in the last year due to budget cuts

   ○ polls show that 65% of the population in this state oppose capital punishment

   ○ the state has hired 25 new judges in the last year to compensate for deaths and retirements

9. The education offered by junior colleges just after World War II had a tremendous practical effect on family-run businesses throughout the country. After learning new methods of marketing, finance, and accounting, the sons and daughters of merchants returned home, often to increase significantly the size of the family's enterprise or to maximize profits in other ways.

   Which of the following statements is best supported by the information above?

   ○ The junior colleges principally emphasized methods of increasing the size of small businesses.

   ○ The business methods taught in the junior colleges were already widespread before World War II.

   ○ The business curricula at junior colleges did not include theoretical principles of management.

   ○ Without the influence of junior colleges, many family-run businesses would have been abandoned as unprofitable.

   ○ Business methods in many postwar family-run businesses changed significantly as a result of the junior colleges.

10. Techniques to increase productivity in the performance of discrete tasks, by requiring less human labor in each step of the production process, are widely utilized. Consultants on productivity enhancement point out, however, that although these techniques achieve their specific goal, they are not without drawbacks. They often instill enough resentment in the workforce eventually to lead to a slowdown in the production process as a whole.

    Which of the following can be reasonably inferred from the statements above?

    ○ Productivity enhancement techniques do not attain their intended purpose and should not be employed in the workplace.

    ○ The fact that productivity enhancement techniques are so widely employed has led to a decline in the ability of American businesses to compete abroad.

    ○ If productivity enhancement consultants continue to utilize these techniques, complete work stoppages will eventually result.

    ○ Ironically, an increase in the productivity of discrete tasks may result in a decrease in the productivity of the whole production process.

    ○ Production managers are dissatisfied with the efforts that productivity enhancement consultants have made to increase productivity.

11. Time and time again, it has been shown that students who attend colleges with low faculty/student ratios get the most well-rounded education. As a result, when my children are ready for college, I'll be sure they attend a school with a very small student population.

    Which of the following, if true, identifies the greatest flaw in the reasoning above?

    ○ A low faculty/student ratio is the effect of a well-rounded education, not its source.

    ○ Intelligence should be considered the result of childhood environment, not advanced education.

    ○ A very small student population does not, by itself, ensure a low faculty/student ratio.

    ○ Parental desires and preferences rarely determine a child's choice of a college or university.

    ○ Students must take advantage of the low faculty/student ratio by intentionally choosing small classes.

12. The increase in the number of newspaper articles exposed as fabrications serves to bolster the contention that publishers are more interested in boosting circulation than in printing the truth. Even minor publications have staffs to check such obvious fraud.

    The argument above assumes that

    ○ newspaper stories exposed as fabrications are a recent phenomenon

    ○ everything a newspaper prints must be factually verifiable

    ○ fact checking is more comprehensive for minor publications than for major ones

    ○ only recently have newspapers admitted to publishing intentionally fraudulent stories

    ○ the publishers of newspapers are the people who decide what to print in their newspapers

13. Our architecture schools must be doing something wrong. Almost monthly we hear of domes and walkways collapsing in public places, causing great harm to human life. In their pursuit of some dubious aesthetic, architects design buildings that sway, crumble, and even shed windows into our cities' streets. This kind of incompetence will disappear only when the curricula of our architecture schools devote less time to so-called artistic considerations and more time to the basics of good design.

    Which of the following, if true, would most seriously weaken the argument above?

    ⬭ All architecture students are given training in basic physics and mechanics.

    ⬭ Most of the problems with modern buildings stem from poor construction rather than poor design.

    ⬭ Less than 50% of the curriculum at most architecture schools is devoted to aesthetics.

    ⬭ Most buildings manage to stay in place well past their projected life expectancies.

    ⬭ Architects study as long and as intensively as most other professionals.

14. World War II had a profound effect on the growth of nascent businesses. The Acme Packaging Company netted only $10,000 in the year before the war. By 1948 it was earning almost 10 times that figure.

    The argument above depends upon which of the following assumptions?

    ⬭ Acme's growth rate is representative of other nascent businesses.

    ⬭ An annual profit of $10,000 is not especially high.

    ⬭ Wars inevitably stimulate a nation's economy.

    ⬭ Rapid growth for nascent businesses is especially desirable.

    ⬭ Acme is not characterized by responsible, farsighted managers.

15. This editorial cannot be a good argument because it is barely literate. Run-on sentences, slang, and perfectly dreadful grammar appear regularly throughout. Anything that poorly written cannot be making very much sense.

    Which of the following identifies an assumption in the argument above?

    ◯ This editorial was written by someone other than the usual editor.

    ◯ Generally speaking, very few editorials are poor in style or grammar.

    ◯ The language of an argument is indicative of its validity.

    ◯ Generally speaking, the majority of editorials are poor in style and grammar.

    ◯ The author of the editorial purposely uses poor grammar to disguise what he knows is a bad argument.

16. All German philosophers, except for Marx, are idealists.

    From which of the following can the statement above be most properly inferred?

    ◯ Except for Marx, if someone is an idealist philosopher, then he or she is German.

    ◯ Marx is the only non-German philosopher who is an idealist.

    ◯ If a German is an idealist, then he or she is a philosopher, as long as he or she is not Marx.

    ◯ Marx is not an idealist German philosopher.

    ◯ Aside from the philosopher Marx, if someone is a German philosopher, then he or she is an idealist.

17. Electrical engineers have developed an energy-efficient type of light bulb that can replace the traditional incandescent bulb. The new bulb, known as the electronic lamp, operates by using a high-frequency radio signal rather than the filament featured in incandescent bulbs. Although the electronic lamp currently costs 20 times as much as its traditional counterpart, its use will prove more cost effective in the long run. While a 100-watt incandescent bulb lasts 6 months if burned for 4 hours daily, a 25-watt electronic lamp used for the same amount of time each day lasts up to 14 years.

    The argument above assumes that

    ○ the typical household use of a light bulb is approximately 4 hours a day

    ○ aside from its greater efficiency, the electronic lamp resembles the incandescent light bulb in most aspects

    ○ the type of light cast by the electronic lamp is different from that cast by an incandescent bulb

    ○ the price of electronic lamps will decrease as they are produced in increasingly greater quantities

    ○ a 100-watt incandescent light bulb does not provide significantly more light than a 25-watt electronic lamp

18. In interviews with jurors inquiring how they arrived at their verdicts, researchers found that 40% of the references jurors made were to factors that had not been included in courtroom testimony. To improve the jury system, the researchers suggested that judges give instructions to the jury at the beginning of a trial rather than at the end. They argued that this would permit jurors to concentrate on the most relevant evidence rather than filling in gaps with their own assumptions, which have little to do with the legality of a case.

    The answer to which of the following questions is LEAST directly relevant to evaluating the researchers' suggestion above?

    ○ Is it possible for a judge to instruct a jury at the end of a trial in such a way that jurors will disregard any irrelevant factors they had been using to weigh the evidence?

    ○ Will a jury that hears a judge's instructions at the beginning of a trial be able to weigh the evidence accordingly once that evidence has actually been presented?

    ○ Will having judges give instructions at the beginning of a trial rather than at the end significantly alter the customary procedures employed by the judicial system?

    ○ When jurors are queried as to how they arrived at their verdicts, does their interpretation of their decision-making process include many references to factors that were not, in fact, influential?

    ○ If jurors hear the judge's instructions at the beginning of a trial, what percentage of the factors that influence their decisions will be matters that were not presented in the evidence?

KAPLAN

19. Privatization of the large state enterprises that comprise the industrial sector in Russia is proceeding slowly, due to competing claims of ownership by various groups. Continued government subsidization of these enterprises creates large deficits that drive up the inflation rate and cause the ruble's value to decline. It is therefore unlikely that the government will make the ruble freely convertible to Western currencies until the question of ownership of state enterprises has been resolved.

    If the author's prediction concerning the ruble is accurate, which of the following conclusions can most reliably be drawn?

    ○ The industrial sector accounts for at least 50% of Russia's economic activity.

    ○ Making the Russian ruble freely convertible to Western currencies will cause the ruble's value to decline.

    ○ The Russian government can indefinitely withstand the expense of subsidiary state enterprises.

    ○ The Russian government is among the groups claiming ownership of certain state enterprises.

    ○ The Russian government is under pressure from the West to make the ruble freely convertible to Western currencies.

20. Attempts to blame the mayor's policies for the growing inequality of wages are misguided. The sharp growth in the gap in earnings between college and high school graduates in this city during the past decade resulted from overall technological trends that favored the skills of more educated workers. Nor can the mayor's response to this problem be criticized, for it would hardly be reasonable to expect him to attempt to slow the forces of technology.

    Which of the following, if true, casts the most serious doubt on the conclusion drawn in the last sentence above?

    ○ The mayor could have initiated policies that would have made it easier for less-educated workers to receive the education necessary for better-paying jobs.

    ○ Rather than cutting the education budget, the mayor could have increased the amount of staff and funding devoted to locating employment for graduating high school seniors.

    ○ The mayor could have attempted to generate more demand for products from industries that paid high blue-collar wages.

    ○ Instead of reducing the tax rate on the wealthiest earners, the mayor could have ensured that they shouldered a greater share of the total tax burden.

    ○ The mayor could have attempted to protect the earnings of city workers by instigating policies designed to reduce competition from foreign industries.

21. In a survey of freshmen at University X, two-thirds claimed never to have plagiarized while in high school. However, the survey may overstate the proportion of freshmen at University X who did not plagiarize in high school because _____.

    Which of the following best completes the passage above?

    ○ some people who do not attend University X probably plagiarized in high school.

    ○ some people who plagiarized in high school may not do so in college.

    ○ some people who claimed to have plagiarized once may have done so many times.

    ○ at University Z, one half of the freshmen admitted to having plagiarized in high school.

    ○ some freshmen who did plagiarize in high school might have claimed on the survey that they did not do so.

22. Smith Products fabricates machine tools that are essentially identical to those produced by Jackson Manufacturing. For both companies, raw materials represent about two-thirds of the cost of manufacturing the machine tools. To gain an edge over Jackson Manufacturing, Smith Products should purchase its raw materials from a new supplier advertising much lower prices.

    Which of the following, if true, would most weaken the argument above?

    ○ Smith Products spends more on employee wages than Jackson Manufacturing does.

    ○ Smith's current supplier provides raw materials of exceedingly high quality.

    ○ The market for machine tools has been declining for several years.

    ○ The new supplier's materials are of low quality and would reduce the lifespan of Smith machine tools by half, causing sales to decline.

    ○ The plant manager for Smith Products is planning to increase the plant's efficiency.

23. According to a recent study, a diet that is free of meat and dairy products greatly reduces the risk of suffering a heart attack. The study cites the fact that only 10% of those who consume such a diet suffer a heart attack at some point in their lives.

    Which of the following would most seriously weaken the argument above?

    ◯ Diets free of meat and dairy are low in calcium, which can lead to bone density decreases.

    ◯ Those who consume only dairy but not meat are twice as likely to suffer a heart attack as those who consume neither meat nor dairy.

    ◯ Some people who consume neither dairy nor meat suffer 2 or more heart attacks over the course of a lifetime.

    ◯ Meat and dairy products are high in low-density cholesterol, which is known to harden arteries and cause other heart problems.

    ◯ 7% of those who consume dairy and meat regularly suffer heart attacks over the course of their lifetime.

24. In 2001, a local high school implemented a new program designed to reduce the incidence of teenage pregnancy. The program, however, failed to produce the desired result. If the program had been successful, the dropout rate for female students would not have increased substantially in 2001.

    The argument in the passage depends on which of the following assumptions?

    ◯ The number of teen pregnancies nationwide increased in 2001.

    ◯ The number of teen pregnancies in 2001 was greater than the number of teen pregnancies in 1991.

    ◯ Teenage pregnancy is a leading reason that female students leave school.

    ◯ The program was mandatory for all female students.

    ◯ Most 2001 female dropouts were not pregnant at any time during the year.

25. In 2001, a local high school implemented a new program designed to reduce the incidence of teenage pregnancy. The program, however, failed to produce the desired result. If the program had been successful, the dropout rate for female students would not have increased substantially in 2001.

    The argument in the passage would be most seriously weakened if it were true that

    ○ the number of female students in the school has remained constant for the past decade

    ○ nationwide, the teen pregnancy rate and the female high school dropout rate both increased significantly in 2001

    ○ some female students who dropped out were pregnant at the time

    ○ many female high school dropouts said that poor economic conditions forced them to leave school and find jobs

    ○ the school also implemented a program designed to reduce the incidence of drug use among teenagers in 2001

26. The workers' union of GrainCorp, a grain-processing plant, is attempting to obtain a pay raise from GrainCorp management. To pressure GrainCorp management into accepting the union's proposal, the president of the union has proposed a boycott against SquareMart food stores, which are owned by MegaFood, the parent company of GrainCorp.

    The answer to which of the following questions is LEAST directly relevant to the union president's consideration of whether a boycott of SquareMart will lead to acceptance of their pay rate proposal?

    ○ Would the loss of business at SquareMart stores materially affect MegaFood?

    ○ Are the staple food products purchased by consumers at SquareMart stores readily available at other stores not owned by MegaFood?

    ○ How many SquareMarts are within the region of the GrainCorp plant?

    ○ Have other unions successfully employed the same strategy?

    ○ Is MegaFood the only corporation that operates both grain-processing plants and food stores?

27. An ecology magazine regularly publishes articles on tree diseases. This year, the number of articles on *Ophiostoma ulmi*, the fungus that causes Dutch elm disease, is significantly smaller than the number of such articles that appeared last year. Clearly, fewer researchers studied *Ophiostoma ulmi* this year than did so last year.

    Which of the following, if true, weakens the above conclusion?

    ○ Many researchers publishing articles are currently studying *Stegophora ulmea*, a fungus that causes elm leaf spot.

    ○ Since its introduction, Dutch elm disease has killed half of the elm trees in North America.

    ○ Research on Dutch elm disease that focuses on prevention receives more funding than research that focuses on finding a cure.

    ○ A new strain of the fungus *Rhytisma acerinum* infested maple trees at an unprecedented rate this year.

    ○ All articles go through at least a one-year review process before publication.

28. Saguaro kangaroo rats generally leave watering holes, where food and water are abundant, during the day, while Sonoran kangaroo rats remain near these same watering holes and continue foraging throughout the day. Although Sonoran kangaroo rats have larger and more frequent litters, they are generally outnumbered by the Saguaro kangaroo rat.

    Which of the following, if true, would best resolve the apparent paradox described above?

    ○ Several species of successful rodents also leave the streams and watering holes during the day.

    ○ The Saguaro kangaroo rat matures much more slowly than the Sonoran kangaroo rat because of its relatively limited food supply.

    ○ Many of the predators of kangaroo rats, such as falcons and rattlesnakes, are only active around streams during the day.

    ○ Saguaro kangaroo rats are more sensitive to sunlight than are Sonoran kangaroo rats.

    ○ Sonoran kangaroo rats are reproductive to a greater age than are Saguaro kangaroo rats.

29. National regulations that limit the sale of meat to within 5 days of packing should be changed. Under optimal conditions, meat kept at 40° F will not spoil for 16 days. If the regulations were changed, prices for meat would drop due to increased shelf life and reduced waste, but the safety of the food supply would not be compromised.

    Which of the following, if true, would most seriously weaken the conclusion drawn above?

    ○ Most consumers keep meat for up to a week before eating it.

    ○ 7 of 10 shopkeepers favor extending the limitation on meat to 9 days.

    ○ Approximately 65% of the meat display cases nationally maintain temperatures between 47 and 54° F.

    ○ Approximately half the meat stored for 25 days is still safe to consume.

    ○ Meat packing operations are more efficient when they can make fewer, larger deliveries than when they must make more frequent, smaller deliveries.

30. The owner of a four-story commercial building discovered termites in the building's first and second floors and called an exterminator. The exterminator pumped gas into the walls on both the first and second floors. Due to the exterminator's work, the termites on those floors were killed quickly.

    Which of the following, if true, most seriously undermines the validity of the explanation for the speed with which the termites were killed?

    ○ The third floor had no termite infestation.

    ○ Even though the exterminator did not pump gas into the walls of the fourth story, the termites there died as quickly as they did on the first and second stories.

    ○ The speed at which termites are killed increases as the concentration of an exterminator's gas increases.

    ○ The speed with which the exterminator's gas kills termites drops off sharply as the gas dissipates throughout the building's walls.

    ○ The exterminator's gas-pumping system works efficiently even when pumping gas into both the first and second stories of the building simultaneously.

31. Recent surveys show that many people who have left medical school before graduating suffer from depression. Clearly, depression is likely to cause withdrawal from medical school.

    Which of the following, if true, would most strengthen the conclusion above?

    ○ Many medical schools provide psychological counseling for their students.

    ○ About half of those who leave medical school report feeling depressed after they make the decision to leave.

    ○ Depression is very common among management consultants who have a similarly difficult work schedule to those of many young doctors.

    ○ Medical students who have sought depression counseling due to family problems leave at a higher rate than the national average.

    ○ Career change has been shown to be a strong contributing factor in the onset of depression.

32. The performance of Southport's two high schools has been quite consistent over the past 5 years. In each of those years, Suburban High has enrolled 40% of Southport's students and produced 75% of the town's high school graduates, while Lakeside High has accounted for the remainder.

    Which of the following can properly be inferred regarding the past 5 years from the passage above?

    ○ The total number of students attending each high school has remained roughly constant.

    ○ Students attending Suburban High come from a larger geographical area than students attending Lakeside High.

    ○ Lakeside High has graduated a lower percentage of its attendees than has Suburban High.

    ○ The respective geographic areas from which the schools draw their student populations have remained unchanged.

    ○ Students attending magnet programs accounted for a higher percentage of the graduating students at Lakeside High than at Suburban High.

33. A chemical company recently introduced a new type of foam spray that it claims will reduce the rate of erosion from the walls of road cuts. A study by the company showed that the rate of erosion was low on a road cut where the foam was applied.

    Which of the following, if true, would most seriously weaken the company's conclusion?

    ◯ Road cuts similar to the one studied typically show low rates of erosion without the foam.

    ◯ Because the foam itself weathers, the foam would have to be reapplied every 4 years to order to maintain protection against erosion.

    ◯ Studies by the company that produces the material are sometimes unreliable because of conflicts of interest.

    ◯ The rate of erosion from the road cut in the study was greater than expected based on computer simulation models.

    ◯ Other foams made from similar materials have failed to halt erosion from certain types of road cuts.

34. A researcher has discovered that steel containing Element X is stronger and more flexible than ordinary steel because Element X reduces the occurrence of microscopic fractures. The level of Element X in much of the steel produced in Canada is naturally high because the ore deposits from which the steel is produced also contain Element X.

    Which of the following can be correctly inferred from the statements above?

    ◯ Steel from Canada is stronger and more flexible than steel from any other country.

    ◯ Steel that is not from Canada is highly likely to develop microscopic fractures after years of use.

    ◯ Producing steel from ore deposits containing Element X is the best way to make steel that is stronger and more flexible.

    ◯ Some steel produced in Canada is less likely to develop microscopic fractures than other steel.

    ◯ Steel produced from Canadian ore deposits contains the highest levels of Element X found in any steel.

KAPLAN

35. The Laysan Rail, an insectivore bird once present on several of the Hawaiian Islands, can no longer be found and is thought to be extinct. Scientists originally thought that a decrease in the amount of ground vegetation available for nesting was responsible for the decline of the bird. However, they now believe that increased competition for food was ultimately responsible for the Laysan Rail's inability to survive.

    Which of the following would best help to account for the change in the accepted explanation for the Laysan Rail's extinction?

    ○ The vegetation on the Laysan Rail's home island was decimated when rabbits were introduced to the island in the 1910s.

    ○ When attempts were made to relocate the Laysan Rail to other islands, the birds lost the geographical cues that they relied on for finding mating sites.

    ○ The Laysan Rail builds nests under dense ground cover to protect the eggs.

    ○ An increase in the use of pesticides resulted in a decrease in the numbers of flies and moths present in the Laysan Rail's territory.

    ○ Many species nested in the same types of vegetation as the Laysan Rail.

36. Retail clothing stores should hold "one-day only" sales to clear merchandise that has been returned because it is defective in some way. The stores should sell this merchandise for up to 70% less than the original retail price. Stores will find these sales to be an effective way of getting rid of defective merchandise as long as they inform customers that the discounted merchandise is non-returnable.

    The author assumes which of the following about the "one-day only" sale merchandise in predicting the effectiveness of these sales?

    ○ The defects in the merchandise are not so significant that customers will be unwilling to pay even the sale price.

    ○ The rate of returns when merchandise is new makes these "one-day only" sales key to a store's profitability.

    ○ Too few shoppers purchase merchandise at full retail price.

    ○ If these sales become popular, stores will have to have them more often.

    ○ The majority of the "one-day only" sale merchandise will be purchased by shoppers who would otherwise not shop at those stores.

37. A brochure for City X highlights the reasons why residents should move there rather than to other cities in the state. One reason that the brochure mentions is the relative ease of finding a job in City X, where the unemployment rate is 4.7% .

    Which of the following statements, if true, casts the most doubt on the validity of the reason to move to City X mentioned above?

    ○ Most of the jobs in City X are hourly rather than salary jobs.

    ○ The state where City X is located has an average unemployment rate of 3.9%.

    ○ Other reasons to move to City X include the school system and easy access to recreational activities.

    ○ The national unemployment rate, calculated during the last census, is 4.3%.

    ○ City Y, located in the same state as City X, recently built a new factory that will employ 5,000 workers.

38. If participation in the honors creative writing class were limited to graduate students and those undergraduates who had received at least a B+ in composition, most of the undergraduate students would be forced to take the regular creative writing class. Such a reduction in undergraduate enrollment would reduce the percentage of failing grades in the honors class.

    Which of the following, if true, would most strengthen the conclusion drawn in Sentence 2 above?

    ○ Graduate students have all scored at least B+ in composition.

    ○ The honors creative writing course is experiencing overcrowding due to increases in graduate enrollment.

    ○ Many undergraduates would work harder to score B+ in composition rather than be excluded from honors creative writing.

    ○ The number of failing grades in honors creative writing has decreased in recent years.

    ○ Undergraduates who scored lower than B+ in composition are responsible for a disproportionate percentage of failing grades in honors creative writing.

39. In a certain state, the rate at which inhabitants of City X contract a certain disease is significantly lower than the rate at which inhabitants of City Y contract the disease. So if a couple originally from City Y relocates to City X and raises a family there, their children will be significantly less likely to contract this disease than they would had they remained in City Y.

    Which of the following, if true, would most seriously weaken the conclusion drawn in the passage?

    ○ Many health experts do not believe that moving to City X will lead to a significant increase in the average person's immunity to the disease.

    ○ The mayor of City Y has falsely claimed that statistics relating to the incidence of the disease in his city are not accurate.

    ○ The lower incidence of the disease in City X can be ascribed mostly to genetically determined factors.

    ○ Some inhabitants of City Y possess a greater immunity to the disease than do the healthiest inhabitants of City X.

    ○ Smog levels in City X are significantly lower than those of any other city in the state.

40. In a certain state, the rate at which inhabitants of City X contract a certain disease is significantly lower than the rate at which inhabitants of City Y contract the disease. So if a couple originally from City Y relocates to City X and raises a family there, their children will be significantly less likely to contract this disease than they would have been if the family had remained in City Y.

    Which of the following statements, if true, would most significantly strengthen the conclusion drawn in the passage?

    ○ The rate at which inhabitants of City X contract the disease will increase as the overall population of City X increases.

    ○ In contrast to City Y, City X is characterized by an abundance of environmental factors that tend to inhibit the occurrence of the disease.

    ○ 23% of those inhabitants of City Y who move to City X live beyond the average life span of native inhabitants of City X.

    ○ Over the last 2 decades, the incidence of the disease has decreased in City Y but has remained unchanged in City X.

    ○ Studies indicate that the incidence of the disease among inhabitants of City X who move to City Y is roughly equal to that of inhabitants of City X who remain in City X.

41. A recently published article on human physiology claims that enzyme K contributes to improved performance in strenuous activities such as weightlifting and sprinting. The article cites evidence of above-average levels of enzyme K in Olympic weightlifters and sprinters.

    Which of the following, if true, would most strengthen the article's conclusion?

    ◯ Enzyme K levels are the most important factor affecting the performance of strenuous activities.

    ◯ Enzyme K has no other function in the human body.

    ◯ Enzyme K is required for the performance of strenuous activities.

    ◯ Enzyme K helps weightlifters more than it helps sprinters.

    ◯ Strenuous activities do not cause the human body to produce unusually high levels of enzyme K.

42. In the state of Michigan, from 1980 to 1989, total spending on books purchased from all sources increased by 34%. But during the same period, spending on fiction books, most of which were purchased from bookstores selling only new books, grew just 16%.

    Which of the following statements about the period from 1980 to 1989 is best supported by the statements above?

    ◯ Spending on nonfiction books increased by more than 34%.

    ◯ Shoppers were more likely to buy fiction books when they went to a bookstore than they were to buy nonfiction.

    ◯ The prices of books purchased at bookstores are higher than those of books purchased elsewhere.

    ◯ Individual spending on books increased, while institutional spending declined.

    ◯ The number of people who bought books from secondhand bookstores increased during this period.

KAPLAN

43. The state legislature has proposed a new law that would provide a tax credit to people who install alarm systems in their homes. Members of the legislature claim that the new law will reduce crime, citing studies showing that crime rates fall as the percentage of homes with alarm systems rises.

    Which of the following, if true, would cast the most doubt on the claim that the new law will reduce crime?

    ○ No law can prevent crime altogether.

    ○ The amount of the tax credit is so low relative to the cost of alarm systems that very few people will install alarm systems in order to obtain this credit.

    ○ Neighborhood crime prevention programs can reduce crime as effectively as alarm systems can.

    ○ The state would have to build more prisons to house all the people caught by the new alarm systems.

    ○ The state cannot afford to reduce taxes any further.

44. Countries A and B are in competition to draw tourists to their countries. In Country A, about 2,500 violent crimes are reported per year. In Country B, about 1,000 violent crimes are reported per year. Trying to draw tourists away from Country A, officials in Country B use these violent crime statistics to claim it has a lower violent crime rate than Country A.

    Which of the following, if true, would expose the flaw in Country B's argument that it has the lower violent crime rate?

    ○ Most violent criminals in Country B are repeat offenders.

    ○ White-collar crime is higher in Country B than in Country A.

    ○ The population of Country A is 20 times greater than the population of Country B.

    ○ Country B has fewer tourists than Country A.

    ○ Country A has a better prison system than Country B.

45. If a poor harvest season in a major corn-producing state results in higher prices for a bushel of corn, corn prices in other states will rise as well, whether or not those states are net importers of corn.

    Which of the following conclusions is best supported by the statement above?

    ⬭ Agricultural commodities companies in states that are not net importers of corn are excluded from the national corn market when there is a disruption in the national corn supply.

    ⬭ National corn supply disruptions have little, if any, effect on the price of local corn as long as the locality is in a state that is not a net importer of corn.

    ⬭ The corn market in any state is part of the national corn market even if most of the corn consumed in the state is produced in the state.

    ⬭ Poor harvesting seasons come at predictable regular intervals.

    ⬭ Higher prices for corn tend to lead to increased prices for livestock, which rely on corn feed.

46. Town X and Town Y are roughly equal in size and local population. A survey was done measuring traffic patterns during the summer months for each of the past 5 years. The survey found that, on average in Town Y, there were 28 minor car accidents in June as well as 28 in July. During the same two months in Town X, the average was only 14 minor car accidents each month. Thus, if the Dentco Autobody Repair franchise were looking to open a new shop in one of the two towns, it would be more likely to succeed in Town Y.

    Which of the following, if true, would most seriously damage the conclusion drawn in the passage?

    ⬭ More people walk to work or use mass transit in Town Y.

    ⬭ The state is planning to add a thruway exit for Town Y.

    ⬭ The traffic volume in Town Y quadruples in the summer because it is a beach town.

    ⬭ In June and July six years ago, Town X had double the amount of accidents than Y.

    ⬭ There are rumors of a megamall possibly being constructed in Town X.

47. Ronald is a runner on the track team and is a great hurdler. All runners on the track team are either sprinters or long distance runners, but a few long distance runners do not run the sprint because they are not fast enough. Hurdlers never run long distance because they lack the endurance necessary. Therefore, Ronald must be fast.

    For the conclusion drawn above to be logically correct, which of the following must be true?

    ○ Sprinters are faster than hurdlers.

    ○ All runners on the track team who run hurdles also run long distance.

    ○ Hurdling requires more endurance than running long distance.

    ○ All sprinters are fast.

    ○ Every runner on the track team who is fast is a sprinter.

48. In the past six pro football drafts, 4 of the 6 players selected by Team A are now starters on the squad. On Team B, only 2 of the 6 players selected in the draft are starters. So, a football player selected by Team A from the draft pool has a higher probability of becoming a starter than if he is selected by Team B.

    Which of the following if true, would be the best reason to reject this argument?

    ○ Two of the four starters on Team A are sons of the coach.

    ○ Team B has a new owner and coaching staff.

    ○ Team B has a new state-of-the-art gym.

    ○ Team B's pick is a quarterback, and the starting quarterback is retiring.

    ○ Team A has had the first draft pick for the past 6 years, while Team B had the last pick. This year it is reversed.

49. The latest census of the town in which Jacob's hardware store is located has revealed that the population of new residents has increased tenfold since 1980. Though Jacob has not encountered any new competition for business during this time period, his inventory records indicate that the average number of lawn-mowers and snowblowers that he sells per year has risen only slightly over the average number of lawn-mowers and snowblowers he sold yearly prior to 1980.

    Which of the following, if true, best explains the discrepancy outlined above?

    ○ Since 1980, many of the single home properties have been subdivided into smaller single home parcels.

    ○ Inflation has caused the prices of the machines to increase every year since 1980.

    ○ All of the housing built in Jacob's town since 1980 has been large apartment complexes.

    ○ The average snowfall since 1980 has decreased from 6 feet per year to 4 feet per year.

    ○ Jacob's store only carries two brands of lawn-mowers and snowblowers.

50. Due to extreme poverty in Italy during the time period between 1870 and 1930, almost 4 1/2 million Italians—most of whom were farmers—immigrated to the United States. The wave from Italy reached its height in the 10-year span between 1920 and 1930, when Italians comprised 12% of the total number of immigrants admitted to the United States. The majority of these Italian immigrants were from Southern Italy and Sicily, and upon their arrival, they settled along the East Coast, with the heaviest concentrations in cities such as New York, Boston, and Philadelphia, though some made the arduous trip across the country to settle in Northern California.

    The statements above, if true, support which of the following?

    ○ The American descendants of those early Italian immigrants outnumber the current population of Italy.

    ○ Many American farmers today are descendants of Italians.

    ○ The strong Euro dollar has contributed to the sharp decline in Italian immigrants.

    ○ An Italian immigrant to America today is still likely to be from Southern Italy or Sicily.

    ○ At the turn of the 19th century, the southern portion of Italy was the country's prominent agricultural region.

ANSWERS AND EXPLANATIONS

1. D	11. C	21. E	31. D	41. E
2. E	12. E	22. D	32. C	42. A
3. C	13. B	23. E	33. A	43. B
4. D	14. A	24. C	34. D	44. C
5. D	15. C	25. D	35. D	45. C
6. C	16. E	26. E	36. A	46. C
7. E	17. E	27. E	37. B	47. D
8. C	18. C	28. C	38. E	48. E
9. E	19. B	29. C	39. C	49. C
10. D	20. A	30. B	40. B	50. E

1. D

An L.A. political candidate who buys saturation radio advertising will get maximum name recognition. In other words, such advertising is sufficient for maximum name recognition. If so, then it must be true that, as (D) says, a candidate can get such recognition without spending on other forms of media.

(A) suggests that radio advertising is the most important factor in L.A. political campaigns, but nothing like this was mentioned in the stimulus, so it's not inferable. Nor were we told the specific results of attaining maximum name recognition, so (B) is out. Similarly, we don't know precisely what is meant by "saturation radio advertising," so we can't infer anything as detailed as (C). Finally, although we know saturation radio advertising is sufficient for getting maximum name recognition, we can't infer that other things, such as the candidate's record mentioned in (E), have little effect on name recognition.

2. E

The evidence discusses attacks by Dobermans, but the conclusion is that dogs—any dogs—are unsafe around little kids. This makes sense only if we assume (E): that Dobermans, in their behavior toward little kids, are generally representative of dogs. A good way of checking assumptions is to see what happens if we take their opposite: If the opposite of a statement weakens the argument, then that statement is assumed; if it doesn't, it's not. Here, if Dobermans' behavior toward small children isn't typical of dogs, the argument falls apart.

(A), whether the attacks were justified, is beside the point. Even if the kids were pulling the dogs' tails, the author's point that the dogs aren't safe still holds. Other pets are beyond the scope, so (B)'s out. As for (C), the argument doesn't deal with the future, so the author needn't assume anything about it. And it certainly wouldn't weaken the argument if, contrary to (D), many of the attacks could not have been prevented, so (D)'s not assumed.

3. C

U.S. law forbids U.S. citizens from engaging in military campaigns against countries unless the United States is at war with those countries. Since no war has been declared between the United States and the Balaland Republic, the author concludes that the recruits being trained to fight against the Balaland Republic are defying U.S. law. But if, as (C) asserts, the recruits are being trained to fight only if a war is declared, then they're not in defiance of U.S. law. Being prepared for battle is different from actually engaging in it.

(A)'s no weakener; we can't assume that the country's escalating civil war justifies military action against it. In (B), severing diplomatic ties doesn't go far enough to show that training recruits is justifiable under U.S. law. As for (D), who funds the rebels was never mentioned by the author and is irrelevant. And as for (E), the author starts off calling for an investigation, so he doesn't assert that charges should be brought without launching an investigation first.

4. D

Since the critics claim, based on the study's results, that the policy of leaving students back doesn't improve their skills, the best restatement of their view is (D). (A) fails for two reasons: one, the critics never hinted that test anxiety was the reason for poor performance, and two, (A) discusses "challenging new material," whereas the tests in question assessed students' basic skills. In (B), we're not interested in students' "true intellectual development"—again, it's their mastery of basic skills. Anyway, (B)'s criticism of standardized test scores tends to go against the critics' argument, which is based on those very scores. The psychological damage of being left back, raised in (C), is well beyond the scope; the critics never hinted at this. Finally, (E) fails because the critics never discussed socioeconomic factors at all—just test scores.

5. D

Most murder victims were killed by people they knew, yet most people are more likely to fear being killed by a stranger. The best way to explain this apparent contradiction is (D): Most people don't believe they fall into the high-risk groups containing murderous friends and relations, but they do think they could be victims of random violence.

As for (A), did these people find it counterintuitive that most murder victims knew their killers? We don't know, so we can't assume they dismissed the statistics. (B)'s too vague to explain the discrepancy. In light of the statistics, people's fear of strangers seems irrational, but is it emotional? A more emotional response might be to become terrified of being killed by one's spouse or best friend. (C) fails because national statistics already exist, as the first sentence makes clear. Finally, (E) might explain why people who knew they might be killed ended up dead, but it doesn't resolve the discrepancy at hand.

KAPLAN

6. C

The author equates the withholding of government funding with censorship. (C), which denies that they're the same thing, destroys the argument. (A) is irrelevant. That the council's actions may reflect majority opinion wouldn't justify what the author considers censorship—her definition isn't dependent on what most people think. (B) complains that the term *obscenity* is used ambiguously, but it's the term *censorship* that's the problem here. (D) misses the whole point; in the author's view, denial of funding amounts to censorship, and (D) simply reaffirms this. And (E), like (A), points to majority opinion, but since the author never denies that most people can agree on what's obscene, this is beside the point.

7. E

First, we need to understand the structure of the argument. Here the statement, "Allowing this would be as disastrous as…" clues us into the author's opinion. Assumption: One needs maturity and experience to design curricula. If the assumption were true, the argument would be strengthened. Check the answer choices, and look for one that affirms the assumption. (A) is just a restatement of the evidence; this choice adds no new information.

In (B) the argument made an analogy: "Allowing students to make their own curricula is as disastrous as letting 3-year-olds choose their own diets." If an argument uses an analogy to make a point, it had better do so effectively. The better the analogy, the stronger the argument. This choice does strengthen the argument by showing the analogy to be true. But the question asks for the best strengthener and a more relevant strengthener may be present.

(C) is a classic faulty comparison choice; it is also out of scope. The author doesn't distinguish between local high school students and average teenagers. Moreover, the focus is on experience and maturity, not intelligence. (D) shifts the focus of the argument from "who should or should not design curricula" to "what kind of curricula is best." Notice the scope change in this choice. It's tempting, especially since it brings up an intelligent point about tailoring to individuals, but that's a topic for a different discussion. The best strengthener is (E), citing the experience needed to design curricula.

8. C

If we can show that something besides the court system may explain the increase in crime (if we can show a different cause for the same effect) we would weaken the argument. The author, after all, assumes that there is no other cause (a common GMAT assumption). Tackle the choices, looking for another cause besides the allegedly lenient court sentences.

(A) is a classic faulty comparison. The argument does not compare one state to another. The argument's scope is the crime rate increase in this state only. In (B), the fact that white collar crime is also on the rise is more of a strengthener than a weakener—maybe it is the leniency in the courtroom that is responsible for an overall crime surge. (C) presents an alternative explanation for the increase in crime. Maybe it is not the judges at all but the fact that there are fewer cops on the street. As for (D), what if 65% of people in the state oppose capital punishment? What if 100% of people in this state oppose capital punishment? This provides little insight into why crime has gone up since last year. (E) tells us that numerous judges have been replaced in the last year. It is possible that the new judges are more lenient, but this would only strengthen the author's conclusion.

9. E

This question asks, "Which of the following is best supported by the information above?" In other words, what can be inferred from the stated material? The author in this question discusses the impact of junior colleges on family-run businesses. Evidence: These colleges introduced people to new methods that were often successfully applied to family-run businesses. Conclusion: These colleges had a tremendous effect on family-run businesses.

A good inference will not go beyond this scope or read too much into particular detail. We go through the choices on Inference questions, because it's hard to predict what the correct answer will be.

In (A) the disqualifying word is *principally*. The information presented does not specify what the junior colleges emphasized. This choice reads too much into the fact that often family businesses increased in size because of the newly acquired knowledge. (B) is wrong because we really can't infer how popular or widespread these methods were before the war. For all we know these could have been revolutionary techniques or well-kept secrets. In (C), we know junior colleges taught new methods of marketing and finance and stuff like that; we do not know how much management theory was or was not presented. This choice relies on data we aren't given—a sure sign of an incorrect or unwarranted inference. In (D), all we are really told is that many family-run businesses became more profitable. It is possible that many family-run businesses could have been abandoned as unprofitable had it not been for the junior colleges, but nothing suggests that there necessarily would have been a significant number of business failures without colleges.

(E) is certainly true. Business methods did change because of the education. Notice how nonbiased this statement is, coming directly from the information given. Often, people find the correct choice to be too obvious in Critical Reasoning questions; often it's just that straightforward.

10. D

Here the author presents the consultants' ideas. Notice the paragraph uses words like *often* and *slowdown*. The correct response should not go beyond such terminology. Consultants' conclusion: Techniques to increase productivity of discrete tasks have drawbacks, even though they accomplish their specific goals. Consultants' evidence: They often instill enough resentment to lead to a slowdown in the production process as a whole.

(A) is a too sweeping a generalization, an unwarranted inference about productivity enhancement techniques. Do these techniques never work? (B) is even further out. Nowhere does the information imply that America is less competitive abroad than before. Since no geographic location is mentioned, this data could have originated in Europe. (C) projects into the future, to an extreme result. All we're told is that sometimes these techniques lead to a slowdown in the production process. (D) uses similar language (and tone) to the original paragraph and remains in scope without bringing in additional information. It is an accurate summary of the text. (E) can almost be disqualified after the first few words. Though it picks up on the negative aspects of productivity enhancement, we can infer nothing about production managers since they are never mentioned. In fact, many production managers may be ecstatic about the efforts that did pay off.

11. C

The evidence says that students who attend colleges with low faculty/student ratios get well-rounded educations, but the conclusion is that the author will send his kids to colleges with small student populations. Since colleges can have the second without necessarily having the first, (C) is correct.

(A) claims that the author confuses cause and effect, but how could getting a well-rounded education cause a low faculty/student ratio? Anyway, the real problem is the scope shift from faculty/student ratios to student populations. As for (B), the author never mentions intelligence at all. (D) fails because it doesn't point to a problem in the reasoning, just in implementing it. And (E) claims students must do something extra to take advantage of the low faculty/student ratio. Since the author never claimed the benefits would be conferred automatically, this isn't a flaw; more importantly, (E) misses the real flaw, which we find in (C).

12. E

Evidence: more newspaper articles exposed as fabrications.

Conclusion: Publishers want to increase circulation, not print the truth. This makes sense only if we assume (E), that publishers decide what to print. If (E) weren't true and this decision were up to someone else, the argument would fall apart.

Since the argument claims only an increase in made-up articles exposed, it's not necessary that they be a recent phenomenon, so (A)'s not assumed. (B) goes too far—it's not necessary that every article be factually verifiable in order for there to have been an increase in fabrications. As for (C), the author's claim that "even minor publications" have fact checkers is meant to emphasize that the publications know they're not printing the truth, not that minor ones are better at fact checking than major ones. And (D) brings up admission of guilt, which the author never mentions—the articles in question were exposed as frauds, not admitted to be frauds.

13. B

Since the author concludes from evidence of collapsing buildings that architecture schools should spend more time teaching "the basics of good design," she obviously assumes that the buildings are falling down because of poor design, not poor construction. (B) destroys the argument by demolishing this assumption.

The author claims architecture schools don't focus enough on basic design, not basic physics and mechanics, so (A)'s no weakener. As for (C), the author never spells out how much of the curriculum should be spent on design, so more than half may not be enough for her. (D) distorts the argument—the author never claimed that most buildings are falling down, so the fact that most of them stay up doesn't matter. As for (E), other professionals are beyond the scope—the issue is how much architecture schools focus on basic design rather than on more lofty artistic concerns.

14. A

The author uses the single case of Acme to conclude that the war profoundly affected "nascent businesses." This assumes that Acme's growth rate is typical, or representative, of such businesses (A); otherwise, why hold it up as an example?

As for (B), the author needn't assume that $10,000 isn't much of a profit. Maybe he thinks it started out high and got even higher. (C), which brings up other wars, is beyond the scope—the argument concerns World War II, period. (D)'s tricky, but it's not assumed. Notice that the author claims only that World War II had a profound, not salutary, effect on nascent businesses, so we don't know just how he feels about rapid growth rates. As for (E), the author needn't assume Acme's managers had nothing to do with the company's success, just that the war also had an effect—and a marked one.

KAPLAN

15. C

The author's claim that the editorial's argument is no good because it is poorly written depends on the assumption that an argument's validity is related to its use of language. After all, if an argument's language didn't indicate its validity, the author's argument wouldn't make any sense at all.

(A)'s not assumed because the argument doesn't concern who's to blame for the bad editorial. (B) and (D) fail because the argument addresses this editorial only, so there's nothing assumed about what happens generally. And (E) goes too far: The author needn't assume that the writer deliberately wrote badly to hide a bad argument, just that, as (C) says, the poor writing indicates a poor argument.

16. E

Read carefully! You're asked to pick the choice from which the statement can be derived, and that's (E): If, as (E) says, anyone who is a German philosopher is an idealist except for the philosopher Marx, then all German philosophers except for Marx are idealists. That being the case, it would certainly be true that, as the stimulus says, with the exception of Marx, all German philosophers—these folks being a subset of all Germans—are idealists. Now while (E)'s claim that all German philosophers are idealists may sound a bit absurd to you (perhaps you know some German philosophers who aren't idealists), we're concerned with strict logic here, not content.

(A) tells us that except for Marx, if someone's an idealist philosopher, then he or she is German, which is precisely the opposite of what we need: Knowing that all idealist philosophers (except Marx) are German doesn't prove that all German philosophers are idealists, because there could be other kinds of German philosophers. Since the stimulus statement tells us that Marx is a German philosopher who's not an idealist, (B), which contradicts this, is wrong. (C) lets us conclude that German idealists who aren't Marx are philosophers, but we need to conclude that German philosophers (except Marx) are idealists. As for (D), like the stimulus statement, it tells us that Marx isn't an idealist German philosopher, but we need a statement that ensures that every other German philosopher besides Marx is an idealist.

17. E

Here we need to identify an assumption. The author attempts to demonstrate that the "electronic lamp" can replace the incandescent bulb (that's the conclusion) because although the electronic lamp now costs much more, it will prove more cost effective *in the long run* (that's a summary of the evidence). He backs up this claim with numbers: A 25-watt electronic lamp can last 28 times longer than a 100-watt incandescent bulb while costing only 20 times as much as the bulb (that's the hard evidence). There's one factor missing from the equation, though, and that's the amount of light the electronic lamp supplies. For the numbers given to support the author's conclusion, the electronic lamp and the normal bulb must each throw about the same amount of light. Otherwise, we might need 15 lamps for every bulb; and if this were the case, the argument would be dead wrong. Unless we assume, as (E) says, that the light produced by the lamp and the bulb is approximately equal, the evidence is meaningless.

(A) isn't assumed because the figure *4 hours a day* doesn't have to represent typical household use; it need only provide a standard by which the lights can be compared. (B) is contradicted by the author. Since the electronic lamp operates by radio waves instead of a filament, it's clear that there are important structural aspects in which it differs from incandescent bulbs. (C) would actually make us doubt the reasonableness of the author's conclusion, so clearly it isn't assumed. If the electronic lamp is supposed to be a replacement for the incandescent bulb, its light should be similar to that produced by the bulb. (D) misconstrues why the electronic lamp is claimed to be cost effective in the long run—the point is that it lasts longer, not that it will become cheaper. The author is arguing that current electronic lamps are more cost effective, not that future lamps will be.

18. C

In order to evaluate the suggestion here, we must identify the problem that the plan is intended to solve, and how it will do so. That's the standard approach to Critical Reasoning arguments that put forth plans and proposals.

After conducting interviews, researchers are alarmed at the extent to which jurors appear to base verdicts on factors outside testimony. Researchers suggest that juries should get instructions at the beginning of a trial rather than at its end, so they can concentrate on relevant evidence. We want the question that is least helpful in evaluating this plan. Questions that are helpful in evaluating the plan will probably test the researchers' understanding of the problem, or test the efficacy of their proposed solution. A good way to test the choices is to check whether "yes" and "no" answers to the question affect the plan's chances of success differently (where, of course, the question allows a "yes" or "no" answer). (C) fails the test. We're interested in whether the plan will be effective, or whether it's necessary, or whether there's a better approach. (C) asks only if implementing the suggestion will alter customary procedures. No matter what the answer to that question is, the researchers' suggestion is unaffected.

If the answer to (A) is yes, then the researchers' plan isn't even necessary—the present system will work if given a little refining. If the answer to (B) is "yes," then the researchers' suggestion is strengthened. If the answer is "no," then the suggestion is worthless. (D) strikes at the reason for developing the plan. If the answer is "yes," that jurors do report factors that weren't really influential to their decision making, then the plan may not be necessary. (E) asks if the plan will work; if jurors still consider many factors that have nothing to do with the evidence even when judges give their instructions ahead of time, then the plan will fail. If, on the other hand, jurors consider far fewer irrelevant factors, then the plan looks good.

19. B

This question asks for the most reliable conclusion based on the author's prediction concerning the ruble. The author describes a chain of cause and effect and ends with a prediction: Competing claims of ownership are slowing efforts to privatize state enterprises; these enterprises must still be subsidized by the government; government subsidies lead to large deficits; deficits drive up the inflation rate; high inflation causes the ruble's value to decline. In a nutshell, the disagreement over ownership is causing the ruble to decline in value. The author's conclusion, which we're told to accept as accurate, is that until the question of ownership has been resolved, the Russian government probably won't make the ruble freely convertible to Western currencies.

Be on the lookout for *new ideas that occur in the conclusion*. Here you should have thought, "What more is going on here? What else is the author assuming?" We want the connection the author sees between the competing claims for ownership and the conclusion's completely new idea of making the ruble freely convertible. Well, her point about the competing claims is that they cause the ruble's value to decline. So look for a choice that connects the action of making the ruble freely convertible to a decline in the ruble's value. (B) fits this scenario by concluding that making the ruble freely convertible to Western currency would also cause the ruble's value to decline, thereby (inferably) making matters worse. (B) explains quite nicely why the state's ownership of enterprises postpones the ruble's convertibility.

If you didn't see (B)'s place in the argument, you could have arrived at it anyway by eliminating the choices that couldn't be correct (a Kaplan method that works rather nicely here). (A) is unwarranted. Nothing in the argument justifies assigning a percentage to the industrial sector. (C) contradicts the spirit of the passage, which says that government subsidies are creating a strain, in the form of large deficits, on the economy. The statement that the government can withstand this strain is definitely farfetched. Contrary to (D), the argument doesn't state that the government is among the parties squabbling over ownership of state enterprises, but only that until the squabble is resolved the enterprises must remain in state hands. (E) would explain why the Russian government might want to make the ruble convertible in the first place, but one, there's no hint of it in the passage, and two, it doesn't jibe with the conclusion that the government will probably wait to make the ruble convertible.

20. A

The Kaplan technique of prephrasing an answer works pretty well here. The author concludes that the mayor isn't responsible for the growing gap in earnings between high school and college graduates. Her evidence is one, that the growing need for technologically skilled workers is responsible, and two, that the mayor can't slow the force of technology. No, probably not, but he can take it upon himself to train the less skilled for better jobs. If that rebuttal occurred to you, you had no trouble finding (A). (A) argues that the mayor could have pursued policies that would have enabled the less educated to receive the education that would qualify them for well-paying jobs. If (A) is true, the author's argument is severely weakened.

(B) is off the mark. The problem addressed in the stimulus isn't the lack of employment for graduating high school students, it's the lack of employment that pays as well as high-skill employment. (C)'s proposal might help create more jobs that pay high blue-collar wages, but we don't know what "high" blue-collar wages are. They could still be far lower than the wages earned by people with college educations, in which case (C) wouldn't really address the inequality of wages. As for (D), the problem the mayor was supposed to solve was unequal wages, and it's not clear that taxing more heavily those with high wages constitutes a solution to that problem. Unskilled workers would still be stuck in low-paying jobs. (E) talks about protecting city workers' earnings, but this refers to all city workers. As such, (E)'s suggestion wouldn't improve the position of high school graduates compared to college graduates, which is what we want.

21. E

The focus of this passage is the accuracy of a particular survey. Any answer choice that doesn't deal directly with the scope of the survey is out of scope of the question. We know that two-thirds of the freshmen on the survey *claimed not* to have plagiarized. We're asked to explain why the true proportion of those who did not plagiarize may actually be lower. The correct choice will be the one that explains the inaccuracy of the survey results, and is within the scope of the passage.

(A) is out of scope; we're only concerned with students at University X who answered the survey. (B) is irrelevant to the argument; the survey is concerned only with how many students plagiarized in high school, not how many may plagiarize in college. (C) doesn't work because the survey asks only whether a student ever plagiarized, not how often. (D) tells us that the proportion of those who did not plagiarize is lower at another school, but that has no bearing on the proportion at University X as reported by the survey. (E) is correct: It tells us that some plagiarizers might have denied doing so on the survey. If that's true, then the survey results are inaccurate and the actual proportion who did not plagiarize is lower than two-thirds.

22. D

The conclusion that Smith Products could gain an advantage by purchasing lower-cost raw materials is based on the evidence that raw materials represent the largest proportion of costs for both Smith and Jackson. For the conclusion to hold, Smith must assume the new raw materials will not have any other negative effects on its business. So, to weaken the argument, look for a choice that casts doubt on this assumption. (D) does so by stating that the low quality of the new materials will cause a drop in sales. If that occurs, using the new supplier will not create an advantage for Smith Products, and so (D) is the answer. (A) and (E) indicate other ways that Smith might gain an advantage, but they don't have any bearing on whether changing suppliers would create an advantage. (B) is similarly irrelevant; even if true, it doesn't provide any reason Smith should not use the new supplier. (C) is out of scope of the argument.

23. E

The conclusion here is that a diet free of meat and dairy products greatly reduces the risk of heart attack, based on the evidence that only 10% of those who omit meat and dairy from their diets suffer heart attacks. The assumption is that more than 10% of those who do eat dairy and meat suffer from heart attacks. If we knew that those who eat meat and dairy are less likely to suffer heart attacks, the assumption would be contradicted and the argument weakened.

(A) is out of scope. A loss of bone density might be an argument against this diet, but it is irrelevant to the passage. (B) comes closer to strengthening the argument than weakening it, by providing evidence that people who eat meat are more likely to have heart attacks. But it is still out of scope, since the passage doesn't mention people who eat meat but not dairy. (C) tells us that some of the people who eat neither meat nor dairy have more than one heart attack. Because we do not have a parallel statistic telling us how many dairy- and meat-eating heart attack sufferers experience more than one heart attack, this information does little to affect the argument in either direction. (D) strengthens the argument because it explains in more detail exactly how meat and dairy consumption is responsible for heart disease. (E) matches our prediction exactly. If we knew that only 7% of those who consume meat and dairy suffer heart attacks, then the fact that 10% of those who *don't* consume such foods suffer heart attacks is not evidence that a diet free of meat and dairy reduces the risk of heart attack.

24. C

This stimulus begins with the conclusion that a 2001 school program to reduce teenage pregnancy was a failure. The evidence is that the female dropout rate increased during 2001. The assumption must be that pregnancy is an important reason for a female to drop out of school. (C) says this correctly.

(A) is out of scope; we're concerned only with the pregnancy numbers in one school, not the numbers nationwide. Though it might be true that an overall increase in nationwide teen pregnancy was somehow related to the failure of the program at this school, any such connection is outside the scope of this argument. (B) is irrelevant: Comparing the number of pregnancies in 2001 to the number in 1991 might be one way of measuring the program's success or failure, but it has nothing to do with the argument that the increased female dropout rate in 2001 proves the program failed. (D) is out of scope because the argument concerns the dropout rate, not the number of students in the program. It could also be rejected on the grounds of "extreme language." (E) provides a reason to doubt the conclusion, as opposed to stating the argument's assumption.

25. D

This question picks up on the same stimulus seen in Question 24. We know that the assumption underlying this argument is that teenage pregnancy is one of the main reasons that females drop out of high school. To weaken the argument, let's find the choice that casts the most doubt on this assumption. (D) tells us that many students dropped out for a different reason: they needed to find a job. If this is true, the assumption that pregnancy is a leading cause of dropouts becomes doubtful, so (D) is correct. (A) contains the common trap of comparing a number with a percent (rate). The increase in the rate has nothing to do with the overall number. (B) is out of scope, since the question doesn't involve nationwide program failure. If anything, that would strengthen the argument by confirming the link between pregnancy and dropout rates. (C) is irrelevant to the argument, and (E) is out of scope.

26. E

The union president needs to decide whether to call for a boycott against SquareMart. According to the question stem, four of the answer choices would clearly help him make this decision, but one answer choice would be much less relevant. With (A), if a loss of business at SquareMart would have a large economic effect on MegaFood, that would be a point in favor of calling for the boycott. So the question in (A) does seem relevant to the decision. With (B), if people have nowhere else to buy their staple food items, they are unlikely to carry out the boycott, which might make the president less likely to suggest it. This question also appears to bear directly on the boycott decision.

As for (C), if the majority of SquareMarts are outside the vicinity of the GrainCorp plant, GrainCorp workers may rarely shop there and a boycott would not affect the company. This is clearly relevant. With (D), if no boycott has ever been effective, there would be little reason for the union president to try this tactic now. (E) is the answer: Whether other companies also own grain processors and food stores seems to have little relevance to the question of whether this boycott would be successful (especially compared to the questions posed in the other choices).

27. E

Conclusion: Fewer researchers studied *Ophiostoma ulmi* this year than last year.

Evidence: This year the number of articles on *Ophiostoma ulmi* is significantly smaller than the number of such articles that appeared last year.

Assumption: Researchers always write and publish articles in the same year the research occurs.

The conclusion is based on the assumption that there's an exact correspondence between the number of articles published on a given topic in a certain year and the number of researchers researching that topic. If, as (E) states, all articles are delayed at least a year, then the number of articles published will not necessarily correspond with the number of researchers. This casts doubt on the assumption, so it is correct.

(A) says nothing about whether the number of researchers studying *Ophiostoma ulmi* increased or decreased. (B) is wrong because the extent of Dutch elm disease is outside the scope of the question, which is only concerned with how many people are studying the fungus that causes the disease. (C)'s information is irrelevant to the actual number of research studies completed. (D) concerns a different type of fungus, so it is incorrect. And, if anything, this would strengthen the argument by giving a possible reason for a decline in research related to *Ophiostoma ulmi*.

28. C

The "apparent paradox" refers to the fact that although Saguaro kangaroo rats have smaller, less frequent litters and spend less time foraging where resources are abundant, they nevertheless outnumber the Sonoran kangaroo rats. We must find an answer choice that explains how this is possible.

(B) and (E) make the paradox even harder to explain. They both discuss further inherent weaknesses of the Saguaro species, which if anything, would lead us to believe that there should be more Sonoran rats, rather than the other way around. (A) isn't relevant to the comparison between the Sonoran and Saguaro species. (D) addresses the wrong question; it may explain why the Saguaro rats leave watering holes during daylight hours, but that doesn't explain why they have greater population numbers. Only (C) provides a plausible explanation. The fact that Sonoran rats spend more time in areas where predators are active could explain why they are outnumbered by the Saguaro rats.

29. C

This argument proposes that the regulations should be changed because meat held at 40° F will last longer than the currently allowed 5 days, and longer storage will result in lower prices for consumers. But this is only true if conditions are optimal; in other words, the assumption is that meat is in fact held at 40° F. (C) contradicts this assumption; if meat is normally displayed at higher temperatures, the proposal to extend the shelf life without reducing food safety will not work. Therefore, (C) is correct.

(A) is out of scope; the period in question is *before sale*, not after sale. Furthermore, suppose the regulations were extended to 9 days; even if consumers then kept the meat for another 7 days, that would still not exceed the 16 days that meat kept at 40° F will last. (B) isn't relevant. (D) ignores the issue of whether meat is actually kept at 40° F and, if anything, would strengthen the argument; if some meat stored up to 25 days is safe to consume, that might argue in favor of changing the 5-day limit. (E) doesn't address the temperature issue and in fact, could strengthen the argument by providing a reason to believe that longer shelf life will result in lower prices.

30. B

The conclusion here that the exterminator's work was responsible for the quick elimination of the termites is supported by the evidence that the exterminator pumped gas directly into the areas where the termites lived. The assumption is that the direct application of gas is faster than other means of extermination. To undermine the argument, let's find the choice that calls this assumption into question.

Taken by itself, (A) is irrelevant. (C) and (D) appear to support, rather than weaken, the argument, because they suggest that a higher density of gas kills termites more rapidly. (E) doesn't weaken the argument because it offers no information to help us compare the speed of termite deaths in gassed and non-gassed areas of the building. (B) is correct: The speed with which the termites in the first and second stories were killed is credited to the gas being injected into those areas. This explanation is weakened if termites are killed equally quickly on another floor, where no gas was injected.

KAPLAN

31. D

Conclusion: Depression causes withdrawal from medical school.

Evidence: Many students who have left medical school are depressed. This assumes that people who begin suffering from depression while in medical school are more likely to leave school than those who don't. The choice that validates this assumption will be the one that most strengthens the argument.

(A) is irrelevant; the counseling provided may or may not be for depression. (B) and (E) support a link between depression and leaving, but in both cases, the depression comes *after* the decision to leave. That's the opposite of what the argument says. (C) is out of scope since we're discussing medical students, not young doctors or consultants. (D) suggests that when some outside event has brought on depression, leaving becomes more likely in the period subsequent to the depression. This confirms that students who are depressed while in school are more likely to drop out.

32. C

The most proper inference will be the choice that MUST be true if the statements in the stimulus are true. Any choices that might be true but do not have to be true can be eliminated.

Suburban High enrolled 40% of the town's students and produced 75% of its graduates, so Lakeside High must have enrolled 60% of the town's students, producing 25% of its graduates. Lakeside has more students but fewer graduates, meaning that it graduated a lower percentage of its attendees than Suburban did. This makes (C) correct.

(A) could be true but doesn't necessarily follow from the stimulus. We know that the *percentage* of enrollees and graduates at each school has been constant, but that doesn't say anything about the total number of students, which may have increased, decreased, or stayed the same. (B), (D), and (E) are out of scope. And we have no information about the geographical areas in which students live, so (B) and (D) are out anyway.

33. A

Conclusion: The foam will reduce erosion from road cuts.

Evidence: On a particular road cut to which the foam was applied, the erosion rate was low. The critical assumption is that that erosion rate on the road that was studied is lower than it would have been without the foam. If that's not true, then the effectiveness of the foam is in doubt.

KAPLAN

By pointing out that road cuts similar to the one tested normally have low rates of erosion without the foam, (A) gives us reason to believe that the erosion on this road would have been the same without the foam. That calls the assumption into question and weakens the argument. (B) is concerned with the long-term use of the foam and its maintenance; even if true, it doesn't contradict the conclusion that the foam will lower erosion at the time that it is applied. (C) doesn't indicate whether *this* study is unreliable, so it is irrelevant. (D) is concerned with an erosion prediction model made by a computer simulation; the fact that the foam is less effective than predicted doesn't mean it's not effective at all. (E) is concerned with other foams, not the one under study.

34. D

We need to find the choice that must logically follow if the stimulus is true. If making steel with Element X reduces the level of microscopic fractures, and if some Canadian steel contains Element X, it follows that some Canadian steel will be less likely to develop such fractures. So (D) can be inferred.

(A) is out of scope and uses extreme language; we can't compare all Canadian steel to all the steel from all other countries. (B) wrongly introduces the idea of "years of use" and "not from Canada," which are outside the scope of the stimulus; we only know specifics about some, not all, Canadian steel and nothing about when fractures might develop. (C) and (E) are too extreme—the stimulus never says steel from ore deposits rich in Element X is the "best," or that it contains more Element X than any other steel.

35. D

Scientists first attributed the bird's extinction to a loss of ground vegetation, which the birds used for nesting, but they now believe that a lack of food (insects) was actually responsible. Let's examine the choices to find one that explains why scientists changed their opinion.

(A) provides evidence that a decrease in vegetation did in fact occur. If anything, that would have *strengthened* the hypothesis that loss of vegetation led to the birds' extinction, rather than causing the scientists to find a new explanation. (B) is out of scope. The passage doesn't concern relocation to other islands, and neither extinction hypothesis has anything to do with mating habits. (C) would strengthen the vegetation hypothesis, by providing evidence of how important the vegetation was to the birds' survival. (E) focuses on other species. Moreover, it supports the vegetation theory, not the food theory. (D) might explain the shift. Since the birds eat insects (Sentence 1), a decrease in the insect population would increase competition for food and could lead to extinction if the birds were not able to compete effectively.

36. A

The author concludes that sales of greatly discounted merchandise would be effective at clearing out defective merchandise, citing as evidence the fact that the merchandise would be non-returnable (final sale). But the sales will only be effective at getting rid of defective merchandise if customers are actually willing to purchase the merchandise; thus, the author must be assuming that nothing will prevent people from actually buying the defective clothing during these one-day sales. (A) states this assumption clearly. As long as the defects aren't so bad that people won't buy the clothing even at a large discount, the sales can be effective.

(B) incorrectly shifts from what the argument discusses (the effectiveness of these sales) to the profitability of the store in general, which is irrelevant to the argument. (C), (D), and (E) are outside the scope of the argument. We aren't given any information about how merchandise sells when it is not on sale, so (C) is incorrect. While it might be true that stores will need to hold these sales more frequently if they become popular, that isn't relevant to the argument that the sales will be effective in clearing out defective merchandise, making (D) incorrect. Finally, we don't know anything about the shoppers going to the sale, so (E) is incorrect.

37. B

The conclusion here is that people should move to City X rather than other cities in the state; City X has a 4.7% unemployment rate, and that makes it relatively easy to find a job there. This is only true if unemployment rates are higher elsewhere. In other words, the assumption is that 4.7% is a low unemployment rate relative to other cities in the state.

We're looking for the statement that weakens this assumption. (B) says that the state has an average unemployment rate of 3.9%, which is lower than that of City X. So, compared to the rest of the state, City X has a higher unemployment rate, which weakens the argument that people should move to City X to take advantage of its low unemployment rate. The exact types of jobs (salary or hourly) available in City X are not part of the argument, so (A) is out of scope. Similarly, other possible reasons to move to City X, such as schools and recreation, are also not at issue, so (C) is incorrect.

(D) cites the national unemployment rate, something out of scope. And (E) is neither mentioned nor relevant to the issue of whether City X's unemployment rate is in fact low.

38. E

The argument here is that eliminating undergraduates who did not receive a B+ or better in composition will reduce the failure rate in the honors class. The assumption must be that undergraduates who did not receive a B+ or better in composition have previously been the ones responsible for the failure rate, and are expected to continue to be responsible if they're allowed in the class. In other words, graduate students and other undergraduates have previously failed less frequently than undergraduates who did not receive a B+ or better in composition. So, to strengthen the conclusion that eliminating the non-B+ students will drive the failure rate down, we need a choice that confirms that the non-B+ students were in fact failing at a proportionally higher rate than the others in the class. This is precisely what (E) does.

(A) seems tempting, but is irrelevant. The passage speaks only of eliminating undergraduates. Graduate students would still be allowed to take the course regardless of their composition grade. Whether or not the honors class is overcrowded in (B) is out of scope; reducing the failure rate, not overcrowding, is the focus of the stimulus. Similarly, (C) tells us nothing about the failure rate in the course. And (D) is wrong because the argument concerns a possible decline in the failure rate after non-B+ students are eliminated, not a decline in the absolute *number* of failures *prior* to the elimination of non-B+ students.

39. C

To weaken the argument, we need to find the choice that contradicts its key assumption. The conclusion is that moving from City Y to City X will lower the likelihood of contracting the disease, since the disease occurs at a much lower rate in City X. The assumption is that the fact of being born in or living in City X reduces the risk of contracting the disease; in other words, environmental factors (such as lifestyle, air quality, health care costs, or some other factor affecting people's lives) in City X are responsible for the low incidence of the disease. Now let's find a choice the makes this assumption unlikely to be true.

(A) is out of scope; the rates of incidence in the two cities, not the opinion of professionals, are at issue here. Also, this type of "appeal to authority" is rarely correct on the GMAT. (B) would strengthen the argument; the statistics state that the incidence is higher in City Y and if the mayor were proven to have *falsely* suggested otherwise, it would still make sense to move to City X, where the incidence is lower. (D) is irrelevant. Even if true, it would not imply that the risk for the average person is lower in City Y.

KAPLAN

(E) is out of scope; we have no information on whether smog has anything to do with the disease in question. Furthermore, this would, if anything, strengthen the conclusion by providing at least one sense in which City X is a more healthful place to live. (C) states that genetic makeup (as opposed to something in the environment) is responsible for the low incidence of the disease in City X. In other words, the risk is determined by genetic factors, not by where one is born or where one lives. This contradicts the assumption that there is something about the environment in City X that lowers the risk of contracting the disease, so (C) is correct.

40. B

This question picks up on the same stimulus seen in Question 39. The key assumption is that environmental factors in City X are responsible for the low incidence of the disease in that city. To strengthen the argument, we need to find the choice that confirms this assumption. And that is what (B) does.

(A) suggests that an increase in population will increase the rate of the disease. This would suggest that newcomers would be more, not less, likely to contract the disease. (C) is too general, speaking of lifespan and not the specific disease in question. (D) is irrelevant; the fact remains that the incidence in City Y is still significantly higher than in City X. (E) would weaken the argument. If City X inhabitants show the same resistance to the disease even in City Y, the reason for their immunity must be inherent—probably genetic, not environmental.

41. E

Because the article claims that enzyme K caused better performance, this is an example of a causality argument—an "X causes Y" situation. The evidence is that Olympic weightlifters and sprinters have above-average levels of enzyme K. To strengthen it, we need to find a choice confirming that X (high levels of enzyme K) does in fact cause Y (better performance).

(A) is out of scope; the article is only concerned with enzyme K, not other factors affecting performance. (B) is irrelevant and uses extreme language. (C) distorts what the article claims; the article says only that enzyme K improves performance, not that it is required. (D) is an irrelevant comparison; both weightlifters and sprinters are presented as equal evidence. (E) states that increased levels of enzyme K are not the result of strenuous activity; this strengthens the conclusion than enzyme K contributes to better performance because the enzyme is found in people who excel at strenuous activities but is not produced by the strenuous activity. Its presence must therefore help performance. If (E) were not true, strenuous activity could actually be causing the increased enzyme levels, and the argument would be weakened because it reversed cause and effect.

42. A

If spending on all books from all sources grew by 34% but spending on fiction books grew only 16%, then spending on other types of books must also have increased. In fact, since all books are either fiction or nonfiction, it must be the case that spending on nonfiction books grew more than 34%. So (A) must be true based on the information in the stimulus.

(C), (D), and (E) introduce the ideas of purchase price, source of spending, and location of purchase. We know only that *some* books were purchased at bookstores; we can infer nothing about where the rest of the books were purchased, who bought them, or how much the books cost. (B) draws the false conclusion that because fiction books were largely bought in bookstores, nonfiction books must not have been. In fact, there's no discussion about where nonfiction books were bought.

43. B

The stimulus cites evidence that an increase in the number of alarm systems does reduce crime. In order for the new law to reduce crime, it must result in an increase in the number of alarm systems installed. The members of the legislature must therefore be assuming that the tax credit will induce people who otherwise would not have installed alarm systems to do so. To cast doubt on this claim, we will need a choice which contradicts this assumption. And that is what (B) does. If the tax credit is too small relative to the cost of the alarm systems, then very few people will be induced to install the systems, and thus the new law will not reduce crime.

(A) uses extreme language and is also out of scope; the issue is whether this particular law can reduce crime, not whether crime can ever be eradicated. (C) presents an irrelevant comparison. Even if it is true, it does not provide any reason for why the new tax law would not reduce crime. (D) is a 180; if the new law reduces crime, the state should need fewer prisons, not more. (E) is both extreme and out of scope.

44. C

The flaw in Country B's argument is that it does not properly distinguish between totals and rates or percentages. Country B has fewer violent crimes, but that doesn't mean that it has a lower crime *rate*, or fewer violent crimes per person. In fact, (C) indicates that Country A's population is so much greater than that of Country B that the percentage of people who are victims of violent crime in Country A is actually lower than it is in Country B. So (C) is correct because it fixes the total/percentage flaw and indicates that Country A has the lower violent crime rate.

KAPLAN

(A), (B), and (E) aren't relevant to the relative rates of violent crime in the two countries. (D) is irrelevant because the crime rates in the two countries are not determined by how many tourists they have but by their total populations.

45. C

The stimulus says that if the price of corn rises in a major corn-producing state because of a poor harvest, the price of corn will increase in other states, whether those states import or grow most of their corn. In other words, the price of corn must somehow be standardized. This implies that all states are part of a national corn market, as in (C).

(A) is a 180; if states that are not importers of corn are not part of the national corn market, their prices won't be affected by a bad harvest in another state, which contradicts the argument. Same thing for (B): The argument states that the price of all corn—local and imported—is affected by a bad harvest in one state. (D) is out of scope; the passage focuses on corn prices, not bad harvests. (E), too, is out of scope, since livestock isn't part of the argument, but it might be tempting; it certainly could be true, but it is incorrect because it is out of scope and doesn't have to be true based on the stimulus. (C) is within the scope and must be true.

46. C

Conclusion: The driving conditions in Town Y are more dangerous than Town X, leading to more frequent occurrences of minor car accidents that will naturally provide more job opportunities for an autobody shop.

Evidence: Indeed, Town Y has averaged twice as many minor car accidents than Town X. However, the figures are only for the two summer months. If the traffic volume quadruples for those two months and there were an average of 28 accidents each month, it can be assumed that for the remaining 10 months there is actually only an average of 7 accidents per month, half the rate of Town X. These numbers would indicate that Dentco should actually open their shop in Town X.

(A) is irrelevant because the higher number of accidents in Town Y still occurred even with the higher number of walkers and those who use mass transit. Because adding a thruway exit for Town Y would only increase the traffic volume, (B) would strengthen the conclusion. (D) doesn't weaken the conclusion because the figures predate the survey, and since then an unspecified condition has influenced the numbers to reverse for five years in a row. Rumors (E) do not qualify as evidence, and therefore do weaken the conclusion.

47. D

Conclusion: Ronald must be fast.

Evidence: We are given that Ronald is a hurdler, and that all the runners on the track team are either sprinters or long distance runners, but no hurdlers are long distance runners. Therefore Ronald, a hurdler, must also be a sprinter. For the conclusion to be logically correct, (D) must be true because if Ronald is a sprinter, and all sprinters are fast, then Ronald must be fast.

(A) makes no sense because the argument states that all hurdlers are sprinters; (B), (C), and (E) directly contradict statements made in the argument.

48. E

Conclusion: This year, the player selected by Team B has a higher chance of becoming a starter than the player selected by Team A.

Evidence: Logically, the person drafted first from a pool of athletes is a better player than the person selected last. Thus, the first pick has a better chance of becoming a starter. In the past, Team A had the first pick; this year however, Team B possesses it.

(A) may jump out as a logical reason to reject this argument, however in a professional sport where winning is the main goal, it is highly unlikely that nepotism would occur; it is more likely that the coach is an ex-professional player and his sons inherited that talent. (B) and (C) are both irrelevant to the argument, because a player's chances of becoming a starter are primarily based on skill, not the owner, coaching staff, or team gym. As for (E), if the starting quarterback is retiring, that position is open, but not enough information is provided to infer that the drafted quarterback has a higher chance of starting than a pick who plays another position. For example, who are the other quarterbacks on Team B? Perhaps one of them is last year's pick.

KAPLAN

49. C

If the vast majority of people who moved into Jacob's town since 1980 moved into apartments, there would be no increase in lawn-mowers or snowblowers because they would have no property that would require the use of the machines in question. Therefore, the demand for those machines bought would not substantially increase, and (C) is the best explanation for the discrepancy. Demand for the products is not diminished by inflation, (B); nor is demand diminished by Jacob's product selection (E), because the given information states that he has not encountered any new competition that would influence his sales. (A) is invalid because the demand for the two products would increase if more single-home properties were created in the town. Besides the fact that (D) does not address the apparent discrepancy in lawn mower sales, it is not a suitable explanation because a decrease in average snowfall would only decrease the demand for snowblowers if it were significant enough for the blowers to be no longer needed. That is not the case here.

50. E

If, as the passage states, that the majority of the Italians that immigrated to the U.S. between 1870 and 1930 were farmers from the south or Sicily, it strongly implies the region of Italy from which they immigrated was primarily agricultural. (E) is correct. It is very possible that (A) is a true statement, but there would need to be current Italian population figures included in the passage to support it—there is not. (C) is also probably true, but the passage doesn't specifically state there was a *sharp decline in Italian immigrants*, so the statement has no support. The fact that the heaviest concentration of Italians settled in cities contradicts choice (B); from this information, it is safe to assume that upon arriving in America, most of the immigrants probably never farmed for a living again. (D) is completely out of scope.

Chapter 5: **Sentence Correction**

- Question Format and Structure
- The 8 Basic Principles of Sentence Correction
- Sentence Correction Rules
- Kaplan's 3-Step Method for Sentence Corrections

The GMAT includes about 16 Sentence Correction questions, which are mixed in with Critical Reasoning and Reading Comprehension. Sentence Corrections test your command of standard written English—the rather formal language that is used in textbooks and scholarly periodicals. It's the language that's used to convey complex information precisely, as opposed to the casual language that we use for everyday communication.

QUESTION FORMAT AND STRUCTURE

The directions for these questions look like this:

> **Directions:** The following question presents a sentence, part or all of which is underlined. Below each sentence you will find five ways to phrase the underlined portion. Choice (A) repeats the original version, while the other four choices are different. If the original seems best, choose choice (A). If not, choose one of the revisions.

This question tests correctness and effectiveness of expression. Choose an answer that follows the norms of standard written English: grammar, word choice, and sentence construction. Choose the answer that produces the most effective sentence, aiming to eliminate awkwardness, ambiguity, redundancy, and grammatical error.

The typical Sentence Correction question contains 2 or more errors. Time is of the essence with these: The sentences vary in length and complexity, so you'll have to move considerably faster on the short ones in order to leave time for the long ones. Here's an example:

Several consumer protecion agencies have filed suit, seeking to bar distributors from advertising treatments for baldness <u>that brings no discernible improvement and may even result in potential harm.</u>

- ◯ that brings no discernible improvement and may even result in potential harm
- ◯ that bring no discernible improvement and may even prove harmful
- ◯ bringing no discernible improvement and even being harmful
- ◯ that brings no discernible improvement and may even potentially result in harm being done
- ◯ that bring no discernible improvement, maybe even resulting in harm

KAPLAN) EXCLUSIVE

Spelling and capitalization are not tested on the GMAT. Certain answer choices differ in their punctuation, but it's never punctuation itself that's being tested.

Sentence Corrections cover a range of grammar and style errors, some of which are so obscure that even good writers commit them. That's the bad news. The good news is that you don't have to be a grammar expert to do well on this section. All you need is a mode of attack and some knowledge about what does—and does not—constitute good GMAT English.

You do not need to know every grammar rule for these questions. Errors reflecting certain rules show up repeatedly on the GMAT.

Another key element in GMAT English is style, or what the directions call "effectiveness of expression." That means English that is clear and exact, and without awkwardness, ambiguity, or redundancy." (Note that it doesn't have to be interesting. In fact, the test is set up to see whether you get worn down by difficult, often boring prose, or whether you rise above that to stay involved—and awake.)

Eliminating wrong answer choices and strategic guessing are keys to unlocking tougher Sentence Corrections. Make an answer grid on your noteboard to keep track of eliminated choices.

THE 8 BASIC PRINCIPLES OF SENTENCE CORRECTION

Here are the basic things that you need to succeed on Sentence Corrections:

1. Understand the directions completely.

There's no greater waste of your precious testing time than rereading the directions. Essentially, you're given a sentence in which some or all the words are underlined. Answer choices (B) through (E) present 4 other ways of expressing the underlined portion, and (A) repeats the original sentence's wording. You have to choose the best version of the sentence. So, if you think that the original sentence is fine and none of the rewrites is better, pick (A). If, however, you feel that the original sentence is awkward or contains a grammatical error, pick the answer that presents the best rewrite.

On a related note, always read the entire original sentence carefully. Don't try to save time by reading only the underlined portion and simply comparing it to the answer choices. You'll need to see how the underlined portion relates to the non-underlined portion.

2. Keep agreement between subject and verb.

Verbs must agree with their subjects. So singular subjects have singular verbs and plural subjects have plural verbs. If you're a native speaker, this is probably so automatic that you may wonder why the GMAT tests it at all. But the test makers craftily separate subject and verb with lots of text, to make it harder to recognize whether the subject and verb agree. Also, it is often hard to tell whether the subject is singular or plural.

KAPLAN) EXCLUSIVE

If the collective noun *audience* or *committee*, for instance, is acting as a unit, it takes a singular verb. Collective nouns are almost always singular in Sentence Corrections.

As a result, Sentence Correction questions often feature separated subjects and verbs, or subjects that aren't obviously singular or plural. You should look out for:

- One or more long modifying phrases or clauses following the subject

- Phrases and clauses in commas between the subject and the verb

- Subjects joined by *either/or* and *neither/nor*

- Sentences in which the verb precedes the subject

- Collective nouns, such as *majority*, *system*, *audience*, and *committee*

Drill: Subject-Verb Agreement

Correct each of the following subject/verb errors.

1. The depletion of natural resources, in addition to the rapid increase in utilization of these resources, have encouraged many nations to conserve energy.

   _____

2. There is, without a doubt, many good reasons to exercise.

   _____

3. Among the many problems plaguing suburbanites is the ubiquity of shopping malls, the increasing cost of gasoline, and the unavailability of mortgages.

   _____

4. The neighbors told police investigators that neither Annette nor her brother are capable of telling the truth.

   _____

5. A majority of the voters want to unseat the incumbent.

   _____

Answers and Explanations

1. *Depletion* is the subject. Correct by changing *have* to *has*, or by changing *in addition to* to *and*.

2. There *are* many good reasons. (A good strategy is to temporarily ignore parts of the sentence that are set off by commas.)

3. If the sentence ended at *malls*, is would be correct. But because there is more than one problem plaguing suburbanites, *are* is the correct verb here.

4. "Neither Annette nor her brother *is* capable." (The verb agrees with whatever follows *nor*. So if it were "Neither Annette nor her friends," *are* would be called for.)

5. As a general rule, the number of the verb depends on the sense of the sentence. Because it is acting as an amorphous mass in this sentence, *majority* is singular: *The majority wants to unseat.*

3. Keep a modifier as close as possible to the word or clause that it modifies.

A modifier is a word, phrase, or clause that describes another part of the sentence, and should be placed as close as possible to whatever it is modifying. Adjectives modify nouns, adverbs modify verbs or adjectives. Modifiers often attach themselves to the closest word. They sometimes appear to modify words they actually don't. Many GMAT modification errors involve misplaced modifiers that occur at the beginning of the sentence.

A long modifier that comes before the beginning of the main clause will seem to modify the subject. A long modifier that comes in the middle or end of the sentence will seem to describe the word immediately before it. Look out for:

- Sentences beginning or ending with descriptive phrases
- *That/which* clauses, especially ones that come at the end of sentences

Drill: Modification

In each of the following sentences, first identify what each clause or phrase is modifying. Then, fix each error you find.

1.   Upon landing at the airport, the hotel sent a limousine to pick us up.

_____

2. Based on the most current data available, the company made plans to diversify its holdings.

    _____

3. Small and taciturn, Joan Didion's presence often goes unnoticed by those she will later write about.

    _____

4. I took several lessons to learn how to play tennis without getting the ball over the net even once.

    _____

5. The house overlooked the lake, which was set back from the shore.

    _____

Answers and Explanations

1. The sentence seems to be saying that the *hotel* landed at the airport. Your common sense will tell you that *upon landing at the airport* really intends to modify the unnamed *we*, instead. So you could say, "Upon landing at the airport, we were met by a limousine sent by the hotel."

2. As written, it sounds as though the company was based on current data. *Based on the most current data available* modifies the subject *company*. Obviously, though, what was based on the data were the *plans*, not the company. So, "Based on the most current data available, plans were made to diversify the company's holdings."

3. It's Joan Didion—*not her presence*—that's small and taciturn. So, "Small and taciturn, Joan Didion often goes unnoticed …"

4. It seems that the author wants to learn how to not hit the ball over the net. It needs to be revised to something like this: "I took many tennis lessons without getting the ball over the net even once."

5. Misplacement produces an absurd image: a lake that's set back from its own shore. Of course, the *which* clause should follow *the house*: "The house, which was set back from the shore, overlooked the lake."

4. A pronoun must agree with its antecedent and refer to only one antecedent.

KAPLAN) **EXCLUSIVE**

Watch out for underlined pronouns. <u>It</u> is well known that <u>they</u> can cause trouble. Pay attention to what comes before and *after* the underline.

Luckily, the GMAT doesn't test every kind of pronoun error. Errors fall into two categories: reference and agreement. Pronoun reference errors mean that a given pronoun does not refer to—or stand for—a specific noun or pronoun in the sentence (its antecedent). The pronouns that cause the most trouble on the GMAT are *it, its, they, their, them, which,* and *that* .

For pronoun agreement errors, it's a question of numbers: Perhaps a pronoun that refers to a singular noun is not in singular form, or a pronoun that refers to a plural noun is not in plural form.

As usual, the GMAT presents camouflaged examples of these two mistakes. Look out for:

- Pronouns, especially *it* and *they*, that are often misused on the GMAT (and in everyday life)

- Pronouns that don't refer to specific nouns or pronouns

- Pronouns that don't agree in person or number with their antecedents

Drill: Pronoun Agreement

Correct the following common pronoun reference errors.

1. Beatrix Potter's stories depict animals in an unsentimental and humorous manner, and she illustrated them with delicate watercolor paintings.

   _____

2. There is no known cure for certain forms of hepatitis; they hope, though, that a cure will be found soon.

   _____

3. If the partners cannot resolve their differences, the courts may have to do it.

   _____

4. In order to boost their name recognition, the Green Party sent canvassers to a busy shopping mall.

_____

5. It is now recognized that the dangers of nuclear war are much graver than that of conventional warfare.

_____

6. Not even your best friend can always be relied on to give one good advice.

_____

Answers and Explanations

1. *She* could refer only to Beatrix Potter, but notice that the proper noun *Beatrix Potter* doesn't exist in the sentence, only *Beatrix Potter's*. There's a second problem: The pronoun *them* seems to refer to animals, though it could logically refer only to stories. Here's a rewrite that solves all the problems: "Beatrix Potter not only wrote stories that depicted animals in an unsentimental and humorous manner, she also illustrated each story with delicate watercolor paintings."

2. It's unclear what *they* refers to. The only plural noun is *forms*, but it can't be the *forms of hepatitis* that are hoping for a cure. It must be *scientists*, or some other group of people: "Scientists hope to find a cure soon for certain types of hepatitis," or "It is hoped that a cure for certain types of hepatitis will be found soon."

3. *It* is the unclear pronoun here. There's no singular noun in the sentence for *it* to refer to. The main clause should read: "…the courts may have to do so."

4. A pronoun or possessive should match the actual form of the noun it refers to. Use *its* and not *their* in place of the Green Party, because *party*, like *majority*, is a singular noun that stands for a collective group: "In order to boost its name recognition, the Green Party…"

5. *Dangers* is plural. So, "…than those of conventional warfare."

6. The sentence can't say your best friend and give one good advice. So, "Not even your best friend can always be relied on to give you good advice," or " Not even one's best friend can always be relied on to give one good advice."

5. Make sure that a verb tense reflects the sequence of events.

A verb tense indicates the order in which separate actions or events occur. Deciding which verb tense is appropriate in a given situation isn't just a matter of grammar, it's also a question of logic. Many GMAT sentences are long and complicated, involving or implying several different actions. The correct tenses make the sequence of events clear.

To determine whether the verbs in a sentence are in the proper tenses, pick one event as a standard and measure every other event against it. Ask yourself whether the other events are supposed to have happened *before* the standard event took place, *after* it took place, or *while* it took place. Those aren't mutually exclusive options, by the way: It is possible in English to have one action start before a second action and continue during that second action.

A frequent GMAT verb error is the inappropriate use of *-ing* forms: "I am going, I was going, I had been going," and so on. As far as the GMAT is concerned, the only reason to use an *-ing* form is to emphasize that an action is continuing or that two actions are occurring simultaneously. Other than that, pick a simpler tense—one that doesn't use the *-ing* form. In other words, avoid *-ing* forms as much as possible. To remember this rule, think of the word *during* and its *-ing* ending. Look out for:

- *-ing* forms
- The appearance of several verbs, indicating events that seem to have happened in sequence or at different times

> ▶ GO ONLINE
>
> Once you have mastered each basic principle, go back to the Diagnostic Quiz and reconsider each question.

Drill: Verb Tense Reflection

Correct each sentence.

1. The criminal escaped from custody and is believed to flee the country.

   _____

2. Some archaeologists believe that the Minoans of 3,700 years ago had practiced a religion that involved human sacrifice.

   _____

3. If the experiment works, it will be representing a quantum leap forward for pharmaceutical chemistry.

   _____

4. He had seen that movie recently, so he doesn't want to see it tonight.

    _____

5. When she retires, she will save enough money to allow her to live comfortably.

    _____

6. She already closed the door behind her when it occurred to her that she wasn't able to get back in later.

    _____

Answers and Explanations

1. *The criminal escaped* uses simple past tense. So, to reflect the logical sequence of events: "...believed to have fled the country."

2. The past perfect verb *had*, plus another verb, is used to indicate a past action taking place before another past action: "He had quit smoking when he died." Here, there's no indication the Minoans practiced human sacrifice for a while and then did something else. So use the simple past *practiced* instead of *had practiced*.

3. The experiment won't be representing a quantum leap, it will *represent* a quantum leap.

4. *Had* plus a past tense verb is used to indicate which of two things that went on in the past occurred earlier. So, "He saw that movie recently, so he doesn't want to see it tonight."

5. Here, we're indicating an action that began in the past but will end in the future. Think of it this way: At some future time, what will have happened? "..., she will have saved enough money."

6. *Closed, occurred,* and *wasn't able to get back in* are all in the simple past tense. But you need to indicate first, that she closed the door before something occurred to her, and second, that she wouldn't be able to do something in the future. "She had already closed behind her when it occurred to her that she wouldn't be able to get back in."

6. Keep similar elements in a sentence parallel to each other.

Similar elements in a sentence—such as items in a list or verbs in a series—must be in similar form, as do two-part constructions (*from…to…or (n)either…(n)or…*). Finally, items linked by *and* should be structurally similar.

Though this principle has several components, the basic concept behind parallelism is pretty simple: Ideas with the same importance and function—nouns, verbs, phrases, or whatever—should be expressed in the same grammatical form. Look out for:

- Lists of items or a series of events
- Such expressions *as both X and Y, either X or Y, prefer X to Y*

Drill: Parallelism among Similar Elements

For each of the following sentences, put parallel items into the same form.

1. The city's decay stems from governmental mismanagement, increasing unemployment, and many businesses are relocating.

   _____

2. Tourists' images of France range from cosmopolitan to the pastoral.

   _____

3. Excited about visiting New York, Jasmine minded neither riding the subways nor to cope with the crowded sidewalks.

   _____

4. To visualize success is not the same as achieving it.

   _____

5. I remember my aunt making her own dandelion wine and that she played the fiddle.

   _____

6. In my favorite Armenian restaurant, the menu is fascinating and the entrées exquisite.

   _____

KAPLAN

Answers and Explanations

1. *Many businesses are relocating* should be written as *business relocation*, to parallel *governmental mismanagement* and *increasing unemployment*.

2. If you say *the* pastoral you have to say *the* cosmopolitan. Or you could say "...cosmopolitan to pastoral."

3. To parallel *riding*, you need *coping*—not *to cope*.

4. *To visualize* should be *visualizing*.

5. It has to be either: "I remember my aunt making...and playing...," or "I remember that my aunt made...and played...."

6. You say *is fascinating*, so you must say *are exquisite*.

7. Compare like things only.

Faulty comparisons account for a significant number of errors in GMAT Sentence Correction questions. Most relate to the very simple idea that you can't compare apples and oranges. Of course you want to compare things that are grammatically similar, but you also want to compare things that are *logically* similar. You can't logically compare, say, a person to a quality or an item to a group. You have to compare one individual to another, one quality to another, one group to another. Look out for:

- Key comparison words, such as *like, as, compared to, less than, more than, other, that of*, and *those of*

Drill: Comparing Like Things

Fix the comparisons in the sentences below.

1. Like a black bear I once saw in the Buenos Aires Zoo, the Central Park Zoo polar bear's personality strikes me as being sadly neurotic.

   _____

2. The article questioned the popularity of jazz compared to classical music.

   _____

3.   The challenger weighed 20 pounds less than that of the defender.

_____

4.   The Boston office contributes less to total national sales than any other U.S. branch.

_____

5.   The host paid more attention to his celebrity guest than the others.

_____

Answers and Explanations

1. *Like* creates a comparison, and you can compare only similar things. Here, you have to compare bears to bears, or personalities to personalities. "Like a black bear I once saw in the Buenos Aires Zoo, the Central Park Zoo polar bear strikes me as being sadly neurotic."

2. "The article questioned the popularity of jazz compared to the popularity [or *that of*] classical music."

3. "The challenger weighed 20 pounds less than the defender did," or "The challenger's weight was 20 pounds less than that of the defender."

4. You want to compare what the Boston office contributes to what any other U.S. branch contributes. Insert *does* after *U.S. branch*. *Does* will stand for *contributes*.

5. A similar problem—you need to repeat the verb after *than* ("than he paid to the others"). Or, refer to the verb by placing *to* after *than* ("than to the others").

8. Use your "ear" for correct idioms.

This eighth (and frequently tested) principle concerns forms of expression that have established themselves in standard English as the "right" way to say things. There's no grammar rule that applies here; it's just that these particular expressions are generally agreed upon as correct by all English speakers.

READ MORE

Read your local newspaper or favorite website to learn idioms. They are tested commonly on the GMAT.

If you're a native English speaker, you probably know most idioms already. You'll hear what's correct and incorrect. If you aren't a native speaker, it's worth taking time to learn these expressions. In fact, keep a notebook and jot them down as you come across them in your practice. Look out for Sentence Corrections that contain idiomatic expressions.

Drill: Correct Idioms

Circle the word(s) that "sound" right in the sentence.

1. Mathew Brady is regarded (as/to be) one of the greatest nineteenth-century American photographers.

2. The destruction of tropical rain forests is generally considered (as/to be/_ _) a major threat to the environment.

3. It took me 4 times as long to write the report collaboratively (than/as) it would have taken me to write it by myself.

4. The Geneva Convention covers such questions (like/as) the proper treatment of prisoners of war.

5. Hiram plays guitar (like/as) his father does.

6. The gas was being produced (in/at) a rate of twelve million cubic feet a day.

7. I prefer Korean food (to/over) Japanese.

8. My mother tried to discourage me (from attending/to attend) law school.

9. Many consumers buy inferior products when forced to choose (among/between) price and value.

10. Off-off-Broadway theaters seat significantly (fewer/ less) patrons than do Broadway theaters.

Answers and Explanations

1. The idiom is *regarded as*.

2. It's *considered a* major threat. While *considered to be* is also correct by most grammarians, it is considered wordy by the GMAT writers, who always prefer to drop the *to be*. And *considered as* is always wrong.

3. The idiom is *as long . . . as*. This test lasted 4 times *as long as* that one did. *As far...as* works in the same way.

4. You have to say "the Geneva Convention covers such questions *as* proper treatment."

5. He plays *as* his father does.

6. It's "*at a* rate of," not "in a rate of."

7. The correct idiom is *prefer…to.*

8. You don't discourage someone *to attend*; you discourage that person *from attending.*

9. Use *between* to distinguish two things, such as *price* and *value* here. Use *among* for more than two things. They divided the pie *between themselves* or *among the 4 of them.*

10. *Fewer* is correct. *Fewer* is used when you can count the items in question (fewer people or lawn-mowers). *Less* is used when the items in question are more abstract in number and cannot be counted (less sand or flour).

 KAPLAN STRATEGY ——————————————————————————

Know this about *which*, *where*, and *when*:

- *Which* must come directly after a comma, and it must refer to the noun just before the comma (except when it follows a preposition, as in the phrase "in which").

- *Where* must refer to an actual location.

- *When* must refer to an actual time reference.

SENTENCE CORRECTION RULES

There are some rules that you should know about certain types of Sentence Correction errors:

Parallel Structure Errors

The key to handling parallel structure questions is *consistency, consistency, consistency.*

Rule 1: Items in a list must have parallel form.

Rule 2: Many two-part constructions set up parallel elements. For instance, "not only...but also," or "from A to B."

Modification Errors

Many modification errors involve misplaced modifiers that appear at the beginning of the sentence.

Rule 1: A modifying phrase must clearly refer to what it modifies, so it must be placed as close as possible to what it modifies.

Rule 2: Adjectives modify nouns, while adverbs modify verbs or adjectives.

Pronoun Errors

The pronouns that cause the most trouble on the GMAT are *it, its, they, their, them, which,* and *that.*

Rule 1: A pronoun must refer unambiguously to a specific noun.

Rule 2: A pronoun must agree in number with the noun it replaces.

Verb Errors

The rules sound simple, but the testmaker has a way of making these errors less than obvious.

Rule 1: A verb must agree with the subject of the sentence. That means plural subjects go with plural verbs, and singular subjects go with singular verbs.

Rule 2: The verb tense must make sense with the rest of the sentence.

KAPLAN'S 3-STEP METHOD FOR SENTENCE CORRECTION

Now we come to the Kaplan method for tackling a Sentence Correction.

Step 1: Read the original sentence carefully, looking for errors.

If you find an error in the sentence, cross out choice (A) immediately because you know it won't be the correct answer choice. Choice (A) will always repeat the wording of the original sentence. If you don't spot an error, go immediately to Step 2.

Step 2: Scan the answer choices.

If the answer choices present a variety of verb tenses or pronouns, for instance, you'll know where to focus your attention. Don't bother reading choice (A), since it's simply a repeat of the original structure. Immediately skip to choice (B).

Step 3: Eliminate choices until only one remains.

If you spot any error in an answer choice, eliminate that choice and move on to the next one. You should be able to eliminate enough answer choices to come up with the correct answer, or at least with a good percentage guess.

Now let's apply the Kaplan Method to a Sentence Correction item:

KAPLAN EXCLUSIVE

Don't overcorrect. Many sentences are correct as written. Choice (A) always reflects the sentence in its original form.

> Several consumer protection agencies have filed suit, seeking to bar distributors from advertising treatments for baldness <u>that brings no discernible improvement and may even result</u> in potential harm.
>
> ○ that brings no discernible improvement and may even result in potential harm
>
> ○ that bring no discernible improvement and may even prove harmful
>
> ○ bringing no discernible improvement and even being harmful
>
> ○ that brings no discernible improvement and may even potentially result in harm being done
>
> ○ that bring no discernible improvement, maybe even resulting in harm

Step 1: Read the original sentence carefully, looking for errors.

The error lies in the second word of the underlined part, *brings*. What *brings* no discernible improvement? Treatments. But you can't say *treatments brings*. The difference in verbs seems to be the issue. So (A), the original structure, can't be correct.

Step 2: Scan the answer choices.

Some choices have *brings*, some have *bring*, and one has *bringing*. Which is correct here?

Step 3: Eliminate choices until only one remains.

The beginning of each choice is a good place to start here, because there are three basic variations. You already know that *brings* is wrong, so you can eliminate (D) without reading any more of it. The answer, of course, turns out to be (B). *Bring* is the verb you need to agree with *treatments*.

SUMMARY

The basic principles of Sentence Correction are:

- Understand the directions completely.
- Keep agreement between subject and verb.
- Keep a modifier as close as possible to the word that it modifies.
- A pronoun must agree with its antecedent and refer to only one antecedent.
- Make sure that a verb tense reflects the sequence of events.
- Keep similar elements in a sentence parallel to each other.
- Compare like things only.
- Use your "ear" for correct idioms.

Common rules for Sentence Correction are:

- For Parallel Structure Errors:

  Rule 1: Items in a list must have parallel form.

  Rule 2: Many two-part constructions set up parallel elements. For instance, "not only...but also," or "from A to B."

- For Modification Errors:

  Rule 1: A modifying phrase must clearly refer to what it modifies, so it must be placed as close as possible to what it modifies.

  Rule 2: Adjectives modify nouns, while adverbs modify verbs or adjectives.

- For Pronoun Errors:

  Rule 1: A pronoun must refer unambiguously to a specific noun.

  Rule 2: A pronoun must agree in number with the noun it replaces.

- For Verb Errors:

  Rule 1: A verb must agree with the subject of the sentence. That means plural subjects go with plural verbs, and singular subjects go with singular verbs.

  Rule 2: The verb tense must make sense with the rest of the sentence.

Kaplan's 3-Step Method for Sentence Corrections is:

Step 1: Read the original sentence carefully, looking for errors.

Step 2: Scan the answer choices.

Step 3: Eliminate choices until only one remains.

PRACTICE QUIZ

Directions: The following question presents a sentence, part or all of which is underlined. Below each sentence you will find five ways to phrase the underlined portion. Choice (A) repeats the original version, while the other four choices are different. If the original seems best, choose (A). If not, choose one of the revisions.

This question tests correctness and effectiveness of expression. Choose an answer that follows the norms of standard written English: grammar, word choice, and sentence construction. Choose the answer that produces the most effective sentence, aiming to eliminate awkwardness, ambiguity, redundancy, and grammatical error.

1. The concert this weekend promises to attract <u>an even greater amount of people</u> than attended the last one.

   ○ an even greater amount of people

   ○ an even larger amount of people

   ○ an amount of people even greater

   ○ a number of people even larger

   ○ an even greater number of people

2. <u>Compared with the time period of John Steinbeck's *The Grapes of Wrath*</u>, the poor of today would be considered wealthy.

   ○ Compared with the time period of John Steinbeck's *The Grapes of Wrath*

   ○ Compared with the time period during which John Steinbeck's *The Grapes of Wrath* took place

   ○ Compared with the characters in John Steinbeck's *The Grapes of Wrath*

   ○ In comparison to the time of John Steinbeck's *The Grapes of Wrath*

   ○ In comparison to John Steinbeck's *The Grapes of Wrath*

3. Although the square root of a negative number has no real value, it is not necessarily true that <u>equations involving imaginary numbers like these are practically inapplicable</u>.

   ○ equations involving imaginary numbers like these are practically inapplicable

   ○ equations involving such imaginary numbers have no practical applications

   ○ equations involving these inapplicable imaginary numbers are practical

   ○ equations involving imaginary numbers such as these are inapplicable practically

   ○ there is no practical applications for equations involving such imaginary numbers as these

KAPLAN

4. Anarchists believe that the ideal society is one
    in which the motivation to maintain law and
    order <u>lies in the innate reasonableness of
    human nature rather than in the threat of
    force</u>.

    ○ lies in the innate reasonableness of
      human nature rather than in the threat of
      force

    ○ lie in the innate reasonableness of human
      nature rather than in the threat of force

    ○ lays in the innate reasonableness of
      human nature rather than the threat of
      force

    ○ lay in the innate reasonableness of
      human nature instead of the threat of
      force

    ○ lies in the innate reasonableness of
      human nature instead of the threat of
      force

5. The public's widespread belief in the existence
    of <u>UFOs and their general curiosity about
    extraterrestrial life has</u> generated considerable
    interest in science fiction.

    ○ UFOs and their general curiosity about
      extraterrestrial life has

    ○ UFOs and they are generally curious
      about extraterrestrial life which has

    ○ UFOs, as well as their general curiosity
      about extraterrestrial life, have

    ○ UFOs, as well as its general curiosity
      about extraterrestrial life, has

    ○ UFOs, as well as general curiosity about
      extraterrestrial life, have

6. In some countries, the political system works
    by a simple logic: the more an organization
    contributes to politicians' campaign funds, <u>its
    interests are better served by the policies and
    actions of the government</u>.

    ○ its interests are better served by the poli-
      cies and actions of the government

    ○ its interests are the better served through
      the policies and actions of the govern-
      ment

    ○ the better its interests are served by the
      policies and actions of the government

    ○ by the policies and actions of the govern-
      ment, its interests being better served

    ○ by the policies and actions of the govern-
      ment, service is the better for its interests

7. Many of the thousands of students currently enrolled in night courses hope <u>for the exchanging of their drab jobs for new careers that are challenging</u>.

   - ⬭ for the exchanging of their drab jobs for new careers that are challenging

   - ⬭ for exchanging drab jobs for new careers that will challenge them

   - ⬭ to exchange their drab jobs with new careers that will be new and challenging

   - ⬭ to exchange their drab jobs for new and challenging careers

   - ⬭ to exchanging their drab jobs and find careers that will be new and challenging

8. Records of the first 736 British convicts deported to Australia reveal <u>convictions for crimes against property in all cases and they ranged</u> from highway robbery to forgery.

   - ⬭ convictions for crimes against property in all cases and they ranged

   - ⬭ convictions in all cases were crimes against property and ranging

   - ⬭ the ranging of convictions for crimes against property in all cases

   - ⬭ that all were convicted of crimes against property ranging

   - ⬭ that all of them had convictions for crimes that were against property; the range was

9. The symptoms of the participants in a recent decongestant effectiveness study, including a required "stuffy nose," <u>parallel that of the multitudes of Americans afflicted with</u> the common cold each winter.

   - ⬭ parallel that of the multitudes of Americans afflicted with

   - ⬭ parallel the multitudes of Americans afflicted with

   - ⬭ parallel those of the multitudes of Americans afflicted with

   - ⬭ parallels those of the multitudes of Americans afflicted from

   - ⬭ parallels that of the multitudes of Americans afflicted from

10. A group of students who have begun to clean up Frederick Law Olmsted's Morningside Park in New York City <u>believes that the park needs not to be redesigned but to</u> be returned to its former condition.

    ○ believes that the park needs not to be redesigned but to

    ○ believe that the park needs to not be redesigned but to

    ○ believes that the park needs not to be redesigned but could

    ○ believe that the park needs to be not redesigned but to

    ○ believe that the park needs not to be redesigned but that it

11. <u>Having recently published a series of science fiction books influenced by Sufism, Doris Lessing will likely</u> be remembered best for her early novels about Africa.

    ○ Having recently published a series of science fiction books influenced by Sufism, Doris Lessing will likely

    ○ Although she has recently published a series of science fiction books influenced by Sufism, Doris Lessing is likely to

    ○ She has recently published a series of science fiction books influenced by Sufism, and Doris Lessing will likely

    ○ In spite of recently publishing a series of science fiction books influenced by Sufism, Doris Lessing should likely

    ○ Recently publishing a series of science fiction books influenced by Sufism, Doris Lessing may likely

12. In February, 1983, brush fires <u>had swept the drought-parched southeastern coast of Australia, at least 69 people being killed, and thousands of homes and acres of farmland were left smoldering.</u>

    ◯ had swept the drought-parched southeastern coast of Australia, at least 69 people being killed, and thousands of homes and acres of farmland were left smoldering

    ◯ swept the drought-parched southeastern coast of Australia, having killed at least 69 people, and thousands of home and acres of farmland were left smoldering

    ◯ swept the drought-parched southeastern coast of Australia, killing at least 69 people, and had left thousands of homes and acres of farmland smoldering

    ◯ swept the drought-parched southeastern coast of Australia, killing at least 69 people, and leaving thousands of homes and acres of farmland smoldering

    ◯ swept the drought-parched southeastern coast of Australia, killing at least 69 people, and left smoldering thousands of homes and acres of farmland

13. Scoliosis, <u>a condition when the spine curves abnormally and throws the body out of line,</u> can cause heart and lung problems as well as physical deformity.

    ◯ a condition when the spine curves abnormally and throws the body out of line

    ◯ an abnormal curvature of the spine that throws the body out of line

    ◯ a condition of the spine curving abnormally and in which the body is thrown out of line

    ◯ where the body is thrown out of line by an abnormal curvature of the spine

    ◯ a condition of an abnormal curvature of the spine throwing the body out of line

KAPLAN

14. Although some ornithologists contend that the precursors of birds are arboreal creatures that glide from tree to tree, others believe that they were runners whose front limbs evolved into wings.

    ○ Although some ornithologists contend that the precursors of birds are arboreal creatures that glide from tree to tree

    ○ However it may be that some ornithologists contend that the precursors of birds were arboreal creatures that glide from tree to tree

    ○ Despite that the precursors of birds were, according to some ornithologists, arboreal creatures that glide from tree to tree

    ○ Although some ornithologists contend that the precursors of birds were arboreal creatures that glided from tree to tree

    ○ According to some ornithologists gliding from tree to tree, the precursors of birds are arboreal creatures, that

15. The newly elected baseball commissioner has asked that a federal arbitrator would mediate negotiations between representatives of the umpire's union, which has threatened to go on strike, and the lawyers representing major league franchise owners.

    ○ that a federal arbitrator would mediate negotiations between representatives of the umpire's union, which has threatened

    ○ that a federal arbitrator mediate negotiations between representatives of the umpire's union, which have threatened

    ○ of a federal arbitrator that he mediate negotiations between representatives of the umpire's union, which have threatened

    ○ a federal arbitrator that he mediate negotiations between representatives of the umpire's union, which has threatened

    ○ a federal arbitrator to mediate negotiations between representatives of the umpire's union, which has threatened

16. In the conflict between the Israelis and the Palestinians, <u>the refusal of each side to acknowledge the other as a legitimate national movement is closer to the heart of the problem than</u> is any other issue.

    ◯ the refusal of each side to acknowledge the other as a legitimate national movement is closer to the heart of the problem than

    ◯ that the refusal of each side to acknowledge the other as a legitimate national movement is closer to the heart of the problem as

    ◯ the refusal of each side to acknowledge another as a legitimate national movement is closer to the heart of the problem than

    ◯ that the refusal of each side to acknowledge another as a legitimate national movement is closer to the heart of the problem than

    ◯ the refusal of each side to acknowledge the other as a legitimate national movement is closer to the heart of the problem as

17. In this year's negotiations, unionized workers will be fighting to improve job security in many industries, but will be seeking large wage increases in some others, <u>as in the prospering telecommunications industry</u>.

    ◯ as in the prospering telecommunications industry

    ◯ such industries like telecommunications, which is prospering

    ◯ as in that of the prospering telecommunications industry

    ◯ as is the prospering telecommunications industry

    ◯ as in an industry like telecommunications, which is prospering

KAPLAN

18. To tackle the issue of Congressional campaign spending is <u>becoming embroiled in a war which is raging between those who support public financing with</u> those who would lift the limits on the amount political parties and individuals may donate.

    ○ becoming embroiled in a war which is raging between those who support public financing with

    ○ becoming embroiled in a war raging among those who support public financing with

    ○ to become embroiled in a war raging between those who support public financing and

    ○ to become embroiled in a war which is raging among those who support public financing and

    ○ becoming embroiled in a war raging between those who support public financing and

19. <u>A scientist has determined that a recently discovered ancient Chinese weapon, buried since approximately 1300 B.C., is encrusted with silk, a fabric previously thought to have been invented 1,000 years later.</u>

    ○ A scientist has determined that a recently discovered ancient Chinese weapon, buried since approximately 1300 B.C., is encrusted with silk, a fabric previously thought to have been invented 1,000 years later.

    ○ Buried since approximately 1300 B.C., an ancient Chinese weapon had been recently determined by a scientist to be encrusted with silk, a fabric previously thought to be invented 1,000 years later.

    ○ A scientist had determined that a recently discovered ancient Chinese weapon is encrusted with silk, a fabric previously thought to be invented 1,000 years later, after having been buried since approximately 1300 B.C.

    ○ After being buried since approximately 1300 B.C., a scientist has determined that a recently discovered ancient Chinese weapon is encrusted with silk, a fabric previously thought to have been invented 1,000 years later.

    ○ A recently discovered ancient Chinese weapon, buried since approximately 1300 B.C., has been determined to be covered with silk by a scientist, a fabric previously thought to have been invented 1,000 years later.

20. <u>When he had run for mayor of Cleveland in 1968,</u> Carl Stokes won the election, proving that an African American candidate can be elected in a city in which African Americans constitute a minority of the population.

    ○ When he had run for mayor of Cleveland in 1968,

    ○ He ran for mayor of Cleveland in 1968, and

    ○ Running, in 1968, for Mayor of Cleveland,

    ○ When he ran for mayor of Cleveland in 1968,

    ○ In 1968 he had run for mayor of Cleveland, and

21. Brief psychotherapy requires far fewer hours and costs far less money than traditional psychoanalysis, and so <u>will hopefully prove to be an effective treatment for many of the large amount</u> of people currently seeking therapy.

    ○ will hopefully prove to be an effective treatment for many of the large amount

    ○ will prove hopefully to be an effective treatment for many of the large amount

    ○ hopefully will prove to be an effective treatment for many of the large number

    ○ will, it is hoped, prove to be an effective treatment for many of the large number

    ○ will, it is hoped, prove to be an effective treatment for many of the large amount

22. <u>Having often been thought of as still a city of working-class neighborhoods, Chicago is increasingly populated by poor people.</u>

    ○ Having often been thought of as still a city of working-class neighborhoods, Chicago is increasingly populated by poor people.

    ○ It is still often thought of as a city of working-class neighborhoods, and Chicago is increasingly populated by poor people.

    ○ In spite of still often being thought of as a city of working-class neighborhoods, the people who populate Chicago are increasingly poor.

    ○ It is still often thought of as a city of working-class neighborhoods, but the people who populate Chicago are increasingly poor.

    ○ Although still often thought of as a city of working-class neighborhoods, Chicago is increasingly populated by poor people.

KAPLAN

23. To control public unease over the regime's impending economic collapse, the government ordered local officials <u>should censor records of what were their communities' unemployment figures</u>.

    ○ should censor records of what were their communities' unemployment figures

    ○ would do the censorship of records of their communities' unemployment figures

    ○ censoring records of unemployment figures in their communities

    ○ the censoring of a record of unemployment figures in their communities

    ○ to censor records of unemployment figures in their communities

24. <u>As a result of having</u> nostrils, called nares, connected to olfactory bulbs that go back to the brain, sharks are capable of smelling even a few molecules of blood in the water.

    ○ As a result of having

    ○ As a result of it having

    ○ Because they have

    ○ Because of having

    ○ Because of their having

25. In the past few months, there has been extensive dispute <u>over if fare hikes should be a first or last recourse</u> in improving the transit system.

    ○ over if fare hikes should be a first or last recourse

    ○ about if fare hikes is a first or last recourse

    ○ about hiking fares being first or last recourses

    ○ over whether fare hikes should be a first or last recourse

    ○ concerning hikes in fares and their being first or last recourses

26. Psycholinguists know that a child produces speech sounds <u>by imitating adults, but they do not know how he learns to distinguish significantly different phonemes or</u> how he comes to ignore meaningless variations between speech sounds.

    ○ by imitating adults, but they do not know how he learns to distinguish significantly different phonemes or

    ○ by imitating adults, but they do not know either how he learns to distinguish significantly different phonemes nor

    ○ through the imitation of adults, but they neither know how he learns to distinguish significantly different phonemes or

    ○ through the imitation of adults, but they do not know either how he learns to distinguish significantly different phonemes nor

    ○ by imitating adults, but they do not know how he learns to distinguish significantly different phonemes nor

27. In response to higher oil prices, window manufacturers have improved the insulating capability of their products; their windows <u>have been built to conserve energy, and they are</u>.

    ○ have been built to conserve energy, and they are

    ○ are built to conserve energy, and they have

    ○ are built to conserve energy, and they do

    ○ are being built to conserve energy, and have

    ○ had been built to conserve energy, and they are

28. Though initially opposed to the measure, the governor approved the new needle-exchange program <u>at the urging of his own doctor, his chief advisers, and a coalition of some</u> 20 social action groups.

   ○ at the urging of his own doctor, his chief advisers, and a coalition of some

   ○ as a consequence of having been urged by his own doctor, his chief advisers, and a coalition of some

   ○ on account of being urged by his own doctor, chief advisers, and a coalition of

   ○ as he was urged to do by his own doctor, his chief advisers, and a coalition of some

   ○ as his own doctor was urging him to do, along with his chief advisers, and a coalition of

29. Since the new manufacturing process for plastic containers was introduced 10 years ago, the average size of plastic manufacturing plants <u>have dropped from 200,000 square feet to 50,000 square feet, an area that is about a football field's size</u>.

   ○ have dropped from 200,000 square feet to 50,000 square feet, an area that is about a football field's size

   ○ have dropped from 200,000 square feet to 50,000 square feet, about the size of a football field

   ○ has dropped from 200,000 square feet to 50,000 square feet, about the size of a football field

   ○ has dropped from 200,000 square feet down to 50,000 square feet, about the size of football field's

   ○ has dropped from 200,000 square feet down to 50,000 square feet, about a football field's size

30. <u>In order to document their contribution to the field of structural engineering, the curators at the university's art museum organized a comprehensive exhibition of the work of leading Swiss designers, including photographs, diagrams and models of their most famous bridges and buildings.</u>

    ○ In order to document their contribution to the field of structural engineering, the curators at the university's art museum organized a comprehensive exhibition of the work of leading Swiss designers, including photographs, diagrams and models of their most famous bridges and buildings.

    ○ In order to document the contribution of the Swiss to the field of structural engineering, the curators at the university's art museum organized a comprehensive exhibition of the work of leading Swiss designers, including photographs, diagrams and models of their most famous bridges and buildings.

    ○ In order to document the contribution of the Swiss to the field of structural engineering, the curators at the university's art museum organized a comprehensive exhibition of the work of leading Swiss designers, including photographs, diagrams and models of its most famous bridges and buildings.

    ○ In order to document their contribution to the structural engineering field, a comprehensive exhibition was organized by the curators at the university's art museum of their photographs, diagrams and models of the most famous bridges and buildings of leading Swiss designers.

    ○ The curators at the university's art museum, in order to document their contribution to the field, organized a comprehensive exhibition of the work of leading Swiss designers, including photographs, diagrams and models of their most famous bridges and buildings.

31. It can be difficult for small investors to sell their shares of stock in companies whose policies they disagree with because small investors' assets are less robust <u>than</u> large investors.

    ○ than

    ○ than those of

    ○ than is true of

    ○ compared with

    ○ relatively to those of

32. Finding itself unable to keep up with the new competitors that had recently entered its industry, the company was forced to begin closing plants, laying off workers, and <u>reduced</u> its research and marketing budgets.

    ○ reduced

    ○ it reduced

    ○ reducing

    ○ would reduce

    ○ it had reduced

33. Those who study ancient European history soon realize that <u>before Greece was Greece, it was a collection of small city-states</u> that were intensely jealous of one another and were only occasionally able to work together for common goals.

    ○ before Greece was Greece, it was a collection of small city-states

    ○ before there was Greece, it was a collection of small city-states

    ○ before Greece, it was a collection of small city-states

    ○ it was a collection of small city-states that was Greece

    ○ Greece became a collection of small city-states

34. <u>Compiled from documents provided by several government agencies</u>, the investigative commission produced a report clearly indicating that federal officials had frequently authorized expenditures far above statutory limits.

    ○ Compiled from documents provided by several government agencies

    ○ Compiling it from several government agencies' documents

    ○ A compilation of documents from several government agencies

    ○ Documents provided by several government agencies

    ○ Working from documents provided by several government agencies

35. In addition to being more expensive than manual research, <u>the compounds identified by machine-based research are often of lower quality than those identified by</u> manual research, which are more likely to become marketable pharmaceutical products.

    ◯ the compounds identified by machine-based research are often of lower quality than those identified by

    ◯ machine-based research often identifies compounds that are of lower quality than those identified by

    ◯ machine-based research is lower in quality than those compounds identified by

    ◯ the compounds identified by machine-based research are often lower in quality than

    ◯ compounds identified by machine-based research often had lower quality than those identified by

36. Since 1993, when it passed a referendum <u>approving casino gambling, the town of Riverside, Missouri was</u> using casino tax revenue to improve its streets, sewers, buildings and other public works.

    ◯ approving casino gambling, the town of Riverside, Missouri was

    ◯ for the approving of casino gambling, the town of Riverside, Missouri was

    ◯ approved casino gambling, the town of Riverside, Missouri has been

    ◯ approving casino gambling, the town of Riverside, Missouri has been

    ◯ approving casino gambling, the town of Riverside, Missouri was to be

37. Disappointed by his students' refusal to complete the assigned reading, <u>a pop quiz from the teacher was chosen to surprise them</u> the next day.

    ◯ a pop quiz from the teacher was chosen to surprise them

    ◯ they were surprised by the choice of a pop quiz from the teacher

    ◯ the teacher chose to surprise them with a pop quiz

    ◯ the teacher was surprised by a pop quiz from them

    ◯ a pop quiz as the choice of the teacher surprised them

KAPLAN

38. Many freshmen find the first year of college quite challenging and are unable to balance responsibilities such as attending class, <u>reading assignments, and to write</u> papers with the wide and sometimes bewildering array of new social opportunities.

    ○ reading assignments, and to write

    ○ reading assignments, and writing

    ○ to read assignments, and write

    ○ to read assignments, and to write

    ○ to read assignments, writing

39. Without hiding the fact that the destruction of Athens <u>was one of their most important objectives</u>, the multitudinous Persian army, led by Xerxes and 9 of his generals, marched westward toward Greece in the spring and summer of 480 BC.

    ○ was one of their most important objectives

    ○ was one of its most important objectives

    ○ was one of the objectives they considered to be most important

    ○ having been one of its most important objectives

    ○ is one of its most important objectives

40. As evidence of sushi's drastically increasing popularity, the most recent studies show that the number of sushi restaurants in the state <u>increased by more than 3 times</u> in the past 5 years.

    ○ increased by more than 3 times

    ○ increased by more than triple

    ○ was increased more than 3 times

    ○ has more than tripled

    ○ was more than tripled

41. Researchers have found that the human body can use protein derived from whey more efficiently than it can use <u>protein from other sources such as soy, eggs or drinking milk</u>.

- ◯ protein from other sources such as soy, eggs or drinking milk
- ◯ protein from other sources like soy, eggs or drinking milk
- ◯ protein from other sources such as soy, eggs or milk
- ◯ protein which it has derived from other sources such as soy, eggs or drinking milk
- ◯ its protein from other sources such as soy, eggs or milk

42. At 60 inmates per 100,000 citizens, Norway has one of the lowest incarceration rates of all Western countries, <u>reflecting their long</u> humanitarian tradition.

- ◯ reflecting their long
- ◯ being a reflection of its long
- ◯ reflection of their long
- ◯ reflecting its long
- ◯ reflecting its greater

43. <u>Despite significant discounts, Detroit automakers were losing</u> U.S. market share to lower-cost rivals from Japan and South Korea, which are gaining ground even while offering smaller discounts.

- ◯ Despite significant discounts, Detroit automakers were losing
- ◯ Despite significant discounts, Detroit automakers are losing
- ◯ Despite significant discounts, the Detroit automakers lost
- ◯ Despite significant discounts, the Detroit automakers continuing to lose
- ◯ The Detroit automakers, despite significant discounts, were losing

44. Sky Airlines recently announced aggressive cost-cutting measures <u>ranging from new airport check-in procedures that encourage passengers to use self-service kiosks and reductions</u> in the size of its fleet.

   ○ ranging from new airport check-in procedures that encourage passengers to use self-service kiosks and reductions

   ○ ranging from new airport check-in procedures that encourage passengers to use self-service kiosks and to reductions

   ○ such as improvement of airport check-in procedures, encouragement of passengers to use self-service kiosks and reducing

   ○ ranging from new airport check-in procedures that encourage passengers to use self-service kiosks to reducing

   ○ ranging from new airport check-in procedures that encourage passengers to use self-service kiosks to reductions

45. The Dancing Doll line sold slightly more than $3.5 million worth of toys last year, 40% more than <u>the Teeny Tiny Trucks line did and nearly 3 times as much as the Basic Blocks line's sales.</u>

   ○ the Teeny Tiny Trucks line did and nearly 3 times as much as the Basic Blocks line's sales

   ○ the Teeny Tiny Trucks did and nearly 3 times what the Basic Blocks' sales were

   ○ the Teeny Tiny Trucks line sold and nearly 3 times as much as Basic Blocks' sales

   ○ the Teeny Tiny Trucks line and nearly 3 times more than Basic Blocks' sales

   ○ the Teeny Tiny Trucks line and nearly 3 times more than the Basic Blocks line

46. It was decided by the National Weather Service to purchase a forecasting system that combines 44 computers linked together with each other to form the world's 6th-largest supercomputer.

   - ○ It was decided by the National Weather Service to purchase a forecasting system that combines 44 computers linked together with each other to form the world's 6th-largest supercomputer.

   - ○ A forecasting system that combines 44 computers linked together with each other to form the world's 6th-largest supercomputer was selected to be purchased by the National Weather Service.

   - ○ It was decided by the National Weather Service to purchase a forecasting system that links 44 computers together to form the world's 6th-largest supercomputer.

   - ○ The National Weather Service decided to purchase a forecasting system that links 44 computers together to form the world's 6th-largest supercomputer.

   - ○ The National Weather Service decided to purchase a forecasting system that combines 44 computers linked together with each other to form the world's 6th-largest supercomputer.

47. The Democratic Republic of Congo not only has one of the world's largest populations, with over 56 million people, but also has one of the world's fastest-growing populations, with an annual growth rate of 3.5%.

   - ○ not only has one of the world's largest populations, with over 56 million people, but also has

   - ○ not only has one of the world's largest populations, with over 56 million people, it also has

   - ○ not only has one of the world's largest populations, with over 56 million people, but moreover it is

   - ○ with 56 million people, making it one of the world's most populous countries, but also has

   - ○ has one of the world's largest populations, with over 56 million people, but also has

KAPLAN

48. <u>Corporation X spends a larger percentage of its revenue on insurance than Corporation Y does on employee salaries.</u>

- ⬭ Corporation X spends a larger percentage of its revenue on insurance than Corporation Y does on employee salaries.

- ⬭ In Corporation X, a larger percentage of the revenues is spent on insurance than is spent on employee salaries in Corporation Y.

- ⬭ In Corporation X they spend a larger percentage of revenues on insurance than Corporation Y does on employee salaries.

- ⬭ A larger percentage of Corporation X's revenue is spent on insurance than Corporation Y spends on employee salaries.

- ⬭ Of the Corporations X and Y, a higher percentage of revenues is spent on insurance by the former than the latter spends on employee salaries.

49. Because the city's files covered only the years 1934 through <u>2002, so the potential buyers were unable to determine the year of originally</u> construction.

- ⬭ 2002, so the potential buyers were unable to determine the year of originally

- ⬭ 2002, and the potential buyers were unable to determine the year of originally

- ⬭ 2002, the potential buyers were unable to determine the year of original

- ⬭ 2002, therefore the potential buyers were unable to determine the year of originally

- ⬭ 2002; therefore, the potential buyers were unable to determine the year of original

50. Museum-goers who glanced up into the building's five-story atrium often <u>notice birds nesting in the rafters, whose behavior was being studied by the museum's staff</u>.

    ○ notice birds nesting in the rafters, whose behavior was being studied by the museum's staff

    ○ notice birds nesting in the rafters, which were being studied by the museum's staff

    ○ notice that birds, whose behavior was being studied by the museum's staff, are nesting in the rafters,

    ○ noticed that birds, whose behavior was being studied by the museum's staff, were nesting in the rafters

    ○ noticed that birds, with the behavior that was being studied by the museum's staff, were nesting in the rafters

ANSWERS AND EXPLANATIONS

1. E	11. B	21. D	31. B	41. C
2. C	12. D	22. E	32. C	42. D
3. B	13. B	23. E	33. A	43. B
4. A	14. D	24. C	34. E	44. E
5. D	15. E	25. D	35. B	45. E
6. C	16. A	26. A	36. D	46. D
7. D	17. A	27. C	37. C	47. A
8. D	18. C	28. A	38. B	48. A
9. C	19. A	29. C	39. B	49. C
10. A	20. D	30. B	40. D	50. D

1. D

Scanning the answer choices, note that 3 choices contain the word *amount* and 2 contain *number*. Because people can be counted, they come in numbers—not amounts. So (A), (B), and (C) are out. And (D)'s *a number of people even larger* could be referring to *bigger* people. (E) is best: "...to attract an even greater number of people" clearly refers to more people.

2. C

In standard English, only similar things can be compared. So "the poor" can be compared only with other people, including fictional characters, (C). People cannot be compared with a "time period," as in (A) and (B); or with a "time," as in (D); or with "a . . . book," as in (E). So: "Compared with the characters in John Steinbeck's *The Grapes of Wrath*, the poor of today would be considered wealthy."

3. B

Choices (A), (C), (D), and (E) use the plural pronoun *these* to refer to the singular noun *square root*. That's not a problem in (B); the phrase *such imaginary numbers* means "numbers like the one mentioned."

4. A

Start by choosing between *lies, lie, lays,* and *lay.* We need a singular, present tense, intransitive verb, so *lies* (A) is correct. (If you're not sure about the difference between *lie* and *lay,* look it up in the dictionary; the distinction is important in Sentence Correction.) Choices (C), (D), and (E) fail to observe parallelism: We have to say that the motivation *lies in* one thing instead of (or rather than) *in* something else.

5. D

The original has two mistakes. First, there's a problem with subject/verb agreement. The subject consists of two nouns, *belief* and *curiosity.* So there's a plural subject but *has* is singular. It is also unclear what *their* refers to—*public* or *UFOs.* Logically, it would seem the reference is to the public, but *public* is singular; so we'd have to use *its,* not *their.* Eliminate (A) right away, on the basis of this one mistake. (B) has no main verb. Also, it's not clear who *they* refers to. (C), (D), and (E) change the sentence's structure so that the word *belief* becomes the only subject—now we need a singular verb. Only (D) contains the singular verb *has.*

6. C

The relevant part begins after the colon: The second part of the sentence begins with *the more,* so idiomatically, *the better* would be the best way to start the second part of the clause after that. The only choice that fits is (C). All other choices muddy the construction, making the sentence awkward and unclear.

7. D

One idiom being tested here is *hope for* versus *hope to.* One can hope for something to happen or for a thing—hope for a peaceful resolution to the problem. One can also hope to do something—hope to travel the world one day.

In this sentence, the students want to do something: change careers. The proper idiom is *hope to.* Eliminate (A) and (B). Another idiom tested here is *exchange for,* so (C)'s *exchange with* is wrong. (E) doesn't specify what the "drab jobs" are being exchanged for.

KAPLAN)

8. D

This sentence attempts to describe the crimes committed by the deported British convicts. The original (A) is awkwardly wordy and the pronoun *they* has more than one possible antecedent. In (B), the verbs linked by *and* aren't parallel; "were convicted" doesn't match "ranging." (C) is awkward and unidiomatic. (E) is wordy, and also, the second part of the sentence doesn't relate clearly to the first part. That raises the question, "The range of what?" (D) is the best choice. Note that it's also the shortest. (The most concise answer choice is often (but not always) the correct answer on the GMAT.)

9. C

This question tests comparison. We have to compare *symptoms* with *symptoms*, not with *multitudes*, so (B) is wrong. *Symptoms* is plural, so the comparison has to be with the plural *those* in (C) or (D), not with the singular *that*, as in (A) and (E). Finally, the correct idiom is *afflicted with*, as in (A), (B), and (C), not *afflicted from*, as in (D) and (E). (C) is correct: "…parallel those of the multitudes of Americans afflicted with the common cold each winter."

10. A

The subject is *group*, which is singular, so the main verb has to be *believes*. Also, the things linked by *not* and *but* have to be in parallel form: the infinitive *to be redesigned* has to be paired with the infinitive *to be returned*. The answer is (A), the original structure.

11. B

(B), using *Although*, makes clear the contrast between Lessing's recent work and her better-known early work. (A), (C), and (E) don't make that contrast clear. Also, *is likely to be* is more idiomatic than *will likely be* in (A) and (C), *should likely be* in (D), or *may likely be* in (E). (B) is correct.

12. D

(A) uses the past perfect *had swept* for no reason, given that there's no sequence of events; they all took place at essentially the same time. (B) illogically implies that the fires killed people before sweeping through the area. Choices (A), (B), (C), and (E) all fail to describe the effects of the fires—the deaths of people and the destruction of property—in parallel form. (D) is correct: "brush fires swept the drought-parched southeastern coast of Australia, killing at least 69 people, and leaving thousands of homes and acres of farmland smoldering."

13. B

When should be used only for references to a time, and *where* should be used only for references to a place, so (A) and (D) are incorrect. (C) and (E) are wordy and awkward.

14. D

Since the sentence is about "precursors" or forerunners, and since the non-underlined part of the sentence uses the past tense verb *were*, the answer has to use *were* as in (D), not *are* as in (A) and (E). Also, *however it may be that* in (B) and *despite that* in (C) are unidiomatic. (E) makes it sound as though the ornithologists are the ones gliding from tree to tree. (D) is correct: "Although some ornithologists contend that the precursors of birds were arboreal creatures that glided from tree to tree, others believe…"

15. E

(A), (C), and (D) are all awkward and unidiomatic. (B) uses an acceptable idiomatic form, *asked that a federal arbitrator mediate*, but it then violates subject-verb agreement by using the plural verb *have* with the singular subject *union*. (E) uses the proper singular verb form *has*, and another acceptable idiomatic expression: "has asked a federal arbitrator to mediate negotiations between representatives of the umpire's union, which…".

16. A

The subject of the sentence is *the refusal*, not *that the refusal*, as in (B) and (D). The idiomatic form of the comparison is *closer…than*, not *closer…as* in (B) and (E). And each of two sides needs to acknowledge "the other," not "another," as in (C) and (D), in order to clarify the relationship between the two sides. (A), the original structure, is correct.

17. A

Such…like in (B) is unidiomatic. *That of* in (C) is illogical: *that* can stand only for *industry*, and it doesn't make sense to talk about the industry of an industry. *Is* in (D) doesn't have an object. In (E), the use of both *as* and *like* is redundant. Also, (B) and (E) both use the phrase *which is prospering*, when the single word *prospering* will do. The most concise choice, (A), is correct.

KAPLAN

18. C

The rule of parallelism demands that the infinitive *to tackle* be paired with the infinitive *to become*, as in (C) and (D), not with the participle *becoming* in the other choices. A war rages between one side *and* another, not between one side *with* another, as in (A) and (B), nor *among those*, as in (D). *Among*, in (B) and (D), should be used only in discussions of 3 or more things; here there are only 2 sides, so *between* is correct. Finally, the phrase *which is* in (A) and (D) can be omitted without the sentence losing anything.

19. A

(B) and (C) contain errors of verb tense. The invention of silk is something that happened in the past, so *be* is wrong. Also, the past perfect *had been* in (B) makes it sound as if the analysis of the weapon took place before its burial, which makes no sense. What's more, (C), (D), and (E) all contain misplaced modifiers. In (C), *after having been buried since approximately 1300 B.C.* seems to modify *silk*; besides, *silk* could hardly have been invented after being buried. In (D), *after being buried since approximately 1300 B.C.* seems to modify *a scientist*. (E) has a nearly identical modification problem. The original structure, (A), is best.

20. D

(D) makes the sequence of events perfectly clear: Stokes ran for mayor at essentially the same time as he won the election. (A) and (E) use the past perfect *had run*, which makes it sound as if Stokes ran for mayor long before actually winning. (C)'s phrasing is awkward and its use of *running* tends to obscure the sense of the victory as the conclusion of the campaign. (B)'s phrasing is awkward and it's unclear who the antecedent of the pronoun *he* is.

21. D

People can be individually counted, so they come in numbers, as in (C) and (D). That means (A), (B), and (E), which all use *amount*, are incorrect. And strictly speaking, the adverb *hopefully* cannot be used to mean "it is hoped." (Though most of us use it this way in everyday speech, standard written English has more rigorous requirements.) That knocks out (C). *Hopefully* can modify only a single verb or adjective—not an entire sentence—in this case, the verb *prove*. So (D) is correct, with "it is hoped" and "the large number (of people)".

22.E

(A) uses the complicated passive construction *having often been thought of* for no good reason; there's no sequence of past events. The point of the sentence is that people now still think something that's no longer entirely correct. (B) leaves unclear what *it* refers to, and also fails to convey the contrast between the truth and what people think. (C) seems to say that *the people* are thought of as a city of working-class neighborhoods. In (D), *it* appears to refer to *the people*. (E) uses the correct sequence of tenses—(simple) past and present—and it also uses the phrase *although still often thought of* to set up the contrast.

23.E

Read the sentence carefully, but don't get preoccupied with correcting it. Get right to the choices. Your ear will tell you that "...ordered local officials *to* censor records" (E) is correct.

24.C

-ing verbs often make sentences or phrases unnecessarily wordy. That's the case here. The answer is a concise choice that eliminates the unnecessary phrase, *As a result of having*. (If you're ever stuck and need to guess, rule out *-ing* answer choices as well as long answer choices.) (C) does this well. It also clears up ambiguity in the sentence by including the pronoun *they*, which refers to sharks in the second half of the sentence.

25.D

The difference between *if* and *whether* is a favorite GMAT issue. A dispute concerns *whether*, not *if*, one alternative or the other is better. As a rule of thumb, *whether* will always beat out *if* on the GMAT. If you can't rely on your ear to rule out funny-sounding constructions like *dispute over if* or *dispute about if*, try to eliminate choices for other reasons. Steer away from really long answer choices like (E) here. And stay away from wordy constructions using *being* as in (C) and (E). (B) has a subject–verb agreement problem: *is* disagrees with *fare hikes*.

26.A

This choice illustrates the importance of knowing your idioms, and of working strategically. Scan the answer choices quickly to zero in on the significant differences, which all occur around *or*. This lets you eliminate all choices but (A) for their incorrect usage. You can't say either…nor in (B) and (D), or neither…or, in (C). Choice (E)'s out as well. Think of it this way: You would say, "They do not know X or Y," not "They do not know X nor Y."

KAPLAN

27. C

The windows in question "have been built to conserve energy, and they are." Are what? Conserving energy, of course. The verb that follows *are* is left out, but its meaning is implied. Problem is, the verb is *to conserve energy*, not *conserving*. *Are* makes no sense. You can't say "they are (conserve energy)." You have to say, "they do (conserve energy)," in (C).

28. A

Here, all the choices except (A) add unnecessary words. In (B), *as a consequence of having been urged* doesn't add anything. In (D), *as he was urged to do* is not so obvious, but still longer than it needs to be. *At the urging* is the most compact and elegant version.

29. C

Notice the descriptive phrase *of plastic manufacturing plants* between the subject *size* and the verb *have dropped*. That's our clue to check for subject–verb agreement. In fact, *size* is singular but *have dropped* is plural. (C) corrects that by using *has*. Furthermore, the phrase *an area that is about a football field's size* is wordy, so look for a choice that improves this construction.

(A) and (B) contain *have*. The remaining choices all use *has*, so they could be correct. But (D) and (E) needlessly add "down after 200,000 square feet," and neither improves the clunky football field construction. (C), on the other hand, does, with "about the size of a football field."

30. B

Pronouns must refer clearly to the nouns they replace. Here, the antecedent for the pronoun *their* in the opening phrase is ambiguous. Are the curators documenting their own contribution or the contribution of the leading Swiss designers? Based on the overall meaning of the sentence, *their* should refer to the designers, not to the curators, so the correct choice must make that clear. Eliminate (E), which retains the ambiguous pronoun *their*.

(C) resolves the problem with *their* in the opening phrase, but then uses *its* in place of *their* at the end of the sentence. (D) makes the sentence extremely awkward by switching the active verb *organized* to the passive verb *was organized*. This also makes *their* even more ambiguous, since it should now technically refer to the exhibition. (B) resolves the ambiguity by replacing *their contribution to the* field with *the contribution of the Swiss to the* field, so it could be the correct choice.

31. B

The fact that the word *than* is underlined is a clue that there may be a comparison problem here. As written, the sentence actually compares the *assets* of small investors to the *large investors* themselves, which doesn't make sense. We need to compare either investors to investors, or assets to assets.

(B) makes the comparison clear: the small investors' assets are less robust *than those of* large investors. (E) fixes the comparison error by adding *of* but *relatively* is grammatically incorrect here. (C) and (D) do not fix the comparison error.

32. C

When you see items in a list, consider whether there is a problem with parallelism. Here we have a list of 3 things the company was forced to do: *close plants, lay off workers*, and *reduce budgets*. In the original sentence, the first 2 items have the gerund *–ing* form (*closing, laying*), so the third item must be *reducing*. (C) is correct.

33. A

The underlined portion includes the pronoun *it*, so let's check for any pronoun-antecedent problems. *It* clearly refers to the noun *Greece* immediately preceding it, so there is no ambiguity. Furthermore, both *it* and *Greece* agree in terms of gender and number, so the sentence appears correct as written. But we'll check the other choices, especially since *before Greece was Greece* might be considered awkward. We might find a choice that improves on this construction.

In (B), *it* no longer has a logical antecedent, because *it* now seems to refer to the time period when Greece did not exist, rather than to the place itself. So (B) is incorrect. With (C), the pronoun has an ambiguous reference. We know from the original sentence that *it* should refer to Greece, but (C) seems to imply that *it* refers to ancient European history, which is illogical. Ancient European history can't be a collection of small city-states.

(D) doesn't have a proper pronoun antecedent. If we replace the pronoun with *Greece*, we end up with a nonsensical sentence: *Greece was a collection of small city-states that was Greece.* (E) changes the meaning of the original sentence by saying that Greece later became a collection of small states. In the end, (A) is best.

34. E

The sentence begins with a long descriptive phrase, so we should check to see if this modifying phrase is being used correctly. The phrase should be modifying the noun that immediately follows it, which in this case is the *investigative commission*. But the commission was not compiled from the government documents; it was the commission's *report*. So the phrase is actually modifying the report, rather than the commission. Since report is not part of the underlined part of the sentence, fixing the sentence by placing report directly after the modifying phrase is not an option. Instead, you'll have to change the phrase so that it modifies commission instead of report.

In (B), the change to compiling—an active participle—and the addition of it means that the phrase does now modify commission, so (B) is possibly correct. But the pronoun is awkward and fairly ambiguous because its antecedent report comes a great distance after it, so see if there's a better option before choosing it.

(C) and (D) do not fix the problem; in (C), the phrase still modifies report and in (D), the phrase doesn't connect grammatically with the sentence at all. (E) changes the phrase so that it modifies commission because the commission must have worked with the documents in order to produce the report. This choice is better than (B) because it avoids the awkwardness of the ambiguous *it*, so (E) is correct.

35. B

As written, "in addition to being more expensive than manual research" incorrectly modifies *compounds*. Manual research should instead be compared to *machine-based research*. So you need the choice that places *machine-based research* directly after the modifying phrase. On this basis, we can eliminate all the choices except (B) and (C).

(C) fixes the modification error, but incorrectly makes *machine-based research* of a lower quality rather than the *compounds identified by machine-based research*. (B) is correct because it places *machine-based research* immediately after the modifying phrase while preserving the original meaning of the sentence.

36. D

The sentence contains two different actions (passing the referendum and improving streets, sewers, and so on), so the verb tenses should indicate the correct timing of these actions. A referendum was passed at one point in time (1993), and improvements have been going on *since*. In the original structure, *was* doesn't indicate the continuation of action implied by *since*.

Has been would be the form to indicate action still continuing. Since (A), (B), and (E) do not include *has been*, they are incorrect. (C) incorrectly changes the active participle *approving* to the passive participle *approved*, so it is not the right choice. (D) fixes the verb tense error and does not introduce any new problems, so it is correct.

37. C

The introductory phrase, "Disappointed by…" is set off from the rest of the sentence by a comma, indicating a possible modification problem. For the modification to be correct, that introductory phrase must modify (or describe) the first word after the comma, which in the original is *pop quiz*. But is it the pop quiz itself that is disappointed? No, the *teacher* is disappointed, so the answer will place *teacher* immediately after the modifying phrase. So we can eliminate (A), (B), and (E).

(D) fixes the modification error but says that the *students surprised the teacher* with a pop quiz, which doesn't make sense. (C) fixes the error and is consistent with the intended meaning of the original sentence, so it is correct.

38. B

The underlined portion of this sentence follows a comma, includes another comma and the conjunction "and," and is preceded by the key words "such as." These clues indicate a series, in which all the elements must have parallel form. The first element is *attending class*. Because it is not underlined, the rest of the series must be adapted to match it. *Reading assignments* matches *attending class*, but *to write* does not, so (A) is out. The answer needs to replace *to write* with *writing*. Only (B) does so.

39. B

The issue here is the pronoun *their*. Usually a pronoun comes after its antecedent, but here the pronoun precedes what it refers to—the singular *Persian army*, not the plural *Xerxes and 9 of his generals*. The answer, then, will use the singular *its* instead of *their*. So (A) and (C) are out.

(D) uses *its*, though it incorrectly changes the verb *was* to the participle *having been* (thus creating a clause without a verb). (E) changes the verb *was* to *is*, and destroys the correct sequence of tenses based on *marched*. (B) is correct.

40. D

The sentence compares the number of sushi restaurants 5 years ago to the number today, telling us that the number today is 3 times as large as the number 5 years ago. But the original version is unidiomatic: a number doesn't increase by more than 3 times. A number "more than triples."

(B) replaces *3 times* with *triple* but incorrectly retains *increased by*. (C) actually says that the number increased on more than 3 different occasions, which is not the same thing as *more than tripling*. (D) and (E) both correctly use *tripled*, but only (D) uses the correct verb. Because the studies have been done in the present, *has...tripled* correctly indicates that the action occurred before the studies were completed.

41. C

The underlined portion contains a list of 3 sources of protein. These 3 sources must have parallel forms, but *soy, eggs,* and *drinking milk* do not. A parallel construction would be *soy, eggs,* or *milk*. So (A), (B), and (D) are out. (E) adds the ambiguous and unnecessary pronoun *its*. (C) is correct.

42. D

The plural pronoun *their* incorrectly refers to the singular *Norway. Their* should be *its*. So (A) and (C) are out. (B) corrects this error but changes *reflection* to the more awkward *being a reflection of*. (E), too, uses the proper pronoun, but the word *greater* changes the meaning of the sentence. That leaves (D), which is the correct choice.

43. B

The sentence contains two different actions, indicating a possible verb tense problem. Because the two actions are happening at the same time, they both require the same tense. Since the second verb *are gaining* is not underlined and cannot be changed, *were losing* must be the one to match *are gaining*, a present-tense verb. (A), (C), and (E) are out, while (D) has no verb, only a participle followed by an infinitive (*continuing to lose*). (B), which uses *are losing*, is the answer.

44. E

The sentence contains two parallel elements—procedures and reductions—that are incorrectly joined by the construction *from…and*. The construction should be *from…to*. Eliminate (A) and (B). (C) changes the parallel structure format with *such as*, but reducing is not parallel with *improvement* and *encouragement*. Moreover, *reducing* can't be followed by the preposition *in*, from the original sentence. Eliminate (C). (D) correctly uses *from…to* but includes the non-parallel *procedures* and *reducing*. That leaves (E), which is correct.

45. E

The word *than* preceding the underlined portion of the sentence tells us that the underlined portion is a comparison. Items compared must be parallel. Here, the money the Dancing Doll (DD) line received from sales is compared to that received by the Teeny Tiny Trucks (TT) and Basic Blocks (BB) lines, so all of these quantities should be stated the same way.

Only the name of the toy line and the amount should change from item to item, and the verb *sold* does not need to be repeated for each item. Since (A) includes *did* with the TT sales but no verb with the BB sales, these forms are not parallel; eliminate (A).

(B) is not parallel because it uses *did* with TT sales and *were* with BB sales. (C) includes *sold* with TT sales, but no additional verb with BB, so it's out. (D) and (E) both eliminate the verbs and make the comparison more parallel by using *more than* for both items, but (D) uses Basic Blocks' sales—something not parallel to Dancing Dolls line and Teeny Tiny Trucks line. (E) uses exactly the same form for all 3 items, so it is correct.

46. D

The original sentence uses the passive voice (*it was decided*), but the GMAT strongly prefers the active voice, which tends to be less wordy. The last part of the sentence, too, is wordy; it isn't necessary to say that the computers are both *combined* and *linked*. (B) rearranges the sentence but doesn't correct either problem. (C) addresses the wordiness issue but not the passive voice, while (E) uses the active voice but remains too wordy. Correct choice (D) addresses both of these errors, converting the passive voice *to active* and simplifying the last part of the sentence.

KAPLAN

47. A

A *not only* construction must be completed with *but also*. The original sentence does so, and has no other errors, so (A) is correct. (B) is missing the *but*. (C) uses *moreover it is*. (E) drops the *not only* while keeping the *but also*. (D), too drops the *not only* but also creates a sentence fragment by changing the verb into a participle (*making*).

48. A

The sentence compares the percentage of revenue that Corporation X spends on insurance with the percentage that Corporation Y spends on salaries. Since these two things have the same form, the comparison is clear and grammatically correct. (A) is correct.

In (B), the phrase *In Corporation X* modifies the rest of the sentence, illogically making it seem as if X spends a percentage of its revenue on employee salaries in Corporation Y. It also needlessly uses the passive voice. In (C), *they* has no clear antecedent. (D) compares Corporation X's percentage with Corporation Y's actual amount. (E) is awkwardly worded and seems to compare a percentage to an amount.

49. C

The first problem here is that the use of *so* to connect the second part of the sentence to the first is unnecessary and incorrect. Since the first part of the sentence (*Because...2002,*) is a dependent clause indicating causation, no further transition is needed between it and the main clause, beginning with *the potential buyers*. The second problem is that *originally* is an adverb, which cannot be used to modify the noun construction; it must become the adjective *original*. Only (C) corrects both problems.

(B) needlessly replaces *so* with the conjunction *and*, and retains *originally*. In (D) and (E), *therefore* is redundant since the sentence already begins with the word *Because*, which indicates the causation.

50. D

There are two problems with this sentence. First, the unchangeable verb *glanced* is in the past tense, but the underlined *notice* is in the present tense. Since museum-goers would *have noticed* the birds at the same time that they *glanced up*, both verbs must be in the past tense. So *notice* must become the past tense *noticed*. On this basis, we can eliminate (A), (B), and (C).

The other problem involves modification. The clause that begins *whose behavior* is intended to describe the *birds*, but since it appears (illogically) to be modifying *rafters*. So the correct choice must place this phrase directly after *birds*. (D) does this, so it is correct. (E) does so, too, but it incorrectly alters the phrase to read *with the* behavior.

Chapter 6: **Reading Comprehension**

- Question Format and Structure
- The 4 Basic Principles of Reading Comprehension
- Reading Comprehension Question Types
- Kaplan's 3-Step Method for Reading Comprehension

Reading comprehension tests critical reading skills. Among other things, it tests whether you can:

1. Summarize the main idea of a passage
2. Differentiate between ideas explicitly stated in a text and those implied by the author
3. Make inferences based on information in a text
4. Analyze the logical structure of a passage
5. Deduce the author's tone and attitude about a topic from the text

In reading comp, you are presented with a reading passage (in an area of business, social science, biological science, or physical science), and then asked 3 or 4 questions about that text. You are not expected to be familiar with any topic beforehand—all the information is contained in the text in front of you. In fact, if you happen to have some previous knowledge about a given topic, it is important that you not let that knowledge affect your answers.

Naturally, some passages will be easier than others, though all will present a challenge. The passages will have a tone and content that one might expect from a scholarly journal.

Expect to see 3 or 4 Reading Comp passages—in areas of business, social science, and natural science—and a total of about 13 questions. You will see only one question at a time on the monitor, however, and you will have to answer each question before you can see the next question. The passage will be visible on one side of the monitor as long as you have a question on that passage.

QUESTION FORMAT AND STRUCTURE

The directions for these questions look like this:

> **Directions:** The questions in this group are based on the content of a passage. After reading the passage, choose the best answer to each question. Base your answers only according to what is stated or implied in the text.

Here's an example of a typical question:

> Which of the following does the author suggest about the importance of the emigration of Southerners to Brazil?
>
> ○ Without the Southern presence, Brazil would never have been settled.
>
> ○ The Southerners' sole purpose in immigrating was to introduce new inventions to the Brazilians.
>
> ○ If the Southerners had not emigrated, they would have gone to prison for war crimes.
>
> ○ Dom Pedro II feared the condition Brazil would be in without the presence of the Americans.
>
> ○ The Southerners' arrival had a great impact on the development of education and agriculture in Brazil.

KAPLAN) EXCLUSIVE

Don't feel that you have to memorize or understand every little thing as you read. You can always refer to the passage to clarify the meaning of a specific detail.

THE 4 BASIC PRINCIPLES OF READING COMPREHENSION

Here are the basic things that you need to succeed on Reading Comprehension:

1. Look for the topic and scope of a passage; the author's purpose and structure; and the author's voice.

Usually we read to learn something or to pass the time pleasantly. Neither of these goals has anything to do with the GMAT. Nor does reading for content. On the GMAT, we don't want to read for overall content—we want to read strategically. There's just no time under strict test conditions to understand everything that's being said, and, as we'll see, no payoff in it either.

So what does GMAT reading involve? Broadly stated, it involves reading to identify 3 general elements: topic and scope, the author's purpose and passage structure, and the author's voice.

Topic and Scope

As you work through the first few sentences of a passage, you need to determine the topic. If it's a science passage, what branch of science is it about? If it's astronomy, what part of astronomy? Stars?

Now, as to scope. Think of scope as a narrowing of the topic. If the topic is industrial safety regulations, what narrower definition can we present that still describes all of the passage? Is there a comparison to another type of safety regulation? Is there a comparison between safety regulations in different historical eras? Is there an analysis of the regulations' histories? Or is the passage concerned only with a small aspect of the regulations—the ones pertaining to pregnant workers, for example?

Notice the questions in the previous paragraph. They may not read well, but we left them that way for a reason. Those questions illustrate the kind of thinking you'll need to do as you work through a passage on Test Day. Once you have the topic and narrowed down its scope, you have finished step 1. But what then? You still don't have a firm grasp of the passage.

KAPLAN

Author's Purpose and Structure

Almost every Reading Comp question hinges on your ability to step back from the text and analyze why the author is writing in the first place. The GMAT demands that you figure out the author's purpose and the passage structure, because that's the best way for the test makers to test how you think about the prose you read.

Like most sophisticated writing, the prose you will see on the GMAT doesn't reveal its secrets so explicitly. Authors always have a purpose, of course, and always have a structural plan for carrying out that purpose, though they don't often announce them. That's your job, as the reader.

Baldly laying out the why and how of a passage up front isn't a hallmark of GMAT Reading Comp passages. And even more important (as far as the test makers are concerned), if ideas were blatantly laid out, the test makers couldn't ask probing questions about them. So, in order to set up the questions—to test how we think about the prose we read—the GMAT uses passages in which authors hide or disguise their statement of purpose and challenge us to extract it. If you came across the following first sentence of a typical passage, could you identify the topic and scope?

> The great migration of European intellectuals to the United States in the second quarter of the 20th century prompted a transmutation in the character of Western social thought.

First, what's the topic? The migration of European intellectuals to the United States in the second quarter of the 20th century. That's clear. Second, what's the scope? (How can we narrow the topic?) Well, the passage looks as if it will discuss the effects of this migration on social thought.

So, using what we know about topic and scope, we can easily deduce why the author is writing. His purpose, we might say, is "to explore how the arrival of European thinkers during the period 1926–1950 changed Western social thought." And notice the implied structure of what will follow. Don't you expect the author to first describe the migration westward and then explain what the "transmutation" was? (And it probably will be in that order; GMAT authors are nothing if not logical.)

The author will never say, "Here's why I write." But unless you figure out why he is writing, you won't be able to analyze why each piece—each paragraph and each detail—is there and how it's being used.

Author's Voice

An important part of critical reading is distinguishing between *factual* assertions and opinions/interpretations. It's the opinions/interpretations that the Reading Comp passages are built on, and you should pay the most attention to them. Let's say you come upon a paragraph that reads:

> The coral polyps secrete calceous exoskeletons, which cement themselves into an underlayer of rock, while the algae deposit still more calcium carbonate, which reacts with sea salt to create an even tougher limestone layer.

A bunch of statements of fact, right? But don't focus on these facts. Keep reading until you get to the more "abstract" author's point: Why he's writing on the topic of coral reef formation. What should grab your attention is the following sentence:

> All of this accounts for the amazing renewability of coral reefs despite the endless erosion caused by wave activity.

Consider how different this sentence is from the earlier, more factual one. The phrase *this accounts for* should tell you, "that's the author talking," saying, "I believe this to be proven cause-and-effect." The same goes for the word *amazing*. It indicates the author's personal interpretation. Your response to this sentence should be: "Okay. But, how so? Where's your evidence?" In other words, as an active reader, you are demanding support for the author's opinions. You're forcing the author to defend his view—to tell you what accounts for the "amazing renewability of coral reefs."

Attacking a passage is what critical reading is all about: stepping back from the sheer factual content, figuring out the author's views on a topic and how she arrived at them, and looking for the evidence that must be provided. Be on the lookout for sentences in which the author's voice is coming through, and try to skip past the sentences that are purely factual or simply there for support.

If you find that you don't personally agree with the author's viewpoints, keep it to yourself. In this situation, that's irrelevant. The questions are going to test your command of the author's views, and you can only get in trouble by imposing your own opinions.

📖 READ MORE

To master understanding on whether an author is speaking in his own voice or is recounting another person's opinion, read music or book reviews.

KAPLAN

2. Get the gist of each paragraph.

The paragraph is the main structural unit of any passage. After you've read the first paragraph of the passage, you need only find the "gist," or general purpose, of each succeeding paragraph and then relate each paragraph to the passage as a whole. Ask yourself:

- Why did the author include this paragraph?
- What shift did the author have in mind when moving on to this paragraph?
- What bearing does this paragraph have on the author's main idea?

This process allows you to create a "mental road map" of the passage. When questions arise that require you to look back at the text, having a road map will help you locate specific references more easily. It is helpful, say, to know that the author's critique of a recommendation is in Paragraph 3. That will help you zero in on the relevant information quickly.

3. Look for the main idea.

At this point, you might be thinking: "But you haven't mentioned the main idea yet; I thought that was crucial." Well, it is and it isn't. If you get in the habit of reading the way we're describing, for purpose and structure, you can't help but notice the author's main idea.

Main idea refers to a single thesis that the author may be trying to prove in the course of the passage. It's always a personal interpretation—a strong point of view that demands evidence. And in the end, it's the main thought that the author wants you to come away with.

Lincoln was the 16th president will never be a main idea on a GMAT Reading Comp passage. Count on it. But *As president, Lincoln set uncomfortable precedents for the curtailing of civil liberties*—now there's a promising main idea! It's a statement that demands evidence (What precedents? Why were they *uncomfortable*?), and an entire 350-word passage might be used to try to prove it true.

Not every reading passage features a strong main idea. Sometimes, the author just sets out to discuss a topic in a style we'd call *storytime*; she has no major axe to grind and she isn't making a super strong argument. When there is a strong main idea, however, the test makers usually highlight it by asking a pointed question, such as:

> Which of the following is the main idea of the passage?

So don't sweat it; "main idea" isn't an especially problematic concept, insofar as GMAT Reading Comprehension is concerned.

4. Don't obsess over details.

On the GMAT, you'll need to read only for short-term—as opposed to long-term—retention. When you finish the questions on a certain passage, that passage is over, gone, done with. You're free to promptly forget everything about it.

What's more, there's certainly no need to memorize details. You always have the option of relocating details if a particular question requires you to do so. If you have a good sense of a passage's structure and paragraph topics and your mental roadmap is clear, then you should have no problem navigating back through the text when the need arises.

 KAPLAN STRATEGY ——————————————

The 4 Basic Principles of Reading Comprehension are:

1. Look for the topic and scope of a passage; the author's purpose and structure; and the author's voice.

2. Get the gist of each paragraph.

3. Look for the main idea.

4. Don't obsess over details.

READING COMPREHENSION QUESTION TYPES

Though you might want to break down the Reading Comp section according to the kinds of passages that appear—business, natural science, and social science—we at Kaplan feel that it's more effective to do so by question type. While passages differ in their content, we read them in essentially the same way, employing the same critical reading techniques for each.

The 4 main question types on GMAT Reading Comp are: **Global**, **Inference**, **Logic**, and **Explicit Detail**.

Global Questions

A Global question asks about the author's overall intentions or ideas. It's scope targets the entire passage. As a rule, any answer choice that focuses on one detail or zeroes in on the content of just one paragraph, will be wrong.

KAPLAN) EXCLUSIVE

Identifying the scope is critical, because most wrong answer choices will be out of scope (too narrow or too broad).

Scanning the verbs in the answer choices is a good way to jump into a Global question. The verbs must agree with the author's tone and structure, so scanning the verbs can narrow down the options quickly. The wrong choices will be too broad or narrow in scope or inconsistent with the author's tone.

Frequently, one of the wrong choices will play on some *side issue* discussed at the tail end of the passage.

Main Idea and Primary Purpose Questions

Global questions fall into two main categories: Main Idea and Primary Purpose. The concepts of *main idea* and *purpose* are inextricably linked, of course, because an author's purpose is usually to convey her main idea.

The format for these question types is pretty self-evident:

- Which one of following best expresses the main idea of the passage?
- The author's primary purpose is to...

Structure Questions

Another type of question asks about the overall structure of a passage:

> Which of the following best describes the organization of the passage?

A passage could be organized in 3 possible ways:

1. **Hypothesis** stated and then **analyzed**

2. **Proposal** evaluated and **alternatives explored**

3. **Viewpoint** set forth and then subsequently **defended**

The answer choices for these question are usually worded very generally, forcing you to recognize the broad layout of the passage (as opposed to the specific content). When scanning the choices, ask yourself: "Was there a hypothesis here? Was there an evaluation of a proposal or a defense of a viewpoint?" These terms might seem similar, but, in fact, they're distinct. Learn to recognize the difference between a proposal, a viewpoint, and so on.

> **GO ONLINE**
>
> Using the questions on your online Practice Test, practice taking notes on a separate sheet of paper. On Test Day, you will not be able to mark the passage directly.

Inference Questions

Inference questions, as you can easily guess, concern inferences arising from the passage. An inference is something that is almost certainly true, based on the passage, but that is contained "between the lines." The answer is something that the author strongly implies or hints at but does not state explicitly. Inference questions ask about large points or small.

Extracting valid inferences from Reading Comp passages requires the ability to recognize that information in the passage can be expressed in different ways. The ability to bridge the gap between the way information is presented in the passage and the way it's presented in the correct answer choice is vital. In fact, Inference questions often boil down to an exercise in "translation."

Regular Inference Questions

The most common type of Inference question asks simply what can be inferred from the passage:

- It can be inferred from the passage that…

- The passage/author suggests that…

- The passage/author implies that…

- The passage supports which one of the following statements regarding…

KAPLAN

Agreement Questions

Agreement questions ask you to find a statement that the author (or a character in the text) would agree with. The question stem usually provides a hint about where in the passage the answer can be found:

> With which one of the following statements…would the author most likely agree?

You need to have a good handle on the author's point of view in order to infer what the author would think about a situation or a new premise. Choose an answer that stays within the scope and tone of the passage. Also, stay away from anything that seems to contradict any of the author's ideas: Those will almost certainly be wrong.

Logic Questions

Logic questions ask why the author does something—why he cites a source, why he includes a certain detail, why he puts one paragraph before another, and so forth. As a result, any answer choice that discusses the actual content or a detail will be wrong. (Question 2 in the upcoming sample passage is a Logic question, so you'll see exactly what one looks like.)

Logic questions will look like this:

- The author refers to/mentions…primarily/most probably in order to…

- Which of the following best describes the relationship of the [first, second, etcetera] paragraph to the rest of the passage?

Just be careful with line references in Logic questions—they'll bring you to the right area, but usually the actual answer will be found in the lines immediately before or after the referenced line.

Explicit Detail Questions

Explicit Detail questions are questions whose answer can be pinpointed in the text. It's fairly simple to identify this type of question from its question stem:

- According to the passage/author…

- The author states that…

- The author mentions which one of the following as…

Often, these questions provide direct clues about where you can find an answer, such as line references or some text that links up with the passage structure.

You may recall that we advised you to skim over details in a Reading Comp passage, and to focus instead on the topic, scope, and purpose. But now, here's a question type that's specifically concerned with details. What's the deal?

The fact is, most of the details in a typical passage are not tested in the questions. Of the few that are, you'll either:

- Remember them from your reading;
- Be given a line reference to bring you right to them; or
- Simply have to find them on your own in order to track down the answer.

If that's the case—if your mental roadmap and understanding of the purpose of each paragraph are both clear in your mind—it shouldn't take long to locate the relevant detail and then choose an answer. So despite this question type, the winning strategy is still to note the purpose of details in each paragraph's argument, but don't memorize the details themselves.

Most students find these questions to be the easiest type of Reading Comp question because they're the most concrete. Unlike inferences, which hide somewhere between the lines, explicit details reside in the lines themselves.

KAPLAN'S 3-STEP METHOD FOR READING COMPREHENSION

There's absolutely nothing to stop you from simply reading a passage from beginning to end and answering the questions. That's as simple as can be, and test takers have been attempting Reading Comp that way for decades. But not the best test takers.

The best test takers use a strategic plan for attacking passages and questions in an aggressive, energetic, and critical way. Working this way pays off because it's the kind of pragmatic and efficient approach that the GMAT rewards—the same type of approach that business schools like their students to take when faced with intellectual challenges.

Step 1: Read the passage critically, creating a Passage Map and noting Topic, Scope, and Purpose.

A passage map will allow you to answer questions about the structure of a passage, and will make it easy to find details in the text. Paraphrase each paragraph, and don't get bogged down in details. Pay attention to structural keywords and phrases, which tell you which way the author is going.

Contrast keywords, such as *but*, *however*, and *on the other hand* tell you that a change in direction follows.

Evidence keywords, such as *because* and *since* tell you that there's a causal relationship between two things in the passage. The author's conclusion is likely to be the result, supported by the evidence that follows the *because*.

Continuation keywords tell you the author is following along the same track. These include *moreover*, *furthermore*, *in addition*, and *also*.

Conclusion keywords point you to the author's main point of a paragraph or the entire passage. Examples include *therefore*, *thus*, and *hence*.

The paragraph is the main structural unit of any passage. After reading paragraph 1, you need only find the "gist," or general purpose, of each succeeding paragraph and then relate each paragraph to the passage as a whole. Ask yourself:

- Why did the author include this paragraph?
- What shift did the author have in mind when moving on to this paragraph?
- What bearing does this paragraph have on the author's main idea?

This process allows you to create a mental road map of the passage, or a passage map. When questions arise that require you to look back at the text, having a map will help you locate specific references more easily. It's helpful, say, to know that the author's critique of a recommendation is in paragraph 3. That will allow you to zero in on the relevant information quickly.

As you read, determine the topic, scope, and author's response. The topic is pretty straightforward; it's the overall subject matter. If it's a science passage, what branch of science does it address? If it's astronomy, what part of astronomy?

Scope is the narrower aspect of the topic that the passage addresses. It is the answer to the question, "What about this topic interests the author?" If the topic is industrial safety regulations, what narrower definition still describes all of the passage? Is there a comparison to another type of safety regulation? Is there a comparison between safety regulations in different historical eras? Is there an analysis of the regulations' effectiveness? Or is the passage concerned only with a small aspect of the regulations—the ones pertaining to pregnant workers, for example? Identifying the scope is critical because most wrong answer choices will be outside the scope (too narrow or too broad).

The purpose is the reason the author has written the piece. What does she intend to do? Many GMAT Reading Comprehension questions hinge on your ability to step back from the text and analyze why the author is writing in the first place and how she puts her text together. If you are stuck on purpose, select a verb that accurately starts your description of the author's purpose: describe, present, compare, propose, analyze, critique, rebut, argue, advocate, explain, etc.

For instance, your road map might look like this:

¶ 1 Problems with electoral college

¶ 2 Alternative 1—Approval voting

¶ 3 Alternative 2—Rank voting

¶ 4 Change unlikely

KAPLAN

Your topic, scope, and purpose might look like this:

Topic: The American presidential election system

Scope: Alternatives for fixing the problems of the current system

Purpose: To describe a problem of the current system and the attributes of two alternative systems

The Passage Map is for your own use for the 5 to 8 minutes you are working on that passage. It can be as cryptic or as complete as you need it to be. Don't waste time writing out entire sentences or details from the passage.

Step 2: Read the question stem, determining what type of question it is.

The next step is to identify the question type: Global, Detail, Inference, Logic. Ask yourself, "What should I do on this question? What is being asked?" Here are some guidelines:

If you see "primary purpose," "main idea," or "appropriate title"	Global Question
If you see direct language such as, "According to the passage,"	Detail Question
If you see "implies" or "suggests"	Inference Question
If you are asked why an author includes a paragraph or detail	Logic Question

Step 3: Answer the question, following the Kaplan strategies for that question type.

Each question type requires a different strategy of attack. Once you have figured out what kind of question you are dealing with, then proceed with the following:

Global Questions

- Use your notes on the Passage Map, topic, scope, and purpose to help you prephrase an answer.

- Then, search the answer choices.

If you can't find your prephrased answer, eliminate answer choices. Common wrong answer choices will misrepresent the scope.

Detail Questions

- Use your Passage Map to locate the relevant text in the passage. If needed, read that portion of the passage again.

- Then, prephrase an answer.

Don't pick an answer choice just because it sounds familiar. Common wrong answer choices will distort real details in the passage.

Inference Questions

- Search for an answer choice that follows from the passage.

It is difficult to prephrase the correct answer to an Inference question. Don't waste your time. Common wrong answer choices will use extreme language or exaggerate views expressed in the passage.

Logic Questions

- Find the answer choice that reflects the author's intentions.

Common wrong answer choices will focus too heavily on specifics: It's not content that's key in Logic questions, but rather the author's motivation for including the content.

Now let's try the method on an actual GMAT-length passage.

Since 1980, the notion that mass extinctions at the end of the Cretaceous period 65 million years ago resulted from a sudden event has slowly gathered support, although even today there is no scientific consensus. In the Alvarez scenario, an asteroid struck the earth, creating a gigantic crater. Beyond the immediate effects
(5)   of fire, flood, and storm, dust darkened the atmosphere, cutting off plant life. Many animal species disappeared as the food chain was snapped at its base.

Alvarez's main evidence is an abundance of iridium in the KT boundary, a thin stratum dividing Cretaceous rocks from rocks of the Tertiary period. Iridium normally accompanies the slow fall of interplanetary debris, but in KT boundary
(10)   strata iridium is 10–100 times more abundant, suggesting a rapid, massive deposition. Coincident with the boundary, whole species of small organisms vanish from the fossil record. Boundary samples also yield osmium isotopes, basaltic sphericles, and deformed quartz grains, all of which could have resulted from high-velocity impact.

(15)   Paleontologists initially dismissed the theory, arguing that existing dinosaur records showed a decline lasting millions of years. But recent studies in North America, aimed at a comprehensive collection of fossil remnants rather than rare or well-preserved specimens, indicate large dinosaur populations existing immediately prior to the KT boundary. Since these discoveries, doubts about
(20)   theories of mass extinction have lessened significantly.

Given the lack of a known impact crater of the necessary age and size to fit the Alvarez scenario, some scientists have proposed alternatives. Courtillot, citing huge volcanic flows in India coincident with the KT boundary, speculates that eruptions lasting many thousands of years produced enough atmospheric debris to cause
(25)   global devastation. His analyses also conclude that iridium in the KT boundary was deposited over a period of 10,000–100,000 years. Alvarez and Asaro reply that the shock of an asteroidal impact could conceivably have triggered extensive volcanic activity. Meanwhile, exploration at a large geologic formation in Yucatan, found in 1978 but unstudied until 1990, has shown a composition consistent with
(30)   extraterrestrial impact. But evidence that the formation is indeed the hypothesized impact site remains inconclusive.

1. It can be inferred from the passage that supporters of the Alvarez and Courtillot theories would hold which of the following views in common?

   ◯ The KT boundary was formed over many thousands of years.

   ◯ Large animals such as the dinosaurs died out gradually over millions of years.

   ◯ Mass extinction occurred as an indirect result of debris saturating the atmosphere.

   ◯ It is unlikely that the specific cause of the Cretaceous extinctions will ever be determined.

   ◯ Volcanic activity may have been triggered by shock waves from the impact of an asteroid.

2. The author mentions "recent studies in North America" (line 16) primarily in order to

   ◯ point out the benefits of using field research to validate scientific theories

   ◯ suggest that the asteroid impact theory is not consistent with fossil evidence

   ◯ describe alternative methods of collecting and interpreting fossils

   ◯ summarize the evidence that led to wider acceptance of catastrophic scenarios of mass extinction

   ◯ show that dinosaurs survived until the end of the Cretaceous period

Step 1: Read the passage critically, creating a Passage Map and noting Topic, Scope, and Purpose.

Take a couple of minutes to read the passage. Aim at the topic, scope, and author's purpose or point of view. Where is the text going? Here's what you should have gotten out of the paragraph on your first pass:

> The topic is clearly announced in the opening sentence: *mass extinctions at the end of the Cretaceous period....* Finding the topic is the first step. At the same time, you want to look for the scope, which is also disclosed in Sentence 1.
>
> Specifically, that same sentence does two things: (1) It introduces the theory that the mass extinctions may have resulted from *a sudden event*; (2) The words *although even today* signal that the passage will explain that there are still differences over what exactly happened. Savvy test takers notice such signal words as they read; they are clues about where the passage is going.
>
> Beyond the first sentence, the paragraph delivers fundamentals about the Alvarez theory of mass extinction. The theory is that an asteroid hit the earth and exploded, filling the atmosphere with dust, which killed off plant life, wrecked the food chain, and caused mass extinctions. Simple enough.

Your Passage Map would look something like this:

¶1 Mass Ext—Alvarez—asteroid

¶2 Alvarez evid—iridium in KT boundary + fossil record

¶3 Paleo- disagree in past, but not now

¶4 Courtillot: volcanoes—atmosph. debris—mass extinction

Not inconsistent with steroid

Topic: Mass extinctions at end of Cret. period

Scope: Whether mass ext. resulted from a single event

Purpose: To evaluate two theories supporting mass extinction as a result of single event

Step 2: Read the question stem, determining what type of question it is.

Now, identify the question type. Question 1 is a clearly an Inference question: it uses the phrase, *can be inferred*.

Question 2 is a Detail question. Specific text and a line reference are included, so you know you are being asked about one detail and are given clues as to the location of the answer.

Step 3: Answer the question, following the Kaplan strategies for that question type.

Depending on the question type, use the appropriate strategy. For question 1, an Inference question, go straight to the answer choices and search for one that follows from the passage. Eliminate all answers that do not follow from the passage. It's usually too difficult to prephrase the correct answer with Inference questions, so don't bother. Common wrong answer choices will use extreme language or exaggerate views expressed in the passage.

Question 2 is a Detail question, so use your Passage Map to locate the relevant text. Go ahead and read that portion of the text again, if you need to. Then, prephrase an answer. Stay clear of an answer choice that just looks familiar: distorted details from the text are commonly placed as traps.

GO ONLINE

Your full-length online Practice Test will give you a sense of how long the Reading Comprehension section will be—and how much endurance you will need.

Now, let's go through the answers and explanations.

1. C

Paragraph 1 describes mass extinctions in the Alvarez scenario as resulting from the devastating effects of atmospheric dust on the food chain. Paragraph 4 describes Courtillot's volcanic theory as an alternative explanation for a similar ecological effect. Therefore, supporters of both theories would agree that atmospheric debris could cause mass extinction. (A) is inconsistent with Alvarez. (B) and (D) contradict both theorists—they agree that the extinctions were pretty sudden and they have clear ideas about causes. (E) contradicts Courtillot, who doesn't buy the asteroid causal notion.

2. D

The gist of Paragraph 3 is that the North American studies are the main reason why initially skeptical paleontologists opened up to the idea of catastrophic mass extinctions. (D) paraphrases the last sentence: "Since these discoveries, doubts about theories of mass extinction have lessened significantly." Beware of choices like (A), (C), and (E). They're baited to sound plausible (i.e., you can infer that the author wouldn't disagree with any of them), but they miss the point that the studies changed people's minds. (B) is inconsistent with the text—the fossil evidence is consistent with catastrophe scenarios, asteroidal or otherwise.

SUMMARY

The basic principles of Reading Comprehension are:

- Look for the topic and scope of a passage; the author's purpose and structure; and the author's voice.
- Get the gist of each paragraph.
- Look for the main idea.
- Don't obsess over details.

The most common question types are:

- Global Questions
- Inference Questions
- Logic Questions
- Explicit Detail Questions

Kaplan's 3-Step Method for Reading Comprehension is:

Step 1: Read the passage critically, creating a Passage Map and noting Topic, Scope, and Purpose.

Step 2: Read the question stem, determining what type of question it is.

Step 3: Answer the question, following the Kaplan strategies for that question type.

PRACTICE QUIZ

Directions: The questions in this group are based on the content of a passage. After reading the passage, choose the best answer to each question. Based your answers only according to what is stated or implied in the text.

Questions 1–7 are based on the following passage:

The rich analyses of Fernand Braudel and his fellow *Annales* historians have made significant contributions to historical theory and research. In a departure from traditional
(5) historical approaches, the *Annales* historians assume (as do Marxists) that history cannot be limited to a simple recounting of conscious human actions, but must be understood in the context of forces and material conditions that
(10) underlie human behavior. Braudel was the first *Annales* historian to gain widespread support for the idea that history should synthesize data from various social sciences, especially economics, in order to provide a
(15) broader view of human societies over time (although Febvre and Bloch, founders of the *Annales* school, had originated this approach). Braudel conceived of history as the dynamic interaction of 3 temporalities. The first of
(20) these, the *événementielle*, involved short-lived dramatic "events," such as battles, revolutions, and the actions of great men, which had preoccupied traditional historians like Carlyle. *Conjonctures* was Braudel's term for larger,
(25) cyclical processes that might last up to half a century. The *longue durée*, a historical wave of great length, was for Braudel the most fascinating of the 3 temporalities. Here he focused on those aspects of everyday life that
(30) might remain relatively unchanged for

centuries. What people ate, what they wore, their means and routes of travel—for Braudel these things create "structures" that define the limits of potential social change for hundreds
(35) of years at a time.

Braudel's concept of the *longue durée* extended the perspective of historical space as well as time. Until the *Annales* school, historians had taken the juridical political
(40) unit—the nation-state, duchy, or whatever—as their starting point. Yet, when such enormous time spans are considered, geographical features may well have more significance for human populations than
(45) national borders. In his doctoral thesis, a seminal work on the Mediterranean during the reign of Philip II, Braudel treated the geohistory of the entire region as a "structure" that had exerted myriad influences on human
(50) lifeways since the first settlements on the shores of the Mediterranean Sea.

And so the reader is given such arcane information as the list of products that came to Spanish shores from North Africa, the
(55) seasonal routes followed by Mediterranean sheep and their shepherds, and the cities where the best ship timber could be bought.

Braudel has been faulted for the imprecision of his approach. With his Rabelaisian delight
(60) in concrete detail, Braudel vastly extended the realm of relevant phenomena; but this very achievement made it difficult to delimit the boundaries of observation, a task necessary to beginning any social investigation. Further,
(65) Braudel and other *Annales* historians minimize the differences among the social sciences. Nevertheless, the many similarly designed studies aimed at both professional and popular audiences indicate that Braudel
(70) asked significant questions which traditional historians had overlooked.

1. The primary purpose of the passage is to

    ○ show how Braudel's work changed the conception of Mediterranean life held by previous historians

    ○ evaluate Braudel's criticisms of tradition- al and Marxist historiography

    ○ contrast the perspective of the *longue durée* with the actions of major historical figures

    ○ illustrate the relevance of Braudel's concepts to other social sciences

    ○ outline some of Braudel's influential conceptions and distinguish them from conventional approaches

2. The author refers to the work of Febvre and Bloch in order to

    ○ illustrate the limitations of the *Annales* tradition of historical investigation

    ○ suggest the relevance of economics to historical investigation

    ○ debate the need for combining various sociological approaches

    ○ show that previous *Annales* historians anticipated Braudel's focus on economics

    ○ demonstrate that historical studies provide broad structures necessary for economic analysis

3. According to the passage, all of the following are aspects of Braudel's approach to history EXCEPT that he

    ○ attempted to unify various social sciences

    ○ studied social and economic activities that occurred across national boundaries

    ○ pointed out the link between increased economic activity and the rise of nationalism

    ○ examined seemingly unexciting aspects of everyday life

    ○ visualized history as involving several different time frames

KAPLAN

4. The passage suggests that, compared to traditional historians, *Annales* historians are

   ○ more interested in other social sciences than in history

   ○ more critical of the achievements of famous historical figures

   ○ more skeptical of the validity of most economic research

   ○ more interested in the underlying context of human behavior provided by social structure

   ○ more inclined to be dogmatic in their approach to history

5. The author is critical of Braudel's perspective for which of the following reasons?

   ○ It seeks structures that underlie all forms of social activity.

   ○ It assumes a greater similarity among the social sciences than actually exists.

   ○ It fails to consider the relationship between short-term events and long-term social activity.

   ○ It clearly defines boundaries for social analysis.

   ○ It attributes too much significance to conscious human actions.

6. The passage implies that Braudel would consider which of the following as exemplifying the *longue durée*?

   I. The prominence of certain crops in the diet of a region

   II. The annexation of a province by the victor in a war

   III. A reduction in the population of an area following a disease epidemic

   ○ I only

   ○ III only

   ○ I and II only

   ○ II and III only

   ○ I, II, and III

7. Which of the following statements is most in keeping with the principles of Braudel's work as described in the passage?

○ All written history is the history of social elites.

○ The most important task of historians is to define the limits of potential social change.

○ Those who ignore history are doomed to repeat it.

○ People's historical actions are influenced by many factors that they may be unaware of.

○ History is too important to be left to historians.

KAPLAN

Questions 8–13 are based on the following passage.

In many underdeveloped countries, the state plays an important and increasingly varied role in economic development today. There are 4 general arguments, all of them related,
(5) for state participation in economic development. First, the entrance requirements in terms of financial capital and capital equipment are very large in certain industries, and the size of these obstacles will serve as
(10) barriers to entry on the part of private investors. One can imagine that these obstacles are imposing in industries such as steel production, automobiles, electronics, and parts of the textile industry. In addition, there
(15) are what Myint calls "technical indivisibilities in social overhead capital." Public utilities, transport, and communications facilities must be in place before industrial development can occur, and they do not lend themselves to
(20) small-scale improvements.

A related argument centers on the demand side of the economy. This economy is seen as fragmented, disconnected, and incapable of using inputs from other parts of the economy.
(25) Consequently, economic activity in one part of the economy does not generate the dynamism in other sectors that is expected in more cohesive economies. Industrialization necessarily involves many different sectors;
(30) economic enterprises will thrive best in an environment in which they draw on inputs from related economic sectors and, in turn, release their own goods for industrial utilization within their own economies.

(35) A third argument concerns the low-level equilibrium trap in which less developed countries find themselves. At subsistence levels, societies consume exactly what they produce. There is no remaining surplus for
(40) reinvestment. As per-capita income rises, however, the additional income will not be used for savings and investment. Instead, it will have the effect of increasing the population that will eat up the surplus and
(45) force the society to its former subsistence position. Fortunately, after a certain point, the rate of population growth will decrease; economic growth will intersect with and eventually outstrip population growth. The
(50) private sector, however, will not be able to provide the one-shot large dose of capital to push economic growth beyond those levels where population increases eat up the incremental advances.

(55) The final argument concerns the relationship between delayed development and the state. Countries wishing to industrialize today have more competitors, and these competitors occupy a more
(60) differentiated industrial terrain than previously. This means that the available niches in the international system are more limited. For today's industrializers, therefore, the process of industrialization cannot be a
(65) haphazard affair, nor can the pace, content, and direction be left solely to market forces. Part of the reason for a strong state presence, then, relates specifically to the competitive international environment in which modern
(70) countries and firms must operate.

8. According to the passage, all of the following are arguments for state economic intervention EXCEPT

⬭ the start-up costs of initial investments are beyond the capacities of many private investors

⬭ the state must mediate relations between the demand and supply sides of the economy

⬭ the pace and processes of industrialization are too important to be left solely to market trends

⬭ the livelihoods and security of workers should not be subject to the variability of industrial trends

⬭ public amenities are required to facilitate a favorable business environment

9. Which of the following best states the central point of the passage?

⬭ Without state intervention, many less developed countries will not be able to carry out the interrelated tasks necessary to achieve industrialization.

⬭ Underdeveloped countries face a crisis of overpopulation and a lack of effective demand that cannot be overcome without outside assistance.

⬭ State participation plays a secondary role as compared to private capital investment in the industrialization of underdeveloped countries.

⬭ Less developed countries are trapped in an inescapable cycle of low production and demand.

⬭ State economic planning can ensure the rapid development of nonindustrialized countries' natural resources.

10. The author suggests all of the following as appropriate roles for the state in economic development EXCEPT

    ○ safeguarding against the domination of local markets by a single source of capital

    ○ financing industries with large capital requirements

    ○ helping to coordinate demand among different economic sectors

    ○ providing capital inputs sufficient for growth to surpass increases in per capita consumption

    ○ developing communication and transportation facilities to service industry

11. The author suggests which of the following about the "technical indivisibilities in social overhead capital" (lines 15–16) and the "low-level equilibrium trap" (lines 35–36)?

    ○ The first leads to rapid technological progress; the second creates demand for technologically sophisticated products.

    ○ Both enhance the developmental effects of private sector investment.

    ○ Neither is relevant to formulating a strategy for economic growth.

    ○ The first is a barrier to private investment; the second can attract it.

    ○ The first can prevent development from occurring; the second can negate its effects.

12. Which of the following, if true, would cast doubt on the author's argument that state participation is important in launching large-scale industries?

    I. Coordination of demand among different economic sectors requires a state planning agency.

    II. Associations of private-sector investors can raise large amounts of capital by pooling their resources.

    III. Transportation and communications facilities can be built up through a series of small-scale improvements.

    ◯ I only

    ◯ II only

    ◯ I and II only

    ◯ II and III only

    ◯ I, II, and III

13. According to the passage, the "low-level equilibrium trap" in underdeveloped countries results from

    ◯ the tendency for societies to produce more than they can use

    ◯ intervention of the state in economic development

    ◯ the inability of market forces to overcome the effects of population growth

    ◯ the fragmented and disconnected nature of the demand side of the economy

    ◯ one-shot, large doses of capital intended to spur economic growth

Questions 14–18 are based on the following passage:

The years following the Civil War in Brazil brought many changes to the Southern states, prompting a large emigration of U. S. citizens—9,000 to 40,000 people—primarily
(5) from the South. In one particular case, this migration of Southerners, many from Alabama and Texas, resulted from direct invitation. Emperor Dom Pedro II of Brazil, in an effort to expand his country, appealed for
(10) colonists from the U.S. South. Dom Pedro II recognized the value these Southerners could have for Brazil in the form of agricultural and educational knowledge. He advertised for citizens from all over the South and even from
(15) some of the Northern states to immigrate to Brazil.

Because they recognized an opportunity to rebuild their lives without yielding their Southern heritage to Northern
(20) "improvements" after the war, many Southerners accepted Dom Pedro's offer. After founding "Vila Americana" (American Town), one of the most important of the "American colonies" in Brazil, the Southern immigrants
(25) did not remain in isolation. They interacted with and even married local Brazilians and other new colonists.

While becoming integrated into the existing society, these colonists maintained their
(30) distinctive American culture. American industrial technology allowed the colonists to improve farming implements, such as ploughs, rakes, harrows, and hoes, for their fellow Brazilians. Housing also improved with
(35) the introduction of chimneys and gutters. The colonists' emphasis on education and industrial skills contributed to Brazil's success in business; many of the country's public transportation systems were built or run by
(40) American-founded companies. Today, Vila Americana, maintaining this original level of excellence, has the highest education and income levels per capita of any city in Brazil.

14. The primary purpose of the passage is to

○ analyze the source of the changes in the lives of Southerners after the Civil War

○ discuss the emigration of U.S. Southerners to Brazil after the Civil War and their benefits to their new country

○ describe how the aftermath of the Civil War changed the lives of all the citizens of the Southern U.S.

○ demonstrate how Brazil adopted the heritage of the Southern U.S. and attracted Southerners wanting to revive the antebellum South

○ account for the mass emigration from the United States that took place following the Civil War, particularly from Alabama and Texas

15. Which of the following does the author suggest about the importance of the emigration of Southerners to Brazil?

    ◯ Without the Southern presence, Brazil would never have been settled.

    ◯ The Southerners' sole purpose in immigrating was to introduce new inventions to the Brazilians.

    ◯ If the Southerners had not emigrated, they would have gone to prison for war crimes.

    ◯ Dom Pedro II feared the condition Brazil would be in without the presence of the Americans.

    ◯ The Southerners' arrival had a great impact on the development of education and agriculture in Brazil.

16. According to the passage, all of the following statements are correct, EXCEPT

    ◯ the Southerners brought their heritage and innovative ideas with them to Brazil

    ◯ many Southerners were looking for a new beginning after the Civil War, independent of Northern interference

    ◯ the influence of the Southerners had a great and lasting effect on Brazil

    ◯ the Southerners fled to Brazil to escape U.S. government policies on farming and education

    ◯ emperor Dom Pedro II invited Southerners and other U.S. citizens to immigrate to his developing country

17. The author states that Southerners moved to Brazil "because they recognized an opportunity to rebuild their lives without yielding their Southern heritage to Northern 'improvements' after the war" in order to

    ◯ explain how fears about losing their traditional culture made Southerners prefer emigration to rebuilding their lives in the U.S.

    ◯ describe the process by which immigrants from Southern U.S. states replaced native Brazilian culture with their own heritage

    ◯ suggest Dom Pedro II's advertising campaign to tempt Southerners to uproot their lives and move to Brazil

    ◯ illustrate the preference native Brazilians had for the heritage of the Southern U.S. over the "improvements" Northerners might provide

    ◯ defend the Southerners from the accusation of a traitorous abandonment of their own country by rationalizing their decision to emigrate

KAPLAN

18. The main purpose of Paragraph 3 is to

    ⬭ rationalize for the reader why Dom Pedro specifically requested that Southerners migrate to his country

    ⬭ describe the benefits that the Southerners conferred on Brazil in various areas

    ⬭ explain the utility of the Southerners' importation of American technology to Brazil's growing agricultural economy

    ⬭ elucidate the colonists' process of choosing to colonize the area of Vila Americana because of its rich agricultural history

    ⬭ argue that Southerners, because they isolated themselves from other inhabitants, had little impact on Brazilian education and agriculture

Questions 19–22 are based on the following passage:

Isolated from the rest of the world by circumpolar currents and ice fields, the Dry Valleys of Antarctica never see snowfall. They are the coldest, driest places on earth, yet this
(5) arid, frigid climate supports several delicate ecosystems. Life in these ecosystems consists of relatively few groups of algae, microorganisms, and invertebrates, as well as plants such as lichen and fungi that live
(10) beneath the surface of rocks, where just enough light penetrates for photosynthesis to occur during the short period each year when meltwater is available. This region has proven interesting specifically to scientists researching
(15) the possibility of life on Mars because the features of the Dry Valleys are strikingly similar to the Martian landscape.

The Dry Valleys' system of lakes provides a particularly interesting area of research. Lake
(20) Hoare boasts a clear ice sun-cover fifteen meters thick that intensifies solar radiation in a way similar to solar panels; summer temperatures in bottom waters can become as high as 25° C, solely from solar heating, and
(25) not geothermal heating. This temperature permits huge mats of cyanobacteria to survive and even thrive on the lake floor. Pieces of this mat occasionally break free, floating up to the underside of the icy lake cover to melt through
(30) the ice toward the surface. The intense Antarctic winds, sweeping across the lake's surface, cause the ice to sublimate—turn directly from ice into vapor—rapidly. Such continuous sublimation should eventually
(35) cause the lake to vanish, but a continuous

trickle of water from a nearby glacier—melted by the sun—refreshes the water. With a constant source of water, however small, and the heat generated by the solar radiation and
(40) retained by insulation from the thick ice cover, this lake offers an odd paradox: thick ice is responsible for maintaining this lake's liquid state.

The ancient river deltas around the slopes of
(45) Lake Fryxell present one feature typical of all river deltas: sediment thick enough to bury fossil life forms. This very thickness, however, makes a formal scientific search for signs of life impracticable. The floor of Lake Vida, on
(50) the other hand, is covered with discrete piles of sediment up to a meter high that have preserved clear signs of life because rocks lying on the lake's surface, heated by sunlight, melt their way through the thick ice cover. Since
(55) smaller rocks, with a larger surface-area-to-volume ratio, get warmer and sink lower than larger rocks, pieces of gravel penetrate by as much as a meter, forming cracks in the ice that cause the finest sediment to sink even deeper.
(60) When the lake dries seasonally, the refined sediment within the ice drops to the lake floor, leaving a protective layer of gravel on top of the finer sediment. Dried bacteria in Lake Vida sediment have been dated back tens of
(65) thousands of years. Some researchers are hoping that exploration of similar terrain on Mars may yield similar results.

KAPLAN

19. According to the passage, thick sediment found in the ancient river deltas of Lake Fryxell

    ○ forms layers of deposits laden with dried bacteria that are tens of thousands of years old

    ○ masks life forms by continuously depositing new layers on top of older ones

    ○ makes it unlikely that scientists will search there for traces of life

    ○ collects liquid water from nearby glaciers warmed by sunlight during the Antarctic summer

    ○ is devoid of life due to the impenetrable barrier formed by the sediment

20. The passage is primarily concerned with

    ○ the adaptations of microorganisms that allow them to live in the Dry Valleys' hostile environment

    ○ the relationship between frozen lakes and glaciers which contributes to the availability of fresh water in the Dry Valleys

    ○ evidence of past and present life forms in the extreme conditions of Antarctica's Dry Valleys

    ○ the evolutionary histories of ancient lakes and the clues they hold about life in cold, dry ecosystems

    ○ the differences and similarities between ancient river deltas and ancient lakes

21. Based on the information in the passage, scientists looking for life on Mars in conditions similar to those in the Dry Valleys would be most likely to find it in which of the following areas?

     ◯ former river deltas

     ◯ circumpolar ice fields

     ◯ larger rocks

     ◯ former glaciers

     ◯ former lakebeds

22. Based on the information in the passage, mounds of sediment found at the bottom of Lake Vida are refined by

     I. Continual sublimation and ice cover
     II. Large pieces of rock decomposing on the lake floor
     III. Cracks formed in the ice by sinking rocks and gravel

     ◯ I only

     ◯ I and II

     ◯ III only

     ◯ II and III

     ◯ I, II, and III

Questions 23–27 are based on the following passage:

History has shaped academic medical centers (AMCs) to perform 3 functions: patient care, research, and teaching. These 3 missions are now fraught with problems
(5) because the attempt to combine them has led to such inefficiencies as duplication of activities and personnel, inpatient procedures that could and should have been outpatient procedures, and unwieldy administrative
(10) bureaucracies.

One source of inefficiency derives from mixed lines of authority. Clinical chiefs and practitioners in AMCs are typically responsible to the hospital for practice issues
(15) but to the medical school for promotion, marketing, membership in a faculty practice plan, and educational accreditation. Community physicians with privileges at a university hospital add more complications.
(20) They have no official affiliation with the AMC's medical school connected, but their cooperation with faculty members is essential for proper patient treatment. The fragmented accountability is heightened by the fact that 3
(25) different groups often vie for the loyalty of physicians who receive research. The medical school may wish to capitalize on the research for its educational value to students; the hospital may desire the state-of-the-art
(30) treatment methods resulting from the research; and the grant administrators may focus on the researchers' humanitarian motives. Communication among these groups is rarely coordinated, and the physicians may
(35) serve whichever group promises the best perks and ignore the rest—which inevitably strains relationships.

Another source of inefficiency is the fact that physicians have obligations to many
(40) different groups: patients, students, faculty members, referring physicians, third-party payers, and staff members, all of whom have varied expectations. Satisfying the interests of one group may alienate others. Patient care
(45) provides a common example. For the benefit of medical students, physicians may order too many tests, prolong patient visits, or encourage experimental studies of a patient. If AMC faculty physicians were more aware of
(50) how much treatments of specific illnesses cost, and of how other institutions treat patient conditions, they would be better practitioners, and the educational and clinical care missions of AMCs would both be better served.

(55) A bias toward specialization adds yet more inefficiency. AMCs are viewed as institutions serving the gravest cases in need of the most advanced treatments. The high number of specialty residents and the presence of burn
(60) units, blood banks, and transplant centers validate this belief. Also present at AMCs, though less conspicuous, are facilities for ordinary primary care patients. In fact, many patients choose to visit an AMC for primary
(65) care because they realize that any necessary follow-up can occur almost instantaneously. While AMCs have emphasized cutting-edge specialty medicine, their more routine medical services need development and enhancement.

(70) A final contribution to inefficiency is organizational complacency. Until recently, most academic medical centers drew the public merely by existing. The rising presence, however, of tertiary hospitals with patient care
(75) as their only goal has immersed AMCs in a very competitive market. It is only in the past several years that AMCs have started to recognize and develop strategies to address competition.

23. The author's attitude toward the inefficiencies at academic medical centers is one of

    ○ reluctant acquiescence

    ○ strident opposition

    ○ agonized indecision

    ○ reasoned criticism

    ○ enthusiastic support

24. The author of the passage would most likely agree with which of the following statements about primary care at AMCs?

    ○ AMCs would make more money if they focused mainly on primary care.

    ○ Burn and transplant patients need specialty care more than primary care.

    ○ AMCs offer the best primary care for most patients.

    ○ AMCs have not tried hard enough to publicize their primary care services.

    ○ Inefficiencies at AMCs would be reduced if better primary care were offered.

25. The author's primary purpose in this passage is to

    ○ discuss the rise and fall of academic medical centers

    ○ explain that multiple lines of authority in a medical center create inefficiencies

    ○ delineate conflicts occurring in academic medical facilities

    ○ examine the differences between academic and other health care entities

    ○ warn that mixed accountabilities result in treatment errors

KAPLAN

26. The author implies which of the following about faculty physicians at AMCs?

    ○ Most of them lack good business sense.

    ○ They put patients' physical health above their hospitals' monetary concerns.

    ○ They sometimes focus on education at the expense of patient care.

    ○ They lack official affiliation with the medical schools connected to AMCs.

    ○ They choose AMCs because follow-up care can be given very quickly.

27. Which of the following would the author probably consider a good strategy for academic medical centers dealing with competition from tertiary hospitals?

    ○ recruiting physicians away from tertiary centers

    ○ increasing the focus on patient care

    ○ sending patients to tertiary facilities

    ○ eliminating specialty care

    ○ reducing dependence on grant money

Questions 28–31 are based on the following passage:

One of the first attempts to peer into the living human brain was carried out by a neurosurgeon named Wilder Penfield in the 1950s. Penfield opened the skulls of conscious
(5) epileptic patients under local anesthesia, and induced a mild electric current into their brains in an attempt to pinpoint the source of seizure activity and then remove that piece of tissue. What he found was even more
(10) remarkable than what he initially set out to do. By stimulating different points on the lower parts of the brain (the temporal lobes), he elicited distinct and vivid memories in his patients. These memories were more precise
(15) than usual memories, and incorporated different modalities such as visual and auditory sense impressions. Penfield's patients reported different types of memories (a moment from childhood, a recollection of a
(20) tune). When the same location in the temporal lobe was stimulated again the same memory reappeared. Could it be that a physical map of memories exists within our brains?
(25) One might mistakenly conclude from Penfield's experiment that particular memories are stored in specific sites in the brain such that the memory of one's grandmother is stored in one area and the
(30) memory of what one had for dinner is stored in another. While this description is imprecise,

the alternative theory, that memory is stored in a unitary superstructure, is also inaccurate. Although it is true that the temporal lobes play
(35) a critical role in memory processes, evidence from brain imaging studies strongly indicates that memory is divided among a range of distinct but interacting neural systems, each contributing to a unique feature of memory.
(40) One system may be involved to a larger extent in encoding or retrieval, while another may deal with the process of consolidating memory. One specific structure is more active in emotional memory, while others are
(45) employed in working memory, semantic memory, and episodic memory. These multiple memory systems are constantly sharing information and modulating one another.

28. A good title for this passage would be

○ The Life and Work of Neurosurgeon Wilder Penfield

○ The Physical Organization of Memory in the Human Brain

○ The Cognitive Functions of the Temporal Lobes

○ Historical Progress in the Search for an Epilepsy Cure

○ Where Are Childhood Memories Located in the Brain?

KAPLAN

29. Which of the following is mentioned in Paragraph 2 with regard to the neural systems of memory?

     ○ A specific brain structure cannot be involved in more than one aspect of memory.

     ○ The same neural system is primarily involved in both emotional memory and semantic memory.

     ○ The lower parts of the brain play a critical role in memory processes.

     ○ There is a specific brain region that stores the memory of last night's dinner.

     ○ Epilepsy will affect the storage and retrieval of memories.

30. When the author talks about a "unitary superstructure," he is referring to

     ○ the brain as a whole

     ○ a theory of memory organization preferred by most scientists

     ○ the cortex of the brain

     ○ a specific brain region in which all memories are stored

     ○ the sum of all memory processes, such as encoding, retrieval, and consolidation

31. All of the following are mentioned in Paragraph 1 as part of the surgical procedure Penfield performed on his patients EXCEPT

     ○ Penfield stimulated different points in his patients' temporal lobes.

     ○ Penfield's epileptic patients were not totally anesthetized during the surgery.

     ○ The patients' brains were given small electric shocks during surgery.

     ○ Penfield removed the pieces of tissue responsible for inducing seizures in his patients.

     ○ The patients' skulls were wide open throughout the surgery.

Questions 32–35 are based on the following passage:

The early 1980's were a time of growing interest in the potential of genetic research. The tedious and painstaking process of analyzing even a short segment of DNA,
(5) however, posed a problem for scientists until 1983, when Kary Mullis happened upon one of the most important ideas ever discovered in the field of genetics. He helped to develop what would eventually be known as the
(10) polymerase chain reaction (PCR), the foundation for a quick and easy process to create multiple copies of DNA from a single strand.

Multiple copies of DNA samples are
(15) necessary for researchers so that they can analyze a DNA sample quickly and with less risk to the original material. To copy a molecule of DNA, its double-helix molecular structure must be unwound into two
(20) matching halves. Each half is then replicated, and the 4 resulting segments are reattached, resulting in two identical copies of the complete DNA strand. Mullis' breakthrough was his discovery that naturally occurring
(25) DNA-copying enzymes known as polymerases could be harnessed to do the job, if pointed to the right stretch of DNA to copy and provided with the right chemical building blocks for making new DNA.

(30) One complicating factor was the extreme sensitivity of the polymerase enzymes to the heat required to unwind DNA segments. When researchers copied a strand of DNA and then wished to make another copy, a new
(35) batch of polymerase was needed, since the heat used in the process kept destroying the previous batch. For each single copy of a piece of DNA, then, a technician had to monitor the heating cycle and add new enzymes.

(40) The discovery of a temperature-resistant polymerase derived from a bacterium that lives in hot springs greatly enhanced the functionality of PCR. This version of the enzyme, able to withstand multiple cycles of
(45) heating and cooling, could make large numbers of copies from a single strand of DNA with minimal human involvement. Using the new process, DNA is heated, unwound, replicated, and reassembled over
(50) and over automatically. At each step, the number of copies is doubled, until millions or billions of copies are created. Scientists can now study a piece of DNA without worrying about damaging or destroying it, since
(55) multiple copies are readily available. The PCR process is not wholly error-free, but without this monumental discovery, genetics as we know it today would not exist.

32. The main function of Paragraph 3 is to

  ◯ examine the need for technicians to be involved in PCR

  ◯ suggest why PCR is not a good method for DNA copying

  ◯ present an alternative to PCR for genetic research

  ◯ explain a problem confronted during the development of PCR

  ◯ identify the complications behind PCR and suggest alternative means

33. The author of the passage would be most likely to agree with which of the following statements?

    ◯ PCR is not error-free, but is as close to flawless as it can possibly be.

    ◯ PCR was introduced for the sole purpose of making technicians' jobs easier.

    ◯ Until PCR, the field of genetics could not exist.

    ◯ PCR made the heating of DNA samples less important.

    ◯ Natural processes can be harnessed for scientific purposes.

34. The author implies that PCR contributed to genetics in all of the following ways EXCEPT for

    ◯ allowing for easy multiple copying of a segment of DNA

    ◯ removing scientists' anxiety about destroying DNA samples

    ◯ eliminating altogether the need to add new enzymes during copying

    ◯ streamlining the process of DNA copying

    ◯ making the copying process workable with minimal human involvement

35. The primary purpose of the passage is to

    ◯ compare two different methods of copying DNA

    ◯ explain the process of PCR and its invention and evolution

    ◯ describe how Kary Mullis came up with the idea for PCR

    ◯ demonstrate the difficulty of copying DNA

    ◯ explore the role of heat and enzymes in DNA replication

Questions 36–38 are based on the following passage:

Many sociologists who examined the phenomenon of secrecy considered secrets morally negative because they defined secrets by their content: if concealed information is
(5) negative, it is "secret"; if it is positive or neutral, it is merely "private." Berlin-born philosopher Georg Simmel (1858–1918) departed from this approach, arguing that a secret is defined not by the kind of
(10) information concealed, but by the fact of concealment. A secret is like a box into which any content can be placed; whatever the content, the box, in itself, is morally neutral. Unlike something locked in a box, however, a
(15) secret is not the internal private knowledge of a single person. Simmel saw secrecy as predicated upon a social relationship: use of the word *secret* demands that more than one person know, but that others be excluded.
(20) When we receive information, to know that it is secret, we must be told not to tell anyone. Furthermore, knowledge of the existence of a secret is separate from knowledge of its content. By removing the moral bias, Simmel's
(25) framework facilitated objective study of secrets. However, Simmel's discussion of disclosure seems to belie his contention that secrets are morally neutral. For him, inherent in every secret lies the possibility, and the
(30) desire, for revelation—regardless of the consequences. This "attraction of the abyss" gives secrets their "moral badness." Since disclosure of a secret is naughty, and secrecy and disclosure must coexist, the immorality of
(35) disclosure taints the secret itself.

One specific example of research into secrecy is Beryl Bellman's study of the "secret societies" of the West African Kpelle: religious associations, segregated by gender, that all
(40) Kpelle are expected to join. Initiated adults learn restricted information such as the true identities of "spirits," society members wearing masks for ceremonies, who are believed to be supernatural beings. Kpelle
(45) ideology holds that the uninitiated do not know that these spirits are really society members. The initiated may not tell a society's secrets to non-members; Kpelle tradition insists that non-members are not allowed to
(50) know. However, Bellman showed that anyone may, in fact, know a society's secrets. The Kpelle word translated as "secret" literally means "you may not speak it." If non-members learn secrets, they are restricted
(55) from revealing that they know by penalties ranging from monetary fines to death. Bellman could write about Kpelle societies without violating their rules by focusing not on the content of the secrets, but on their
(60) form. Bellman's realization shows that the mechanism of Kpelle secrecy relies on Simmel's model: the importance of keeping of secrets (nondisclosure) as a social act with rules and consequences carries the burden of
(65) morality rather than the personal, internal knowledge of the content of the secret.

KAPLAN

36. The "abyss" referred to by Simmel (line 32) is best defined as

    ○ a deed that is both exciting and dangerous

    ○ the ultimate punishment established for telling a secret

    ○ the gap between early models of secrecy and his approach

    ○ the distance between two people that is bridged by sharing a secret

    ○ a feature of the topography in Western Africa

37. Based on the passage, which of the following situations would most clearly violate the rules of a Kpelle secret society?

    ○ A foreign scholar publishes a book about the organization of Kpelle secret societies

    ○ A woman claims she knows the details of men's initiation rituals

    ○ A man learns the ritual knowledge of a women's secret society

    ○ Two women are overheard discussing the identities of their secret society's "spirits"

    ○ A secret is passed on with the words "don't tell anyone, but…"

38. From the information in this passage, the author would be most likely to agree with which of the following statements?

    ○ Secrets contain personal information but lies can be about anything.

    ○ The best social scientists' work must contain no contradictions.

    ○ All Kpelle adults know the secrets of the secret societies.

    ○ Sociologically, how people behave is at least as important as what they know.

    ○ It is impossible to eliminate a moral dimension from the concept of secrets.

Questions 39–44 are based on the following passage:

The study of the outbreak of Severe Acute Respiratory Syndrome (SARS) between late fall 2002 and the summer of 2003 is a fascinating look into how exponentially fast
(5) contagious viruses can spread throughout the world's population if unchecked. Before the virus was officially contained, there were a reported 8,442 confirmed cases of SARS, of which 916 were fatal—a mortality rate of
(10) roughly 10%. Of all the SARS-related deaths, however, age seems to play the most important factor: almost 50% of the SARS fatalities were over 65 years old.

SARS is a viral infection of the respiratory
(15) system caused by a coronavirus known as the SARS-associated coronavirus (SARS-CoV). Coronaviruses are also believed to be the root of almost all the common colds found in humans. SARS is spread through close contact
(20) with an infected person; it's possible to contract SARS by simply talking in close proximity to an infected person, touching them, or touching a surface contaminated with the respiratory droplets propelled by a
(25) sneeze or a cough. Following exposure to SARS-CoV, it usually takes between 2 to 10 days for symptoms to arise. The first symptoms are comparable to coming down with the flu. One may suffer from fever,
(30) headache, muscle pains, shortness of breath, sore throat, and a dry cough. Many SARS patients eventually develop pneumonia. Of all these symptoms, though, the only one that is universal among all confirmed SARS patients is
(35) a very high fever, usually well over 100° F.

The first recorded case of SARS occurred in November 2002 in Foshan City in China's southern province of Guangdong. Analysis conducted by the World Health Organization

(40) (WHO) has revealed several groups of outbreaks in different areas of Guangdong during this time period, yet curiously, no links have been uncovered among those first initial human cases, and they seem to have occurred
(45) independently of each other. However, scientists have discovered the SARS virus in 3 different animals that were being sold in the live markets of Guangdong at the time, each considered a delicacy in China.

(50) SARS seems to have been spread outside of the province by a Chinese doctor who treated Guangdong SARS patients and unknowingly became infected himself. The doctor went to Hong Kong to attend a wedding, where he
(55) stayed on the 9th floor of the Metropole Hotel. At the Metropole, he somehow transmitted SARS to 16 other hotel guests, all who stayed on the ninth floor. Those infected guests were the original seed that spread the virus to
(60) almost 30 countries, with the largest number of cases found in Mainland China, Hong Kong, Taiwan, Singapore, and Canada. Of those original 16 guests was a Chinese-American businessman who transmitted the
(65) virus to 20 hospital workers in Singapore. He was then transferred to a Hong Kong hospital where he died, but his suspicious illness and death sparked an investigation by the WHO into SARS that brought the virus to the
(70) world's attention.

After the virus was recognized as a threat to worldwide health, a global mobilization effort led by the WHO to contain the disease quickly stopped SARS in its tracks. The WHO declared
(75) that the virus was officially contained on July 5, 2003. Though the spread of the virus has been thwarted, it still remains one of the most potentially dangerous viruses in the world. Accordingly, global health authorities are
(80) constantly on alert for another possible outbreak.

KAPLAN

39. Based on information from the passage, approximately how many people over the age of 65 fatally contracted the SARS virus?

    ○ 8,400

    ○ 4,200

    ○ 900

    ○ 450

    ○ 90

40. The discussion in Paragraph 2 about how SARS is spread through close contact serves which of the following functions within the passage?

    ○ It illustrates the need for hospital staff to be well protected against possible infection when dealing with SARS cases.

    ○ It lists the different possible "close contact" scenarios.

    ○ It demonstrates how easily the virus is spread from person to person.

    ○ It offers a comparison of SARS to the common cold.

    ○ It contradicts earlier theories of how the virus is spread.

41. It can be inferred from the passage that

    ○ the first SARS cases may have occurred by eating infected meat

    ○ doctors are very close to discovering a SARS vaccine

    ○ the Chinese doctor purposely spread the SARS virus

    ○ SARS no longer poses a threat to the global population

    ○ the WHO mishandled the SARS outbreak

42. According to the passage, all of the following are true of the Chinese-American businessman EXCEPT that:

    ○ he was a guest on the ninth floor of the Metropole Hotel.

    ○ he died in a hospital in Singapore.

    ○ his death sparked a WHO investigation into SARS.

    ○ before he died, he had a very high fever.

    ○ he had been to both Hong Kong and Singapore.

43. The passage provides support for which of the following statements?

    ○ The risk of dying from SARS decreases with age.

    ○ It is impossible to track the origins of an outbreak.

    ○ Coronaviruses are the most deadly strain of virus.

    ○ Males are more susceptible to the SARS virus than females.

    ○ Healthcare professionals need to be especially wary of possible SARS infection.

44. Which of the following provides the most appropriate title for the passage?

    ○ Serial Killer: the anatomy of the 2003 SARS Outbreak

    ○ The Ninth Floor

    ○ SARS: an animal-human link?

    ○ The Global Impact of the SARS Virus

    ○ Conquering SARS

Questions 45–50 are based on the following passage:

At last count in the year 2004, it was estimated that there were over 800 million mobile phone users worldwide, almost one-eighth of the global population. Underscoring
(5) this dramatic number is a growing suspicion that the radiation emitted by these mobile phones may be dangerous to humans. There is no doubt that the body absorbs varying levels of radiation emitted by cell phones, but the
(10) question is, do these levels pose a health risk?

Mobile phones employ radio waves, more specifically, radiofrequency (RF) energy, to wirelessly transmit voice data and other information between handsets and base
(15) stations. The Food and Drug Administration (FDA) and the Federal Communications Commission (FCC), share the responsibility of making sure every cell phone sold in the United States complies with certain safety
(20) guidelines that limit a person's exposure to RF energy. The amount of RF energy absorbed by a human body when in contact with a cell phone is measured by a unit known as the Specific Absorption Rate (SAR). A phone
(25) deemed "safe" by the FCC must not have a SAR level higher than 1.6 watts per kilogram (1.6 W/kg). Deeming a phone "safe," however, is misleading. The FDA states that though there is "no hard evidence of adverse health
(30) effects [of cell phone use] on the general public," they urge further research into the subject. This statement is vague at best, and rather than answering our question, it brings up a number of others.

(35) This vague stance by the FDA and FCC derives from the fact that most of the research findings on the possible negative affects of cell phone radiation have been controversial. An example of this was a study conducted on rats
(40) in 1995 at the University of Washington in Seattle by a research team headed by Henry Lai. Lai's team concluded that the exposure of rats to RF energy within the FCC cell phone SAR limits resulted in DNA breaks in the rats'
(45) brain cells. Such breaks could be linked to cancer and brain tumors. With good reason, these findings garnered much media attention; but they could never be clinically replicated, which cast serious doubt upon
(50) them. It is worth nothing, however, that one of the studies that tried to confirm Lai's findings was conducted by a group funded by the cell phone manufacturer Motorola.

The use of cell phones has only recently
(55) become widespread. Regardless of what research may indicate, time will offer the true answer as to whether cell phones are indeed dangerous. Let's hope, unlike the smoking of cigarettes 50 years ago, the outcome does not
(60) reach us too late.

45. The author's primary purpose in the passage is to

   ⬭ dispel rumors about the negative side effects of cell phone use

   ⬭ illustrate how the risks associated with using a cell phone outweigh the phone's positive uses

   ⬭ describe how cell phones transmit voice data and other information

   ⬭ discuss her personal views on the subject of cell phone radiation

   ⬭ address the question of whether or not cell phone use is unhealthy

46. It can be inferred from the passage that a phone deemed "safe" (line 25) by the FCC would actually be better described as

   ⬭ probably safe

   ⬭ possibly safe

   ⬭ completely safe

   ⬭ somewhat dangerous

   ⬭ extremely dangerous

47. According to the passage, which of the following is true?

   ⬭ Cell phone batteries utilize the power of RF energy.

   ⬭ The FCC would consider a cell phone with a SAR level of 1.5 W/kg as unsafe.

   ⬭ Henry Lai concluded that the exposure of rats to RF energy could be linked to cancer and brain tumors in rats.

   ⬭ The FDA and FCC believe that further cell phone research is unnecessary.

   ⬭ Smaller cell phones have higher SAR ratings.

48. According to information from the passage, it can be inferred that which of the following devices also emit RF energy?

   ◯ a standard wall phone

   ◯ a television broadcast tower

   ◯ a DVD player

   ◯ a radio speaker

   ◯ an internet router

49. The author most probably notes in lines 50–53 that "one of the studies that tried to confirm Lai's findings was conducted by a group funded by the cell phone manufacturer Motorola" to suggest

   ◯ a possible bias on the part of the confirmation group

   ◯ that Lai was a disgruntled ex-employee of Motorola

   ◯ Cell phone manufacturers are actively trying to sabotage radiation research

   ◯ that Motorola is looking for alternatives to RF energy

   ◯ Lai's research team lied about their findings

50. The author draws a comparison between cigarettes and cell phones in the final sentence of the passage in order to

   ◯ illustrate a historical precedent

   ◯ demonstrate how quickly a person becomes hooked on their phone

   ◯ display her dislike for both

   ◯ make a point about social etiquette

   ◯ exaggerate the issue to help her illustrate a point

ANSWERS AND EXPLANATIONS

1. E	11. E	21. E	31. D	41. A
2. D	12. D	22. C	32. D	42. B
3. C	13. C	23. D	33. E	43. E
4. D	14. B	24. E	34. C	44. A
5. B	15. E	25. C	35. B	45. E
6. A	16. D	26. C	36. A	46. B
7. D	17. A	27. B	37. B	47. C
8. D	18. B	28. B	38. D	48. B
9. A	19. C	29. C	39. D	49. A
10. A	20. C	30. D	40. C	50. A

Fernand Braudel Passage: Questions 1–7

This social science passage explains the ideas of historian Fernand Braudel, and how they differ from traditional historians. Notice that all the French expressions are explained in plain English.

1. E

Primary purpose is another term for main idea. The purpose (main idea) of this passage is to explain how Braudel's ideas were a departure from traditional approaches to history. (A) and (D) focus on details, and (B) and (C) focus on inaccurately stated details.

2. D

Febvre and Bloch are mentioned only in Paragraph 1. There, it's said that they "originated [Braudel's] approach."

3. C

Here, you need the detail *not* mentioned in the passage. (A) is mentioned in Paragraph 1, (D) and (E) in Paragraph 2, and (B) in Paragraph 3.

4. D

In this Inference question, correct choice (D) refers to a point made in the opening paragraph. ("[H]istory...must be understood in the context of forces and material conditions that underlie human behavior.") (A) is wrong because there's no indication that the *Annales* historians were more interested in other social sciences than in history (they were historians, after all). (E) is wrong because, though it's clear that the *Annales* historians had a dogma of their own, there's no indication that they were any more dogmatic than anyone else.

5. B

Criticism of Braudel's perspective can be found in the last paragraph, which says that *Annales* historians "minimize the differences between social sciences." (C), (D), and (E) are contradicted by the passage. (A) is correct, but it's not really a criticism. (B) is best.

6. A

The *longue durée* is defined in Paragraph 2. Item I gives us the example of a *longue durée* that's actually given in the passage at line 31. Item II, as a dramatic, one-time event, is an example of what Braudel calls the *événementielle*. Item III describes a change, not necessarily permanent, in response to a specific event, so this is probably an example of *conjoncture*.

7. D

(A) and (B) are defensible claims, and (C) and (E) are familiar sayings, but none are supported by the passage. (D) accurately states the assumptions underlying Braudel's work (see in particular lines 3–10).

State Role in Development Passage: Questions 8–13

This passage presents 4 reasons for government participation in economic development in underdeveloped countries. (1): The capital required for development is more than private investors can muster. (2): Several sectors of the economy must be coordinated. (3): A large boost is necessary to put the economy beyond the stage at which increased populations eat-up increased capital. (4) The state can best oversee development in such a way as to make the country competitive in an international market.

8. D

You need to find a reason that's not given in the passage. (A) and (E) are mentioned in Paragraph 1, (B) in Paragraph 2, and (C) in Paragraph 4.

9. A

The passage as a whole presents reasons state intervention is necessary for the industrialization of many less developed countries. (B) introduces the idea of outside assistance, (C) contradicts the passage by saying that state participation is not as important as private investment, (D) says that less developed countries can't be industrialized at all, and (E) overstates the case with the words "can ensure."

10. A

You need what's not in the passage. (B) and (E) are mentioned in Paragraph 1, (C) in Paragraph 2, and (D) in Paragraph 3. "Safeguarding against the domination of local markets by a single source of capital" is not mentioned.

11. E

"Technical indivisibilities in social overhead capital" and "low-level equilibrium trap" refer to problems in underdeveloped countries that can make state participation necessary. (E) says that the technical indivisibilities can prevent development from occurring, and the low-level equilibrium can negate its effects. The wrong answer choices all say that at least one of these things are good, or at least neutral.

12. D

We're looking for statements that essentially weaken the author's argument (something that's often tested in Critical Reasoning, too). Statement I (Coordination of demand…) is not part of the correct answer, because it restates the author's opinion. Because (A), (C), and (E) all include Statement I, they're out. Statement II (Associations of private-sector investors…) contradicts the author's statement, in Paragraphs 1 and 3, that only the government can come up with the amount of capital necessary to launch large-scale industries. Statement III (Transportation and communications facilities…) also contradicts the author's statement, in Paragraph 1, that transportation and communications facilities "do not lend themselves to small-scale improvements." Correct choice (D) specifies accurate Statements II and III.

KAPLAN

13. C

The quoted phrase comes from Paragraph 3; it explains how economic growth in subsistence-level economies tends to produce population growth, which negates the effects of the economic growth.

Civil War in Brazil Passage: Questions 14–18

The passage talks about emigration from the American South to Brazil, and the contributions the emigrants made to their new country.

14. B

(A) is out of scope: the passage focuses on what happened to one group of Southerners who emigrated to Brazil, not on the source of changes in all Southerners' lives. (C) is out of scope for the same reason. (D) distorts Paragraph 2: There is no suggestion that Brazil adopted the heritage of the antebellum South. And though Paragraph 1 does mention emigration from Alabama and Texas, the passage does not account for all of the emigration from the U.S. after the Civil War, as (E) suggests, only emigration from the South to Brazil. (B) is correct.

15. E

The answer to this inference question will be well-supported by information in the passage; the wrong answers will not. (A) is extreme, since Brazil was already inhabited when the Southerners arrived. (B) is also extreme: Though the Southerners brought new inventions, this wasn't their sole purpose in immigrating. (C) is outside the scope, as is (D): The focus of Dom Pedro's appeal for immigrants was his desire to expand his country, not his fears for it. (E) is correct: It reflects statements in Paragraph 3 about the Southerners' influences on Brazilian society.

16. D

(D) is the only choice that has no support in the passage. (A) and (C) are both supported by Paragraph 3, which talks about the benefits the Southerners brought with them and their lasting effect. (B) is supported by the beginning of Paragraph 2, where the author says that the Southerners "recognized an opportunity to rebuild their lives…." Choice (E) is also incorrect, because the author specifically states that Dom Pedro advertised for colonists.

17. A

This question asks why the author makes a certain statement. Though the quote itself mentions nothing about fears, from the phrase "without yielding their Southern heritage," we can infer that Southerners expected to have to give up their heritage but preferred not to. (B), while it mentions Southern heritage, distorts the passage; Southerners influenced Brazilian culture, but didn't replace it with their own. (C) is tempting in that the quote directly follows the sentence that mentions Dom Pedro advertising for colonists, but the passage never suggests that the Southerners' desire to be free of Northern influence was suggested by Dom Pedro. (D) is a distortion; Brazilians' preferences are never mentioned in the passage. And (E) is out of scope. The answer is (A).

18. B

Paragraph 3 focuses on the benefits that the Southern immigrants conferred on Brazil. (A) is incorrect because Dom Pedro's appeal is the focus of Paragraph 1, not 3. (C) is too narrow; only one sentence in Paragraph 3 discusses the technology imported to Brazil. Furthermore, the agricultural economy in general is never a topic in the passage. (D) is out of scope, and (E) is the complete opposite of what the author suggests. The answer is (B).

Dry Valleys of Antarctica Passage: Questions 19–22

The passage is concerned with signs of life—both currently living organisms and fossilized ones—in the Dry Valleys of Antarctica.

19. C

The first step is to locate the reference to sediment in the river deltas of Lake Fryxell. Paragraph 3 tells us that the thickness of these sediments "makes a formal scientific search for signs of life impracticable." This supports (C).

(A) is a distortion. Part of (B) may be right, but the other part is wrong: it is unclear whether new layers are still being deposited on top of old ones. (D) distorts information about Lake Hoare from Paragraph 2. (E) is extreme: the passage says that it would be difficult to detect life here, but does not say that the sediment is devoid of life.

KAPLAN

20. C

(A) is out of scope: Adaptations of organisms are never considered. (B) is too narrow, since it refers to material mentioned only at the end of Paragraph 2. (D) is out of scope, and (E), like (B), is too narrow: Differences between ancient lakes and river deltas are discussed only briefly, and only in relation to the search for fossil evidence. (C) is correct. The author introduces the topic in Paragraph 1, and gives examples in Paragraphs 2 and 3.

21. E

The last sentence of Paragraph 1 states that the Dry Valleys are of particular interest to scientists looking for life on Mars because the Valleys' features resemble those of the Martian landscape. Paragraph 2 describes the ecosystem found in Lake Hoare. Paragraph 3 describes how evidence of life is well preserved on the floor of Lake Vida. This focus on lakebeds makes (E) the answer.

(A) is contradicted in Paragraph 3, which says that deltas typically bury fossil life forms too deeply to be easily found. (B), (C), and (D) each represent distortions of details mentioned in the passage. The first sentence of the passage says that circumpolar currents and ice fields surround the Dry Valleys, but there is never a mention of "circumpolar ice fields." Paragraph 3 mentions the different amounts of heat absorbed by larger and smaller rocks, and Paragraph 1 mentions that some life forms live beneath the surface of rocks, but there is no suggestion that larger rocks would be especially good places to look for life. Glaciers are mentioned in Paragraph 2 as a source of fresh water for Lake Hoare, but are never described as actually containing life.

22. C

The question asks about the piles of sediment found at the bottom of Lake Vida, which are discussed in Paragraph 3. Statement I is a reference to Lake Hoare, described in Paragraph 2, and so isn't relevant to the sediment in Lake Vida. Statement II is unsupported; nowhere does the passage describe "large pieces of rock decomposing on the lake floor." Only Statement III is correct, and so (C) is correct: Paragraph 3 implies that the sediment is "refined" as it settles into cracks formed by small rocks and gravel that have worked their way down into the ice. The small size of these cracks allows only the finest of sediment to fall through.

KAPLAN

Academic Medical Center Passage: Questions 23–27

The passage offers specific criticisms of the inefficiencies at AMCs, and suggests certain improvements.

23. D

We could say that the author does not approve of the current situation, but does not condemn AMCs altogether. (A) is incorrect since the author does not accept the status quo. (B) is extreme—the author's tone is not "strident." (C) is way off: the author is calm and certain of his positions. (E) misses the author's critical attitude toward the problems at AMCs. (D) is correct: the author presents particular criticisms, backed up by clearly explained reasons.

24. E

Since this is an inference question, we need the answer choice that is best supported by what the author says about primary care at AMCs. Primary care is addressed, in comparison to specialization, in Paragraph 4.

(A) is incorrect since the passage offers no evidence that a shift to focusing on primary care would increase AMCs' revenue. (B) is out of scope; we learn nothing about what type of care a given patient needs. (C) and (D) are also out of scope. Moreover, (C) is extreme. Only (E) is supported by the passage: we're told that strong specialty care biases are a source of inefficiency, and that primary care services need development and enhancement.

25. C

Paragraph 1 tells us that the text will discuss the inefficiencies that have resulted from the combined presence of 3 missions in academic medical centers. This is supported by the remaining paragraphs, where 4 sources of inefficiency are explored. (A) is way too broad. (B) focuses on one source of inefficiency, discussed in Paragraph 2, but doesn't encompass the larger scope of the passage. And while (D) is mentioned briefly in the passage, it is not the main point. (E) is out of scope. (C) correctly captures the author's intention of explaining challenges faced by AMCs tasked with multiple missions.

26. C

The answer here must be clearly supported by evidence from the text. (A) and (B) are extreme and go beyond anything in the passage. (D) is a distortion of a detail in Paragraph 2, which describes only community physicians with privileges at an academic hospital, not faculty physicians at AMCs. (E) is another distortion, this time of a point in Paragraph 4, which discusses why some patients choose AMCs for primary care. (C), on the other hand, is supported in Paragraph 3; we're told that physicians may "order too many tests, prolong a visit, or encourage experimental studies of a patient" for educational purposes.

27. B

(A) is not supported in the text; nowhere are we told that the physicians at tertiary hospitals would somehow be desirable to AMCs. (C) would assist the tertiary facilities, rather than help the AMCs. (D) is too extreme to follow from anything in the passage. (E) distorts the mention of grant money in Paragraph 2; there is no reason to think that less grant money would make AMCs more competitive. (B) is correct: Since the tertiary hospitals' "only goal" is patient care (Paragraph 5), it makes sense that AMCs should focus more on patient care as a response to competition from the other hospitals.

Human Brain Passage: Questions 28–31

The passage discusses the way memory is organized in the human brain and where it is stored.

28. B

A question about a title is a global question, and it needs a global answer. (A) wrongly focuses on Penfield, who only comes into Paragraph 1. (C) is out of scope: we're focused on memory, not the general question of the temporal lobes and their cognitive functions. (D) and (E) are also out of scope, with each referring to a single detail in the passage. (B) is correct.

29. C

Paragraph 2 states that "the temporal lobes play a critical role in memory processes," and from Paragraph 1 we already know that the temporal lobes are located in the lower parts of the brain. So (C) is correct.

(A) is too extreme: The passage says that "one system may be involved to a larger extent in encoding or retrieval," and "one specific structure is more active in emotional memory," but we don't know that specific structures cannot ever be involved in more than one memory-related task. (B) is a 180: At the end of Paragraph 2, we're told that "[a] specific structure is more active in emotional memory, while others are employed in working memory, semantic memory and episodic memory." Thus, both functions are not primarily mediated by the same structure. (D) is also incorrect: the author rejects this kind physical map of memory in the first sentence of Paragraph 2. (E) is totally out of scope, as epilepsy itself isn't mentioned in connection with memory processes.

30. D

Here, you need to simply define a phrase as used by the author. A "unitary superstructure" where all memories are stored is mentioned as an alternative theory for an earlier described one: that "particular memories are stored in specific sites in the brain." So we can conclude that a memory superstructure will hold all memories in one place. This is a reference to a specific brain region, as (D) indicates. It is not a reference to the brain as a whole, as in (A). The author goes on to say that this superstructure theory is inaccurate; we have no reason to think that this superstructure theory is preferred by most scientists, so (B) in incorrect. (C) is never mentioned in the text, and (E) refers to cognitive processes rather than a physical brain region; we have no evidence that this is what the unitary superstructure refers to.

31. D

The passage tells us that "[b]y stimulating different points on the lower parts of the brain (the temporal lobes) [Penfield] elicited distinct and vivid memories in his patients." That's what is described in (A), so we can rule it out. We're also told that patients were given local, not total, anesthesia, confirming choice (B). And we know that Penfield used a mild electric current on his patients' brains, (C).

What about (D)? We know that Penfield's operations were "an attempt to pinpoint the source of seizure activity and then remove that piece of tissue." But the passage never tells us whether he succeeded in achieving this goal. So (D) is the answer. As for (E), we're told in the second sentence that this was the case.

DNA Passage: Questions 32–35

This challenging passage tries to explain the discovery and importance of PCR in moving forward DNA research.

32. D

Paragraph 3 describes a complication in the PCR process, posed by the fact that heat is needed to unwind the DNA, but also destroys the polymerase enzymes used in copying. (D) closely matches this, making it the best answer. (A) is a trap—the need for technicians' involvement is mentioned in the last sentence, but it is not the main thrust of the paragraph. (B) is extreme: the paragraph doesn't say PCR is not a good method for DNA copying, only that there are certain difficulties that must be dealt with. And neither (C) nor (E) are mentioned in Paragraph 3.

33. E

(A) might be tempting, given that the last sentence of the passage says that PCR is not error-free, but it's only half-right: The passage doesn't suggest that the author thinks that PCR is close to flawless. (B) is too extreme: Nowhere does the author suggest that PCR was introduced only to make things easier for technicians. (C) distorts the last sentence (…without PCR, "genetics as we know it today would not exist,") but that doesn't mean that there was no genetic research at all before PCR came along. (D) is a 180: heating is a vital part of PCR. (E) is supported by what the author tells us about Kary Mullis' breakthrough— that it involved harnessing natural enzymes for the purpose of DNA copying and analysis.

34. C

(A), (B), and (E) are supported in the last paragraph. (D) is implied by the fact that less human involvement is necessary; so, the process is more streamlined than it used to be. With (C), we're told that heat-resistant polymerases can "withstand multiple cycles of heating and cooling, "and thus" could make large numbers of copies from a single strand of DNA with minimal human involvement," but nowhere does it say that the need to add new enzymes has been eliminated altogether. This answer is too extreme.

35. B

(A) is out of scope, as we're told almost nothing about methods of DNA copying other than PCR. (C) is too narrow (because Kary Mullis' discovery of PCR is only one part of the passage) and also out of scope (we aren't told how he came up with the idea). Neither (D) nor (E) accurately captures the passage's focus on the function and development of PCR. (B) is the answer.

Secrecy Passage: Questions 36–38

This passages speaks of Georg Simmel's beliefs about secrecy. According to Simmell, the "social form" of secrets was more compelling than their content. He supports this theory by citing the example of the West African Kpelle.

36. A

Simmel uses *abyss* to refer to the temptation to tell a secret despite possible adverse consequences, (A). All the other answer choices, while playing on the literal meaning of *abyss* (a seemingly bottomless pit), are out of scope.

37. B

Bellman's work (Paragraph 2) shows that the key part of a secret in Kpelle society is disclosure; the secret can be revealed by initiates only under certain circumstances. If non-initiates know a secret, they must pretend they don't. The situation in (B) is a direct violation of this prohibition—a woman claiming to know men's secrets would violate Kpelle taboos, even if she doesn't actually know what she claims to know or reveal the secret.

The other answer choices do not violate the rules of Kpelle secrecy. (A) describes Bellman's own work, which we're told in Paragraph 2 is permitted by Kpelle secrecy rules. (C) might not be considered desirable, but as long as the man doesn't tell anyone that he knows about women's secret rituals, he hasn't violated the rules. Likewise, we cannot say that (D) violates Kpelle secrecy rules—if only other initiated women are present, this situation would be perfectly permissible. (E) is out of scope; this type of opening phrase is not mentioned as part of the Kpelle rules.

38. D

(A) distorts Sentence 1, which describes a position that Simmel disagreed with; the author believes Simmel's approach allows "an objective study of secrets" (line 25), so she probably agrees more with Simmel than with the older attitude toward secrets. (B) is extreme and out of scope. (C) is too extreme, since we don't know if all adults know the secrets. (E) is a 180: the author seems to endorse Simmel's general, non-moral approach to secrets, even if Simmel does diverge from this position in one instance. (D) is correct: Simmel made an important contribution to the study of secrecy by separating secrets from their content; the essence of the secret is the prohibition on disclosure. At the end of Paragraph 2, there is discussion of why the methodology has been so helpful for Bellman's work. Clearly, the author considers that the separation of secrets' form and content is an important insight.

SARS Passage: Questions 39–44

This passage discusses the origins of the 2002 SARS outbreak.

39. D

It's easy to get caught up in all the different figures found in this passage, but Paragraph 1 clearly states that of the 916 reported SAR deaths, "almost 50% …. were over 65 years old." Half of approximately 900 is 450, (D). (A) is an approximation of the stated number of total confirmed SARS cases found in line 8. (B) is found by approximating half of the total number of confirmed SARS cases, not the fatalities. (C) is an approximation of the stated number of total SARS fatalities found in line 9. (E) is roughly 10% of the SARS fatalities.

40. C

The purpose of the passage is to illustrate how quickly a contagious virus such as SARS can spread throughout the global population. The examples of "close contact"—simply talking to or touching an infected person—help to support this purpose by illustrating the ease with which the virus can be transmitted. So, (C) is correct. (A), while certainly true, is incorrect because it is not discussed in the passage. (B) simply summarizes the discussion in question, it does not describe the discussion's function within the passage. (D) distorts facts regarding coronaviruses. (E) is incorrect because no *earlier theories* of SARS transmission are discussed.

41. A

Paragraph 3 states that the initial human SARS cases in Quangdong "curiously" occurred independently of each other, but at that time, certain animals "considered to be delicacies" in Guangdong were known to have a version of the SARS virus. Though it is never stated outright in the passage, one can easily assume that these initial SARS patients could have caught the virus from eating the meat of these "delicacies"; therefore, (A) is the best answer.

(B) and (C) are incorrect because in the passage there is no mention or suggestion of a possible SARS vaccine or malicious intentions on the part of the Chinese doctor. (D) is directly contradicted by the final sentence. And (E) is contradicted as well: the passage states that shortly after the WHO became aware of the virus, it led a worldwide effort that "quickly stopped SARS in its tracks."

42. B

Of all the choices, the only one not supported by facts from the passage is choice (B). For the Chinese-American businessman to be able to transmit "the virus to 20 hospital workers in Singapore," he certainly must have been in a hospital there, however, the very next sentence states that from Singapore he was "transferred to a Hong Kong hospital where he died."

(A) is incorrect because the passage states that the businessman was one of the original 16 guests infected by the Chinese doctor "who stayed on the ninth floor" of the Metropole. (C) is true, and therefore incorrect, because it basically paraphrases lines 67–68: "his suspicious illness and death sparked an investigation by the WHO." (D) is incorrect: paragraph 2 states that the only universal symptom among all SARS patients is a very high fever, and this can be applied to the Chinese-American businessman. (E) has already been established as incorrect in the answer summary above. He was in hospitals in Singapore and Hong Kong.

43. E

The idea presented in the second paragraph that SARS is easily transmitted through close contact is demonstrated in the passage by the cases of the Chinese doctor and the 20 hospital workers in Singapore who contracted the virus after coming in contact with SARS patients. These examples offer strong support for the statement made in (E); healthcare professionals seem to be especially at risk, and therefore need to be especially wary.

(A) is incorrect, since information on SARS mortality rates in the first paragraph demonstrates that the risk of dying from SARS *increases* with age. (B) is incorrect, since the passage relates how the WHO were able to track the SARS virus back to the earliest of outbreaks in Foshan City. (C) is too extreme. As for (D), there is insufficient evidence to support this statement.

KAPLAN

44.A

A global question such as this one asks you to look at the passage as a whole, usually to ascertain its purpose, or, as in this title-related question, sum up its main idea. The main idea of this passage is that an unchecked, highly contagious virus like SARS can spread throughout the world in just a few short months. The choice that best relates this main idea and sums up the theme of the overall passage is (A).

(B) and (C) address only details in the passage. (D) is incorrect because while there is enough information to draw conclusions about the global impact of SARS, the topic is barely addressed here.

Mobile Phone Passage: Questions 45–50

This passage addresses the radiation emitted by cell phones, and its possible side effects.

45.E

The author reveals her primary purpose for writing the passage when she states "There is no doubt that the body absorbs varying levels of radiation emitted by cell phones, but the question is, do these levels pose a health risk?" She then uses the rest of the passage to address this question. Therefore, choice (E) is correct.

46.B

In lines 26–34, the author characterizes the deeming of a cell phone "safe," as misleading because of the FDA's rather vague statement that there is "no hard evidence of adverse health effects [of cell phone use] on the general public." The key here is the phrase "no hard evidence." This could be translated into "so far there is no evidence to prove cell phones are unsafe." That evidence may one day arrive, but it may never arrive. So it is *possible* that they are safe, but it has yet been proven. (B) is your answer.

There is no evidence to support (A), (D), and (E), so all incorrect. (C) is directly contradicted by the author's statement that to deem a cell phone "safe" is misleading.

47. C

This is a detail question that asks you to sift through false distracters to find your answer, which is (C). This question also illustrates why it is very important to read each question carefully. True, lines 48–49 state that Henry Lai's findings could "never be clinically replicated," however, that does not alter the fact that Lai made his conclusions based on them. (A) is incorrect because RF energy is used for the cell phone's communications (line 13), not as a power source for the battery. (B) is incorrect because a SAR level of 1.5 W/kg is below the FCC's "safe" limit of 1.6 W/kg. (D) is contradicted by the text, which says that both organizations "urge further research." (E) is out of scope.

48. B

Paragraph 2 states that "Mobile phones employ radio waves, more specifically, radiofrequency (RF) energy, to wirelessly transmit voice data and other information between handsets and base stations." The key phrase in this sentence is *wirelessly transmit*; you must look to the choices to find the one that also employs wireless transmission. Of the choices, your best answer is (B).

(A) is out because a standard wall phone utilizes telephone lines to transmit voice data. (C) is out of scope. With (D), a radio receives radio waves (RF energy) that contain sound data and converts it to sound waves; the radio's speakers just *amplify* the converted data. (E) could be correct if the router was wireless, however, that is never specified so this choice is wrong.

49. A

This question asks you to infer why the author would note Motorola's affiliation with the confirmation group. Of the choices, (A) and (C) should catch your attention. Of the two, (A) is better because its neutral tone matches the passage's tone better than the accusatory tone of (C). (B) and (D) are out of scope. (C), though not a stretch, is a bit extreme to fit the passage. Plus, such an implication would probably have some precedent somewhere in the text; there is none. With (E), the fact that Lai's findings could not be replicated does not mean he was lying.

50. A

The comparison between cigarettes and cell phones is a good one because 50 years ago or so, many people smoked cigarettes unaware of how dangerous they were, until it was too late. The author, by making this comparison, is illustrating a historical precedent for what our ignorance of the effects RF radiation may lead to. (B) is incorrect: Like cigarettes, there are many people who seemingly cannot live without cell phones, but this is never discussed. (C) is out of scope. With (D), there is certainly a comparison to make between second-hand smoke and obnoxious cell phone behavior, but that is out of scope. And with (E), the implication of the comparison is not an exaggeration. It is possible that the effects of RF energy upon human health could rival that of smoking.

Chapter 7: **Quantitative Section Strategies and Practice**

- **How to Manage the Quantitative Section**
- **How the Quantitative Section Is Scored**

A little less than half of the GMAT multiple-choice questions are Quantitative (math) questions. You'll have 75 minutes to answer 37 math questions in two formats: Problem Solving and Data Sufficiency. These two formats are mingled throughout the Quantitative section, so you never know what's coming next. Here's what you can expect to see.

Quantitative Question Type	Approximate Number of Questions
Problem Solving	22
Data Sufficiency	15
Total:	**37 questions in 75 minutes**

The range of math topics tested on the GMAT is actually fairly limited. The same concepts are tested again and again in remarkably similar ways.

Arithmetic is the most commonly tested topic in GMAT math, covering about half of all the questions. **Algebra** is second, covering about one quarter of the questions. Fewer than one-sixth of all GMAT math questions are geometry questions. The other questions relate to a variety of less frequently tested topics, such as graphs and logic.

The good news is that if you're comfortable with arithmetic and algebra, you've already taken a big step toward doing well on the GMAT. Don't worry if you haven't done math in school for a long time. You're using it all the time in daily life; every time you leave a 15% tip you're practicing one of your most important GMAT math skills—percents. And to help you brush up on math concepts, we've included Kaplan's GMAT Math Reference in the back of the book.

In the next few chapters, we'll show you strategies for specific Quantitative question types. But first, let's look at some techniques for managing the whole section.

HOW TO MANAGE THE QUANTITATIVE SECTION

The best way to attack the computer-adaptive GMAT is to exploit the way it determines your score. Here's what kind of rules you're dealing with:

1. For any unanswered questions at the end of a section (that is, if time runs out), you get a double penalty. The penalty is harsher for unanswered questions than it is for incorrectly answered questions. Pace yourself to make sure that you get through the whole set in the allotted time.

2. There is no going back to check your work. You cannot go back to double-check your earlier answers. So if you get to the end of a set early, you won't be able to use the remaining time to check your answers.

3. Earlier questions in a section are worth more points than the later questions. The value of each question decreases as you progress in a section.

Since early questions are worth more than later ones, spend more time on the first 10–15 questions. Try not to guess, when possible, and double-check your answers before moving one. These questions are crucial in determining your ability estimate, so invest the necessary time trying to answer them correctly.

 READ MORE

For capsule summaries of the math topics that appear on the GMAT, go to the Math Reference at the end of this book.

At the same time, don't forget that you are being timed. Pace yourself so that you have time to mark an answer for every question in the section, because you will be *penalized for questions you don't reach*. If you don't have time to think through every question, guess during the final minutes allotted so that you can get to the end of the section.

In addition, know your math skills cold before going into the exam. A basic knowledge of certain math skills are expected on the GMAT, yet many students neglect to review. On a paper test, you could skip a math question you couldn't solve; however, on the CAT, you cannot skip any questions. In other words, you'll be required to answer the question in front of you before moving forward. In other words, it is more important that you review basic math skills before Test Day.

Guessing

Of course you'll find that you have to occasionally guess. But you should never just guess at random. Narrowing down the answer choices first is imperative. Otherwise, your odds of getting the right answer will be pretty slim. Follow this plan when you guess:

1. Eliminate answer choices you know are wrong. Even if you don't know the right answer, you can often tell that some of the answer choices are wrong. For instance, on Data Sufficiency questions, you can eliminate at least two answer choices by determining the sufficiency of one statement.

2. Avoid answer choices that make you suspicious. These are the answer choices that just "look wrong" or conform to a common wrong-answer type. For example, if only one of the answer choices in a Problem Solving question is negative, chances are that it will be incorrect.

3. Choose one of the remaining answer choices.

Avoid the Penalty

There is a penalty for not completing a section. *Every question left unanswered at the end of a section is **twice as damaging** to your score as an incorrect answer.* So clearly, it's crucial that you answer all of the questions. If you have only a minute or two left, and you have questions remaining, guess at random to get to the end of the section.

Experimental Questions

About 25% of the questions on the test are experimental—questions that the test makers are checking out for possible use on future tests. These questions are not weighed into your score. The problem is, though, that there is no way for you to identify them, so treat every question the same way.

HOW THE QUANTITATIVE SECTION IS SCORED

The Quantitative section of the GMAT is quite different from the Quantitative sections of most paper-and-pencil tests. The major difference between the test formats is that the CAT "adapts" to your performance. Each test taker is given a different mix of questions depending on how well he is doing on the test. The questions get harder or easier depending on whether the current question is answered correctly or not. Your score is not directly determined by how many questions you get right, but by how hard the questions you get right are.

When you start a section, the computer:

- Assumes you have an average score (500)

- Gives you a medium-difficulty question. About half the people who take the test will get this question right, and half will get it wrong

What happens next depends on whether you answered the question correctly.

If you answer the question correctly:

- Your score goes up

- You are given a slightly harder question

If you answer a question incorrectly:

- Your score goes down

- You are given a slightly easier question

This pattern continues for the rest of the section. Every time you get the question right, the computer raises your score, then gives you a slightly harder question. Every time you get a question wrong, the computer lowers your score, then gives you a slightly easier question. In this way the computer tries to "home in" on your score.

Theoretically, as you get to the end of a section, you will reach a point where every time the computer raises the difficulty level of a question, you get it wrong, but every time it lowers the difficulty level of a question, you get it right. Your score at this point will supposedly be an accurate measure of your ability.

Chapter 8: **Problem Solving**

- Question Format and Structure
- The 4 Basic Principle of Problem Solving
- Kaplan's 4-Step Method for Problem Solving

Problem solving questions test basic math skills; an understanding of elementary mathematical concepts, and the ability to reason quantitatively.

Some questions require only simple computations or manipulations; others require multi-step problem solving.

The format is simple: a standard multiple-choice question with five answer choices. To answer a question, select the best of the answer choices.

QUESTION FORMAT AND STRUCTURE

The instructions for the Problem Solving Questions look like this:

Directions: Solve the problems and choose the best answer.

Note: Unless otherwise indicated, the figures accompanying questions have been drawn as accurately as possible and may be used as sources of information for answering the questions.

All figures lie in a plane except where noted.

All numbers used are real numbers.

GO ONLINE

Your downloadable study sheet summarizes many key math principles and strategies.

There are about 22 Problem Solving questions on each GMAT Quantitative section. The directions indicate that some diagrams on the GMAT are drawn to scale, which means that you can use them to estimate measurements and size relationships. Other diagrams are labeled "Not drawn to scale," so you can't "eyeball" them. In fact, when a diagram says "Not drawn to scale," the unpredictability of the picture is often the key to the problem.

The directions also let you know that you won't have to deal with imaginary numbers, such as $\sqrt{-1}$, and that you'll be dealing with flat figures, such as squares and circles, unless they tell you otherwise.

THE 4 BASIC PRINCIPLES OF PROBLEM SOLVING

By adopting a systematic approach to Problem Solving, you will have a clear, concise method for thinking your way to a response. You won't waste time by attacking a problem in a tentative or haphazard manner. A systematic approach will ensure that you find the most efficient solution to the problem and that you make as few careless and unnecessary errors as possible.

1. Develop the ability to decipher question stems quickly.

With practice, you'll quickly recognize exactly what you're being asked. For example, you might get this question early on during the GMAT.

> At a certain diner, Joe ordered 3 doughnuts and a cup of coffee and was charged $2.25. Stella ordered 2 doughnuts and a cup of coffee and was charged $1.70. What is the price of 2 doughnuts?
>
> ○ $0.55
> ○ $1.00
> ○ $1.10
> ○ $1.30
> ○ $1.80

Did you read carefully and avoid the potential trap? You're asked for the price of 2 doughnuts, not 1 doughnut. Many GMAT Problem Solving questions invite you to misread them. If you're careless when you read the question—for instance, solving for the price of 1 doughnut in this example—you can be sure that the test maker will include that answer among the four wrong answer choices.

2. Decide how much effort to put into each question.

Depending on where you are on the test, you might be better off guessing and saving time for other questions. Only you know what type of questions give you particular trouble. If you're not that good at ratios and hit a ratio question in the second half of the test, you should move through it quickly to allow time to answer other questions more completely.

3. Consider alternative methods.

If the question seems as if it will take too long to solve, look for shortcuts. There are many different ways to solve a given math question. Remember, you're not looking for an ideal method for everybody but the fastest method for you. Time is a key element on standardized exams, so you should maximize the value of your time with shortcuts or alternative methods. The Kaplan Method is all about time management. The right method is whatever method is quickest for you.

In the doughnut example above, you could power your way through using algebra and substitutions:

$$3d + 1c = 2.25, \text{ therefore } c = 2.25 - 3d$$
$$2d + 1c = 1.70$$

Now, substituting for c:

$$2d + (2.25 - 3d) = 1.70$$
$$2d - 3d = 1.70 - 2.25$$
$$-d = -0.55$$
$$d = 0.55; \text{ therefore } 2d = 1.10.$$

A better way might be to notice that Joe orders the same thing Stella does, *except that he orders 1 more doughnut.* So the difference in the price of their orders, in dollars, is 2.25 − 1.70, or 0.55, is just the price of one doughnut. Algebraically, this looks like:

$$
\begin{array}{r}
(3d + 1c = 2.25) \\
-(2d + 1c = 1.70) \\
\hline
d \qquad = 0.55
\end{array}
$$

The lesson: It saves time to *think* about what you're doing before setting up your equations.

Picking Numbers

Picking Numbers is a powerful alternative to solving problems by brute force. Rather than trying to work with unknown variables, you pick concrete values for the variables. Any answer choice that does not work for the concrete values cannot be the correct answer.

How does Picking Numbers work?

- Pick simple numbers to stand in for the variables. The usefulness of the strategy depends in large part on your ability to pick convenient numbers.

- Try all the answer choices, ditching those that don't agree with the question information. Remember to keep the values you've picked for the variables constant throughout the problem.

- Try different values when more than one answer choice works. Sometimes more than one choice will give the right answer. If that happens, pick some new numbers. The correct choice must work for all possible numbers.

When you encounter a problem that contains variables, think of Kaplan alternative approaches to Problem Solving. Very often, Picking Numbers and substituting is quicker than any mathematical calculation.

Now let's try using the Picking Numbers technique on a few problems. You might run into this kind of question:

> Carol spends $\frac{1}{4}$ of her savings on a stereo and $\frac{1}{3}$ less than she spent on the stereo for a television. What fraction of her savings did she spend on the stereo and television?
>
> ○ $\frac{1}{4}$
>
> ○ $\frac{2}{7}$
>
> ○ $\frac{5}{12}$
>
> ○ $\frac{1}{2}$
>
> ○ $\frac{7}{12}$

In this case, the common denominator is 12; so let the number 12 (12 dollars) represent Carol's total savings. That means she spends $\frac{1}{4}$ × 12 dollars, or 3 dollars, on her stereo, and $\frac{2}{3}$ × 3 dollars, or 2 dollars, on her television. That comes out to be 3 + 2 = 5 dollars; that's how much she spent on the stereo and television combined. You're asked what *fraction* of her savings she spent. Because her total savings is 12 dollars, she spent $\frac{5}{12}$ of her savings; (C) is correct. Notice how picking a common denominator for the variable (Carol's savings) made it easy to convert each of the fractions $\left(\frac{1}{4}$ and $\frac{2}{3} \times \frac{1}{4}$ of her savings$\right)$ to a simple number.

A tricky part of this question is understanding how to figure the price of the television. Remember your first Basic Principle of Problem Solving: Understand exactly what's being asked. The television does not cost $\frac{1}{3}$ of her savings, it costs $\frac{1}{3}$ *less* than the stereo; that is, it costs $\frac{2}{3}$ as much as the stereo.

A quick overview could have helped you eliminate (A), (D), and (E). (A) is too small; the stereo alone costs $\frac{1}{4}$ of her savings. (D) and (E) are too large, because the television costs LESS than the stereo, so the two together must cost less than 2 × $\frac{1}{4}$, or half, of Carol's savings.

KAPLAN EXCLUSIVE

With fractions, a lowest common denominator is often a good number to pick.

This next problem is of medium difficulty:

If $a > 1$, what is the value of $\dfrac{2a + 6}{a^2 + 2a - 3}$?

○ a

○ $a + 3$

○ $\dfrac{2}{a - 1}$

○ $\dfrac{2a}{a - 3}$

○ $\dfrac{a - 1}{2}$

If a question has variables in the answer choices, that's your signal it can be attacked by Picking Numbers.

Note the condition you're given: $a > 1$. You might start by picking 2 for a. Then the expression we're given is $\dfrac{2(2) + 6}{(2)^2 + 2(2) - 3}$. This equals $\dfrac{10}{5}$, or 2. Check the answer choices: which of the expressions equals 2 when $a = 2$? Unfortunately, both (A) and (C) equal 2. This narrows the possibilities down to (A) and (C). When you have more than one answer choice that gives the right answer, you have to pick another number.

Try $a = 3$. Then the expression in the question stem is $\dfrac{2(3) + 6}{(3)^2 + 2(3) - 3}$. This equals $\dfrac{12}{12}$, or 1.

Now when $a = 3$, (A) has value of 3 and (C) has value of 1, so (C) is the correct answer.

Remember to try out *all* the answer choices with the Picking Numbers strategy. If you neglected to do this, you might have picked (A) before seeing that (C) also works with $a = 2$.

You might run into the following difficult problem.

> A car rental company charges for mileage as follows: x
> dollars per mile for the first n miles and $x + 1$ dollars per
> mile for each mile over n miles. How much will the
> mileage charge be, in dollars, for a journey of d miles,
> where $d > n$?
>
> ○ $d(x + 1) - n$
> ○ $xn + d$
> ○ $xn + d(x + 1)$
> ○ $x(n + d) - d$
> ○ $(x + 1)(d - n)$

Picking Numbers can often simplify complex word problems.

This is a late problem, so you know to expect traps. Reading it might make your head spin, but it becomes much simpler when you substitute numbers for the variables. For instance, suppose you pick $x = 4$, $n = 2$, $d = 5$. The problem now reads: 4 dollars per mile for the first 2 miles, and 5 dollars a mile for each mile over 2 miles. How much will the mileage charge be for a journey of 5 miles? That's easily calculated: the first 2 miles cost 2 × 4 dollars and the remaining 3 miles cost 3 × 5 dollars for a total cost of 8 + 15, or 23 dollars. Of the answer choices, only (A) has value 23 when $x = 4$, $n = 2$, and $d = 5$. Without the Picking Numbers strategy at their disposal, many test takers might be stumped by a question like this one on Test Day. With the Picking Numbers strategy in mind, however, *you* can answer it fairly quickly.

Picking Numbers is almost always the best way to attack odd/even questions. The following problem is of medium difficulty.

> If a and b are odd integers, which of the following is an
> even integer?
>
> ○ $a(b - 2)$
> ○ $ab + 4$
> ○ $(a + 2)(b - 4)$
> ○ $3a + 5b$
> ○ $a(a + 6)$

You can run through the answer choices quite quickly using the picking numbers strategy. Try $a = 3, b = 5$. Only (D), $9 + 25 = 34$, is even. There's no trick here; this question simply rewards the careful test taker.

Backsolving

Backsolving is a strategy that allows you to use the answer choices to work backward through the question stem. You plug the answer choices into the question to see which one works. The answer choice that agrees with the information in the question stem is correct. You've probably used this strategy unconsciously when you ran into a multiple-choice question that you found difficult. Backsolving can save a great deal of time if you use it wisely. It is an exceptional method for solving questions when you have no idea where to begin on a problem.

KAPLAN) EXCLUSIVE

Start with choice (B) or (D) when Backsolving. The choices are arranged in ascending or descending order, so if the middle choices are not correct, you'll likely be able to determine whether you have to go up or down in value.

We want you to learn to use Backsolving systematically. On the GMAT, answers are arranged in ascending or descending order. Start Backsolving with choice (B) or choice (D). If that isn't the answer, you'll usually be able to tell whether the correct answer is larger or smaller, which means you'll have narrowed the choices down.

Solve the following problem by Backsolving; this problem is of medium difficulty.

A crate of apples contains one bruised apple for every 30 apples in the crate. If 3 out of every 4 bruised apples are considered unsaleable, every unsaleable apple is bruised, and there are 12 unsaleable apples in the crate, how many apples are there in the crate?

○ 270
○ 360
○ 480
○ 600
○ 840

Start Backsolving with choice (B). Suppose that there are 360 apples in the crate. Then $\frac{360}{30}$ apples, or 12 apples, are bruised. Then $\frac{3}{4}$ of 12 apples, or 9 apples, are unsaleable. This is too few unsaleable apples. So (B) is too small. We can eliminate (A) and (B). Now let's look at (D). Suppose there are 600 apples in the crate. Then $\frac{600}{30}$ apples, or 20 apples, are bruised. Then $\frac{3}{4}$ of 20 apples, or 15 apples, are unsaleable. This is too many unsaleable apples. So (D) is too large. (C) must be correct.

This is also a medium-difficulty problem.

> What is the value of x if $\dfrac{x+1}{x-3} - \dfrac{x+2}{x-4} = 0$?
>
> ○ −2
> ○ −1
> ○ 0
> ○ 1
> ○ 2

Backsolving is often simpler and faster than solving equations (especially when the equations look like this).

Since (D) looks easier to work with than (B), let's start with that.

$$\frac{1+1}{1-3} - \frac{1+2}{1-4} = \frac{2}{-2} - \frac{3}{-3} = -1 - (-1) = 0. \text{ Bingo!}$$

4. Guess if you're stumped.

If you simply cannot solve an equation using regular math or an alternative method, sometimes that's the time to make an educated guess. The key to good guessing is the elimination of wrong answer choices. Many questions will have answer choices that are obviously wrong or don't make sense. If you can eliminate some wrong choices using common sense, make a good guess and move on.

For example, try to eliminate some answer choices on the following medium-difficulty question.

> A container holding 12 ounces of a solution that is 1 part alcohol to 2 parts water is added to a container holding 8 ounces of a solution that is 1 part alcohol to 3 parts water. What is the ratio of alcohol to water in the resulting solution?
>
> ○ 2:5
>
> ○ 3:7
>
> ○ 3:5
>
> ○ 4:7
>
> ○ 7:3

Right away you can eliminate (E). It's the only choice that has more alcohol than water; not only does it stand out from the other answer choices because it is the only one that represents a fraction greater than 1, but it doesn't make sense because both solutions had less alcohol than water. You can use common sense to eliminate some other choices. One of the solutions is 1:2 alcohol to water, the other is 1:3. A combination of the two should have a ratio somewhere between 1:2 and 1:3. But (C) and (D) both have a higher proportion of alcohol than the 1:2 solution, so you can eliminate them. Guess (A) or (B); you have a 50 percent chance of being right.

(Point of information: The answer is (B). The 12-ounce solution has 4 oz alcohol and 8 oz water. The 8 oz solution has 2 oz alcohol and 6 oz water. Add the amounts of alcohol and water for a solution with 6 oz alcohol and 14 oz water for a ratio of 3:7 alcohol to water.)

Guessing can also be useful on Roman numeral questions. If you can figure out one statement, you can eliminate a few answer choices. Try the following medium-level Roman numeral question.

If $x - y = 8$, which of the following must be true?

    I. Both x and y are positive.

   II. If x is positive, y must be positive.

  III. If x is negative, y must be negative.

    ◯ I only

    ◯ II only

    ◯ III only

    ◯ I and II

    ◯ II and III

You want to figure out one statement and thus eliminate as many answer choices as you can while doing as little work as possible. Statement II occurs in three answer choices, so we'll try it. You can use the Picking Numbers technique to evaluate the truth of this statement. Can II be false? Can you pick numbers to fit the equation such that x is positive and y is negative? Suppose $x = 2$. Then $y = -6$. So II need not be true. That eliminates (B), (D), and (E), and leaves you with a 50-50 shot at guessing.

As a matter of fact, you've done better than that. Did you notice? If II can be false, if it's possible for x to be positive and y to be negative, then Statement I need not be true either, and the answer is (C).

An important point to take with you about guessing is that it works in alliance with the techniques we've discussed. Don't guess blindly: Use anything you can—common sense, Picking Numbers, Backsolving—to eliminate some choices and improve your odds.

You've already seen how Problem Solving techniques can help your guessing. But what happens when you're totally at a loss? Suppose you were confronted with the following medium-difficulty question.

If a and b are prime numbers, such that $a > b$, which of the following cannot be true?

    ◯ $a + b$ is prime.

    ◯ ab is odd.

    ◯ $a(a - b)$ is odd.

    ◯ $a - b$ is prime.

    ◯ a^b is even.

KAPLAN

KAPLAN EXCLUSIVE

A prime number is a positive integer that has only 2 positive factors—itself and 1. The first eight prime numbers are 2, 3, 5, 7, 11, 13, 17, and 19.

Guessing anything when you have no clue at all is usually smart—with one exception. Let's say you were totally clueless on this problem beyond knowing the definition of a prime number. If you were the test maker and your goal was to make some students spend too much time on a problem, where would you hide the answer? In a problem in which there's no alternative but to work with the answer choices to solve, the answer will more often than not be (D) or (E). So if you decide to guess, which should you guess? (Or if you decide to solve it, where should you begin trying out answer choices?) How about (E)? For the record, the answer *is* (E): Because a can't be even ($a > b$), no integer power of a can be even.

By now you've seen that there's more than one way to solve a math problem. Your concern is to pick the one that will solve the problem fastest for you. You can always, at a minimum, get started on a problem, eliminate a few answer choices, and guess.

 **KAPLAN STRATEGY**

The 4 basic principles for success in Problem Solving are:

- Develop the ability to decipher question stems quickly.
- Decide how much effort to put into each question.
- Consider alternative methods (Picking Numbers or Backsolving).
- Guess if you're stumped.

KAPLAN'S 4-STEP METHOD FOR PROBLEM SOLVING

Now that you've got a grip on the basic principles of Problem Solving, let's look at how to attack the questions you'll see on the test.

1. Read through the whole question.

Determine exactly what the question is asking. Is the question or situation complicated?

2. Decide how much effort to put into the question.

Is this the sort of question you normally do well on? Will you be able to solve it quickly? Be aware of where you are in the test and how much time you have left.

3. Choose the fastest approach to the answer.

Choose the approach that you feel most comfortable with. Questions are often deliberately confusing and contain traps for the unwary.

4. Select an answer.

Answer every question. Eliminate answer choices whenever you can. The more unlikely answer choices you can eliminate, the better your chances of guessing correctly. And if you're running out of time and several questions remain, make sure to answer each question by guessing something.

Now, try the 4-Step Method on the following example:

If $w > x > y > z$ on the number line and y is halfway between x and z, and x is halfway between w and z, then $\dfrac{y-x}{y-w} =$

- $\dfrac{1}{4}$
- $\dfrac{1}{3}$
- $\dfrac{1}{2}$
- $\dfrac{3}{4}$
- 1

Step 1: Read through the whole question.

You should immediately notice that the question has four variables and that you need to figure out the relative values for x, y, and w.

Step 2: Decide how much effort to put into the problem.

It's up to you, but let's go for it.

Step 3: Choose the fastest approach to the answer.

This could have been a long day at the office if you didn't see that Picking Numbers is the fastest way here. The question essentially gives you instructions on how to Pick Numbers. Say $z = 2$ and $y = 4$; then $x = 6$. That would make $w = 10$, so: $\frac{y-x}{y-w} = \frac{4-6}{4-10} = \frac{-2}{-6} = \frac{1}{3}$. If you missed this strategy you might have elected to skip this one and come back later.

Step 4. Select an answer.

Eliminate unlikely choices, and guess. If you're running out of time, guess something.

Now that you have a handle on Problem Solving, try the Practice Quiz.

_____

SUMMARY

The 4 basic principles for success in Problem Solving are:

- Develop the ability to decipher question stems quickly.
- Decide how much effort to put into each question.
- Consider alternative methods (picking numbers or backsolving).
- Guess if you're stumped.

Kaplan's 4-Step Method for Problem Solving is:

Step 1: Read through the whole question.
Step 2: Decide how much effort to put into the question.
Step 3: Choose the fastest approach to the answer.
Step 4: Select an answer.

KAPLAN

PRACTICE QUIZ

Directions: Solve the problems and choose the best answer.

1. $7.38 + 10.075 =$

    ○ 10.813

    ○ 17.113

    ○ 17.355

    ○ 17.383

    ○ 17.455

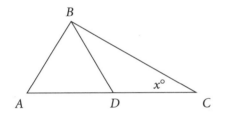

2. In the diagram above, if $AB = AD = BD = DC$, then $x =$

    ○ 30

    ○ 35

    ○ 40

    ○ 45

    ○ 60

3. If $2x - 4y = -2$ and $3x - 2y = 3$, then $2y + x =$

    ○ $\dfrac{3}{2}$

    ○ 2

    ○ $3\dfrac{1}{2}$

    ○ 5

    ○ $5\dfrac{1}{2}$

KAPLAN

4. Joan spends 20 percent of her income on taxes and 20 percent of the remainder on rent. What percent of her income does she spend on rent?

   ○ 8%

   ○ 10%

   ○ 16%

   ○ 20%

   ○ 24%

5. An overnight courier service charges $5.00 for the first 2 ounces of a package and $0.75 for each additional ounce. If there is a 6 percent sales tax added to these charges, how much does it cost to send a 6-ounce package?

   ○ $4.24

   ○ $8.00

   ○ $8.48

   ○ $9.28

   ○ $10.60

6. If $\dfrac{3M}{2N} = 0.125$, what is the value of N in terms of M?

   ○ $\dfrac{M}{8}$

   ○ $\dfrac{8}{M}$

   ○ $4M$

   ○ $8M$

   ○ $12M$

7. Company C sells a line of 25 products with an average retail price of $1,200. If none of these products sells for less than $420, and exactly 10 of the products sell for less than $1,000, what is the greatest possible selling price of the most expensive product?

  ○ $2,600

  ○ $3,900

  ○ $7,800

  ○ $11,800

  ○ $18,200

8. If $\frac{n}{2}$ is an even integer, what is the remainder when n is divided by 4?

  ○ 0

  ○ 1

  ○ 2

  ○ 3

  ○ 4

9. A certain industrial loom weaves 0.128 meters of cloth every second. Approximately how many seconds will it take for the loom to weave 25 meters of cloth?

  ○ 178

  ○ 195

  ○ 204

  ○ 488

  ○ 512

10. If $a - b = \dfrac{a^2 - b^2}{b^2 - a^2}$ and $b^2 - a^2 \neq 0$, then $b - a =$

    ○ -1

    ○ 0

    ○ 1

    ○ 2

    ○ It cannot be determined from the information given.

11. If a sequence of consecutive integers of increasing value has a sum of 63 and a first term of 6, how many integers are in the sequence?

    ○ 11

    ○ 10

    ○ 9

    ○ 8

    ○ 7

12. A cube of white chalk is painted red, and then cut parallel to a pair of parallel sides to form two rectangular solids of equal volume. What percent of the surface area of each of the new solids is not painted red?

    ○ 15%

    ○ $16\dfrac{2}{3}\%$

    ○ 20%

    ○ 25%

    ○ $33\dfrac{1}{3}\%$

13. Ann and Bob drive separately to a meeting. Ann's average driving speed is greater than Bob's average driving speed by one-third of Bob's average driving speed, and Ann drives twice as many miles as Bob. What is the ratio of the number of hours Ann spends driving to the meeting to the number of hours Bob spends driving to the meeting?

   ○ 8:3

   ○ 3:2

   ○ 4:3

   ○ 2:3

   ○ 3:8

14. If $0 < p < 1$, which of the following has the least value?

   ○ $\dfrac{1}{p^2}$

   ○ $\dfrac{1}{\sqrt{p}}$

   ○ $\dfrac{1}{p^2 + 1}$

   ○ $\dfrac{1}{\sqrt{p + 1}}$

   ○ $\dfrac{1}{(p + 1)^2}$

15. In a certain game, each player scores either 2 points or 5 points. If n players score 2 points and m players score 5 points, and the total number of points scored is 50, what is the least possible positive difference between n and m?

   ○ 1

   ○ 3

   ○ 5

   ○ 7

   ○ 9

KAPLAN

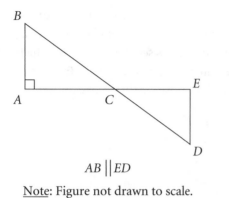

$AB \parallel ED$

Note: Figure not drawn to scale.

16. In the figure above, $ED = 1$, $CD = 2$, and $AE = 6\sqrt{3}$. What is the perimeter of $\varnothing ABC$?

   ○ $3\sqrt{3}$

   ○ $5\sqrt{3}$

   ○ $10\sqrt{3}$

   ○ $15 + 5\sqrt{3}$

   ○ $25\sqrt{3}$

17. James's library contains reference, biography, and fiction books only, in the ratio of 1:2:7, respectively. If James's library contains 30 books, how many biographies does he own?

   ○   2

   ○   3

   ○   4

   ○   6

   ○   10

18. Which of the following fractions is smaller than $\frac{2}{5}$?

   ○ $\frac{7}{16}$

   ○ $\frac{4}{11}$

   ○ $\frac{3}{7}$

   ○ $\frac{4}{9}$

   ○ $\frac{9}{20}$

19. A sink contains exactly 12 liters of water. If water is drained from the sink until it holds exactly 6 liters of water less than the quantity drained away, how many liters of water were drained away?

    ◯ 2

    ◯ 3

    ◯ 4.5

    ◯ 6

    ◯ 9

20. In a certain state, a person may inherit up to $8,000 tax free, but any amount in excess of $8,000 is taxed at a rate of 6 percent. If Tony inherits a total of $11,500, how much tax will he have to pay?

    ◯ $210

    ◯ $270

    ◯ $300

    ◯ $420

    ◯ $510

21. The amount of gas in a gas storage tank is halved by draining 15 gallons of gas from it. If p gallons of gas are then added to the tank, how many gallons of gas are there in the storage tank?

    ◯ $15 + p$

    ◯ $30 - p$

    ◯ $30 + p$

    ◯ $2p - 30$

    ◯ $p - 15$

KAPLAN

22. A rectangular parking space is marked out by painting three of its sides white. If the length of the unpainted side is 9 feet, and the sum of the lengths of the painted sides is 37 feet, what is the area of the parking space in square feet?

   ○ 46

   ○ 81

   ○ 126

   ○ 252

   ○ 333

$x\%$	on time
43%	up to 15 minutes delayed
17%	15–30 minutes delayed
12%	30–60 minutes delayed
3%	more than 60 minutes delayed

23. The chart above describes departures from a certain airport on a certain day. If 1,200 flights were delayed, how many flights departed on time?

   ○ 250

   ○ 300

   ○ 350

   ○ 400

   ○ 900

24. Cheese, bologna, and peanut butter sandwiches were made for a picnic in a ratio of 5 to 7 to 8. If a total of 120 sandwiches were made, how many bologna sandwiches were made?

   ○ 15

   ○ 30

   ○ 38

   ○ 42

   ○ 48

25. If a rectangle with width 49.872 inches and length 30.64 inches has an area that is 15 times the area of a certain square, which of the following is the closest approximation to the length, in inches, of a side of that square?

    ○ 5

    ○ 10

    ○ 15

    ○ 20

    ○ 25

26. If $y = -(4 - 5)$, then $y =$

    ○ −2

    ○ −1

    ○ 0

    ○ 1

    ○ 2

27. If a store purchases a sweater for a wholesale price of $36.00 and then sells the sweater at a retail price of $50.00, what is the approximate percent increase in the price?

    ○ 18%

    ○ 24%

    ○ 33%

    ○ 34%

    ○ 39%

28. What is the ratio of $\frac{37}{5}$ to the product $6\left(\frac{37}{5}\right)$?

    ○ $\frac{1}{6}$

    ○ $\frac{1}{5}$

    ○ $\frac{5}{6}$

    ○ $\frac{6}{5}$

    ○ 37

29. What is the greatest integer that is a sum of four different prime numbers, each less than 14?

    ○ 36

    ○ 40

    ○ 44

    ○ 48

    ○ 52

30. A church collected exactly $303 from its members during a service. If each member contributed at least $2, what is the greatest number of members that could have attended this particular service?

    ○ 149

    ○ 150

    ○ 151

    ○ 152

    ○ 153

31. $\dfrac{5.005}{2.002} =$

   ⚪ 2.05

   ⚪ 2.50025

   ⚪ 2.502

   ⚪ 2.5025

   ⚪ 2.5

32. How many different subsets of the set {10, 14, 17, 24} are there that contain an odd number of elements?

   ⚪ 3

   ⚪ 6

   ⚪ 8

   ⚪ 10

   ⚪ 12

33. If a student allocated one-half of her annual budget for rent, one-quarter for tuition, one-fifth for living expenses, and the remaining $1,000 for recreation, what was her total annual budget?

   ⚪ $10,000

   ⚪ $15,000

   ⚪ $20,000

   ⚪ $50,000

   ⚪ $200,000

34. Which of the following must equal zero for all real numbers x?

    I. $x^3 - x^2$
    II. x^0
    III. x^1

  ◯ None

  ◯ I only

  ◯ II only

  ◯ I and II only

  ◯ II and III only

35. The population of City A is three times the population of City B. Together, Cities A and B have twice the population of City C. What is the ratio of the population of City C to the population of City B?

  ◯ 1:4

  ◯ 1:2

  ◯ 2:1

  ◯ 3:1

  ◯ 4:1

36. If the fraction $\dfrac{m}{n}$ is negative, which of the following cannot be true?

  ◯ $\dfrac{n}{m} > \dfrac{m}{n}$

  ◯ $mn < 0$

  ◯ $n - m > 0$

  ◯ $mn^3 > 0$

  ◯ $m - n > 0$

37. The speed of a train pulling out of a station is given by the equation $s = t^2 + t$, where s is the speed in kilometers per hour, and t is the time in seconds from when the train starts moving. The equation holds for all situations where $0 \leq t \leq 4$. In kilometers per hour, what is the positive difference in the speed of the train 4 seconds after it starts moving compared to the speed 2 seconds after it starts moving?

- ○ 0
- ○ 6
- ○ 14
- ○ 20
- ○ 38

38. If Lisa walks t blocks in 3 minutes, how many minutes will it take her to walk s blocks at the same rate?

- ○ $\dfrac{s}{3t}$
- ○ $\dfrac{3s}{t}$
- ○ $\dfrac{3}{st}$
- ○ $\dfrac{3t}{s}$
- ○ $\dfrac{t}{3s}$

39. A chemist has 10 liters of a solution that is 10 percent nitric acid by volume. He wants to dilute the solution to 4 percent strength by adding water. How many liters of water must he add?

- ○ 15
- ○ 18
- ○ 20
- ○ 25
- ○ 26

KAPLAN

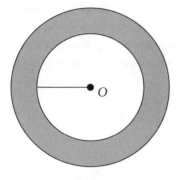

40. In the figure above, a circular swimming pool (the unshaded area) is surrounded by a circular walkway (the shaded area). Both the circular swimming pool and the entire circular region consisting of the swimming pool and the walkway have the center O. If the radius of the swimming pool is 10 meters and the width of the walkway is 5 meters, how many square meters greater than the surface area of the swimming pool is the area of the walkway?

○ 25π

○ 50π

○ 100π

○ 125π

○ 225π

41. Molly purchased Brand A binders at $8.00 a piece and Brand B binders at $5.60 a piece. If she bought a total of 12 binders for $84.00, how many Brand A binders did she buy?

○ 2

○ 5

○ 6

○ 7

○ 10

42. The host of a dinner party must determine how to seat himself and 5 guests in a single row. How many different seating arrangements are possible if the host always chooses the same seat for himself?

○ 6

○ 15

○ 21

○ 120

○ 720

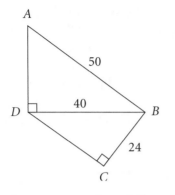

43. What is the perimeter of quadrilateral *ABCD* above?

   ○ 106

   ○ 114

   ○ 120

   ○ 127

   ○ 136

44. A local farmer grows wheat on land he rents for a fixed cost of $200,000 per year. The variable cost of growing one bushel of wheat is $10. In a certain year, the farmer grows and sells 50,000 bushels of wheat and makes a profit of $150,000, after paying the fixed cost to rent the land. If every bushel sold for the same price, what was the selling price, in dollars, of a bushel of wheat?

   ○ 3

   ○ 7

   ○ 11

   ○ 13

   ○ 17

45. In a rectangular coordinate system, triangle *ABC* is drawn so that one side of the triangle connects two points on the *y* axis, *A*(0, 2) and *B*(0, −4). If point *C* has coordinates (*c*, 0) where *c* > 0, and the area of *ABC* is 21, then *c* =

   ○ $\dfrac{7}{3}$

   ○ 7

   ○ $\sqrt{53}$

   ○ $\sqrt{65}$

   ○ 21

KAPLAN

46. A company received two shipments of ball bearings. In the first shipment, 1 percent of the ball bearings were defective. In the second shipment, which was twice as large as the first, 4.5 percent of the ball bearings were defective. If the company received a total of 100 defective ball bearings, how many ball bearings were in the first shipment?

   ○ 990

   ○ 1,000

   ○ 2,000

   ○ 3,000

   ○ 3,500

47. If $x + y = 2$, and $x^2 - xy - 10 - 2y^2 = 0$, what does $x - 2y$ equal?

   ○ 0

   ○ 1

   ○ 2

   ○ 5

   ○ 10

48. The average speed of a certain train was measured every 6 minutes and was found to have increased by 3 miles per hour during each successive 6-minute interval after the first interval. If in the third 6-minute interval its speed was 24 miles per hour, how many miles did the train travel in the first 6-minute interval?

   ○ 0.6

   ○ 1.2

   ○ 1.8

   ○ 2.4

   ○ 3.0

49 If the product of the integers a, b, c, and d is 546, and if $1 < a < b < c < d$, what is the value of $b + c$?

    ⬭ 273

    ⬭ 185

    ⬭ 21

    ⬭ 10

    ⬭ 4

50. In a certain laboratory, chemicals are identified by a color-coding system. There are 20 different chemicals. Each one is coded with either a single color or a unique two-color pair. If the order of colors in the pairs doesn't matter, what is the minimum number of different colors needed to code all 20 chemicals with either a single color or a unique pair of colors?

    ⬭ 5

    ⬭ 6

    ⬭ 7

    ⬭ 20

    ⬭ 40

KAPLAN

ANSWERS AND EXPLANATIONS

1. E	11. E	21. A	31. E	41. D
2. A	12. D	22. C	32. C	42. D
3. D	13. B	23. D	33. C	43. E
4. C	14. E	24. D	34. A	44. E
5. C	15. B	25. B	35. C	45. B
6. E	16. D	26. D	36. D	46. B
7. D	17. D	27. E	37. C	47. D
8. A	18. B	28. A	38. B	48. C
9. B	19. E	29. A	39. A	49. D
10. C	20. A	30. C	40. A	50. B

1. E

It doesn't get any more basic than this, which is why you need to be on the lookout for silly errors. If you wanted to double-check your decimal arithmetic, you could reason that 7.38 plus the integer 10 is going to be 17.38. Therefore, since we're adding more than 10, (A), (B), and (C) are all out. Adding 0.075 to 0.38 is actually 0.455, so (E) gets the nod.

2. A

This question quickly tests your knowledge of a few triangle "rules." Triangle *ABD* is an equilateral triangle, which means that in addition to having sides of the same length, it has angles of the same measure (namely, 60°). Triangle *BDC* is an isosceles triangle, meaning that it has two sides of the same length, and that the angles opposite these sides are of the same measure. This allows us to conclude that angle *DBC* is *x*° also. Angle *BDC* is supplementary to angle *BDA*, so its measure and angle *BDA*'s measure sum to 180°. Therefore, the measure of angle *BDC* is 180° − 60°, which is 120°. (Angle *BDA*, remember, is 60°.) So, if angle *BDC* is 120°, then the other two angles in triangle *BDC* must sum to 60°. Since they are equal angles, each is half of 60°, or 30°.

3. D

Two equations, two variables. We can express one variable in terms of the other using one equation, and then plug this expression for the variable we solved for into the other equation, but there's a faster method. If we subtract the first equation from the second, we get—on the left side—exactly the expression that we are asked the value of:

$$3x - 2y = 3$$
$$\underline{- (2x - 4y = -2)}$$
$$x + 2y = 5$$

Although the order of x and y is reversed from the expression in the question, the left side of the last equation contains the same expression. Choice (D) it is.

4. C

If Joan spends 20 percent of her income on taxes, then the remainder is 80 percent of her income, which is $0.8x$. If she spends 20 percent of this remaining 80 percent on rent, she spends:

$$0.2(0.8x) = 0.16x$$

$0.16x$ is 16 percent of x. Sixteen percent of her income goes to rent.

5. C

Take it one step at a time. We want to send a 6-ounce package. The first 2 ounces cost $5.00. Each of the remaining 4 ounces costs $0.75. So the total for all 6 ounces, exclusive of tax is:

$$\$5.00 + 4(\$0.75) = \$8.00$$

To this is added a 6 percent tax, resulting in a total cost of:

$$\$8.00 + 0.06(\$8.00) =$$
$$\$8.00 + \$0.48 = \$8.48.$$

6. E

We want to isolate N. First we'll multiply both sides by $2N$ in order to get rid of the denominator.

$$\frac{3M}{2N} = 0.125$$
$$3M = 2N(0.125)$$
$$3M = 0.25N$$
$$\frac{3M}{0.25} = N$$
$$12M = N$$

7. D

Since the 25 products sell at an average of $1,200, to buy one of each we'd have to spend $25 \times \$1,200 = \$30,000$. We want to find the greatest possible selling price of the most expensive product. The way to maximize this price is to minimize the prices of the other 24 products. Ten of these products sell for less than $1,000, but all sell for at least $420. This means that (in trying to minimize the price of 24 items) we can have 10 sell at $420. That leaves 14 more that sell for $1,000 or more. So, in order to keep minimizing, we'll price these at $1,000. That means that, out of the $30,000 we know it will take to purchase one of each item, at least $10(\$420) + 14(\$1,000) = \$18,200$ is needed in order to purchase the 24 other items. The final, most expensive item can thus cost as much as $\$30,000 - \$18,200 = \$11,800$.

8. A

You either see this one right away, through your knowledge of number properties, or you just Pick Numbers. Any even integer multiplied by 2 will be evenly divisible by 4 because either the even integer itself is already divisible by 4 or it leaves a remainder of 2 when divided by 4. If it leaves a reminder of 2, then when this number is multiplied by 2, we'll have 2 remainders of 2, which when divided by 4 leaves no remainder. If you didn't see that, you could have Picked Numbers for n that resulted in an even integer when divided by 2 and seen what happens:

$$\frac{4}{2} = 2; \qquad \frac{4}{4} = 1$$
$$\frac{8}{2} = 4; \qquad \frac{8}{4} = 2$$
$$\frac{12}{2} = 6; \qquad \frac{12}{4} = 3$$
$$\frac{16}{2} = 8; \qquad \frac{16}{4} = 4$$

KAPLAN

Already we can see the pattern: When divided by 2, only multiples of 4 will result in an even integer. Multiples of 4, of course, will have a remainder of 0 when divided by 4.

9. B

Work = Rate × Time. The work here is 25 meters; the rate is 0.128 meters/second; we want to solve for the number of seconds:

25 meters = 0.128 meters/second × y seconds

$$\frac{25 \text{ meters}}{0.128 \text{ meter/second}} = y \text{ seconds}$$

$$y = \frac{25}{0.128} \approx 195$$

10. C

Notice that $a^2 - b^2$ is the negative of $b^2 - a^2$. That is, $a^2 - b^2 = -(b^2 - a^2)$. From $a - b = \frac{a^2 - b^2}{b^2 - a^2}$, we have $a - b = \frac{-(b^2 - a^2)}{b^2 - a^2}$. Then $a - b = -1$. Multiplying both sides by -1, we have $(-1)(a - b) = (-1)(-1)$, $-(a - b) = 1$, $-a + b = 1$, and $b - a = 1$.

11. E

It may look ugly, but it's easiest to just add up the integers, stopping when the sum hits 63:

$$6 + 7 = 13$$
$$13 + 8 = 21$$
$$21 + 9 = 30$$
$$30 + 10 = 40$$
$$40 + 11 = 51$$
$$51 + 12 = 63$$

The sequence runs from 6 to 12, which is 7 integers total.

12. D

If you aren't good at visualizing, you might want to scratch out a figure:

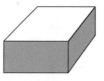

In the figure above, meant to represent one of the two half cubes, the three unseen sides (the back, bottom, and left side) are also red (shaded). It's the top—the surface that used to be "inside" the cube—that's still white. Let's count up the surfaces, calling a full cube face (a face on the original cube) 1 unit. Then let's find the areas of the faces of the half cube.

We have the bottom and top here, which makes 2 square units. Each of the other four faces has an area of half a square unit, so that's another 2 square units. The total surface of the half cube, then, is 4 square units. One whole cube face (the top), which has an area of 1 square unit, is still white, so $\frac{1}{4}$ or 25 percent of the surface area is not red.

13. B

Picking Numbers is the strategy that works here. Since Ann drives $\frac{1}{3}$ faster than Bob, let's pick a number for Bob that's a multiple of 3. Why not 3? Let's say that Bob drives 3 miles per hour. Then Ann drives $\frac{1}{3}$ faster, or 4 miles per hour.

Now, the other information we have to consider is how far each travels. Ann drives twice as far as Bob. Let's pick 12 as the number of miles she drives (it's a multiple of both 3 and 4, the numbers we've already chosen—that's usually a good idea). If Ann drives 12 miles, then Bob drives 6 miles.

So now how much time will each spend driving? Ann will drive 12 miles at 4 miles per hour:

4 miles per hour $\times x$ hours $=$ 12 miles
$$4x = 12$$
$$x = \frac{12}{4}$$
$$x = 3$$

Bob will drive for 6 miles at 3 miles per hour:

3 miles per hour × x hours = 6 miles

$$3x = 6$$
$$x = \frac{6}{3}$$
$$x = 2$$

So the ratio of the amount of time that Ann will drive to amount of time that Bob will drive is 3:2.

14. E

Since p is a positive fraction less than 1, let's pick a value for it. Since we'll be taking a root (in choices (B) and (D)), let's choose $\frac{1}{9}$, which is convenient for (B). Notice that since all of the choices are fractions whose numerators are 1, we need compare only the denominators. To find the smallest value, we'll want the fraction with the largest denominator. So the question is essentially asking which denominator is largest. (A)'s is $\left(\frac{1}{9}\right)^2 = \frac{1}{81}$. (B)'s is $\sqrt{\frac{1}{9}} = \frac{1}{3}$. (B)'s is larger. (C)'s denominator is (A)'s but with 1 added. That'll be a number larger than 1 (namely $1\frac{1}{81}$), so (C)'s is clearly larger than (B)'s. The denominator of (E) is $\left(\frac{1}{9} + 1\right)^2 = \left(\frac{10}{9}\right)^2 = \frac{100}{81} = 1\frac{19}{81}$, which is greater than the denominator of (C). Since $p + 1$ is greater than 1, the denominator of (E)—which is the square of $p + 1$—must be greater than the denominator of (D), which is the positive square root of $p + 1$. Since (E) has the largest denominator, it's the smallest fraction.

15. B

The quickest solution is to pick numbers for n and m. Since $n = 1$ and $m = 1$ would amount to 7 points, and since we want to minimize the difference between n and m, and since $50 \div 7$ is just a bit more than 7, we'll start with values near 7.

The key is to discover what values for n, when multiplied by 2 points, will leave a multiple of 5 as the remaining points. The solution turns out to be 5 for n (10 points), which allows 8 for m (40 points). That's a total of 50 points, and the positive difference between the two values is only 3. If you investigate further, you find that it's impossible for there to be a difference of only 1 (choice (A)).

16. D

The key is to recognize similar triangles. If *AB* is parallel to *ED*, then the alternate interior angles are equal: Angle *ABC* is equal to angle *CDE* and right angle *BAC* is equal to angle *CED*. Angle *BCA* is opposite angle *ECD* so the two of them are equal. Once we see that the triangles are similar, we know that the ratio between their corresponding sides is the same for all 3 pairs of sides. That, in turn, tells us that the same ratio will hold for their perimeters (which are, after all, just the sums of the sides).

Further inspection shows us that triangle *CED* is a special right triangle. With a leg of length 1 and a hypotenuse of length 2, the other leg (side *CE*) must be $\sqrt{3}$. Now if *CE* plus *AC* is $6\sqrt{3}$, and *CE* alone is just $\sqrt{3}$, then *AC* must be $5\sqrt{3}$. *AC* is the side corresponding to *CE*. Therefore, whatever ratio exists between the lengths of these sides also exists between the perimeters. Since *AC* is 5 times the length of *CE*, the perimeter of triangle *BAC* is 5 times that of triangle *CED*. Triangle *CED* has a perimeter of $1 + 2 + \sqrt{3}$, or $3 + \sqrt{3}$. Five times this is $15 + 5\sqrt{3}$.

17. D

Since a ratio gives relative size rather than absolute size, we need to figure out what number, multiplied by the ratio, will give us the actual number of each type of book. Of course, we're only concerned with one type of book—biographies. If we call the unknown number *x*, we can create an algebraic equation. $1x + 2x + 7x$ is equal to the total number of books, which we've been told is 30. Therefore, $x + 2x + 7x = 30$; $10x = 30$; $x = 3$. So James owns $2(3) = 6$ biographies.

As a savvy Kaplan test taker, you might have solved this even more quickly, *by noticing that the parts of the ratio (1, 2, and 7) add up to 10*. So for every 10 books there must be 1 reference, 2 biographies, and 7 fiction books. Since there are 30 books, which is 3×10, we can find the actual number of any type of book by multiplying that part of the ratio by 3.

18. B

When you see a question like this on the day of the test (and you will), compare fractions as quickly as possible. For choice (A), the least common denominator of $\frac{2}{5}$ and $\frac{7}{16}$ is 5×16, or 80, so convert $\frac{2}{5}$ to $\frac{32}{80}$ and convert $\frac{7}{16}$ to $\frac{35}{80}$; $\frac{35}{80}$ is obviously larger than $\frac{32}{80}$. For (B), the least common denominator of $\frac{2}{5}$ and $\frac{4}{11}$ is 5×11, or 55. Convert $\frac{2}{5}$ to $\frac{22}{55}$ and convert $\frac{4}{11}$ to $\frac{20}{55}$; $\frac{20}{55}$ is less than $\frac{22}{55}$. That is, $\frac{4}{11}$ is less than $\frac{2}{5}$, so (B) is correct and we don't have to check the other choices.

19. E

The key to this somewhat confusing word problem is to concentrate on what the question asks for: the quantity of water drained away, which we'll call x. We're told that x liters of water are drained away, and $x - 6$ liters are left. So x (the number of liters taken away) plus $x - 6$ (the number of liters left) equals 12 (total liters originally in the sink). Therefore, $x + (x - 6) = 12$, $x + x - 6 = 12$, $2x - 6 = 12$, $2x = 18$, and $x = 9$.

We can also use Backsolving here. Start with (B). If 3 liters were drained, then $12 - 3 = 9$ liters remain. The amount of water remaining is not 6 liters less than the amount of water drained away. Choice (B) is too small. We can eliminate (A) and (B). Next move on to (D). If 6 liters were drained, then $12 - 6 = 6$ liters remain. The amount of water remaining is not 6 liters less than the amount of water drained away. (D) is too small. Choice (E) must be correct.

Just for the sake of discussion, let's check (E). If 9 liters were drained, $12 - 9 = 3$ liters remain. Since the 3 liters that remain is 6 liters less than the 9 liters drained, we see that (E) is correct.

20. A

The only trick here is understanding what quantity is being taxed: the amount of inheritance in excess of $8,000. Tony will have to pay the 6 percent inheritance tax on $11,500 − $8,000, or $3,500. The problem then becomes a matter of straightforward calculation: 6 percent of $3,500 is just $0.06 \times \$3,500$, which is 6×35, or $210. *In percent word problems, always make sure you're taking the proper percent of the proper quantity.*

21. A

The key is interpreting the first sentence, which tells you how many gallons of gas are left in the tank after 15 gallons are drained. Since draining 15 gallons cuts the amount of gas in half, there must originally have been 2×15, or 30 gallons in the tank. After the 15 gallons are drained away, there are 15 gallons left. (This should be intuitively obvious. If it's not, you can set up an algebraic equation, letting x stand for the amount in the tank at the beginning: $x - 15 = \frac{1}{2}x$; $\frac{1}{2}x = 15$; $x = 30$.) Since p gallons are added to the 15 gallons left in the tank, the number of gallons at the end is $15 + p$.

If for some reason you were confused by the wording of this problem you should at least have been able to narrow it down to (A) and (C). Since p gallons of gas are added to some other quantity, the correct answer should be in the form of some non-negative quantity plus p.

22. C

The key to solving this one is knowing that the opposite sides of a rectangle are equal in length. If the unpainted side is 9 feet long, then the opposite, painted side is also 9 feet long. The total length of the three *painted* sides is 37 feet; this means that the other two painted sides are 37 − 9 (the length of the painted side opposite the unpainted side) = 28 feet in length combined. Since these two sides are also opposite and equal, each one is $\frac{28}{2} = 14$ feet long. The area of the rectangle is then 14 (the length of one of the two painted sides) × 9 (the length of one of the other sides—only one of which is painted) = 126 square feet.

23. D

The chart tells us what percent of the flights were late, and the text tells us what number of flights were late (the number of flights that the percentage represents). We have to figure out the number of flights that were *not* late (that were on time). $43\% + 17\% + 12\% + 3\% = 75\%$ of the flights were late. That's a nice, neat percentage, representing $\frac{3}{4}$. So $\frac{3}{4}$ of the flights were late, which means $\frac{1}{4}$ of the flights were on time. That makes the calculation very easy: 1,200 flights were late, which is equal to $\frac{3}{4}$ of all the flights. Call the total number of flights F. Then, since 1,200 flights is equal to $\frac{3}{4}$ of all the flights, we can write the equation $\frac{3}{4}F = 1,200$. Solve for F. We have:

$$\frac{3}{4}F = 1,200$$
$$3F = 1,200(4)$$
$$3F = 4,800$$
$$F = \frac{4,800}{3} = 1,600$$

The total number of flights is 1,600. We know that of all the flights were on time. So the number of flights that were on time is $\frac{1}{4}F = \frac{1}{4}(1,600) = 400$.

24. D

There's a shortcut to solving this one. We're told that cheese, bologna, and peanut butter sandwiches are made in the ratio of 5 to 7 to 8. Every time they make 5 cheese sandwiches, they also have to make 7 bologna and 8 peanut butter sandwiches. So there must be 5x cheese sandwiches (and we don't know what x is at this point), 7x bologna sandwiches, and 8x peanut butter sandwiches. How many bologna sandwiches were made? Well, the number of bologna sandwiches must be some multiple of 7. Only choice (D), 42, is a multiple of 7.

If you didn't notice that, you'd have solved the problem algebraically, which is also pretty simple. If you add 5x, the number of cheese sandwiches, 7x, the number of bologna sandwiches, and 8x, the number of peanut butter sandwiches, you get 120 total sandwiches. In other words: $5x + 7x + 8x = 120$, $20x = 120$, $x = 6$. So there were $7(6) = 42$ bologna sandwiches.

25. B

Follow the question carefully. We're ultimately interested in the length of a side of "a certain square." We've been given a clue: the square's area is $\frac{1}{15}$ the area of a rectangle measuring 49.872 by 30.64. Fortunately, we've been told we need only the "approximate" length of a side, so we can work with approximates throughout. The area of the rectangle, then, is approximately 50 × 30, or 1,500. The area of the square will be approximately $\frac{1}{15}$ of that, or 100. The length of the side of a square is always the positive square root of the area (side × side = area), so this square has sides of approximately 10 inches.

26. D

To solve this equation, we need to follow the order of operations and simplify the expression inside the parentheses first. Since $4 - 5 = -1$, we can restate the original equation as $y = -(-1)$, or $y = 1$. Choice (D) is correct.

27. E

We can calculate a percent increase by dividing the increase in price by the original price. In this, the price went from $36 to $50, so the increase is $50 - 36 = 14$. The original value was $36, so the fractional increase is $\frac{14}{36}$, or $\frac{7}{18}$.

To convert a fraction (or decimal) to a percent, multiply that fraction (or decimal) by 100. So $\frac{7}{18} = \frac{7}{18} \times 100 = \frac{7}{9} \times 50 = \frac{350}{9} =$ approximately 38.89%. This is closest to choice (E).

28. A

Ratios are just another way of expressing fractions.

Therefore, the ratio $\left(\frac{37}{5}\right) : 6\left(\frac{37}{5}\right)$ is the same as the fraction $\dfrac{\left(\frac{37}{5}\right)}{6\left(\frac{37}{5}\right)}$. The term $\frac{37}{5}$ cancels out, leaving us with just $\frac{1}{6}$, which is (A).

29. A

Prime numbers are integers by definition, so any sum of four primes will therefore be an integer. We want to find the largest sum of four primes, each of which is less than 14, so we'll need the four largest prime numbers less than 14. The largest is 13, and then, working backward, the next three primes are 11, 7, and 5. Now we just need to add them up: $13 + 11 + 7 + 5 = 36$. That matches (A).

30. C

We're asked to find the greatest number of people who could have contributed to the $303 collected at the church service. In order to do so, we must assume that each person gave the minimum amount possible, according to the terms of the problem.

In this case, we can divide the total amount collected, $303, by the minimum contribution per member, $2, to find the maximum number of members:

$$\frac{\text{Total Contrib}}{\text{Contrib/Member}} = \frac{\$303}{\$2} = \frac{300}{2} + \frac{3}{2} = 150 + 1.5 = 151.5$$

Since we cannot have a fraction of a person, the minimum number of members must have been 151, choice (C).

We could also have backsolved here, starting with (B). If 150 people made the minimum contribution of $2, that would be 150 × $2 = $300, which is $3 short of the total. So (B) is too small. Let's try (D). If 152 people made the minimum contribution of $2, they would have contributed 152 × $2, or $304, too much. (D) is too large. Choice (C) must be correct.

31. E

When we see what appears to be a lengthy arithmetic problem, we should look for ways to simplify the work. When fractions are involved, think about factoring the numerator and denominator, looking for terms that will cancel out.

In this case, $5.005 = 5 \times 1.001$ and $2.002 = 2 \times 1.001$. So, we can rewrite the original fraction as $\dfrac{5.005}{2.002} = \dfrac{5(1.001)}{2(1.001)} = \dfrac{5}{2} = 2.5$. Choice (E) is correct.

32. C

A subset of an original set is any set that contains one or more elements of the original set, but no elements of any other set. So {10, 14} is a subset of the original set in this problem, but {5, 10, 14} is not because 5 was not in the original set.

We need to determine the number of subsets that have an odd number of elements. So for this four-member set, we need to determine the number of subsets that have 1 or 3 elements.

There are 4 subsets that contain exactly one element: {10}, {14}, {17}, and {24}.

To find the number of three-element subsets, we can think of this as a combinations problem. The order of the elements is not important—the set {10, 14, 17} is the same as the set {10, 17, 14}—so the question becomes, How many ways are there to choose 3 elements from a set of 4, when order doesn't matter?

The combinations formula is $\dfrac{n!}{k!(n-k)!}$ where n is the number of elements in the original set and k is the number of elements in the subset. Here $n = 4$ and $k = 3$, so the number of combinations is $\dfrac{4!}{3!(4-3)!} = \dfrac{4 \times 3 \times 2 \times 1}{(3 \times 2 \times 1)(1)} = 4$.

So, there are 4 one-element subsets and 4 three-element subsets, for a total of 8 subsets with an odd number of elements.

Instead of using the combinations formula, we could also have listed all the subsets of {10, 14, 17, 24} that contain 3 elements. Those subsets are:

{10, 14, 17}
{10, 14, 24}
{10, 17, 24}
{14, 17, 24}

So, when you also consider the 4 subsets with 1 element, there are 8 subsets of {10, 14, 17, 24} that contain an odd number of elements.

33. C

The student's budget is divided among four items: rent, tuition, living expenses, and recreation, with the cost of each item representing a fraction of the total cost. Since the four items represent the total budget, the four fractions must add up to 1. We know three of the fractions, and we can find the fraction allocated for recreation as follows.

We know that (Rent Fraction) + (Tuition Fraction) + (Living Expenses Fraction) + (Recreation Fraction) = 1. If we let r represent the Recreation Fraction and replace the other fractions with the numbers given in the problem, we have $\frac{1}{2} + \frac{1}{4} + \frac{1}{5} + r = 1$.

Thus, $r = 1 - \frac{1}{2} - \frac{1}{4} - \frac{1}{5}$. The least common multiple of 1, 2, 4, and 5 is 20, so we can rewrite all the fractions with a denominator of 20 to get $r = \frac{20}{20} - \frac{10}{20} - \frac{5}{20} - \frac{4}{20} = \frac{1}{20}$.

So, we know that the $1,000 spent on recreation equals $\frac{1}{20}$ of the total budget. If x is the total budget, we have the equation: $\frac{1}{20}(x) = 1,000$. Multiplying both sides by 20, we have $x = 20,000$.

34. A

For a Roman numeral problem, we want to find the statement that appears in the most choices and work with it first; if we can eliminate it, we can quickly reduce the number of possible choices.

Here, statement II shows up three times, so let's start there. By definition, any nonzero number raised to the exponent zero is equal to 1, so x^0 cannot equal zero. So, we can eliminate (C), (D), and (E). Based on the remaining choices, we can see that either statement I must equal zero, or none of the statements must equal zero.

Our next step is to evaluate statement I. Let's Pick Numbers. If x is 1, then $x^3 - x^2$ is $1 - 1 = 0$. But if we try $x = 2$, we find that $x^3 - x^2 = 2^3 - 2^2 = 8 - 4 = 4$. So this statement might be equal to zero, but it doesn't have to be. So, we can eliminate (B). In fact, none of the statements has to be zero, so (A) is correct.

35. C

Let a be the population of City A, let b be the population of City B, and let c be the population of City C. Since a is three times larger than b, $a = 3b$, and the population of A and B together is $3b + b$, or $4b$.

Furthermore, since the population of A and B together is twice the population of C, we can write the equation $4b = 2c$, or $c = 2b$. Dividing both sides by b gives $\frac{c}{b} = 2$, and therefore the ratio of c to b is 2:1.

Alternatively, we could solve this problem by Picking Numbers. For City A, pick any small number easily divisible by 3; in fact, picking 3 will work well. If the population of A is 3, then the population of B must be 1, and their combined population must be 4. Since C's population is half that of A and B together, it must be 2. Thus the ratio of C to B is 2:1.

36. D

This is a number properties question, so Picking Numbers will work. Since m divided by n must be negative, one of the two numbers m or n must be negative and the other must be positive. So, we'll test two pairs of numbers: $m = 3$, $n = -1$ and $m = -3$, $n = 1$. Because the question asks "which of the following," we can start with choice (E).

(E): Using the first pair of values, $m - n = 3 - (-1) = 4$. That's greater than zero, so (E) could be true; there is no need to test the second pair. We can eliminate (E).

Testing (D), we find

$$(3)(-1)^3 = (3)(-1) < 0, \text{ and } (-3)(1)^3 = (-3)(1) < 0$$

So, both pairs give values less than zero, so (D) is not true in either case. Therefore, (D) is the answer. This can be confirmed either by testing the other choices or by recognizing that since one and only one of the two numbers must be negative, and any negative number cubed will still be negative, mn^3 will either involve multiplying a positive m times a negative n^3 or a negative m times a positive n^3, and therefore the product mn^3 could never be positive.

37. C

This situation seems complicated, but with a little translation we can simplify it. We have an equation that tells us how fast the train is moving at any time: $s = t^2 + t$. For example, when t is 0 (before the train starts moving), the speed is $t^2 + t = 0^2 + 0 = 0$, as we would expect. After one second, the speed would be $t^2 + t = 1^2 + 1 = 2$ kilometers per hour.

To answer the question, all we need to do is find the positive difference between the train's speed at 4 seconds and at 2 seconds.

$$2 \text{ seconds: } t = 2, \text{ so } s = t^2 + t = 2^2 + 2 = 4 + 2 = 6$$
$$4 \text{ seconds: } t = 4, \text{ so } s = t^2 + t = 4^2 + 4 = 16 + 4 = 20$$

The positive difference between the two speeds is $20 - 6 = 14$, so (C) is the answer.

38. B

Let's use the formula Distance = Speed × Time. In this case, we want to find the time required to walk s blocks, so let's divide both sides of the formula by Speed to get $\frac{\text{Distance}}{\text{Speed}} = \text{Time}$. We are told that the distance is s blocks, so we just need to find Lisa's speed.

If we go back to the distance formula and divide both sides by Time, we see that $\text{Speed} = \frac{\text{Distance}}{\text{Time}}$. Lisa walked t blocks in 3 minutes, so her speed is $\frac{t \text{ blocks}}{3 \text{ minutes}} = \frac{t}{3}$ blocks per minute. So, $\frac{\text{Distance}}{\text{Speed}} = \frac{s \text{ blocks}}{\frac{t}{3} \text{ blocks per minute}} = (s)\left(\frac{3}{t}\right) = \frac{3s}{t}$ minutes.

Choice (B) is correct.

Because there are variables in the answer choices, we could also have Picked Numbers. Since it takes her 3 minutes to walk t blocks, let's pick a value for t that's divisible by 3, such as $t = 6$. If Lisa walks 6 blocks in 3 minutes, her rate is 2 blocks per minute. Now pick a value for s that is divisible by 2. If $s = 10$ blocks and her speed is 2 blocks per minute, the time required is 5 minutes. We now substitute $t = 6$ and $s = 10$ into the choices. The one which results in a value of 5 will be the correct choice:

(A): $\frac{s}{3t} = \frac{10}{(3)(6)} = \frac{10}{18}$, which is not 5. Eliminate (A).

(B): $\frac{3s}{t} = \frac{(3)(10)}{6} = \frac{30}{6} = 5$, so (B) is correct.

Test the remaining choices only if time permits.

39. A

The amount of nitric acid will be the same before and after additional water is added. To determine the amount of nitric acid present, we multiply the original volume, 10 liters, by the percent acid, 10 percent. This gives us (10 liters)(10% nitric acid) = (10)(0.10) = 1 liter of nitric acid.

Since the dilution is made by adding water, the new 4 percent solution will contain more water than the old solution, but will still contain the same 1 liter of nitric acid. If x represents the liters of water added, the new solution will have a total volume of $(10 + x)$ liters. Thus, in the new solution, 1 liter of nitric acid will be 4 percent of the solution. Dividing 1 liter by the new total volume, we have $\frac{1}{10 + x} = 0.04$.

To solve for x, we can multiply both sides by $10 + x$ to get $1 = 0.04(10 + x)$, or $1 = 0.4 + 0.04x$. Now, we subtract 0.4 from both sides to get $0.6 = 0.04x$. Dividing both sides by 0.04, we have $x = 15$, which is choice (A).

40. A

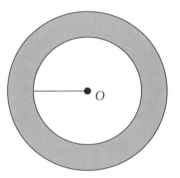

We need to find both the area of the walkway and the surface area of the pool and then find the difference between the two. Let's take the area of the pool first. The area of a circle with a radius r is πr^2, and we know that the pool has a radius of 10 meters. Thus, the area of the circular swimming pool is $\pi(10)^2 = \pi(100) = 100\pi$.

Since the pool has a radius of 10 meters and the walkway is 5 meters wide, the radius of the region consisting of the circular swimming pool together with the walkway is $10 + 5 = 15$ meters. Therefore, the area of this circular region is $\pi(15)^2 = \pi(225) = 225\pi$. We now subtract the area of the pool from this area to find the area of the walkway. We find that $225\pi - 100\pi$, or 125π, is the area of the walkway.

Now we need the difference between the area of the walkway and the area of the pool, which is $125\pi - 100\pi$, or 25π. So (A) is correct.

Be careful to avoid the trap answers. Choice (C) is the area of the pool; Choice (D) is the area of the walkway; Choice (E) is the area of the entire circular region.

41. D

This classic word problem can be solved algebraically. If we let $a =$ the number of Brand A binders and $b =$ the number of Brand B binders, we can write two equations. For the number of binders purchased, we have $a + b = 12$, and for the amount spent we have $\$8a + \$5.60b = \$84$.

In order to use combination to solve the equations, we need one of the variables to have the same coefficient in both equations so that it will cancel out. If we multiply the first equation by 8, we get $8(a + b) = 8(12)$, or $8a + 8b = 96$.

So, we can write the two equations as follows:

$$8a + 8b = 96$$
$$8a + 5.60b = 84$$

If we subtract the bottom equation from the top one, we get $(8a - 8a) + (8b - 5.60b) = 96 - 84$, or $2.4b = 12$. If we divide both sides by 2.4, we are left with $b = 5$. Thus, Molly must have purchased $12 - b = 12 - 5 = 7$ Brand A binders. Thus choice (D) is the correct answer.

42. D

Because the question asks how many *arrangements* are possible, we know that the order in which the guests are seated matters, and therefore, that we're dealing with a *permutation* problem.

To compute the number of permutations, all we need to do is determine the number of possible ways to fill each seat, and then multiply the possibilities together. In this case, there are 5 seats to be filled; although there are 6 people in total, the host will always take the same spot, so only five seats can be changed.

Picture a row of 6 chairs with the host in one chair and 5 empty chairs. Any of the 5 guests could sit in the first empty chair, so there are 5 possibilities for the first seat. Now there are 4 guests left, so there are 4 possibilities for the second seat. Similarly, there will be 3, 2, and then 1 possibility, for the remaining seats.

Now all we need to do is multiply the possibilities together: $(5)(4)(3)(2)(1) = 120$, so there are 120 possible seating arrangements. (D) is correct. Avoid trap answer (E), which represents the number of arrangements possible if the host does not always take the same seat.

43. E

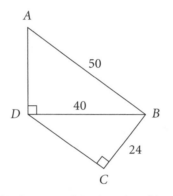

The perimeter of a quadrilateral is the sum of the lengths of its sides. For *ABCD*, the perimeter is $AB + BC + CD + DA$. From the figure, we know that $AB = 50$ and $BC = 24$. So, we need to find the lengths of *CD* and *DA*.

To find the length of *DA*, let's consider right triangle *ABD*. This triangle is a multiple of the 3-4-5 right triangle with each member of the 3 : 4 : 5 ratio multiplied by 10. Since $BD = 40 = 4 \times 10$ and $AB = 50 = 5 \times 10$, *DA* must have a length of $3 \times 10 = 30$.

Now let's consider right triangle *BCD*. This triangle is also a multiple of the 3-4-5 right triangle. However, in this triangle, each member of the 3 : 4 : 5 ratio is multiplied by 8. Since $BC = 24 = 3 \times 8$ and $BD = 40 = 5 \times 8$, *CD* must have a length of $4 \times 8 = 32$.

Now we have the lengths of all the sides of quadrilateral *ABCD*: $AB = 50$, $BC = 24$, $CD = 32$, and $DA = 30$. So the perimeter of quadrilateral *ABCD* is

$$AB + BC + CD + DA = 50 + 24 + 32 + 30 = 136$$

44. E

With numbers in the answer choices, the Backsolving approach will work. We'll test the choices to find a price per bushel that results in a profit of $150,000. Profit will be calculated by multiplying the price per bushel by the number of bushels and then subtracting the variable costs ($10 per bushel) and the fixed cost to rent the land.

Starting with (B), if the price of one bushel is $7, the farmer's total revenue will be 50,000 × $7 = $350,000. Total costs will be ($10 × 50,000) + $200,000 = $700,000. We are told that the farmer made a profit of $150,000, but if choice (B) were correct, costs ($700,000) would actually be higher than revenue ($350,00), so he would have lost money. So he must have sold the wheat at a price higher than $7 per bushel. We can eliminate (A) and (B).

Moving to (D), if the price is $13, total revenue will be $650,000, still less than costs. Thus (E) must be the answer. In fact, with a price of $17 per bushel, revenue would be 50,000 × $17 = $850,000, and profit would be $850,000 − $700,000 = $150,000, which matches the conditions given in the problem.

Algebraically, if p = selling price per bushel in dollars and Profit = Revenue − Fixed Cost − Variable Cost, the following equation can be written: $150,000 = 50,000p − 200,000 − (50,000 × 10)$. Solving this for p will result in $850,000 = 50,000p$ or $p = 17$.

45. B

For triangle ABC, let's call the side that lies on the y-axis between $A(0,2)$ and $B(0,−4)$ the base of the triangle.

Since the distance between these two points is 6, we can say that the base of the triangle is 6 units in length. Because the base lies along the y-axis, the height will therefore be the distance from the y-axis to the third point, $C(c, 0)$. Since c represents the distance from the y-axis to point C, finding the height will give us the value of c, because c is positive. Now we use the formula for the area of a triangle, $\frac{1}{2}$(base)(height). In this case, the base is 6 and the area is 21, so $\frac{1}{2}(6)$(height) = 21, $\frac{1}{2}(6)(c) = 21$, and $3c = 21$, so $c = 7$.

The answer is (B).

46. B

To solve algebraically, let x represent the number of ball bearings in the first shipment. Because the second shipment was twice as large as the first, $2x$ will be the number in the second shipment. In each shipment, the number of defective ball bearings received will be the percent defective multiplied by the number of ball bearings in the shipment. A total of 100 defective ball bearings were received, which is equivalent to 1% of the first shipment plus 4.5% of the second shipment. We can sum all this up in the following equation:

$$100 = (0.01)(x) + (0.045)(2x)$$

We can now solve for x. Let's first simplify the right side to get $100 = 0.01x + 0.09x$. Combining like terms, we have $100 = 0.10x$, or $x = 1,000$, which represents the size of the first shipment.

Avoid the trap answers (C) and (D), which are the sizes of the second shipment and the two shipments combined, respectively.

47. D

We have two equations and two variables, but because the second equation is not linear, we can't solve directly for x and y. Instead, since the second equation is a quadratic equation, we should think about factoring.

If we add 10 to both sides of the second equation, we get $x^2 - xy - 2y^2 = 10$. Now, the left side looks like a quadratic expression that we can factor with reverse FOIL. Since we could get the x^2 term by multiplying x and x, we know both factors will contain x. Next we need to determine what two factors multiplied together will give us $-2y^2$. We need either $-2y$ and y or $2y$ and $-y$. Since the coefficient of the xy term is negative, we should choose $-2y$ and y, because the sum of the outer and inner products will give us $-xy$. Thus, the factorization of $x^2 - xy - 2y^2$ is $(x + y)(x - 2y)$; if we expand this using FOIL, it will equal $x^2 - xy - 2y^2$.

Now, notice that both factors of $x^2 - xy - 2y^2$ appear in the question stem. We are told that $x + y = 2$ and we are asked to find the value of $x - 2y$.

We can find the value of $x - 2y$ if we return to the quadratic equation. We know that $(x + y)(x - 2y) = 10$. Since $x + y = 2$, we can replace $(x + y)$ with 2, giving us $2(x - 2y) = 10$, or $(x - 2y) = 5$. So (D) is correct.

KAPLAN

48. C

We need to find the distance traveled in the first 6-minute interval. Because Distance = Rate × Time and we already know that the time is 6 minutes, all we need to do is find the train's speed (its rate) during the first interval in order to find the distance.

We are given that the train's average speed increased by 3 miles per hour during each interval. During the third interval, its average speed was 24 miles per hour. So in the second interval, its speed must have been 24 − 3 = 21. Similarly, its speed in the first interval must have been 21 − 3 = 18 miles per hour.

Now we have time (6 minutes) and speed (18 miles per hour). But the time is in minutes and the speed is in miles per hour. We can't calculate the distance unless we convert the time to hours or the speed to miles per minute. An hour has 60 minutes, so 6 minutes is $\frac{6}{60} = \frac{1}{10}$ of an hour. Therefore, the distance is $\frac{1}{10}$ hours × 18 miles per hour $= \frac{18}{10} = 1.8$ miles. So (C) is correct.

49. D

The stem gives us one equation, $abcd = 546$, and asks us to find $b + c$. There is no way to solve directly for b and c, but we know they must be factors of 546, so let's start by factoring 546. Since it's even, one factor must be 2, so $546 = (273)(2)$. Now factor 273 by dividing it by 3: $273 = (91)(3)$. Now factor 91; its factors are 13 and 7. Putting this all together, the factors of 546 are 2, 3, 7, and 13. All of these are prime, so 546 cannot be factored any further.

Now go back to the equation we were given: $abcd = 546$. Since the prime factors of 546 are 2, 3, 7, and 13, it must be the case that $(2)(3)(7)(13) = abcd$. Since we are told that $1 < a < b < c < d$, it must also be the case that b and c are the middle 2 factors. Thus, $b = 3$ and $c = 7$. So $b + c = 10$, and (D) is correct.

50. B

Because the order of colors in the pairs doesn't matter, the number of two-color codes that can be made will be the number of ways one can select two colors from the total number of colors; that is, the number of combinations of two colors that can be created.

Now, knowing that we're looking for the minimum number of colors that could be used, we can backsolve starting with (B). If 6 colors are used, we'll need at least $20 - 6 = 14$ combinations, so we use the combinations formula with $n = 6$ and $k = 2$. We get $\dfrac{6!}{2!(6 - 2)!}$ $= \dfrac{6!}{2!4!} = 15$. That's one more than the 14 we needed, so (B) is correct. We need at least 6 different colors to color-code all 20 chemicals.

If guessing on this problem, we could have eliminated (D) and (E). Because some chemicals will use pairs of colors, there is no need to have as many colors as chemicals, (D), or more colors than chemicals, (E).

Chapter 9: **Data Sufficiency**

- Question Format and Structure
- The 5 Basic Principles of Data Sufficiency
- Kaplan's 3-Step Method for Data Sufficiency
- Value Questions
- "Yes or No" Questions
- Guessing in Data Sufficiency

Data Sufficiency is just a fancy name for a skill that you use all of the time, and it's one that's actually very important in business. The basic idea is to determine when you have enough information to make a decision or solve a problem. The big difference between Data Sufficiency on the GMAT and most of the "data sufficiency" problems you come across in real life is that the GMAT problems are concerned solely with math facts and relationships.

Let's say you want to know whether a particular manager is doing a good job in her department. If you were informed that her department spent $50,000 more than it took in this year, would you be justified in saying that she was doing a bad job? Of course not—there could be all kinds of factors causing the loss that were beyond her control. For instance, the department might have spent $250,000 more than it took in last year when she wasn't in charge, and so she could be making great improvements, even though the department is still losing money.

Data Sufficiency questions measure your ability to recognize what information is relevant to a problem, and to determine at what point there is sufficient information to solve the problem. The questions are accompanied by some initial information and two statements, labeled (1) and (2). You must decide whether the statements provide enough data to allow you to answer the question.

 GO ONLINE

You'll need to use your noteboard often with Data Sufficiency questions. Work through the CAT-like questions online, so you can practice switching between paper and screen.

QUESTION FORMAT AND STRUCTURE

The instructions for the Data Sufficiency section on the GMAT look like this:

Directions: In each of the problems, a question is followed by two statements containing certain data. You are to determine whether the data provided by the statements are sufficient to answer the question. Choose the correct answer based upon the statements' data, your knowledge of mathematics, and your familiarity with everyday facts (such as the number of minutes in an hour or cents in a dollar). You must indicate whether:

- Statement (1) ALONE is sufficient, but statement (2) is not sufficient.
- Statement (2) ALONE is sufficient, but statement (1) is not sufficient.
- BOTH statements TOGETHER are sufficient, but NEITHER statement ALONE is sufficient.
- EACH statement ALONE is sufficient.
- Statements (1) and (2) TOGETHER are NOT sufficient.

Note: Diagrams accompanying problems agree with information given in the questions, but may not agree with additional information given in statements (1) and (2).

All numbers used are real numbers.

Confused? No wonder. The directions for these questions are pretty complicated. Let's look at a simple example.

$A \qquad B \qquad C$

What is the length of segment *AC*?

(1) *B* is the midpoint of *AC*

(2) *AB* = 5

Statement (1) tells you that B is the midpoint of AC, so $AB = BC$ and $AC = 2AB = 2BC$. Since statement (1) does not give a value for AB or BC, you cannot answer the question using statement (1) alone. Statement (2) says that $AB = 5$. Since statement (2) does not give you a value for BC, the question cannot be answered by statement (2) alone. Using both statements together you can find a value for both AB and BC; therefore you can find AC, so the answer to the question is choice (C).

THE 5 BASIC PRINCIPLES OF DATA SUFFICIENCY

1. Know the Data Sufficiency answer choices cold.

The directions and answer choices for Data Sufficiency questions never change. As we pointed out earlier, you can't afford to fumble with the answer choices on test day. You've got to become familiar with them now, so you can save time and minimize errors when you actually take the test.

Let's take another look at the five answer choices:

- ○ Statement (1) ALONE is sufficient, but statement (2) is not sufficient.
- ○ Statement (2) ALONE is sufficient, but statement (1) is not sufficient.
- ○ BOTH statements TOGETHER are sufficient, but NEITHER statement ALONE is sufficient.
- ○ EACH statement ALONE is sufficient.
- ○ Statements (1) and (2) TOGETHER are NOT sufficient.

A statement provides sufficient information only if it leads to one and only one answer to the question. For example, if a question asked "What is the value of x?" and a statement told you that x was equal to either 1 or 2, that statement would *not* be sufficient to answer the question.

2. Learn to work with the stem and two statements.

There are two basic questions that you must ask yourself on every Data Sufficiency question: Can you answer the question using the information from statement (1) only? Can you answer the question using the information from statement (2) only? If the answer to both of these questions is "no," then you ask yourself a third question: Can you answer the question if you combine the information from both statements?

KAPLAN

Let's look at an example:

> **Stem** If Augie's restaurant needs daily revenues of at least $3,000 to cover operating costs, is the restaurant making a profit from its operations?
>
> **Statement** (1) At Augie's restaurant, the average amount that each customer spends is $10.00.
>
> **Statement** (2) An average of 400 customers per day dine at Augie's restaurant.

1. Can you answer the question in the stem using only the information from statement (1)? *No.* You don't know how many customers come to the restaurant per day.

2. Can you answer the question using only the information from statement (2)? No. You don't know how much the customers will spend. (*You must ignore what statement (1) tells you when you consider statement (2).*)

Now, because the answer to both of these questions is "no," you must ask yourself a third question:

3. Can you answer it if you combine the information from both statements? *Yes.* You can determine that the restaurant makes a profit because you know that revenues are higher than $3,000 (400 customers per day × $10.00 per customer = an average of $4,000 per day).

3. Know the two types of Data Sufficiency questions.

You should start to conceptualize Data Sufficiency questions into two types—those for which you have to consider the statements in combination, and those for which you don't. Recall the first two questions about statement (1) and statement (2) we asked about Augie's restaurant. Had the answer to either of these questions been "yes," we wouldn't have had to ask the third question—the one that involved combining the statements. If at least one of the statements is sufficient, your answer can be only (A), (B), or (D), depending on whether statement (1) is sufficient or statement (2) is sufficient or both are sufficient. Only in a case (such as Augie's) in which neither statement is sufficient do you have to consider the statements in combination. These, then, are the two "types" of Data Sufficiency question:

READ MORE

Read—and reread—the directions for Data Sufficiency: they are crucial to your understanding of the questions.

- At least one of the statements is sufficient, and the answer is either (A), (B), or (D).

- Neither statement by itself is sufficient, forcing you to the additional step of combining the statements in order to choose between (C) and (E).

4. Know the topics.

As with the other GMAT question types, knowing what to expect from Data Sufficiency is half the battle. In addition to knowing the question type and how to deal with it efficiently (which we'll discuss shortly), it also helps to know the topics that you're likely to be tested on. The more you know about the inner workings of the GMAT, the better you can budget your time and maximize your score. The following table shows what topics are tested on Data Sufficiency and with what frequency:

Ratios, Rates, Percentages	30%
Algebra	25%
Number Properties	25%
Geometry	15%
Other	5%

5. Think sufficiently.

Get into the habit of thinking about the sufficiency of information from the moment you read the question. The goal of the following exercise is getting you to think about what sort of information you need to answer a question, not about what the answer is. Read each statement below and ask yourself whether that statement alone is enough to answer the question. Don't bother about coming up with an actual value.

> A particular company made a profit of 4.5 million dollars in 1991. What was the value of its profit in 1993?

Can you answer this question if you know that:

1. The company earned 10 percent less profit in 1991 than in 1993?

2. In 1993, the company earned the same amount of profit as in 1992?

3. The company's profit was larger in 1993 than in 1991?

4. In 1991, the company's profit was $4.5 million less than in 1993?

KAPLAN

Statement 1 is sufficient. You could solve this by letting the 1993 profit equal x and solving the equation for x : 4.5 million $= 0.9x$.

Statement 2 is insufficient. How much did the company earn in 1992? There's no way to tell.

Statement 3 is insufficient. Larger, but by how much?

Statement 4 is sufficient. You could add another $4.5 million to 1991's $4.5 million profit.

(♟) KAPLAN STRATEGY ———————————————————

The 5 Basic Principles of Data Sufficiency are:

- Know the Data Sufficiency answer choices cold.
- Learn to work with the stem and two statements.
- Know the two types of Data Sufficiency questions.
- Know the topics.
- Think sufficiently.

KAPLAN'S 3-STEP METHOD FOR DATA SUFFICIENCY

This is the essential systematic approach to mastering Data Sufficiency. Use this approach for every Data Sufficiency question. It will allow you to answer questions quickly and will guarantee that you avoid the common GMAT mistake of subconsciously combining the statements instead of using them separately.

Here's how the method works:

Team X won 40 basketball games. What percent of its basketball games did Team X win?

(1) Team X played the same number of basketball games as Team Y.

(2) Team Y won 45 games, representing 62.5 percent of the basketball games it played.

Step 1: Focus on the question stem.

First think about what information would be sufficient to answer the question. You must be able to decipher the question stem quickly and focus on what information is needed to answer it. Do you need a formula? Do you need to set up an equation? Do you need to know the value of a variable?

You should be able to recognize this sample question as a percent question. (Helpful hint: Percent × Whole = Part.) You're given the part (the number of games team X won) and asked for the percent (that is, the percentage of its games that team X won). What do you need? The whole—the total number of games team X played.

Step 2: Look at each statement separately.

Be sure you ignore the other statement! Remember, while determining the sufficiency of a particular statement, you must not carry over the other statement's information. When you look at statement (1), cover up statement (2), and vice versa. That's a practical and easy way to avoid falling into this very, very common GMAT error. As you evaluate each statement, eliminate the appropriate answer choices.

In our example, with (1) we know that Team X played the same number of games as Team Y, but we don't know what that number is. With (2), we get plenty of information about Team Y, but nothing at all that relates to Team X. So neither statement by itself is sufficient.

Step 3: Look at both statements in combination.

You need to proceed to Step 3 only when both statements (1) and (2) are insufficient. This happens less than half the time. Note that if you reach this point on a problem, you know the answer is either (C) or (E). When considering the two statements together, simply treat them and the stimulus as one long problem and ask yourself: Can it be solved? STOP as soon as you know whether it can be solved! Don't carry out any unnecessary calculations.

In general, these questions are a lot easier when taken in parts; don't try to cram all the information into your head at once. In the example, when we combine the two statements, we know that the number of games Team X played is the same as the number Team Y played, *and* we can find out how many games Team Y played by using the percent formula (Percent × Whole = Part; 62.5% × Games Played = 45). Therefore, we can figure out how many games Team X played, which is all we need to know in order to figure out what percent of its games Team X won. So we have the answer for this example, (C), without doing any calculation at all.

The key to doing well in Data Sufficiency is becoming adept at determining the sufficiency or insufficiency of the statements without doing unnecessary calculations. It just takes practice.

Here's how the 3-Step Method works.

If $2b - 2a^2 = 18$, what is the value of b?

(1) $a^2 = 1,156$

(2) $a > 0$

◯ Statement (1) ALONE is sufficient, but statement (2) is not sufficient.

◯ Statement (2) ALONE is sufficient, but statement (1) is not sufficient.

◯ BOTH statements TOGETHER are sufficient, but NEITHER statement ALONE is sufficient.

◯ EACH statement ALONE is sufficient.

◯ Statements (1) and (2) TOGETHER are NOT sufficient.

Step 1: Focus on the question stem.

What would we need to get the value of b? We need the value of the equation's only other variable, a.

Step 2: Look at each statement separately.

(1) alone does give us what we need. We could just substitute the value statement (1) gives for a^2 into the equation and solve. Right off that eliminates choices (B), (C), and (E). (2) alone, however, gives us nothing, because a could be 1 or 1,000,000. So eliminate (D) and the answer is (A).

Step 3: Look at both statements in combination.

There is no Step 3 for this problem. Remember, Step 3 is necessary only when neither statement by itself is sufficient, which is true less than half the time (about 40 percent of the time, actually).

Now let's look at another problem, which is easier than it looks. When a question appears to be complicated, take it apart and deal with it piece by piece. Keep focused on exactly what information you need in order to solve the problem.

A certain company produces exactly three products, X, Y, and Z. In 1990, what was the total income for the company from the sale of its products?

(1) In 1990, the company sold 8,000 units of product X, 10,000 units of product Y, and 16,000 units of product Z.

(2) In 1990, the company charged $28 per unit for product X, and twice as much for product Z.

◯ Statement (1) ALONE is sufficient, but statement (2) is not sufficient.

◯ Statement (2) ALONE is sufficient, but statement (1) is not sufficient.

◯ BOTH statements TOGETHER are sufficient, but NEITHER statement ALONE is sufficient.

◯ EACH statement ALONE is sufficient.

◯ Statements (1) and (2) TOGETHER are NOT sufficient.

Step 1: Focus on the question stem.

What do you need to solve this problem? You need to know the total income of the company from the three products, and so far you've been told nothing.

Step 2: Look at each statement separately.

(1) by itself is insufficient; it gives you just the number of **units** of each product, but it says nothing about income. Eliminate choices (A) and (D). (2) by itself is also insufficient; it gives you the price per unit of X and Z, but it doesn't even mention Y. Eliminate choice (B) as well.

Step 3: Look at both statements together.

Both together still leave us lacking the unit price of Y, and so we have no way of figuring the income derived from the sale of Y. The statements together are insufficient and the answer is (E).

Note that focusing on exactly what you needed to answer the question—the total income from all three products—allowed you to avoid wasting time calculating the profits for *X* and *Z*. You knew that without *Y*, such calculations were fruitless. You can avoid calculations (on a math test no less) by determining exactly what information you need to solve the problem. Then you can recognize straight off when you have that necessary information. When you use the three-step method and take an overview of the problem at the beginning (our Step 1), you save yourself unnecessary labor.

> A number of bacteria were placed in a petri dish at 5:00 A.M. If the number of bacteria in the petri dish grew for 5 days, by doubling every 12 hours, how many bacteria were in the petri dish at 5:00 P.M. on the third day?
>
> (1) From 5:00 A.M. to 5:00 P.M. on the second day the number of bacteria increased by 100 percent.
>
> (2) 20 bacteria were placed in the petri dish at 5:00 A.M. the first day.
>
> ○ Statement (1) ALONE is sufficient, but statement (2) is not sufficient.
>
> ○ Statement (2) ALONE is sufficient, but statement (1) is not sufficient.
>
> ○ BOTH statements TOGETHER are sufficient, but NEITHER statement ALONE is sufficient.
>
> ○ EACH statement ALONE is sufficient.
>
> ○ Statements (1) and (2) TOGETHER are NOT sufficient.

Step 1: Focus on the question stem.

You're given a description of how the number of bacteria grows, and the time at which the growth started. You're asked for the number of bacteria at the end of the growth. You need to know a number: How many bacteria did they start with?

Step 2: Look at each statement separately.

Forget what (1) gives us; you have to realize what it doesn't: anything about numbers, so it is insufficient. (As a matter of fact, it just repeats the information in the stimulus that the number of bacteria doubles every 12 hours.) Eliminate choices (A) and (D). (2) gives us exactly what we're looking for—the number of bacteria in the dish at the beginning. You *could* do calculations from here to get the actual numbers, but because you *know* that you could, you don't have to bother. So choice (B) is the answer, and we can skip step 3.

As you'll see in the next example, geometry also shows up on Data Sufficiency. Be very careful with any diagrams you are given! Things may not be what they seem. Try the problem below. (Helpful hint: The key to multiple figures is to pass information from one figure to the next.)

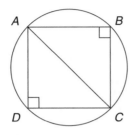

If points A, B, C, and D are points on the circumference of the circle in the figure above, what is the area of $ABCD$?

(1) The radius of the circle is $\dfrac{\sqrt{2}}{2}$.

(2) $ABCD$ is a square.

◯ Statement (1) ALONE is sufficient, but statement (2) is not sufficient.

◯ Statement (2) ALONE is sufficient, but statement (1) is not sufficient.

◯ BOTH statements TOGETHER are sufficient, but NEITHER statement ALONE is sufficient.

◯ EACH statement ALONE is sufficient.

◯ Statements (1) and (2) TOGETHER are NOT sufficient.

Step 1: Focus on the question stem.

Be careful! The trap is that many, if not most, students will assume that *ABCD* is a square. You can't trust diagrams in Data Sufficiency. Straight lines are straight, that's true, and angles marked as right angles are right angles, but they want to test your ability to look at a shape and re-imagine it based on the facts, and this is how they do it. Here you could slide the points around the circumference without changing the angle measures, so *ABCD* may not be a square. So if we can confirm that *ABCD* is a square, we will need either a radius, a diameter (*AC*), or a side. (Note: We know *AC* is a diameter because angle *ADC*—and angle *ABC*, for that matter—is a right angle. Whenever a right angle is inscribed in a circle, the two chords that form this right angle are the legs of a right triangle with a hypotenuse that is a diameter of the circle.) If we can confirm that *ABCD* is a rectangle, we'll need the length of two sides, or the length of one side together with a radius or a diameter.

Step 2: Look at both statements separately.

Statement (1) gives you the radius, but you still don't know whether *ABCD* is a square, so you can't calculate its area from the length of diameter *AC*. Insufficient: Eliminate (A) and (D). Statement (2) tells you *ABCD* is indeed a square but not how big a square. Because (2) provides no numbers, it is insufficient, and we can eliminate (B).

Step 3: Look at both statements together.

With the two statements together, however, we have what we were looking for. We know *ABCD* is a square, we have the length of its diagonal *AC* (which is also the diameter of the circle; remember to pass information between figures), so we're set. The answer is (C).

KAPLAN EXCLUSIVE

Diagrams in Data Sufficiency may not be drawn to scale, so don't assume anything just by the way they look.

If you drew a complete blank on the geometry in this problem, don't worry. Geometry is a fairly small part of GMAT and should never become your top priority. Moreover, you could have eliminated some answer choices even if you know almost nothing about squares and circles. You might have been baffled by (1), but look at (2). No numbers! There are no numbers in the stimulus either, so (2) can't possibly be sufficient to provide a number for the area. So you could eliminate (B) and (D), which leaves you with a one-in-three chance of guessing correctly.

VALUE QUESTIONS

Many GMAT Data Sufficiency questions ask for the value of a particular variable. When they ask for a value on GMAT Data Sufficiency, it means the one and only value. Statement (1) and statement (2) will never give contradictory values for the same variable.

The next example is a fairly basic value problem.

What is the value of x?

(1) $x^2 - 9 = 16$

(2) $3x(x - 5) = 0$

○ Statement (1) ALONE is sufficient, but statement (2) is not sufficient.

○ Statement (2) ALONE is sufficient, but statement (1) is not sufficient.

○ BOTH statements TOGETHER are sufficient, but NEITHER statement ALONE is sufficient.

○ EACH statement ALONE is sufficient.

○ Statements (1) and (2) TOGETHER are NOT sufficient.

Step 1: Focus on the question stem.

No question about what you need; you're looking for x. Don't expect to be given the value directly, though (that almost never happens), but instead a way of finding it, perhaps through an equation.

Step 2: Look at each statement separately.

Statement (1) is an example of a dangerous GMAT trap. The minute you see x^2 in Data Sufficiency, expect a trap. Here, $x^2 = 25$, but x can equal +5 or −5. So (1) is not sufficient; eliminate choices (A) and (D).

As for (2), again you have two possible values for x: 0 and 5. So, (2)'s insufficient, and we eliminate (B).

Step 3: Look at both statements together.

Many students may jump to the conclusion that the answer must be (E) when they see what looks like three possible values for *x* (−5, 0, +5). But look carefully at what's going on. (1) says *x* is either +5 or −5; (2) says *x* is either 0 or +5. *Both* these statements must be true, and that means the only possible value for *x* is +5. We know that *x* can't be 0, because that contradicts statement (1), and *x* can't be −5, because that contradicts statement (2). If in one statement the variable has two values, and in the other statement the variable has two values, but the statements share just one value, then these statements are sufficient for answering the question.

Here's another value problem:

> If z is an integer, what is the units' digit of z^3 ?
>
> (1) z is a multiple of 5.
>
> (2) $\sqrt{z}$ is an integer.
>
> ○ Statement (1) ALONE is sufficient, but statement (2) is not sufficient.
>
> ○ Statement (2) ALONE is sufficient, but statement (1) is not sufficient.
>
> ○ BOTH statements TOGETHER are sufficient, but NEITHER statement ALONE is sufficient.
>
> ○ EACH statement ALONE is sufficient.
>
> ○ Statements (1) and (2) TOGETHER are NOT sufficient.

Step 1: Focus on the question stem.

The question isn't actually asking for *z*, though of course figuring out *z* would do it. We're looking for the value of a digit of z^3; on the GMAT that's a pretty strong signal that we're going to be dealing with the concept of multiples.

Step 2: Look at each statement separately.

KAPLAN) EXCLUSIVE

If you are asked for the value of a particular variable, you must identify one and only one value.

How does the concept "multiple of 5" in (1) relate to the units' digit (what we're looking for)? All multiples of 5 (and of course that includes the cubes of all multiples of 5) have units' digits of 0 or 5. Therefore, (1) tells us only that the units' digit of z^3 is 0 or 5. It's insufficient, so eliminate (A) and (D). In statement (2), z^3 can have different units' digits. If you can't see this immediately, it becomes obvious when you pick a couple of numbers: say $z = 1$, then the units' digit of z^3 is 1. Say $z = 100$, then the units' digit of z^3 is 0. So statement (2) is insufficient, and we can eliminate (B).

Step 3: Look at both statements together.

Even when you combine the statements you can still have 0 and 5 as possible values for the units' digit of z^3 (again, pick numbers, say $z = 25$, and $z = 100$). The statements taken together are insufficient, and (E) is correct. As you can see, some Data Sufficiency problems cannot be intuited. In such cases, picking numbers is really the only way to go. If more than one value works for a statement, then that statement is insufficient.

"YES OR NO" QUESTIONS

Usually about a third of the Data Sufficiency questions you'll see on the GMAT are "Yes or No" questions. Although these questions are sometimes hard to get a handle on immediately, don't get into the habit of giving up on them too easily. The important thing is to remember that they're looking for a definite, unambiguous "yes" or a definite, unambiguous "no." Generally, if a statement provides sufficient information, the answer to the question is almost always "yes." But don't forget that a solid "no" is adequate too.

Here's a fairly basic "yes or no" question.

Is $4 + \dfrac{n}{6}$ an integer?

(1) n is a multiple of 3.

(2) n divided by 6 has a remainder of 0.

○ Statement (1) ALONE is sufficient, but statement (2) is not sufficient.

○ Statement (2) ALONE is sufficient, but statement (1) is not sufficient.

○ BOTH statements TOGETHER are sufficient, but NEITHER statement ALONE is sufficient.

○ EACH statement ALONE is sufficient.

○ Statements (1) and (2) TOGETHER are NOT sufficient.

Step 1: Focus on the question stem.

Simple. We need to know whether n is a multiple of 6, because the 4 is an integer (if $\frac{n}{6}$ is an integer, $\frac{n}{6} + 4$ is an integer).

Step 2: Look at each statement separately.

(1) is insufficient; n could be 3, 9, 15, etcetera, in which case $\frac{n}{6}$ is not an integer; or it could be 6, 12, 18, etcetera, in which case $\frac{n}{6}$ is an integer. Eliminate choices (A) and (D).

(2) tells us that n is a multiple of 6 by the definition of multiples of 6, so it's sufficient (the answer to the question is "yes"); (B) is the answer and we can skip step 3.

Note that Picking Numbers came in handy again, but remember: If you pick numbers, you must be thorough. You must pick different types of numbers: Here in statement (1) it was important that you picked both odd and even multiples of 3.

The following is a middle-level "yes or no" question, one that involves the common GMAT concepts of primes and odds-and-evens. When the GMAT brings the primes together with a question about oddness and evenness, it's a pretty sure bet that the answer is going to test whether you know that 2 is the only even prime.

If x and y are prime numbers, is $y(x - 3)$ odd?

(1) $x > 10$

(2) $y < 3$

    ◯ Statement (1) ALONE is sufficient, but statement (2) is not sufficient.

    ◯ Statement (2) ALONE is sufficient, but statement (1) is not sufficient.

    ◯ BOTH statements TOGETHER are sufficient, but NEITHER statement ALONE is sufficient.

    ◯ EACH statement ALONE is sufficient.

    ◯ Statements (1) and (2) TOGETHER are NOT sufficient.

Step 1: Focus on the question stem.

We're asked whether the product $y(x-3)$ is odd. We can answer that if we know either that *both $x - 3$ and y are odd*, which would mean that the product is odd, or by showing that *either $x - 3$ or y is even*, which would mean that the product is even (because an even integer times any integer is even).

Step 2: Look at each statement separately.

(1): If x is a prime greater than 10, then x is an odd prime. Therefore $x - 3$ is even, and $y(x - 3)$ must also be even, so (1) is sufficient. Eliminate answer choices (B), (C), and (E). (2) tells us that y is 2, the only prime less than 3, so y is even. Once again this is sufficient to prove that $y(x - 3)$ is even. Eliminate (A). (D) is the answer.

Note that these statements were sufficient to answer the question in the negative, which is rare but does happen. A "no" is as good as a "yes" for sufficiency in answering "yes or no" questions.

Try this next "yes or no" question, which is basic. It's a natural for the picking numbers strategy.

▶ GO ONLINE

The answer choices in Data Sufficiency take a little getting used to. Use your Diagnostic Quiz to memorize them before Test Day.

Is the product of x, y, and z equal to 1?

(1) $x + y + z = 3$

(2) x, y, and z are each greater than 0.

○ Statement (1) ALONE is sufficient, but statement (2) is not sufficient.

○ Statement (2) ALONE is sufficient, but statement (1) is not sufficient.

○ BOTH statements TOGETHER are sufficient, but NEITHER statement ALONE is sufficient.

○ EACH statement ALONE is sufficient.

○ Statements (1) and (2) TOGETHER are NOT sufficient.

Step 1: Focus on the question stem.

You want the product *xyz*; that may mean knowing the values of *x*, *y*, and *z* or it may mean having some other way of determining their product (if you were told $xy = 1$, for instance, you wouldn't need to know the values of *x* and *y* separately).

Step 2: Look at each statement separately.

When you run into a straightforward question like this, it sometimes pays to give some thought to the math oddity that's being tested. Here the test makers know that some people will pick only positive integers. You, on the other hand, should always be aware of the importance of picking negative numbers, fractions, and zero.

(1): Pick a couple of possibilities for *x*, *y*, and *z*; remember to try fractions, negative numbers, and zero, as well as positive integers. If $x = 1$, $y = 1$, and $z = 1$, then *xyz* does equal 1. But if $x = 3$, $y = 0$, $z = 0$, then *xyz* does not equal 1. (1) is insufficient. Eliminate (A) and (D).

(2) is obviously insufficient; you could have $x = y = z = 1$ again, where *xyz* does equal 1, or you could have $x = y = z = 100$, and *xyz* equals 1,000,000. Eliminate (B).

Step 3: Look at both statements together.

Combining the steps is still insufficient. You could again pick $x = y = z = 1$, which makes *xyz* equal 1. You could also pick $x = 2$, $y = \frac{1}{2}$, $z = \frac{1}{2}$, which makes $xyz = \frac{1}{2}$. So the two statements together don't tell us if $xyz = 1$, and the answer is (E).

GUESSING IN DATA SUFFICIENCY

When you run into a real horror-show question, like the following, don't forget to use sound Data Sufficiency guessing strategy. That means skipping a statement that looks too daunting and trying to eliminate some answer choices by looking at the easier statement. Try your hand at the tough question below. Don't try to solve it; instead see if you can narrow the possibilities down quickly.

What was the maximum temperature in City A on Saturday, May 14?

(1) The average (arithmetic mean) of the maximum daily temperatures in City A from Sunday May 8 to Saturday, May 14 was 72°, which was two degrees less than the average (arithmetic mean) of the maximum daily temperatures in City A from Monday, May 9 to Friday, May 13.

(2) The maximum temperature on Saturday, May 14 was 5° greater than the maximum temperature in City A on Sunday, May 8.

◯ Statement (1) ALONE is sufficient, but statement (2) is not sufficient.

◯ Statement (2) ALONE is sufficient, but statement (1) is not sufficient.

◯ BOTH statements TOGETHER are sufficient, but NEITHER statement ALONE is sufficient.

◯ EACH statement ALONE is sufficient.

◯ Statements (1) and (2) TOGETHER are NOT sufficient.

Even on a difficult question, you can still use the Three-Step Method.

Step 1: Focus on the question stem.

Clear enough: We need a number—the maximum temperature on a certain date. It's hard to say what sort of information we might need to answer this, before we look at the statements.

Step 2: Look at each statement separately.

(1): This is a mess. You're in a hurry. Skip it and look at statement (2), which only compares the maximum on May 14 with the maximum on May 8, without telling us what that earlier temperature was. There's no way you can get a number from statement (2), so it's insufficient. That eliminates (B) and (D), so guess from the remaining choices.

On harder questions, answer choices tend to be more sufficient than they might seem, so don't choose (E). Pick between (A) and (C), depending on how much you think you can extract from the first statement, and lean toward (A). In this case, the answer is (C), though historically (A) has been slightly more common in this GMAT situation.

Don't let this one leave you with a bad taste in your mouth; you're unlikely to run into anything as horrible as statement (1) on test day. The point of this exercise is to show you that even if you do hit something this bad, you're still in control. You work the odds, you look for the strategic approach, and you increase your likelihood of picking up a point.

Here's the solution. Working with statement 1, if the average maximum temperature from May 8 to May 14 was 72°, then the sum of the maximum temperatures of those days is $7 \times 72 = 504°$. If the average maximum temperature from May 9 to May 13 was 72 + 2, or 74°, then the sum of the maximum temperatures of those days was $5 \times 74 = 370°$.

The difference between those numbers is just the sum of the maximum temperature on May 8, which we'll call x, and the maximum temperature on May 14, which we'll call y (since these two days were left out of the second time period). So $x + y = 504 - 370 = 134$. But statement (2) tells us that $y - x = 5$. We have the two different linear equations $x + y = 134$ and $y - x = 5$. These equations lead to a single value for y, so the statements taken together are sufficient.

This example demonstrates how guessing can be more practical for some questions. By looking at only one statement you can narrow the possibilities down to 2 or 3 choices. This can be a great help, particularly on difficult problems for which you think you might have to guess. But you must be sure you know the rules absolutely cold by test day.

- If statement (1) is sufficient, eliminate (B), (C), and (E): the answer must be (A) or (D).

- If statement (2) is sufficient, eliminate (A), (C), and (E): the answer must be (B) or (D).

- If statement (1) is insufficient, eliminate (A) and (D): the answer must be (B), (C), or (E).

- If statement (2) is insufficient, eliminate (B) and (D): the answer must be (A), (C), or (E).

Helpful Hint: If statement (1) looks too confusing, don't skip the problem. Look at statement (2); sometimes it's a lot easier. If you can figure out if even one statement is sufficient or insufficient, you've enormously improved the odds of guessing correctly.

SUMMARY

The 5 basic principles of Data Sufficiency are:
- Know the Data Sufficiency answer choices cold.
- Learn to work with the stem and two statements.
- Know the two types of Data Sufficiency questions.
- Know the topics.
- Think sufficiently.

Kaplan's 3-Step Method for Data Sufficiency are:

Step 1: Focus on the question stem

Step 2: Look at each statement separately.

Step 3: Look at both statements in combination.

The most common question types are:
- Value questions
- "Yes or No" questions

PRACTICE QUIZ

Directions: In each of the problems, a question is followed by two statements containing certain data. You are to determine whether the data provided by the statements are sufficient to answer the question. Choose the correct answer based upon the statements' data, your knowledge of mathematics, and your familiarity with everyday facts (such as the number of minutes in an hour or cents in a dollar). You must indicate whether:

- ○ Statement (1) ALONE is sufficient, but statement (2) is not sufficient.
- ○ Statement (2) ALONE is sufficient, but statement (1) is not sufficient.
- ○ BOTH statements TOGETHER are sufficient, but NEITHER statement ALONE is sufficient.
- ○ EACH statement ALONE is sufficient.
- ○ Statements (1) and (2) TOGETHER are NOT sufficient.

Note: Diagrams accompanying problems agree with information given in the questions, but may not agree with additional information given in statements (1) and (2).

All numbers used are real numbers.

Example:

$$A \qquad B \qquad\quad C$$

What is the length of segment *AC*?

(1) *B* is the midpoint of *AC*

(2) *AB* = 5

Explanation: Statement (1) tells you that B is the midpoint of *AC*, so *AB* = *BC* and *AC* = 2*AB* = 2*BC*. Since statement (1) does not give a value for *AB* or *BC*, you cannot answer the question using statement (1) alone. Statement (2) says that *AB* = 5. Since statement (2) does not give you a value for *BC*, the question cannot be answered by statement (2) alone. Using both statements together you can find a value for both *AB* and *BC*; therefore you can find *AC*, so the answer to the problem is choice (C).

You must indicate whether:

◯ Statement (1) ALONE is sufficient, but statement (2) is not sufficient.

◯ Statement (2) ALONE is sufficient, but statement (1) is not sufficient.

◯ BOTH statements TOGETHER are sufficient, but NEITHER statement ALONE is sufficient.

◯ EACH statement ALONE is sufficient.

◯ Statements (1) and (2) TOGETHER are NOT sufficient.

1. What is the ratio of the discounted price of an item to the list price?

   (1) The discounted price is $4 less than the list price.

   (2) The discounted price is 20 percent less than the list price.

   ◯

   ◯

   ◯

   ◯

   ◯

2. Does $x = y$?

   (1) $x^2 - y^2 = 0$
   (2) $(x - y)^2 = 0$

   ◯

   ◯

   ◯

   ◯

   ◯

3. Does rectangle A have a greater perimeter than rectangle B?

   (1) The length of a side of rectangle A is twice the length of a side of rectangle B.

   (2) The area of rectangle A is twice the area of rectangle B.

   ◯

   ◯

   ◯

   ◯

   ◯

KAPLAN

You must indicate whether:

○ Statement (1) ALONE is sufficient, but statement (2) is not sufficient.

○ Statement (2) ALONE is sufficient, but statement (1) is not sufficient.

○ BOTH statements TOGETHER are sufficient, but NEITHER statement ALONE is sufficient.

○ EACH statement ALONE is sufficient.

○ Statements (1) and (2) TOGETHER are NOT sufficient.

4. How many students scored less than the average (arithmetic mean) of the class on a test?

   (1) The average arithmetic mean of the class was 83.

   (2) Fourteen students scored above the average arithmetic mean of the class.

   ○
   ○
   ○
   ○
   ○

5. If $ab < ac$, which is greater, b or c?

   (1) $a < 0$

   (2) $c < 0$

   ○
   ○
   ○
   ○
   ○

6. If p, q, and r are even numbers, and $2 < p < q < r$, what is the value of q?

   (1) $r < 10$

   (2) $p < 6$

   ○
   ○
   ○
   ○
   ○

You must indicate whether:

⬭ Statement (1) ALONE is sufficient, but statement (2) is not sufficient.

⬭ Statement (2) ALONE is sufficient, but statement (1) is not sufficient.

⬭ BOTH statements TOGETHER are sufficient, but NEITHER statement ALONE is sufficient.

⬭ EACH statement ALONE is sufficient.

⬭ Statements (1) and (2) TOGETHER are NOT sufficient.

7. If there are 250 words on each page, how many pages can Michael read in an hour?

  (1) There are 25 ten-word lines on each page and there is nothing else on each page.

  (2) Michael can read 30 ten-word lines per minute.

  ⬭

  ⬭

  ⬭

  ⬭

  ⬭

8. Is $m > n$?

  (1) $\dfrac{3}{7} < m < \dfrac{5}{7}$

  (2) $\dfrac{2}{7} < n < \dfrac{4}{7}$

  ⬭

  ⬭

  ⬭

  ⬭

  ⬭

9. What is the value of $a^4 - b^4$?

  (1) $a = 3$

  (2) $b = a$

  ⬭

  ⬭

  ⬭

  ⬭

  ⬭

KAPLAN

You must indicate whether:

⬭ Statement (1) ALONE is sufficient, but statement (2) is not sufficient.

⬭ Statement (2) ALONE is sufficient, but statement (1) is not sufficient.

⬭ BOTH statements TOGETHER are sufficient, but NEITHER statement ALONE is sufficient.

⬭ EACH statement ALONE is sufficient.

⬭ Statements (1) and (2) TOGETHER are NOT sufficient.

10. If R is an integer, is R evenly divisible by 3?

(1) $2R$ is evenly divisible by 3.

(2) $3R$ is evenly divisible by 3.

⬭

⬭

⬭

⬭

⬭

11. Susan flipped a fair coin N times. What fraction of the flips came up heads?

(1) $N = 24$

(2) The number of flips that came up tails was $\frac{3}{8}N$.

⬭

⬭

⬭

⬭

⬭

12. If the vertices of quadrilateral $PQRS$ above lie on the circumference of a circle, is $PQRS$ a square?

(1) Side PS is equal in length to a radius of the circle.

(2) The degree measure of minor arc QR is 45°.

⬭

⬭

⬭

⬭

⬭

You must indicate whether:

◯ Statement (1) ALONE is sufficient, but statement (2) is not sufficient.

◯ Statement (2) ALONE is sufficient, but statement (1) is not sufficient.

◯ BOTH statements TOGETHER are sufficient, but NEITHER statement ALONE is sufficient.

◯ EACH statement ALONE is sufficient.

◯ Statements (1) and (2) TOGETHER are NOT sufficient.

13. If he did not stop along the way, what speed did Bill average on his 3-hour trip?

    (1) He traveled a total of 120 miles.
    (2) He traveled half the distance at 30 miles per hour, and half the distance at 60 miles per hour.

    ◯
    ◯
    ◯
    ◯
    ◯

14. What is the value of $\dfrac{x+z}{x-y}$?

    (1) $x + z = 3$
    (2) $y + z = 2$

    ◯
    ◯
    ◯
    ◯
    ◯

15. If x is a positive integer less than 10, and $x + 2$ is a prime number, what is the value of x ?

    (1) $x + 3$ is the square of an integer.
    (2) $x + 7$ is the cube of an integer.

    ◯
    ◯
    ◯
    ◯
    ◯

You must indicate whether:

- ○ Statement (1) ALONE is sufficient, but statement (2) is not sufficient.
- ○ Statement (2) ALONE is sufficient, but statement (1) is not sufficient.
- ○ BOTH statements TOGETHER are sufficient, but NEITHER statement ALONE is sufficient.
- ○ EACH statement ALONE is sufficient.
- ○ Statements (1) and (2) TOGETHER are NOT sufficient.

16. On a certain construction crew there are 3 carpenters for every 2 painters. What percent of the entire crew are carpenters or painters?

    (1) Eighteen percent of the crew are carpenters.
    (2) Twelve percent of the crew are painters.

    ○
    ○
    ○
    ○
    ○

17. A rectangular aquarium provides 36 square centimeters of water-surface area per fish. How many fish are there in the aquarium?

    (1) The edges of the aquarium have lengths of 60, 42, and 30 centimeters.
    (2) The aquarium is filled to a depth of 40 centimeters.

    ○
    ○
    ○
    ○
    ○

You must indicate whether:

- ⬭ Statement (1) ALONE is sufficient, but statement (2) is not sufficient.
- ⬭ Statement (2) ALONE is sufficient, but statement (1) is not sufficient.
- ⬭ BOTH statements TOGETHER are sufficient, but NEITHER statement ALONE is sufficient.
- ⬭ EACH statement ALONE is sufficient.
- ⬭ Statements (1) and (2) TOGETHER are NOT sufficient.

18. At Consolidated Foundries, for a resolution to become policy, a quorum of at least half the 20 directors must pass the resolution by at least a two-thirds majority. At a meeting of the board of directors, did resolution X pass or fail?

    (1) Ten directors voted for the resolution.

    (2) Seven directors voted against the resolution.

    ⬭
    ⬭
    ⬭
    ⬭
    ⬭

19. Is $x + y$ positive?

    (1) $x - y$ is positive.

    (2) $y - x$ is negative.

    ⬭
    ⬭
    ⬭
    ⬭
    ⬭

You must indicate whether:

○ Statement (1) ALONE is sufficient, but statement (2) is not sufficient.

○ Statement (2) ALONE is sufficient, but statement (1) is not sufficient.

○ BOTH statements TOGETHER are sufficient, but NEITHER statement ALONE is sufficient.

○ EACH statement ALONE is sufficient.

○ Statements (1) and (2) TOGETHER are NOT sufficient.

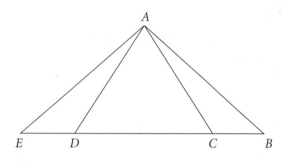

20. In the figure above, segments AD and AC divide $\angle EAB$ into three nonoverlapping angles that are equal in measure. Are AE and AB equal in length?

    (1) $AD = AC$

    (2) $AC = CB$

    ○
    ○
    ○
    ○
    ○

21. If x and y are positive, x is what percent of y?

    (1) $x = \dfrac{1}{16}$

    (2) $\dfrac{x}{y} = 4$

    ○
    ○
    ○
    ○
    ○

22. A shopper bought a tie and a belt during a sale. Which item did he buy at the greater dollar discount?

    (1) He bought the tie at a 20 percent discount.

    (2) He bought the belt at a 25 percent discount.

    ○
    ○
    ○
    ○
    ○

You must indicate whether:

○ Statement (1) ALONE is sufficient, but statement (2) is not sufficient.

○ Statement (2) ALONE is sufficient, but statement (1) is not sufficient.

○ BOTH statements TOGETHER are sufficient, but NEITHER statement ALONE is sufficient.

○ EACH statement ALONE is sufficient.

○ Statements (1) and (2) TOGETHER are NOT sufficient.

23. Joyce has a recipe for a batch of brownies and a recipe for a coffee cake. How many cups of flour does her recipe for a batch of brownies require?

    (1) When Joyce bakes a batch of brownies and a coffee cake following her recipes, she uses a total of $4\frac{1}{2}$ cups of flour.

    (2) When Joyce bakes 2 batches of brownies and 3 coffee cakes following her recipes, she uses a total of 11 cups of flour.

    ○
    ○
    ○
    ○
    ○

24. Calvin has a total of 64 compact discs and cassettes. How many compact discs does he have?

    (1) If he buys 10 more cassettes, he will have 58 cassettes.

    (2) He has three times as many cassettes as compact discs.

    ○
    ○
    ○
    ○
    ○

You must indicate whether:

○ Statement (1) ALONE is sufficient, but statement (2) is not sufficient.

○ Statement (2) ALONE is sufficient, but statement (1) is not sufficient.

○ BOTH statements TOGETHER are sufficient, but NEITHER statement ALONE is sufficient.

○ EACH statement ALONE is sufficient.

○ Statements (1) and (2) TOGETHER are NOT sufficient.

25. Is the volume of cube A greater than the volume of cube B?

    (1) The volume of cube A is 160 percent of the volume of cube B.

    (2) The volume of cube B is 62.5 percent of the volume of cube A.

    ○
    ○
    ○
    ○
    ○

26. If m is a positive integer, is m^3 an odd integer?

    (1) m is an even integer.
    (2) $\sqrt{m}$ is an even integer.

    ○
    ○
    ○
    ○
    ○

27. Is p positive?

    (1) The square of p is positive.
    (2) The reciprocal of p is negative.

    ○
    ○
    ○
    ○

You must indicate whether:

◯ Statement (1) ALONE is sufficient, but statement (2) is not sufficient.

◯ Statement (2) ALONE is sufficient, but statement (1) is not sufficient.

◯ BOTH statements TOGETHER are sufficient, but NEITHER statement ALONE is sufficient.

◯ EACH statement ALONE is sufficient.

◯ Statements (1) and (2) TOGETHER are NOT sufficient.

28. There are two lines at an airline ticket counter. The first line contains exactly 20 people, two of whom are flying to Taipei. What percent of the people in the second line are flying to Taipei?

    (1) There are twice as many people flying to Taipei in the second line as in the first line.

    (2) The total number of people in both lines is 36, and the total number of people in both lines who are flying to Taipei is 6.

    ◯
    ◯
    ◯
    ◯
    ◯

29. What is the value of m if $m = \dfrac{4c}{5d}$ and d is not equal to zero?

    (1) $c = 10d$
    (2) $c = 2$

    ◯
    ◯
    ◯
    ◯
    ◯

30. What is the value of $2x - y$?

    (1) $x + y = 12$
    (2) $x - y = 4$

    ◯
    ◯
    ◯
    ◯
    ◯

KAPLAN

You must indicate whether:

○ Statement (1) ALONE is sufficient, but statement (2) is not sufficient.

○ Statement (2) ALONE is sufficient, but statement (1) is not sufficient.

○ BOTH statements TOGETHER are sufficient, but NEITHER statement ALONE is sufficient.

○ EACH statement ALONE is sufficient.

○ Statements (1) and (2) TOGETHER are NOT sufficient.

31. Are at least 20 percent of the people in City H who are at least 30 years old bilingual?

    (1) In City H, 30 percent of the population is at least 30 years old.

    (2) In City H, of the population 30 years old or older, 18 percent of the women and 17 percent of the men are bilingual.

    ○

    ○

    ○

    ○

    ○

32. What is the value of the product DE?

    (1) $ABCD > 0$
    (2) $BCDE = 0$

    ○

    ○

    ○

    ○

    ○

33. What is the value of x?

    (1) $2x + 4y = 3$
    (2) $3(x + 2y) = 6y - x$

    ○

    ○

    ○

    ○

    ○

You must indicate whether:

◯ Statement (1) ALONE is sufficient, but statement (2) is not sufficient.

◯ Statement (2) ALONE is sufficient, but statement (1) is not sufficient.

◯ BOTH statements TOGETHER are sufficient, but NEITHER statement ALONE is sufficient.

◯ EACH statement ALONE is sufficient.

◯ Statements (1) and (2) TOGETHER are NOT sufficient.

34. Of the members of a marching band, what percentage are boys who play trombone?

    (1) 30 percent of the members of the band play trombone.
    (2) 60 percent of the members of the band are boys.

    ◯
    ◯
    ◯
    ◯
    ◯

35. If m and n are both positive, what is the value of $m\sqrt{n}$?

    (1) $\dfrac{mn}{\sqrt{n}} = 10$
    (2) $\dfrac{m^2 n}{2} = 50$

    ◯
    ◯
    ◯
    ◯
    ◯

36. At a certain restaurant, the total price for one hamburger and one drink is $3.50. How much does one drink cost?

    (1) If the price of the drink were half of its present price, the price of a drink would be one-fifth of the price of a hamburger.
    (2) The cost of one hamburger and two drinks is $4.50.

    ◯
    ◯
    ◯
    ◯
    ◯

You must indicate whether:

○ Statement (1) ALONE is sufficient, but statement (2) is not sufficient.

○ Statement (2) ALONE is sufficient, but statement (1) is not sufficient.

○ BOTH statements TOGETHER are sufficient, but NEITHER statement ALONE is sufficient.

○ EACH statement ALONE is sufficient.

○ Statements (1) and (2) TOGETHER are NOT sufficient.

37. The price per share of stock A increased by 25 percent during the same period of time that the price per share of stock B decreased by 25 percent. The original price per share of stock A was what percent of the original price per share of stock B?

    (1) The increased price per share of stock A was equal to the decreased price per share of stock B.

    (2) The increase in the price per share of stock A was $\frac{3}{20}$ of the original price per share of stock B.

    ○
    ○
    ○
    ○
    ○

38. A bag of coins contains only nickels, dimes, and quarters. There are 38 coins in all. What is the total value of all the coins in the bag?

    (1) Quarters account for half the value of the coins in the bag.

    (2) The value of all the dimes equals the value of all the nickels.

    ○
    ○
    ○
    ○
    ○

You must indicate whether:

   ⬭ Statement (1) ALONE is sufficient, but statement (2) is not sufficient.

   ⬭ Statement (2) ALONE is sufficient, but statement (1) is not sufficient.

   ⬭ BOTH statements TOGETHER are sufficient, but NEITHER statement ALONE is sufficient.

   ⬭ EACH statement ALONE is sufficient.

   ⬭ Statements (1) and (2) TOGETHER are NOT sufficient.

39. Is the integer x a multiple of 5 ?

   (1) x divided by 3 leaves a remainder of 2.

   (2) x divided by 4 leaves no remainder.

   ⬭

   ⬭

   ⬭

   ⬭

   ⬭

40. Megacorp International spent a total of $90,000,000 on television, magazine, and billboard advertising combined. How much of the total was spent on television advertising?

   (1) The total spending for billboard and magazine advertising was 20% less than the amount spent on television advertising.

   (2) The company spent 50% more on magazine advertising than on billboard advertising.

   ⬭

   ⬭

   ⬭

   ⬭

   ⬭

41. The integer x is even and the integer y is odd. Is the integer z odd?

   (1) $xyz + 1$ is odd.

   (2) $xy + xz + yz$ is even.

   ⬭

   ⬭

   ⬭

   ⬭

   ⬭

   ⬭

You must indicate whether:

○ Statement (1) ALONE is sufficient, but statement (2) is not sufficient.

○ Statement (2) ALONE is sufficient, but statement (1) is not sufficient.

○ BOTH statements TOGETHER are sufficient, but NEITHER statement ALONE is sufficient.

○ EACH statement ALONE is sufficient.

○ Statements (1) and (2) TOGETHER are NOT sufficient.

42. What is the area of the floor in Dan's rectangular bedroom that will not be covered by a particular rectangular rug?

    (1) The area of the floor in Dan's bedroom is 300 square feet.

    (2) After the rug is placed in Dan's room, there will be a 24-inch strip of exposed floor between the rug and the wall along all sides of the rug.

    ○
    ○
    ○
    ○
    ○

43. If x and y are both positive, what percent of x is y?

    (1) $10x - 15y = 0$
    (2) $4x^2 = 9y^2$

    ○
    ○
    ○
    ○
    ○

44. A right triangle has sides of lengths A and $2B$ and hypotenuse of length $A + B$. What is the perimeter?

    (1) $A = 3$
    (2) $A = \dfrac{3B}{2}$

    ○
    ○
    ○
    ○
    ○

You must indicate whether:

- ⬭ Statement (1) ALONE is sufficient, but statement (2) is not sufficient.
- ⬭ Statement (2) ALONE is sufficient, but statement (1) is not sufficient.
- ⬭ BOTH statements TOGETHER are sufficient, but NEITHER statement ALONE is sufficient.
- ⬭ EACH statement ALONE is sufficient.
- ⬭ Statements (1) and (2) TOGETHER are NOT sufficient.

45. If x is positive, is x prime?

    (1) x^3 has *exactly* four distinct positive integer factors.

    (2) $x^2 - x - 6 = 0$

    ⬭

    ⬭

    ⬭

    ⬭

    ⬭

46. If x is not equal to zero, is $\dfrac{1}{x} > 1$?

    (1) $\dfrac{y}{x} > y$

    (2) $x^3 > x^2$

    ⬭

    ⬭

    ⬭

    ⬭

    ⬭

47. At the beginning of last year, a car dealership had 150 cars in stock, which the dealership had purchased for $20,000 each. During the same year, the dealership made only one purchase of cars. What is the total amount spent by the dealership on the cars it had in stock at the end of last year?

    (1) Last year the dealership purchased 50 cars for $18,000 each.

    (2) Last year the total revenue from the sale of cars was $180,000.

    ⬭

    ⬭

    ⬭

    ⬭

    ⬭

KAPLAN

You must indicate whether:

◯ Statement (1) ALONE is sufficient, but statement (2) is not sufficient.

◯ Statement (2) ALONE is sufficient, but statement (1) is not sufficient.

◯ BOTH statements TOGETHER are sufficient, but NEITHER statement ALONE is sufficient.

◯ EACH statement ALONE is sufficient.

◯ Statements (1) and (2) TOGETHER are NOT sufficient.

48. What is the minimum number of rectangular shipping boxes Company L will need in order to ship 120 packages that are rectangular solids, all of which have exactly the same dimensions?

    (1) The dimensions of each package are 3 inches in length, 4 inches in depth, and 6 inches in height.

    (2) Each box is a cube with an edge of length one foot.

    ◯
    ◯
    ◯
    ◯
    ◯

49. If set Z has a median of 19, what is the range of set Z?

    (1) $Z = \{18, 28, 11, x, 15, y\}$

    (2) The average (arithmetic mean) of the members of set Z is 20.

    ◯
    ◯
    ◯
    ◯
    ◯

50. If each of a, b, and c is positive, and $a = 5b + 7c$, what is the value of $\frac{a}{b}$?

    (1) $2b + 5c = 50$

    (2) $3b - 5c = 0$

    ◯
    ◯
    ◯
    ◯
    ◯

ANSWERS AND EXPLANATIONS

1.	B	11.	B	21.	B	31.	B	41.	B
2.	B	12.	D	22.	E	32.	C	42.	E
3.	C	13.	D	23.	C	33.	B	43.	D
4.	E	14.	C	24.	D	34.	E	44.	A
5.	A	15.	D	25.	D	35.	D	45.	B
6.	A	16.	D	26.	D	36.	D	46.	B
7.	B	17.	E	27.	B	37.	D	47.	E
8.	E	18.	B	28.	B	38.	C	48.	C
9.	B	19.	E	29.	A	39.	E	49.	C
10.	A	20.	A	30.	C	40.	A	50.	B

1. B

We need to determine a ratio.

(1) *Insufficient.* Merely knowing that there is a four dollar difference won't suffice. The list price could be $40, making the ratio 36:40, which is 9:10. Or the list price could be $10, making the ratio 6:10.

(2) *Sufficient.* Knowing the percentage difference, as opposed to the actual dollar difference, allows us to determine the ratio. The ratio between a quantity and another quantity 20 percent less than the first is 10:8, or 5:4.

2. B

We want to know whether x equals y. If and only if a statement allows us to answer "yes" definitively, or to answer "no" definitively, is it sufficient.

(1) *Insufficient.* There's a common trap here, one you need to learn for test day. It may look like the two variables are equal, but not necessarily. All the statement tells us is that x^2 is equal to y^2. That doesn't mean that x equals y, because one could be negative and the other positive. Suppose x equals 2; y could also equal 2, or it can equal −2.

(2) *Sufficient.* This tells us that $(x − y)(x − y) = 0$. So, $x − y = 0$. The only way the difference between the two variables can be 0 is if they are equal.

3. C

Perimeter, remember, is the sum of the lengths of the sides. We'll need to consider different rectangles to test whether the statements are sufficient.

(1) *Insufficient.* The two rectangles could be exactly the same. Let's say they are both 5 by 10. In this case the question is answered "no." On the other hand, *B* could be 5 by 10 while *A* is 10 by 10. In this case, the answer is "yes."

(2) *Insufficient.* This one is tricky. The key though, is to envision a very long, thin rectangle for *B*. If it is 50 by 1, its perimeter is greater than a rectangle *A* that is 10 by 10, even though *B*'s area is only half that of *A*. The answer then would be "no." It's easy to see how the answer could be "yes," as it's not hard to envision *A* as having a greater perimeter in addition to its greater area.

Since neither is sufficient, we have to combine them. If we combine the two, however, we can answer the question. If *A* has one side twice the length of one of *B*'s, and *A*'s area is twice that of *B*, then the other side of *A* is equal to the other side of *B* and *A* must have a greater perimeter.

4. E

The question is clear: How many students scored less than the average?

(1) *Insufficient.* Merely knowing the average tells us nothing about how anyone scored. There could be a lot of students under the average, or only a few.

(2) *Insufficient.* There could be any number of number of students under the average.

Combining the statements still leaves the question unanswered. Fourteen students above 83 could be balanced by a lot of students under 83 or very few who happen to have scored way under 83. We don't even know what those 14 scores were.

5. A

A key here will be determining whether *a* is positive or negative. If we know that, we'll be able to divide both sides of the inequality and settle the issue. (Remember, if you divide both sides of an inequality by a negative number, you must reverse the direction of the inequality sign. Since we don't know whether *a* is positive or negative, we cannot do the division yet.)

(1) *Sufficient*. If *a* is negative, we can cancel it from both sides of the inequality as long as we reverse the inequality. We're left with $b > c$, and the question is answered.

(2) *Insufficient*. The fact that *c* is negative tells us nothing. Let's say *a* is 1. Then it's just a straight comparison between *b* and *c*, and *c* is greater. On the other hand, suppose *a* is −1. In this case, we get $-b < -c$. Divide by −1 and we find that *b* is greater.

6. A

We know that all three variables are even numbers greater than 2, and that *q* is greater than *p* but less than *r*. Notice also that we cannot assume *p*, *q*, and *r*, are consecutive even numbers.

(1) *Sufficient*. If *r* is less than 10, it can be only 8. So *p* and *q*, respectively, must be 4 and 6.

(2) *Insufficient*. If *p* is less than 6, it can be only 4. However, *q* can be any even number greater than 4, and *r* can be any even number greater than 6.

7. B

To find the number of pages per hour that Michael reads, we need a rate. Most helpful would be words per hour, but in fact, any rate will do—words per day, year, etcetera.

(1) *Insufficient*. This tells us merely how the words are arranged on the page. It provides no information about Michael's reading speed.

(2) *Sufficient*. This is a rate, exactly what we wanted. Since we know that he reads 300 words per minute, and the question told us there are 250 words per page, we can compute how many pages he reads per hour. On Test Day you wouldn't bother doing this computation. For the record, it's

$$\frac{300 \text{ (words/min.)} \times 60 \text{(min./hour)}}{250 \text{ (words/page)}} = 72 \text{ (pages/hour)}.$$

8. E

Not much to pull out of the question; on to the statements.

(1) *Insufficient.* Spend no time thinking about this. Since n is never mentioned, the statement cannot be sufficient.

(2) *Insufficient.* Same principle here. We get a range of values for n, but are told nothing about m.

In combining the two statements, we want to see whether we can have m greater than n and also have m not greater than n. If we can, the answer is (E); if we can't, it's (C). Certainly m can be greater. It could be just less than $\frac{5}{7}$ and thus greater than the entire range of values for n. The question then becomes: Can n be greater than or equal to m? Yes, n could be just a hair less than $\frac{4}{7}$, while m is just a hair more than $\frac{3}{7}$. (With $\frac{10}{21}$ for m and $\frac{11}{21}$ for n, both statements are true and $n > m$.) The answer is (E).

9. B

We need to know, or be able to derive, the values of both a^4 and b^4, or the difference between them.

(1) *Insufficient.* This allows us to derive a value for a^4, but tells us nothing about b^4. Therefore, we can't determine the difference between the two.

(2) *Sufficient.* If the variables are equal, then their values when raised to the fourth power are equal, and so $a^4 - b^4 = 0$.

10. A

There isn't anything special to pull out of this question. We just want to know whether R is a multiple of—evenly divisible by—3.

(1) *Sufficient.* Since the quantity $2R$ is divisible by 3, one of those two factors (2 or R) must be divisible by 3. (If you don't see this, plug in some numbers and try it out.) Since 2 isn't evenly divisible by 3, R must be.

(2) *Insufficient.* Similar reasoning is at work here. We know that the quantity $3R$ is evenly divisible by 3, which means that at least one of the factors (3 or R) must be divisible by 3. The problem, though, is that 3 is evenly divisible by 3, making it impossible for us to tell whether R is also evenly divisible by 3.

11. B

The fraction described is just the number of times the coin came up heads over the number of flips, *N*. Of course, this fraction can be determined from different types of information.

(1) *Insufficient*. This tells us how many coin tosses there were, but leaves us clueless as to how many came up heads. (Note that you cannot infer that 12 of the tosses were heads just because the coin is described as "fair." Although a fair coin tends to come up heads half the time, in any given series of flips the number of times it comes up heads can vary significantly.)

(2) *Sufficient*. By telling us what fraction came up tails, this statement tells us what fraction came up heads. Since only heads or tails is possible, and since $\frac{3}{8}$ were tails, the remaining $\frac{5}{8}$ were heads.

12. D

PQRS is described only as a quadrilateral, which means that none of its sides needs to be the same length as any other. We want to know whether or not it's also a square, meaning that all four sides are the same length. (Because the quadrilateral is inscribed in a circle, we don't need to worry about whether the angles are all 90°; if the four sides are all the same length, the angles must each be 90°.) Notice how Data Sufficiency diagrams can be misleading. *PQRS* could look quite different from what's depicted. It could look like this:

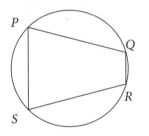

(1) *Sufficient*. Interestingly, the answer to the question turns out to be "no." That's unusual, but it does happen. In order for *PQRS* to be a square, all four sides must have the same length. This is impossible if *PS* is equal to the circle's radius. Draw in the triangle formed by *PSR*. If it's half of a square, it has to be an isosceles right triangle. Is it? The hypotenuse *PR* is equal to the diameter. If *PS* and *SR* are each equal to the radius—half of the diameter—the triangle collapses. The sum of any two sides of a triangle must be greater than the third; here the sum of two sides equals only the third.

(2) *Sufficient*. In order for *PQRS* to be a square, the degree measure of all four minor arcs (*PQ*, *QR*, *RS*, and *SP*) must be one quarter of the circle. Since every circle is 360°, the degree measure of each of the arcs would have to be 90°. Since minor arc *QR* is 45°, *PQRS* isn't a square.

KAPLAN

13. D

We want Bill's average rate. The rate formula is: *Distance = Rate × Time*. We know the time (3 hours), so merely finding out the distance he traveled would be sufficient.

(1) *Sufficient*. Exactly as hoped for. With the distance known, we could plug it into the rate formula and compute Bill's rate. We won't, however, because all we need to know is that we could solve for the rate; doing so would waste valuable time.

(2) *Sufficient*. If he covered the same distance at 30 mph as he did at 60 mph, he must have been traveling at 30 mph for twice as long as he was at 60 mph. Given that he traveled for 3 hours, he traveled at 30 mph for 2 hours and 60 mph for 1 hour. That comes to 120 miles total distance, and again we can solve for the rate.

14. C

We need values for these variables, or at least values for the numerator $x + z$ and the denominator $x - y$ of the fraction.

(1) *Insufficient*. This supplies the numerator, but as we have no idea what the value of the denominator is, we cannot evaluate the fraction.

(2) *Insufficient*. We cannot determine the value of either part of the fraction.

Since we know the value of the numerator from statement (1), combining the two is just a matter of trying to determine the value of the denominator, $x - y$. As it turns out, we can do this. Statement (2) can be rewritten as $z = 2 - y$. Substituting that value for z into statement (1) yields: $x + 2 - y = 3$. Subtracting 2 from both sides yields $x - y = 1$. We now have a value for the denominator as well as the numerator, so we can find the value of the fraction.

15. D

This question is worth working out ahead of time. For x to be less than 10 and for $x + 2$ to be prime, x must be 1, 3, 5, or 9. Those are the only numbers that fit the description. Answering the question, then, will really be a matter of seeing whether the statements narrow x down to only one of these.

(1) *Sufficient*. Just plug in the values above: $1 + 3 = 4$; $3 + 3 = 6$; $5 + 3 = 8$; $9 + 3 = 12$. Only 4 is the square of an integer, so we know the value of x.

(2) *Sufficient*. Just plug in the values again: $1 + 7 = 8$; $3 + 7 = 10$; $5 + 7 = 12$; $9 + 7 = 16$. Only 8 is the cube of an integer, so again we know the value of x.

16. D

We want to know what percent of the crew is made up of carpenters and painters. Because we're given the ratio of carpenters to painters, if we're told how many there are of either, we can compute the total of both. We'd still need to know, though, how many people are in the crew because there could be people in the crew who are not carpenters or painters. Another way to solve this would be to get a ratio for the total crew to either the carpenters or the painters. This additional ratio would allow us to compute the percent of the crew that is comprised of carpenters and painters.

(1) *Sufficient.* This is essentially a ratio between carpenters and the whole crew. For every 100 members of the crew, there are 18 carpenters. From the question itself, we can determine that 12% of the whole crew are painters, so the percentage of the whole crew that carpenters and painters is (18% + 12% = 30%).

(2) *Sufficient.* Same idea, just the other way around. If 12 percent are painters, then 18 percent are carpenters (this comes from the 3:2 ratio) and so 30 percent are either carpenters or painters.

17. E

It's simple division, once you've figured out what needs to be divided. The number of fish will be determined by dividing 36 (each fish's allotment) into the number of square centimeters of "water-surface area." All we need, essentially, is that—the amount of surface area the water in the tank has. As the tank is a rectangle, we'll need to know the length, width, and depth of the water.

(Note: The volume of the water won't be sufficient. The same volume can have different surface areas.)

(1) *Insufficient.* Here's a tricky one. These dimensions provide the surface area of the tank, but not of the water. Since we don't know how full the tank is, we can't solve for surface area.

(2) *Insufficient.* This gives us the depth of the water, but without its length or width, we can't determine its surface area.

You might have thought that combining the two would do the trick, since we know the tank's dimensions and how deep the water is. The problem, though, is that we don't know which dimension is which. That is, we don't know whether the 40 cm deep water has a surface area of 60 cm by 30 cm, or 42 by 30. (The surface area can't be 60 by 42, because that would leave 30 for the depth, yet we know the depth of the water is 40.) Until we learn the length and width of the tank, we don't have sufficient information.

18. B

The rules say that a resolution must be passed by at least two-thirds of half of the 20 directors. Half of 20 is 10, and two-thirds of that is $6\frac{2}{3}$. Since we can't have fractional directors, we're left with 7—the absolute minimum number of directors required to pass a resolution. Of course, if more directors are voting, more votes are needed to pass the resolution. Twenty directors voting, for example, would require 14 votes in favor.

(1) *Insufficient*. Ten votes might or might not pass a resolution, depending on how many directors vote. If only 10 vote, it passes; if 20 vote, it doesn't.

(2) *Sufficient*. Seven votes against means that even if all 20 directors vote, a $\frac{2}{3}$ majority is impossible. The resolution doesn't pass.

19. E

The best strategy is to "pick numbers."

(1) *Insufficient*. Pick 10 for x and 5 for y. This satisfies the statement and would allow us to answer "yes" to the question. We can't stop here, though; we have to try different values to see if we can answer the question "no." Try 5 for x and -10 for y. These values satisfy statement (1) but allow us to answer the question "no."

(2) *Insufficient*. Try the same values: 10 for x and 5 for y. Those values allow us to answer "yes" to the question. But we need to consider other values. If we set x equal to 5 and y equal to -10, we can answer "no" to the question.

The values that we used to show that each statement by itself is insufficient can be used to show that both statements taken together are insufficient. Thus, if $x = 10$ and $y = 5$, then both statements are true and the answer to the question is "yes." If $x = 5$ and $y = -10$, then both statements are true and the answer to the question is "no." The statements taken together are insufficient. As it turns out the two statements are equivalent. So they are just as insufficient together as each is separately.

20. A

Triangles *EAD*, *DAC*, and *CAB* have an equal angle. Since we want to know if two of them have an equal side, we should think in terms of isosceles triangles.

(1) *Sufficient*. This tells us that the middle triangle (*ACD*) is isosceles. The angles facing the two equal sides are, therefore, equal (these are angles *ACD* and *ADC*). Since these angles are equal, their supplementary angles (*ADE* and *ACB*) are also equal. Since those two supplementary angles are equal, the third and final angles (*AED* and *ABC*) in the two outside triangles must also be equal. Looking at the whole figure then, we see that triangle *ABE* is isosceles. Therefore, *AE* is equal to *AB*.

(2) *Insufficient.* This allows us to conclude that angles *CAB* and *CBA* are equal, but that's of no help. We learn nothing more about triangle *ADE*, so we cannot answer the question.

21. B

From the stem: *x* and *y* are positive. We want to know the percent of *y* that *x* is. That's most easily thought of as a fraction: $\frac{x}{y}$. If you thought of it that way, you probably jumped to statement (2) first.

(2) *Sufficient.* If we're given a value for $\frac{x}{y}$, we can determine the percent we're asked about. This is, in fact, how you would do so—you'd divide *x* by *y*. In fact, and know this for GMAT day, we could also have solved for the percent if we'd been given the value for the reciprocal, for $\frac{x}{y}$. Eliminate (A), (C), and (E).

(1) *Insufficient.* The value of *x* has been given, but the value of *y* has not, and thus the desired percent cannot be found. Choose (B).

22. E

From the stem: We can see that we want to compare the number of dollars discounted from the price of the tie with the number of dollars discounted from the price of the belt. Notice that we need dollars discounted; mere percentages won't suffice. Also notice that since we aren't given information on either item, a statement can be sufficient only if it talks about both items or compares the two items.

(1) *Insufficient.* Only information about the tie is given. We know nothing about the belt. Eliminate (A) and (D).

(2) *Insufficient.* Only information about the belt is given. We know nothing about the tie. Eliminate (B).

In combination: All we can determine is that a greater percentage discount was obtained on the belt. Whether this translates into a greater dollar discount cannot be determined. Twenty percent of the tie's original price may amount to more or fewer dollars than 25 percent of the belt's original price. Choose (E).

23. C

Your Data Sufficiency sense probably alerted you to the fact that this looks very much like a setup for an algebra problem. We should be ready to work with equations, employing *b* for brownies and *c* for coffee cakes.

(1) *Insufficient.* One batch of brownies (*b*) and one coffee cake (*c*) together require 4.5 cups of flour. We get one equation, $b + c = 4.5$, with two variables. We can't solve for either variable. Eliminate (A) and (D).

(2) *Insufficient*. Same story. Two batches of brownies and three coffee cakes together require 11 cups of flour. Therefore, $2b + 3c = 11$. We can't solve the problem for either variable. Eliminate (B).

In combination: Since the equations are different, and since there are only two variables, we can solve for the values of the variables. Remember, you can solve for a variable if you have as many different first-degree equations as you have variables in the equations. Choose (C).

24. D

From the stem: Since Calvin has 64 total discs and cassettes, the number of his discs (d) plus the number of his cassettes (c) equals 64: $d + c = 64$. Thus, to find the number of discs, we need only *one* more first-degree equation with d or c or both in it. (It must be a different equation, of course.)

(1) *Sufficient*. Here's a different equation: $c + 10 = 58$. We could solve for c and plug that value into our original equation to solve for d. There's no need, though, to actually find the value of d. Merely seeing that we have two different equations with two variables is enough. Eliminate (B), (C), and (E).

(2) *Sufficient*. Same story: $c = 3d$. This is another, different equation and so we can solve for d. Choose (D).

25. D

Since this is a yes-no question, we won't necessarily have to find the exact volume of each cube; all we need is the relationship between the two volumes.

(1) *Sufficient*. Statement (1) tells us directly that cube A has a larger volume than cube B, since 160 percent is greater than 100 percent. The answer to the question is "yes." Statement (1) is sufficient, so we can eliminate choices (B), (C), and (E).

(2) *Sufficient*. Statement (2) tells us directly that cube B has a smaller volume than cube A, since 62.5 percent is less than 100 percent. Thus, cube A has a greater volume and the answer to the question is "yes." (D) is correct.

26. D

Because $m^3 = m \times m \times m$, m^3 will be odd if m is odd and m^3 will be even if m is even. Thus, the question is really asking if m is odd.

(1) *Sufficient.* Statement (1) says that m is even, so it can't be odd. Thus statement (1) is sufficient to answer "no" to the question. Eliminate (B), (C), and (E).

(2) *Sufficient.* In statement (2), if the positive square root of m is an even integer, then m must be the product of two even integers and therefore m must be even. So m is *not* odd; the answer to the question is "no." (D) is correct.

27. B

This is a yes-no question, so the answer must be always yes or always no in order to have sufficiency.

(1) *Insufficient.* Statement (1) tells us that the square of p is positive, or $p^2 > 0$. This means that p could be positive or negative; when we square either a positive or a negative we always get a positive. The only thing we really learn from statement (1) is that p is not 0. So, we can't answer the question definitively. Statement (1) is insufficient; eliminate (A) and (D).

(2) *Sufficient.* Statement (2): The reciprocal of p is $\frac{1}{p}$. If $\frac{1}{p}$ is negative, then since the numerator 1 is positive, p itself must be negative. Since p must be negative, the answer to the question is always no. Choice (B) is correct.

28. B

To find the percentage of people in the second line flying to Taipei, we need to know how many people are in the second line and how many of them are flying to Taipei. The stem gives us information only about the first line, so let's go on to the statements.

(1) *Insufficient.* Statement (1) tells us that four people in the second line are flying to Taipei but gives us no information about how many people are in this line, so the statement is insufficient. Eliminate (A) and (D).

(2) *Sufficient.* Statement (2): Since there are 36 people in the two lines combined and there are 20 people in the first line, there must be $36 - 20 = 16$ people in the second line. Similarly, 6 people in total are flying to Taipei and 2 of them are in the first line, so 4 of them must be in the second line. So, statement (2) tells us how many people are in the second line and how many of them are flying to Taipei; therefore it is sufficient. Choice (B) is correct.

29. A

The stem gives us one equation, $m = \frac{4c}{5d}$, and asks us to find a value for m. To do this, we need to find two more linear equations involving the variables c and d or some other information that allows us to find the value of the expression $\frac{4c}{5d}$.

(1) *Sufficient.* Let's replace c in our original equation with $10d$. Doing so gives us $m = \frac{4(10d)}{5d}$. The d terms cancel out, leaving us with $m = \frac{4(10)}{5} = 8$. So, statement (1) is sufficient. Eliminate (B), (C), and (E).

(2) *Insufficient.* If we replace c with 2 in the original equation, we have $m = \frac{4(2)}{5d}$. We still have one equation and two variables, so we can't solve for m.

30. C

Although finding the values of x and y will definitely give us sufficiency, we won't need the individual values if we can find a value for the expression $2x - y$. So, we'll be looking either for information on x and y or on the expression $2x - y$.

(1) *Insufficient.* This gives us one equation with two variables, so we have no way to solve for x and y. We also can't rearrange the equation to isolate the expression $2x - y$, so statement (1) is insufficient. Eliminate (A) and (D).

(2) *Insufficient.* We have basically the same story. With only one equation, we can't solve for x and y, and the equation also cannot be solved for $2x - y$. So, statement (2) is also insufficient. Eliminate (B).

When we combine the statements, we have two distinct linear equations and two variables, so we can solve for x and y. So (C) is the correct choice.

31. B

Since this is a yes-no question, we don't need to find the exact percentage of people 30 and over who are bilingual. We only need to know for sure whether the number is at least 20 percent.

(1) *Insufficient.* Statement (1) tells us what percent of the population is 30 years old or older. But this statement tells us nothing about how many people are bilingual, so it is insufficient. Eliminate choices (A) and (D).

(2) *Sufficient.* Statement (2) tells us that the percentage of women 30 and over who are bilingual is less than 20 percent and that the percentage of men 30 and over who are bilingual is also less than 20 percent. Since neither group is at least 20 percent bilingual, the total population (women and men) of people 30 and over must be less than 20 percent bilingual. Thus, we can definitely say that the answer to the question is "always no." Statement (2) is sufficient, and (B) is correct.

32. C

We don't get much information from the question stem other than the fact that we are looking for the values of D and E or their product, so let's go right to the statements.

(1) *Insufficient.* Since the product $ABCD$ is greater than zero, we know that none of these four variables can be equal to zero. So, D isn't zero, but we don't know anything about E or the product DE, so statement (1) is insufficient. We can eliminate (A) and (D).

(2) *Insufficient.* Since the product $BCDE$ is equal to zero, at least one of these four variables must be zero, but that's as far as we can go with this statement. It does not give us the value of DE, so it is also insufficient.

Taking the statements together, we know from statement (1) that A, B, C, and D are all *not* equal to zero, and from statement (2) that at least one of B, C, D, and E must be equal to zero. So E must be zero, and the product DE must also be zero. The two statements together are sufficient, and (C) is correct.

33. B

We are given no information about x in the stem, so we'll have to go right to the statements to find the value of x.

(1) *Insufficient.* Statement (1) gives us one equation involving x and y. We don't have enough information to solve for x and y with only one equation, so this statement is insufficient. Eliminate (A) and (D).

(2) *Sufficient.* Statement (2) appears to be another equation with two variables, but let's simplify it to see what's going on. First, expand the left side by multiplying out the 3. This gives us $3x + 6y = 6y - x$. Now, if we subtract $6y$ from both sides, we have $3x = -x$. Adding x to both sides gives us $4x = 0$, so x must be zero. Thus statement (2) is sufficient, and (B) is correct.

34. E

To answer the question, we'll need information on how many boys play trombone and on how many people are in the band.

(1) *Insufficient.* Statement (1) tells us only that 30 percent of the people in the band play trombone. It doesn't tell us how many band members there are or how many band members are boys who play trombone. Nor does it tell us what percent of all the band members are boys who play trombone. Statement (1) is insufficient. Eliminate (A) and (D).

(2) *Insufficient.* Statement (2) tells us that 60 percent of the members of the band are boys. It doesn't tell us what percent or fraction of the boys play trombone. So statement (2) is insufficient. Eliminate (B).

Taking the statements together, we know that 30 percent of the members of the band play trombone and that 60 percent of the members of the band are boys. Yet we have no information about what percent or fraction of the 30 percent of the band members who play trombone are boys, and we have no information about what percent or fraction of the 60 percent of the band members who are boys play trombone. The statements taken together are insufficient.

35. D

For sufficiency, we need to find either the values for m and n or the value of $m\sqrt{n}$ itself.

(1) *Sufficient.* We have only one equation and two variables, so we can't solve for m and n.

Instead, let's see if we can work with the equation to find a value for $m\sqrt{n}$. If we multiply the left side by $\dfrac{\sqrt{n}}{\sqrt{n}}$, we get $\dfrac{mn\sqrt{n}}{(\sqrt{n})(\sqrt{n})} = 10$, or $\dfrac{mn\sqrt{n}}{n} = 10$. We can cancel an n from the numerator and denominator on the left side, leaving us with $m\sqrt{n} = 10$. Thus statement (1) is sufficient.

(2) *Sufficient.* Again, we can't find m and n, so let's solve for $m\sqrt{n}$. If we multiply both sides by 2, we have $m^2n = 100$. Taking the positive square root of both sides gives us $m\sqrt{n} = 10$, which is the same thing we found from statement (1). Each statement by itself is sufficient, so (D) is correct.

36. D

Let's say that h is the price of one hamburger, in dollars, and d is the price of one drink, in dollars. We need to be able to find the value of d. We know that $h + d = 3.50$, so as we evaluate the statements, we'll be looking for an additional linear equation involving h and d.

(1) *Sufficient.* Half the present price of the drink would be $\frac{1}{2}d$ and one-fifth of the price of a hamburger is $\frac{1}{5}h$. So, statement (1) tells us that $\frac{1}{2}d = \frac{1}{5}h$. This gives us the second equation we were looking for, so we could solve for the value of d. Statement (1) is sufficient. We can eliminate (B), (C), and (E).

(2) *Sufficient.* Algebraically, this statement says that $h + 2d = 4.50$. Again, we have an additional distinct linear equation, so this statement is also sufficient. (D) is correct.

37. D

Percents are just another way of expressing fractions; if we know one, we know the other. So we can think of the question stem as "The original price per share of stock A was what *fraction* of the original price per share of stock B?"

Let a represent the original per share of stock A and let b represent the original per share of stock B. To answer the question, we need to find the fraction $\frac{a}{b}$. In other words, dividing a by b tells us what fraction of b is represented by a.

(1) *Sufficient.* Statement (1) says that (a plus 25% of a) is equal to (b minus 25% of b). Expressing this as an equation, we have $a + 0.25a = b - 0.25b$. This is one equation with two unknowns. While we cannot solve this equation for the values of either a or b, sometimes one equation with two variables can be solved for an expression containing both variables. Here, we have $a + 0.25a = b - 0.25b$, which is equivalent to $1.25a = 0.75b$. Dividing by b gives us $\frac{1.25a}{b} = 0.75$, and then dividing by 1.25 gives us $\frac{a}{b} = \frac{0.75}{1.25}$. There is no need to simplify any further. We have found the fraction we were looking for. Statement (1) is sufficient. Eliminate (B), (C), and (E).

(2) *Sufficient.* Statement (2) says that $0.25a = \left(\frac{3}{20}\right)b$. The fraction $\frac{3}{20}$ is equivalent to 0.15, so we have $0.25a = 0.15b$, or $\frac{0.25a}{b} = 0.15$. Dividing by 0.25, we get $\frac{a}{b} = \frac{0.15}{0.25}$. There is no need to simplify further. As with statement (1), finding the fraction is enough to show sufficiency. Both statements alone are sufficient, so (D) is correct.

Notice that statement (1) and statement (2) both gave us the same value for $\frac{a}{b}$, as they must:

$$\frac{0.75}{1.25} = \frac{(0.15)(5)}{(0.25)(5)} = \frac{0.15}{0.25}$$

38. C

There are three types of coins in the bag, but we don't know how many of any kind there are, so we have three variables: the number of quarters, the number of dimes, and the number of nickels. Let's represent these with the variables q, d, and n respectively.

Since quarters are worth 25 cents, dimes 10 cents, and nickels 5 cents, we can say that the total value of the coins in the bag, in cents, will be $25q + 10d + 5n$. To find the total value, we'll need values for all three variables, which means we'll need three distinct linear equations involving these variables. We can get one equation from the stem: $q + d + n = 38$. In order to be sufficient, the statements will have to give us two more equations.

(1) *Insufficient.* This means that the value of all the quarters, $25q$, is equal to the value of the nickels and dimes together, $10d + 5n$. So we have one equation: $25q = 10d + 5n$. But that's not enough; we need two more equations, and statement (1) gives us just one. So statement (1) is insufficient. We can eliminate (A) and (D).

(2) *Insufficient.* Statement (2): Here, we can say that $10d = 5n$. Again, we have only one additional equation, so statement (2) is also insufficient. We can eliminate (B).

When we take the statements together, we have two more equations: $25q = 10d + 5n$ and $10d = 5n$. Combining these equations with the equation $q + d + n = 38$ is sufficient to solve for the values of q, d, and n, so (C) is correct.

39. E

This is a yes-no question, so either "always yes" or "always no" is required for sufficiency. When working with multiples and remainders, Picking Numbers is a good strategy. We'll use the statements to determine what numbers we can pick for x.

(1) *Insufficient.* If x divided by 3 leaves a remainder of 2, then x must be 2 greater than some multiple of 3. The multiples of 3 are 3, 6, 9, 12, 15, 18, etc., so x could be 5, 8, 11, 14, 17, 20, and so on. Some of these possible values of x are multiples of 5 (for example, 5 and 20), but others (8, 11, etc.) are not. So we cannot definitively answer the question, meaning that (1) is insufficient. Eliminate (A) and (D).

(2) *Insufficient.* Approach statement (2) in the same way. If there is no remainder when x is divided by 4, then x is a multiple of 4, such as 4, 8, 12, 16, 20, and so on. Once again, x might or might not be a multiple of 5, so (2) is also insufficient. Eliminate (B).

Now look at the statements together. We need to consider only those numbers that appear in both of our sets. There are two ways we could have sufficiency: either every number that appears in both sets *is* a multiple of 5 (sufficient-yes), or every number that appears in both sets is *not* a multiple of 5 (sufficient-no). The first two numbers that appear in both sets are 8 and 20. If $x = 8$, x is not a multiple of 5, but if $x = 20$, x is a multiple of 5. We still can't answer the question. Even when taken together, the statements are insufficient.

40. A

Let's use the variables t, m, and b to represent the amounts, in dollars, spent on television, magazine, and billboard advertising respectively. So then $t + m + b = 90$ million. As we evaluate the statements, we will be looking for information that would allow us to solve this equation for the value of t, the amount spent on television advertising.

(1) *Sufficient.* Statement (1) tells us that magazine and billboard advertising were 20 percent less than television advertising. In other words, magazine and billboard advertising were equal to 80 percent of television advertising. Stated as an equation, we have $m + b = 80\%$ of t, or $m + b = 0.80t$. So, we can replace $m + b$ in our original equation with $0.80t$. This gives us $t + 0.80t = 90$ million. We could certainly solve this for t, so statement (1) must be sufficient. We can eliminate (B), (C), and (E).

(2) *Insufficient.* Statement (2) tells us only that $m = 1.50b$. Replacing m in our original equation gives us $t + 1.50b + b = 90$ million. We still have two variables and only one equation, so we can't solve for t. Thus statement (2) is insufficient.

KAPLAN

41. B

This is a yes-no question involving odds and evens. We can apply the odd/even rules, such as odd × odd = odd, or we can Pick Numbers.

(1) *Insufficient.* Statement (1) tells us that $xyz + 1$ is odd. Only an even number plus 1 will yield an odd number. So xyz must be even. We know from the stem that x is even, y is odd, and z is an integer, so for xyz we have an even integer × an odd integer × an integer = an even integer. Since the product already includes one even number (x), the result must be even whether z is odd or even.

Let $x = 2$ and $y = 3$. So $xyz = (2)(3)z = 6z$, which will be even regardless of the value of z, because the product of any even integer and any integer will always be even. If $z = 1$, $6z = 6$, which is even. If $z = 2$, $6z = 12$, which is also even. So we can't determine if z is odd or even. Statement (1) is insufficient; eliminate (A) and (D).

(2) *Sufficient.* In statement (2) we'll keep in mind the same rule that any integer times an even integer is even. We know x is even, so xy and xz are both even. Thus we have even + even + yz = even. An even plus an even will be even, so we can simplify the situation to even + yz = even. So yz must be even, because the sum of two even numbers will be even, but the sum of an even and an odd will be odd.

Now, if yz must be even and we know from the stem that y is odd, then z itself must be even. In other words, we now know that z is NEVER odd, so statement (2) is sufficient. Based on statement (2), the answer to the question is *no*. Choice (B) is correct.

42. E

(1) *Insufficient.* To solve, we'll need to know the dimensions of Dan's room and the rug itself. Statement (1) tells us the total area of Dan's room but nothing about the size of the rug, so it is insufficient. Eliminate (A) and (D).

(2) *Insufficient.* Statement (2) tells us how wide the exposed area is, but without also knowing the length and width of the room or the rug, we cannot calculate the uncovered area. So statement (2) is also insufficient. Eliminate (B).

Statements (1) and (2): Now we know the area of the room and the width of the exposed space, but because there are many different room dimensions that could result in an area of 300 square feet, the statements together are insufficient.

Pick numbers to confirm this. Suppose the room is 30 × 10. Since 24 inches is 2 feet, there will be 2 feet exposed on all sides, so the dimensions of the rug must be $30 - 2 - 2 = 26$ and $10 - 2 - 2 = 6$. The area of the rug is 156 square feet, so the exposed area is $300 - 156 = 144$ square feet.

But the room could also be 20×15 (among other possibilities). In this case, the rug would be 16×11, with an area of 176. The exposed area would be $300 - 176 = 124$ square feet.

Since there is more than one possible value for the exposed area, the statements taken together are insufficient. Choice (E) is correct.

43. D

To find the percent of x that y is, we need to find a value for the fraction $\frac{y}{x}$. Note that we don't have to find the actual values of x and y.

(1) *Sufficient.* Statement (1) can be written as $10x = 15y$. Since we have one equation and two variables, we can't find x and y, but we don't have to. We can solve the equation for the expression $\frac{y}{x}$. First, divide both sides by x to get $10 = \frac{15y}{x}$. Now divide both sides by 15 and we have $\frac{10}{15} = \frac{y}{x}$. There's no need to simplify further; we see that we can get the fraction we need, so we know that statement (1) is sufficient.

(2) *Sufficient.* To evaluate statement (2), let's rewrite the equation $4x^2 = 9y^2$ by $(2x)^2 = (3y)^2$. Since x and y are positive, $2x$ and $3y$ are positive. This gives us $2x = 3y$. Again, we can't solve for x and y, but we can solve for $\frac{x}{y}$. So statement (2) is also sufficient and (D) is correct.

If we solve for $\frac{y}{x}$ in statement (2), we will get $\frac{y}{x} = \frac{2}{3}$, which is consistent with the value for $\frac{y}{x}$ of $\frac{10}{15}$ that we found from statement (1), since $\frac{2}{3} = \frac{10}{15}$.

44. A

The perimeter of the triangle is the sum of the lengths of the sides, or $A + 2B + (A + B)$. To find a value for the perimeter, we need to find values for A and B. To do so, we'll need some equations involving these two variables. The fact that the problem concerns a right triangle is a clue that we should use the Pythagorean theorem to set up an equation involving A and B.

The Pythagorean theorem tells us that for any right triangle, $x^2 + y^2 = z^2$ where x and y are the legs and z is the hypotenuse. So, replacing these variables with the ones from the problem, we have $A^2 + (2B)^2 = (A + B)^2$.

Using FOIL to expand the right side gives us $A^2 + (2B)^2 = A^2 + 2AB + B^2$, or $A^2 + 4B^2 = A^2 + 2AB + B^2$. Subtracting A^2 from both sides yields $4B^2 = 2AB + B^2$, or $3B^2 = 2AB$. Dividing both sides by $2B$ gives us $\frac{3B}{2} = A$.

We now have one linear equation involving A and B. When we evaluate the statements, all we need for sufficiency is one more linear equation with these variables (or the value of either one of the variables). That will be enough to allow us to solve for their values and thus find the perimeter.

(1) *Sufficient.* Statement (1) gives us the value of A, so we could solve for B because $\frac{3B}{2} = A$. Thus we could find values for A and B. Statement (1) is sufficient.

(2) *Insufficient.* Statement (2) is identical to the equation we found using the Pythagorean theorem, so it provides no additional information and is insufficient. Choice (A) is correct.

45. B

We have a yes-no question, so we'll need to know if x is always prime or never prime. When working with primes, keep in mind that 2 is the smallest prime number and the only even prime. Other than that, all we know from the stem is that $x > 0$, so let's evaluate the statements.

(1) *Insufficient.* Can we find any prime values for x such that x^3 has four distinct factors? If $x = 2$, which is prime, then $x^3 = 2^3 = 8$, which has four distinct factors (1, 2, 4, and 8). So, it's *possible* that x is prime. But does it have to be prime? Let's consider other positive numbers with four distinct factors. The smallest such number is 6 (its factors are 1, 2, 3, and 6), so suppose $x^3 = 6$. In this case, $x = \sqrt[3]{6}$, which is not even an integer, much less a prime number. So we've found both prime and non-prime values for x that make (1) true. Therefore, (1) is insufficient to determine whether or not x is prime. Eliminate (A) and (D).

(2) *Sufficient.* In this case, we can solve the equation to find possible values for x. If we subtract 6 from both sides, we get $x^2 - x - 6 = 0$. Factor the left side using reverse FOIL to get $(x - 3)(x + 2) = 0$. So, the equation has one negative root and one positive root, meaning that there are two possible values for x, one negative and one positive. The stem tells us that x must be positive, so there is actually only one possible value of x. Since we could find exactly one value for x, we can answer the question definitively; if we know what x is, we know whether or not it is prime. So statement (2) is sufficient.

46. B

Though the question stem seems straightforward, we can do a lot with it because of the fraction and the inequality. You are asked if $\frac{1}{x} > 1$. For this to be true, x itself must be positive. If x were negative, then $\frac{1}{x}$ would be negative, so $\frac{1}{x}$ could not be greater than 1. Now, if x is positive, we can multiply both sides of $\frac{1}{x} > 1$ by x to get rid of the fraction without worrying about reversing the direction of the inequality sign. Doing this will give us $1 > x$, or $x < 1$. Putting this all together, we know that for $\frac{1}{x} > 1$ to be true, x must be positive and less than 1. In other words, we can restate the question more simply as follows: is $0 < x < 1$? We'll have sufficiency if x is either always or never a positive number less than 1.

(1) *Insufficient.* We can eliminate y by dividing both sides by y, but since we don't know if y is positive or negative, we have to consider both cases. If it is positive, we get $\frac{1}{x} > 1$, but if y is negative, we get $\frac{1}{x} < 1$. So we cannot answer the question definitively, meaning that statement (1) is insufficient. Eliminate (A) and (D).

(2) *Sufficient.* For statement (2), we know from the stem that x is not 0. So x^2 is positive. Dividing both sides of the inequality $x^3 > x^2$ by x^2, we have $x > 1$. So we will never have $0 < x < 1$, meaning that the answer to the question is "no." Statement (2) is sufficient, and (B) is correct.

47. E

To answer the question, we need to know the amount spent by the dealership on all the cars it had in stock at the end of last year.

(1) *Insufficient.* Statement (1) tells us about cars purchased during the year but gives us no information about how many were sold. Thus, we can't determine how many were in stock at the end of the year. Statement (1) is insufficient. Eliminate (A) and (D).

(2) *Insufficient.* Statement (2) tells us only how much money the dealership received from the sale of cars. Since we don't know how much each car sold for, we can't determine the number of cars sold or the number in stock at the end of the year. Thus statement (2) is insufficient, and we can eliminate (B). We could also have determined that this statement is insufficient because it does not give us any information about how many cars were purchased or how much was spent on them.

Combining the statements, there still is no information about the number of cars the dealership had in stock at the end of last year or the amount spent on each of these cars in stock at the end of the year. The statements taken together are insufficient.

48. C

We need to know how many packages will fit inside one shipping box. If we have this number, we can divide the total number of packages (120) by the number per shipping box to find out how many shipping boxes are needed. So as we evaluate the statements, we'll need to know the dimensions and volume of both the packages and the shipping boxes; only with that information will we be able to determine how many packages can fit in one shipping box.

(1) *Insufficient.* Statement (1) gives us the dimensions of each package, from which we could calculate the volume if we multiplied the dimensions together. But without any information about the dimensions of the shipping boxes, statement (1) is insufficient. Eliminate (A) and (D).

(2) *Insufficient.* Statement (2) tells us that the volume of the shipping boxes is one cubic foot. Since the boxes are cubes, their dimensions must be 1 foot by 1 foot by 1 foot. But without any information about the packages, statement (2) is also insufficient. Eliminate (B).

When we combine the statements, we see that we have everything we need. Statement (1) tells us the dimensions and therefore the volume of each package; statement (2) gives us the dimensions and volume of the shipping boxes. This is sufficient to answer the question, so (C) is correct. There is no need to do the actual calculations.

Notice that if we convert the box dimensions to inches, we see that they are $12 \times 12 \times 12$. Thus, each dimension of the shipping boxes is an exact multiple of the corresponding dimension of the packages, $3 \times 4 \times 6$. So we know that the packages will fit precisely into the shipping boxes with no wasted space. And thus the volume of one shipping box divided by the volume of one package will tell us exactly how many packages will fit inside one box. If we did the calculations, we would find that

$$\frac{\text{Box volume}}{\text{Package volume}} = \frac{12 \times 12 \times 12}{3 \times 4 \times 6},$$

which will simplify to $4 \times 3 \times 2 = 24$. Thus, 24 packages will fit in one box, and 120 packages will fit inside $\frac{120}{24} = 5$ boxes.

49. C

The range of a set is the difference between the largest and smallest values in the set. From the stem, we know that the median, or middle value, is 19, but nothing about the largest and smallest values, so let's go on to the statements.

(1) *Insufficient.* Let's first put the known elements of the set in ascending order. Excluding x and y, the set is {11, 15, 18, 28}. Since the median is 19 and there is an even number of terms, the average of the two middle terms must be 19. There are already two numbers less than 18, so if either x or y is less than 18, then 18 becomes the fourth term in the set. If that happens, the median would be the average of 18 and some number less than 18—and so the median could never be 19. Therefore, neither x nor y can be less than 18.

Given that 18 must be the third term in the set, it must also be the case that either x or y (or both) must be 20, in order for the median to be 19. So let's say that $x = 20$; now the set, excluding y, is {11, 15, 18, 20, 28}. But where does y fit in? All we can say is that y must be 20 or more. If y is 20, the range is $28 - 11 = 17$. But y could also be the largest value. If y is 30, the range is $30 - 11 = 19$. We can't determine a single value for the range based on statement (1), so the statement is insufficient.

(2) *Insufficient.* There is no definite relationship between the mean and the median. The set could be {18, 19, 23} but it also could be {17, 19, 24}. Both sets have a median of 19 and a mean of 20, but the range of the first set is $23 - 18 = 5$ and the range of the second set is $24 - 17 = 7$. In fact, we could write many sets that have a median of 19 and a mean of 20, each with a different range. So statement (2) is insufficient.

Statements (1) and (2) together: From statement (1), we know the set has 6 elements and that either x or y must be 20. From (2), we know that the average is 20. For a set of 6 elements with an average of 20, the sum of the numbers must be $6 \times 20 = 120$ (the average formula tells us that the sum of the terms of the set equals the average of the terms in the set times the number of terms in the set).

So, it must be the case that $11 + 15 + 18 + 28 + x + y = 120$, or $x + y = 48$. Since we know that either x or y must be equal to 20, let's say that $x = 20$. So, we have $20 + y = 48$, or $y = 28$. Thus, the set is {11, 15, 18, 20, 28, 28}. The range must be $28 - 17 = 11$, so the statements together are sufficient. (C) is correct.

50. B

We will be able to find the value of $\frac{a}{b}$ if we can find the values of both a and b. Let's divide both sides of the equation $a = 5b + 7c$ by b. Then $\frac{a}{b} = \frac{5b + 7c}{b}$. From the equation $\frac{a}{b} = \frac{5b + 7c}{b}$, we see that we will also be able to find the value of $\frac{a}{b}$ if we can find the values of both b and c. We can rewrite the equation $\frac{a}{b} = \frac{5b + 7c}{b}$. We have $\frac{a}{b} = \frac{5b + 7c}{b}$, $\frac{a}{b} = \frac{5b}{b} + \frac{7c}{b}$, $\frac{a}{b} = 5 + \frac{7c}{b}$, and $\frac{a}{b} = 5 + 7\left(\frac{c}{b}\right)$. From the equation $\frac{a}{b} = 5 + 7\left(\frac{c}{b}\right)$, we see that we will also be able to find the value of $\frac{a}{b}$ if we can find the value of $\frac{c}{b}$. Now let's look at the statements.

Statement (1) gives us the equation $2b + 5c = 50$. We cannot solve the two equations $a = 5b + 7c$ and $2b + 5c = 50$ with three variables for the values of any of a, b, and c. Furthermore, we cannot solve these two equations for the value of $\frac{a}{b}$ and we cannot solve these two equations for the value of $\frac{c}{b}$. Statement (1) is insufficient. We can eliminate choices (A) and (D). We can also show that statement (1) is insufficient by Picking Numbers. The values $b = 10$ and $c = 6$ satisfy the equation $2b + 5c = 50$ of statement (1). From the equation $a = 5b + 7c$ of the question stem, we find that when $b = 10$ and $c = 6$, $a = 92$. In this case, $\frac{a}{b} = \frac{92}{10} = \frac{46}{5}$. The values $b = 20$ and $c = 2$ also satisfy the equation $2b + 5c = 50$ of statement (1). From the equation $a = 5b + 7c$ of the question stem, we find that when $b = 20$ and $c = 2$, $a = 114$. In this case, $\frac{a}{b} = \frac{114}{20} = \frac{57}{10}$. So different values for $\frac{a}{b}$ are possible. Again, statement (1) is insufficient.

Statement (2) says that $3b - 5c = 0$. Adding $5c$ to both sides of this equation, we have $3b = 5c$. Dividing both sides of this equation by 5, we have $\frac{3b}{5} = c$. Dividing both sides of this equation by b, we have $\frac{3}{5} = \frac{c}{b}$. Thus, $\frac{c}{b} = \frac{3}{5}$. We have the value of $\frac{c}{b}$. We can find the value of $\frac{a}{b}$. It is not necessary to actually find the value of $\frac{a}{b}$ by substituting $\frac{3}{5}$ for $\frac{c}{b}$ in the equation $\frac{a}{b} = 5 + 7\left(\frac{c}{b}\right)$. Knowing that we could is enough. Statement (2) is sufficient. Choice (B) is correct.

KAPLAN

Chapter 10: **Word Problems**

- Word Problems Translation Table
- The 3 Basic Principles of Word Problems
- Kaplan's 4-Step Method for Word Problems in Problem Solving
- Kaplan's 3-Step Method for Word Problems in Data Sufficiency

Word problems appear throughout the Quantitative section. Because word problems can be particularly tricky, we're going to discuss them separately in this section. We'll begin by looking at word problems in Problem Solving format.

The primary skill used in word problems is to take a tedious, little story and conceptualize it mathematically. If you have trouble with word problems, it's probably because you're having trouble with this technique. Don't get frustrated. Just keep practicing until you can see a word problem and visualize the math as you are reading. That is, if you get a problem that tells you, "George has ten dollars less than twice as much as Bill," you should be thinking, "Oh, I'll use G for how much George has, and B for how much Bill has. *Twice as much as Bill* means $2B$, and *ten dollars less* means -10, so $G = 2B - 10$." Once you have mastered this skill, you will have mastered the most difficult part of GMAT word problems.

Word problems are ultimately an exercise in translation. The actual math in GMAT word problems tends to be fairly easy—it's the translation that's often the hard part. All of us, at some time or other, come across a word problem that makes us scratch our head and ask, "What are these people talking about?!" The word problems translation table on the next page should help.

WORD PROBLEMS TRANSLATION TABLE

English	Math
Equals, is, was, will be, has, costs, adds up to, the same as, as much as	$=$
Times, of, multiplied by, product of, twice, double, by	$\times$
Divided by, per, out of, each, ratio	$\div$
Plus, added to, and, sum, combined	$+$
Minus, subtracted from, smaller than, less than, fewer, decreased by, difference between	$-$
A number, how much, how many, what	x, n, etcetera

THE 3 BASIC PRINCIPLES OF WORD PROBLEMS

1. Before plunging into word problems, read through the entire question and the answer choices to gain a general understanding of the situation.

Some people follow this principle instinctively. If you are such a person, great! If you aren't, you need to practice until it becomes a reflex. This step shouldn't take more than 10 to 15 seconds.

2. Always keep track of exactly what you're after.

Locate the specific question itself: Exactly what is it asking? To solve word problems efficiently, it helps to make sure you know exactly what the question is asking.

3. Learn to recognize the types of problems that you find easy and those that you find difficult.

You should ask yourself whether the question is one that you normally do well on. If this is the type of question you typically ace and if you think you will be able to solve it quickly, go ahead and tackle it. If you think the question looks complicated or you have less confidence solving this particular type of question and if it isn't one of the first few questions, eliminate answer choices and guess.

KAPLAN'S 4-STEP METHOD FOR WORD PROBLEMS IN PROBLEM SOLVING

Step 1: Look for the best approach to the question—and apply it.

In most cases the best approach to use in solving word problems is to translate the prose into a mathematical equation. But sometimes you can solve the problem by using an alternative method, such as picking numbers and backsolving.

Step 2: Reread the question, figuring out what you're given and what you need to know.

Before trying to solve the problem, be sure that you know exactly what information the problem gives you and what you need to figure out yourself.

Step 3: Translate the problem from English to an equation.

Your ability to translate word problems from prose to math is the single most important skill that you need to develop to master this problem type. For geometry word problems, you'll need to translate from English to a diagram.

Step 4: If you're stuck translating, or if you just don't understand the problem, consider using an alternative method.

Sometimes translating is too complicated, or the problem doesn't click for you. You can use such alternative methods as picking numbers or backsolving.

Go through this fairly typical word problem about age, referring to the Word Problem Translation Table if you need to. Then compare how you translated the word problem with how Kaplan translated it.

> Jacob is now 12 years younger than Michael. If in 9 years Michael will be twice as old as Jacob, how old will Jacob be in 4 years?
>
> ⬯ 3
> ⬯ 7
> ⬯ 15
> ⬯ 21
> ⬯ 25

KAPLAN

Here's Kaplan's solution:

Jacob's age	is now	Michael's age	(but) 12 years younger
J	$=$	M	-12

In this case, we switched the order of the sentence as we translated it from English to math. "12 years younger than Michael" became "Michael's age (but) 12 years younger."

Sometimes the order of the terms in English will differ slightly from the order in math. If you get confused, pick some sample values: If Michael is 15 years old, then Jacob is 12 years younger, or 3. Therefore, $J = M - 12$.

To continue, here's the rest of the solution.

Michael	in 9 years	will be	twice as old as Jacob
M	$+9$	$=$	$2(J + 9)$

So we know that: $J = M - 12$ and $M + 9 = 2(J + 9)$. The question asks for $J + 4$. Solve for J by substituting.

$$J = M - 12$$
$$J + 12 = M$$

$$M + 9 = 2(J + 9)$$
$$(J + 12) + 9 = 2J + 18$$
$$J + 21 = 2J + 18$$
$$J + 3 = 2J$$
$$3 = J$$
$$7 = J + 4$$

Remember that we're looking for $J + 4$, not J, so (B) is correct.

Another way to solve this problem is by combining the equations. When you have two equations, you can add or subtract them from one another just as though they were regular numbers. You just have to set it up right, with like variables directly above one another.

$$M + 9 = 2J + 18$$
$$- (M - 12 = J)$$
$$\overline{21 = J + 18}$$
$$3 = J$$
$$7 = J + 4$$

So that's how to translate word problems into math. We said before that we'd look at how Kaplan's math strategies can be applied to word problems. The two most useful are Picking Numbers and Backsolving. Let's look at them now and later turn to detailed attacks on two of the most annoying types of GMAT word problems.

Picking Numbers

There are two times to pick numbers. First, when the problem is made easier by trying out possibilities rather than by hassling with the algebra involved. Second, when you simply don't understand the algebra and cannot solve the problem. What you do in either case is pick a few simple numbers—keeping them small, if possible, so the arithmetic will be simple—and do to them what has been described in the word problem.

KAPLAN EXCLUSIVE

Tips for Picking Numbers: For percents problems, use 100. For fractions problems, use the least common denominator.

Here are a few guidelines for when to plug in numbers and what numbers you should try:

- In problems involving **percents**, a good number to start with is often 100, because it is so easy to find a percent of 100.

- In problems with two or more **fractions**, try using the least common denominator of the fractions involved.

- Picking numbers is almost always the fastest way to do problems about **remainders.**

- In algebra, in which the problem and its answer choices are all expressed in terms of **variables** such as x or y, you can avoid algebra by simply making up values for x and y. When you plug in numbers for the variables and do the arithmetic involved, you will get another number as a result. Take the numbers you used for x and y and plug them into the variables in the answer choices—assuming only one choice results in the same number as in the problem, that choice is the answer. (Avoid using 0 or 1, because they have special properties. Often, when you use 0 or 1, more than one answer choice will work, and then you have to try plugging in another number to decide between the remaining choices.)

Let's take a look at Picking Numbers in action.

> The value of a certain antique car increased by 30 percent from 1986 to 1990 and then decreased by 20 percent from 1990 to 1994. The car's value in 1994 was what percent of its value in 1986?
>
> ○ 90%
>
> ○ 100%
>
> ○ 104%
>
> ○ 110%
>
> ○ 124%

Let's say the car was originally worth $100: $100 in 1986. It increases by 30% of $100, or $30, which means it was worth $130 in 1990. Then it decreases 20%: $\frac{1}{5} \times 130 = 26$. So it decreased by $26. Therefore it was worth $104 in 1994. The car was worth $104, which is 104% of $100. The answer, therefore, is (C).

Try each of the next two word problems on your own, using the strategy of picking numbers. Feel free to refer back to the bullet point guidelines for picking numbers on the previous page. After you've worked through each question, consult the Kaplan solution.

> At an international dinner $\frac{1}{5}$ of the people attending were from South America. If the number of North Americans at the dinner was $\frac{2}{3}$ greater than the number of South Americans, what fraction of people at the dinner were from neither South America nor North America?
>
> ○ $\frac{1}{5}$
>
> ○ $\frac{2}{5}$
>
> ○ $\frac{7}{15}$
>
> ○ $\frac{8}{15}$
>
> ○ $\frac{2}{3}$

You should notice immediately that the problem contains two fractions: $\frac{1}{5}$ and $\frac{2}{3}$. The least common denominator is 15, so let's say the total number of people at the dinner was 15. That means we have 3 South Americans in the room. We also have North Americans numbering two-thirds more than that, or $3 + \frac{2}{3}(3)$, which is 5. So there were 8 people from South America or North America, which means 7 people were not from either place. So $\frac{7}{15}$ of the people in the room were from neither South America nor North America. The correct answer, therefore, is (C).

Here's another Picking Numbers example.

> If the price of item X increased by 20%, and then by a further 20%, what percent of the original price is the increase in price?
>
> ⬭ 24%
>
> ⬭ 40%
>
> ⬭ 44%
>
> ⬭ $66\frac{2}{3}$%
>
> ⬭ 140%

Let's say the price was originally $100. It increases by 20% of $100 (which is $20), so now the price is $120. The price then increases by 20% of $120 $\left(\frac{1}{5} \times \$120 = \$24\right)$, which means an increase of $24. So the price is now $144, or 44% more than its original price of $100. The correct answer, therefore, is (C).

Backsolving

You will remember that in backsolving, you plug in the answer choices and see which one works. This approach might seem time-consuming, but you already know that you can make it more efficient (the choices are almost always in ascending or descending order). Assume they're in ascending (increasing) order. Start with choice (B). If that's too small, try (D). If (D) is too large, we know it must be (C).

It takes a while to get used to backsolving, but with practice it can be nearly as fast as solving the problem the traditional way. Follow along as we backsolve through this word problem:

> An insurance company provides coverage for a certain dental procedure according to the following rules: the policy pays 80% of the first $1,200 of cost, and 50% of the cost above $1,200. If a patient had to pay $490 of the cost for this procedure himself, how much did the procedure cost?
>
> ◯ $1,200
> ◯ $1,300
> ◯ $1,500
> ◯ $1,600
> ◯ $1,700

Because the policy pays 80% of the first $1,200 of cost, the patient must pay 20% of $1,200. One-fifth of $1,200 is $240.

Let's try (B). If the procedure cost $1,300, then the patient pays: $240 + 50% of $100; $240 + $50 = $290, which is too small.

We need a larger number, so try (D). If the procedure cost $1,600, then the patient pays: $240 plus 50% of $400, which is $240 + $200, totalling $440—too small. The answer must be (E).

Rate Problems

Some word problems deal with rates. Don't let them psych you out because they aren't really that difficult. They typically spell out some kind of rate early in the problem, like the following example. Follow along as we show you two ways to solve this typical rate problem.

If José does GMAT word problems at a constant rate of 2 problems every 5 minutes, how many seconds will it take him to do N problems?

- $\frac{2}{5}N$

- $2N$

- $\frac{5}{2}N$

- $24N$

- $150N$

There are two common ways of doing rate problems: algebraically and by plugging in numbers. Let's try both for the problem above.

Algebraic Solution

Let's call the number of seconds that we've been asked to find T.

$$\frac{2}{5(60)} = \frac{N}{T}$$

Now we cross multiply and solve for T.

$2T = 300N$

$T = 150N$

The answer is (E).

Picking Numbers Solution

Let's say that $N = 2$. That means José does exactly 2 problems every 5 minutes, or 300 seconds (5 × 60 seconds = 300 seconds). Now look for the answer choices that yield 300 when N = 2. The only one that does is (E), so that must be the answer.

By the way, here's a tip while we're on the topic of rates: It'll help if you know the Distance formula, $D = R \times T$, as it usually shows up once or twice on the test. It just means that the distance you traveled equals the rate you were going at multiplied by the time it took you to get there. For instance, if you travel for 2 hours at 30 miles per hour, then you travel 2 × 30, or 60 miles.

KAPLAN

Work Problems

Word problems involving work occasionally show up on the GMAT. They will be easy if you use this formula:

> The reciprocal of the time it takes everyone working together = the sum of the reciprocals of the times it would take each working individually. (The reciprocal of A is $\frac{1}{A}$.)

Now let's look at a problem and use the formula.

> Working together, John, David, and Roger require $2\frac{1}{4}$ hours to complete a certain task, if each of them works at his respective constant rate. If John alone can complete the task in $4\frac{1}{2}$ hours, and David alone can complete the task in 9 hours, how many hours would it take Roger to complete the task, working alone?
>
> ⬭ $2\frac{1}{3}$
>
> ⬭ $4\frac{1}{2}$
>
> ⬭ $6\frac{3}{4}$
>
> ⬭ 9
>
> ⬭ 12

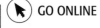 **GO ONLINE**

Use your online study sheet to review math facts and formulas.

Here's the solution, employing the work equation.

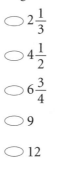

$$\frac{1}{T} = \frac{1}{J} + \frac{1}{D} + \frac{1}{R}$$

$$\frac{1}{2.25} = \frac{1}{4.5} + \frac{1}{9} + \frac{1}{R}$$

$$\frac{4}{9} = \frac{2}{9} + \frac{1}{9} + \frac{1}{R}$$

$$\frac{1}{9} = \frac{1}{R}$$

$$R = 9$$

An alternative approach to this kind of problem that some find intuitive and quick is to break down the work on an hour-by-hour basis.

Take David first. By himself, he could do the entire task in 9 hours. Therefore, during every *single* hour that the guys work together, David will be doing $\frac{1}{9}$ of the task ($\frac{1}{9}$ is just the reciprocal of 9). In the second hour he'll do another $\frac{1}{9}$. And in that extra $\frac{1}{4}$ hour, he'll do $\frac{1}{4}$ $\times \frac{1}{9}$ or $\frac{1}{36}$ of the task. Add them up: David will be doing $\frac{1}{9} + \frac{1}{9} + \frac{1}{36} = \frac{1}{4}$ of the entire task during the period in question.

How about John? He's much faster than David. Working alone, he could do the entire task in $4\frac{1}{2}$ (or $\frac{9}{2}$) hours. So during each hour he works, he'll do the reciprocal of $\frac{9}{2}$, or $\frac{2}{9}$ of the task. Multiply that $\frac{2}{9}$ of a task per hour by the $2\frac{1}{4}$ hours the guys work, and you see that John himself will account for $\frac{2}{9} \times \frac{9}{4}$, or $\frac{1}{2}$ the task. With David and John accounting for $\frac{1}{4}$ and $\frac{1}{2}$ of the task respectively, that leaves exactly $\frac{1}{4}$ of the task to be performed by Roger. You can either see that this means that Roger and David work at the same rate—so it'll take Roger 9 hours, too—or just divide $2\frac{1}{4}$ hours by $\frac{1}{4}$ task to get 9 hours per task, choice (D).

Note that even where backsolving helps, it does not absolve you of thoroughly understanding the question. You must understand what's being asked before you can apply backsolving.

KAPLAN'S 3-STEP METHOD FOR WORD PROBLEMS IN DATA SUFFICIENCY

Data Sufficiency word problems are a little different from other types of word problems. They often require very little calculation, and if you attack them without thinking first, you will nearly always waste time and end up crunching numbers.

If a Data Sufficiency word problem is based on some kind of formula, such as the distance formula ($D = RT$) or the area of a circle, ask yourself what kind of information would give you the area of a circle. Then, if statement (1) tells you the circle's circumference, don't calculate! It is sufficient to know that you could have calculated. Your motto should be, "Think—don't crunch!"

Here's Kaplan's method for approaching these problems.

Step 1: Quickly skim the question stem.

Determine what you're looking for and what kind of information would be sufficient to find it. Often that information will be the missing variable in a common formula, such as the distance formula or the average formula.

Step 2: If stuck, try translating the question stem and the statements into math.

If a statement clearly isn't sufficient, though, don't waste time trying to translate it. Instead move on.

Step 3: If and when each statement is insufficient by itself and you need to consider the statements together, think of the problem as one long word problem and translate it as one unit.

You should keep in mind what kind of information is needed to answer the question. Do only as much work as you need in order to determine sufficiency and remember to ignore the other statement!

Let's put these strategies into practice. Try the two problems below. Try to conceptualize what you need, without actually solving for it. Keep the relevant formulas in mind and ask yourself, "What do I need?" and "What kind of statement would give it to me?"

If there are 32 guests at a party, what is the average (arithmetic mean) age of the guests?

(1) The sum of the ages of the guests is 1,536 years.

(2) The youngest guest, Tracy, is 24 years old and the oldest guest, Pat, is 68 years old.

○ Statement (1) by itself is sufficient to answer the question, but statement (2) by itself is not.

○ Statement (2) by itself is sufficient to answer the question, but statement (1) by itself is not.

○ Statements (1) and (2) taken together are sufficient to answer the question, even though neither statement by itself is sufficient.

○ Either statement by itself is sufficient to answer the question.

○ Statements (1) and (2) taken together are not sufficient to answer the question, requiring more data pertaining to the problem.

Remember the average formula:

$$Average = \frac{Sum\ of\ the\ terms}{Number\ of\ terms} = \frac{Sum}{32}$$

So we just need the sum to calculate the average. Does either of the statements give us the sum? Yes, Statement (1) does. Statement (2) does not give us the sum; there's no way to figure it out from (2) because the guests in between can be of all sorts of ages. So the answer is (A).

Here's a second example.

> A rectangle has length y feet and width z feet. What is its area in square feet?
>
> (1) z is the reciprocal of y.
>
> (2) The fence around the perimeter of the rectangle is 720 feet.
>
> ◯ Statement (1) by itself is sufficient to answer the question, but statement (2) by itself is not.
>
> ◯ Statement (2) by itself is sufficient to answer the question, but statement (1) by itself is not.
>
> ◯ Statements (1) and (2) taken together are sufficient to answer the question, even though neither statement by itself is sufficient.
>
> ◯ Either statement by itself is sufficient to answer the question.
>
> ◯ Statements (1) and (2) taken together are not sufficient to answer the question, requiring more data pertaining to the problem.

First recall the formula for the area of a rectangle:

Area = length × width

Here you might want to draw a picture of a rectangle with the length and width labeled y and z respectively.

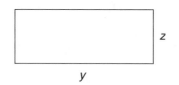

This would be a hard problem, but if you focus on what you need to know, you're less likely to be fooled. We need the area of this rectangle, which is length × width or, in this case, $y \times z$. We need a number. Would statement (1) give us a number? It's not clear on a first glance, so let's test it:

$z = \dfrac{1}{y}$, so $y \times z = y \times \dfrac{1}{y} = 1$. The area must be 1, and Statement (1) is sufficient.

How about Statement (2)? It gives us the perimeter. But this doesn't give us $y \times z$. It tells us that $2(y + z) = 720$, or $y + z = 360$. But this doesn't tell us the individual values of y and z, or the product of y and z, so this statement is insufficient. (A) is correct.

Remember this mathematical principle: Whatever number of different variables you need to solve for, you will need **that same number of different equations** relating at least one of those variables.

There are usually a few tough Data Sufficiency problems that can be made easy by applying this principle and the Kaplan Method for Data Sufficiency Word Problems. If you get such a problem, ask yourself, "How many variables do I need to solve for? How many equations do I have?"

The following is a typical question involving simultaneous equations.

> Jessica has a limited investment portfolio of stocks and bonds. If she sells half her stocks, how many stocks and bonds will she be left with?
>
> (1) If she were to buy six more stocks, she would have twice as many stocks as bonds.
>
> (2) If she were to triple the number of her bonds, she would have three less than twice the number of her stocks.
>
> ⬯ Statement (1) by itself is sufficient to answer the question, but statement (2) by itself is not.
>
> ⬯ Statement (2) by itself is sufficient to answer the question, but statement (1) by itself is not.
>
> ⬯ Statements (1) and (2) taken together are sufficient to answer the question, even though neither statement by itself is sufficient.
>
> ⬯ Either statement by itself is sufficient to answer the question.
>
> ⬯ Statements (1) and (2) taken together are not sufficient to answer the question, requiring more data pertaining to the problem.

We get one equation in Statement (1) and another equation in Statement (2). You need both equations to answer the question, so you need both statements. The answer is (C). Thus, you solve a difficult problem in 10 seconds, and the time you save can help you get another question right.

Try to apply these techniques as best you can on the Practice Test. Use the Math Reference in the next chapter to brush up on any basic concepts that are troubling you.

SUMMARY

The 3 Basic Principles of Word Problems are:

1. Before plunging into word problems, read through the entire question and the answer choices to gain a general understanding of the situation.

2. Always keep track of exactly what you're after.

3. Learn to recognize the types of problems that you find easy and those that you find difficult.

Kaplan's 4-Step Method for Word Problems in Problem Solving is:

Step 1: Look for the best approach to the question—and apply it.

Step 2: Reread the question, figuring out what you're given and what you need to know.

Step 3: Translate the problem from English to an equation.

Step 4: If you're stuck translating, or if you just don't understand the problem, consider using an alternative method.

Kaplan's 3-Step Method for Word Problems in Data Sufficiency is:

Step 1: Quickly skim the question stem.

Step 2: If stuck, try translating the question stem and the statements into math.

Step 3: If and when each statement is insufficient by itself and you need to consider the statements together, think of the problem as one long word problem and translate it as one unit.

Chapter 11: **Analytical Writing Assessment (AWA) Strategies and Practice**

- **Essay Format and Structure**
- **The 4 Basic Principles of Analytical Writing**
- **How the AWA Is Scored**
- **Kaplan's 5-Step Method for Analytical Writing**
- **Breakdown: Analysis of an Issue**
- **Breakdown: Analysis of an Argument**

The AWA is the first task on the GMAT. After you are situated at your computer workstation, you will be presented with the two essays assignments: an *Issue* essay and an *Argument* essay. You will have 30 minutes to complete each one.

For both essays, you will have to analyze a given topic and then type your essay into a simple word processing program. It allows you to do only basic functions:

- Insert text
- Delete text
- Cut and paste
- Undo the previous action
- Scroll up and down on the screen

Spelling check and grammar check functions are not available in the program, so you will have to check those things carefully yourself.

KAPLAN EXCLUSIVE

A slow typing speed could lower your score. If you're not comfortable typing an essay that's several paragraphs long, take the time to practice before Test Day.

KAPLAN

Strategically, assuming your typing skills are adequate, you don't have to do much of anything differently on the CAT than you would when writing an essay on computer. First, write your outline on noteboard. Doing this on paper will help you to visually grasp the development and scope you'll need for the essay. Then, spend 5 minutes developing your ideas. Once the development has been done, jump back on the computer and spend 20 minutes on the actual composition. The last 5 minutes should be spent on proofreading .

The two essays can appear in either order on your exam. Since the two require different specific tasks, make sure you look at the directions.

ESSAY FORMAT AND STRUCTURE

At the start of the AWA, you'll be given a brief tutorial on how to use the word processor. If you are concerned that you do not type on the computer very fast, you should spend some time practicing typing with full-page text documents between now and Test Day.

Analysis of an Issue Essay

For the Issue essay, you will be given a statement that expresses an opinion about something. Your task is to communicate your own view on the issue. Whether you agree or disagree with the opinion on the screen is irrelevant—what matters is how well you support your view with relevant examples and statements. For instance:

> "Everyone in this country over the age of 12 should be required to perform a minimum amount of public service. Such a required contribution would not only help society as a whole, it would also add to the individual's character."
>
> Discuss the extent to which you agree or disagree with the opinion stated above. Support your views with reasons and/or examples from your own experience, observations, or reading.

Whether you agree that all citizens—even youth—should be required to perform public service does not matter here. What matters is, How convincing an argument can you make for either side? If you can come up with more support and evidence to argue *against* a public service requirement, then that's the side you should choose.

Analysis of an Argument Essay

The other assignment is the "Argument" essay. Here, you'll have to assess the logic of a certain argument. It doesn't matter whether you truly agree or disagree with what you see on the screen—it's just how convincing you make your argument. For instance:

> The following appeared in a memo from the CEO of Hula Burger, a chain of hamburger restaurants.
>
> "Officials in the film industry report that over 60% of the films released last year targeted an age 8–12 audience. Moreover, sales data indicate that, nationally, hamburgers are the favorite food among this age group. Since a branch store of Whiz Vid Video Store opened in town last year, hamburger sales at our restaurant next door have been higher than at any other restaurant in our chain. Because the rental of movies seems to stimulate hamburger sales, the best way to increase our profits is to open new Hula Burger restaurants right nearby every Whiz Vid Store."
>
> Discuss how well reasoned you find this argument. In your discussion be sure to analyze the line of reasoning and the use of evidence in the argument. For example, you may need to consider what questionable assumptions underlie the thinking and what alternative explanations or counterexamples might weaken the conclusion. You can also discuss what sort of evidence would strengthen or refute the argument, what changes in the argument would make it more logically sound, and what, if anything, would help you better evaluate its conclusion.

In your opinion, is this a solid argument? Or does it have holes? Whatever you decide, you will need to support your opinion with specific explanations and examples. You cannot get away with just "filler" or "fluff" here—you will need to be concrete.

THE 4 BASIC PRINCIPLES OF ANALYTICAL WRITING

GMAT writing is a two-stage process: First you decide what you want to say about a topic, and then you figure out how to say it. If your writing style isn't clear, your ideas won't come across, no matter how brilliant they are.

 READ MORE

Turn to the Editorials or Op–Ed page of your local newspaper. There should be some good examples of clear, concise language.

Good GMAT English is not only grammatically correct; it is also clear and concise. The following principles will help you to express your ideas clearly and effectively.

1. Your control of language is important.

Writing that is grammatical, concise, direct, and persuasive displays the "superior control of language" (as the test makers term it) that earns top GMAT Analytical Writing scores. To achieve effective GMAT style in your essays, you should pay attention to the following points.

Grammar

Your writing must follow the same general rules of standard written English that are tested by Sentence Correction questions. If you're not confident of your mastery of grammar, review the Sentence Correction section.

Diction

Diction means word choice. Do you use the words *affect* and *effect* correctly? What about *its* and *it's*, *there* and *their*, *precede* and *proceed*, *principal* and *principle*, and *whose* and *who's*?

Syntax

Syntax refers to sentence structure. Do you construct your sentences so that your ideas are clear and understandable? Do you vary your sentence structure, sometimes using simple sentences and other times using sentences with clauses and phrases?

2. Keep things simple.

Perhaps the single most important thing to bear in mind when writing a GMAT essay is to keep everything simple. This rule applies to word choice, sentence structure, and organization. If you obsess about how to spell an unusual word, you can lose your flow of thought. The more complicated your sentences are, the more likely they'll be plagued by errors. The more complex your organization gets, the more likely your argument will get bogged down in convoluted sentences that obscure your point.

Keep in mind that simple does not mean *simplistic*. A clear, straightforward approach can still be sophisticated and convey perceptive insights.

3. Minor grammatical flaws won't harm your score.

Many test takers mistakenly believe they'll lose points over a few mechanical errors. That's not the case. The GMAT essays asked of you should be *final first drafts*. This means that a couple of misplaced commas, misspellings, or other minor glitches aren't going to heavily affect your score. Occasional mistakes of this type are acceptable. In fact, according to GMAC, a top-scoring essay may well have a few minor grammatical flaws.

Provided you don't make grammatical or spelling mistakes consistently, the essay graders won't be looking to deduct points for minor errors. But if your essays are littered with misspellings and grammar mistakes, the graders may conclude that you have a serious communication problem.

So be concise, forceful, and correct. An effective essay wastes no words, makes its point in a clear, direct way, and conforms to the generally accepted rules of grammar and form.

4. Keep sight of your goal.

Remember, your goal isn't to become a prize-winning stylist. It's to write two solid essays that will convince B-school admissions officers you can write well enough to clearly communicate your ideas to a reader—or business associate. GMAT essay graders don't expect rhetorical flourishes, but they do expect effective expression.

♟ KAPLAN STRATEGY ——————————————————————

The 4 Basic Principles of Analytical Writing are:

1. Your control of language is important.

2. Keep things simple.

3. Minor grammatical flaws won't harm your score.

4. Keep sight of your goal.

HOW THE AWA IS SCORED

Your essays will be graded on a scale from 0 to 6 (highest). You'll get one score, which will be an average of the scores that you receive for each of the two essays. Your essay will be graded by a human grader as well as a computerized essay grader (the "e-rater"). If the human and the e-rater agree on a score, that's the grade your essay will receive. If they disagree by more than one point, a second human will grade the essay to resolve any differences.

The e-rater was designed to make the same judgments that a good human grader would make. In fact, part of GMAC's argument for the validity of the e-rater is the fact that in the vast majority of cases the e-rater gives the same grade a human would give. Even so, there are steps you can take to improve your chances of getting a great score from the e-rater. The computer is not a great judge of creativity or humor, but it does know what it likes. We'll have more to say on this topic later in this chapter, but here are some tips to get started with:

- Before you begin to write, outline your essay. Good organization always counted, and now it's more important than ever.

- Since your essay will be compared against other essays, think about the points that the best essays will make.

- The length of your essay is not a factor; the computer does not count the number of words in your response.

- Use transitional phrases like *first, therefore, since,* and *for example* so that the computer can recognize structured arguments.

- Avoid spelling and grammar errors. Though the e-rater doesn't grade spelling per se, it could give you a lower score if it can't understand you or thinks you used the wrong words.

KAPLAN'S 5-STEP METHOD FOR ANALYTICAL WRITING

Here's the deal: You have a limited amount of time to show the business school admissions people that you can think logically and express yourself in clearly written English. They don't care how many syllables you can cram into a sentence or how fancy your phrases are. They care that you're making sense. Whatever you do, don't hide beneath a lot of hefty words and abstractions. Make sure that everything you say is clearly written and relevant to the topic. Get in there, state your main points, back them up, and get out.

Step 1: Digest the Issue/Argument.

- Read it through to get a sense of the scope of the matter.

- Note any terms that are ambiguous and need defining.

- Frame the issue/argument.

Step 2: Select the Points You Will Make.

- In the "Analysis of Issue" essay, think of the arguments for both sides and make a decision as to which side you will support or the exact extent to which you agree with the stated position.

- In the "Analysis of Argument" essay, identify all the important gaps between the evidence and the conclusion. Think of remedies for the problems you discover.

Step 3: Organize.

- Outline your essay.

- Lead with your best arguments.

- Think about how the essay as a whole will flow.

Step 4: Write/Type.

- Be direct.

- Use paragraph breaks to make your essay easier to read.

- Make transitions, link related ideas; it will help your writing flow.

- Finish strongly.

Step 5: Proofread.

- Save enough time to read through the entire essay.

- Have a sense of the errors you are liable to make.

As explained before, the two essay types you'll write—Issue and the Argument—require generally similar tasks. You must analyze a subject, take an informed position, and explain that position in writing. The two essay types, however, require different specific tasks.

BREAKDOWN: ANALYSIS OF AN ISSUE

The stimulus and question stem of an Analysis of an Issue topic will look something like this:

> Many assert that individuals allowed to work flexible schedules at home will be both more productive and happier than colleagues working under more traditional arrangements. But others assert that the close supervision of an office workplace is necessary to ensure productivity and quality control and to maintain morale.
>
> Which argument do you find more compelling, the case for flexible work conditions or the opposing viewpoint? Explain your position using relevant reasons or examples drawn from your own experience, observations, or reading.

The Stimulus

In this example, the stimulus consists of a few sentences that discuss two points of view on a general issue. Sometimes the stimulus is a single sentence. You don't need prior knowledge of any specific subject matter to discuss the issue.

The first sentence or two introduces the general issue and expresses one point of view. Sometimes, a key word—here, it's the word but—will signal the introduction of the contrasting point of view. In other cases, the transition might not be so obvious. The last part of this stimulus presents the contrary view of the issue.

The Question Stem

The stem asks you which of the two viewpoints you find more convincing and instructs you to explain your position using reasons or examples. Though the specific wording will vary for each question, the basic task will be essentially the same.

Exactly what are you being asked to do here?

> Which argument do you find more compelling, the case for flexible work conditions or the opposing viewpoint?

Translation: There are two conflicting viewpoints here. Take one side or the other.

> Explain your position using relevant reasons or examples drawn from your own experience, observations, or reading.

Translation: Argue your position, using specific examples. Support your points with evidence.

Not all issue topics will look exactly like our example. Some may present only a sentence in which the two conflicting viewpoints are not specified. For instance:

> Allowing individuals to work flexible schedules is an idea that makes sense.

Notice how this is just a reworking of our original topic. Here, the two viewpoints are implicit, so your task includes a little digging: What are the two viewpoints? From here, your basic task is the same. Explain what the issue is and make a case for one opinion on that issue.

Now let's use the 5-Step Method on the Analysis of an *Issue* topic we saw before:

> Many assert that individuals allowed to work flexible schedules at home will be both more productive and happier than colleagues working under more traditional arrangements. Others assert that the close supervision of an office workplace is necessary to ensure productivity and quality control and to maintain morale.
>
> Which argument do you find more compelling, the case for flexible work conditions or the opposing viewpoint? Explain your position using relevant reasons or examples drawn from your own experience, observations, or reading.

1. Digest the issue.

It's simple enough. Some people think flexible schedules make for happier and more productive workers. Other people think a traditional office workplace makes for happier and more productive workers. Your job, as stated in the second paragraph, is to pick one of the sides and defend it.

2. Select the points you will make.

So which side do you take? Remember, this isn't about showing the admissions people what your politics are—it's about showing you can formulate an argument and write it down. Think through the pros and cons of each side, and choose the side for which you have *more relevant things to say*. For this topic, that process might go something like this:

Arguments for flexible schedules:	Arguments for office workplace:
• People feel more valued, work better	• People less likely to waste time if boss is there
• Decreases absence due to child care emergencies, etc.	• People need to feel part of team to be happy
• People happier if they don't have to commute	• More supervision and quality control possible

Again, it doesn't matter which side you take.

Suppose that in this case, you decide to argue in favor of traditional office workplaces. You are being asked why traditional schedules lead to greater happiness and productivity. Happiness and productivity are the ends you're arguing toward, so don't list them as supporting arguments.

3. Organize your argument.

You've already begun to think out your arguments—that's why you picked the side you did in the first place. Now's the time to write them all out, including ones that weaken the opposing side.

Traditional office workplaces lead to greater happiness and productivity because:

- People work harder under supervision (more productive)
- People need co-workers, team spirit (happier)
- People who work at home feel isolated (weakens opposing argument)
- Healthier to separate work and home life (happier, weakens opposing argument)
- Other staff members present for problem solving (more productive)
- Greater technical resources in office environment (more productive)

4. Compose your essay.

Remember, open up with a general statement and then assert your position. From there, get down your main points. Your essay for this assignment might look like this:

Many companies face the decision to either allow employees flexible work schedules or to maintain traditional work environments. A close examination of the issue reveals that workers are happier and more productive in a traditional office environment.

A main reason that people are happier in traditional offices is the team spirit and personal satisfaction that come from working in a group. People who spend their workday at home are more likely to feel isolated from the company and divorced from the final product. Additionally, people who work in an office environment are more likely to form close friendships with co-workers than those who are rarely in the office, an occurrence that fosters greater happiness and stability within the company.

The bottom line for businesses is, of course, productivity, and there are several reasons why the traditional workplace promotes greater productivity than work at home. One reason is the increased resources the workplace provides. An office space is more likely to have better technical resources than a home work space. Also, the company staff provides problem-solving resources to which a home worker would not have direct access.

Traditional work space is far better from a managerial standpoint, as well. An office environment makes for easier supervision and quality control. Managers can make sure employees aren't wasting time or doing shoddy work. Also, a manager can more quickly spot and fix problems if they are occurring in the office, increasing productivity significantly.

While there are arguments to be made for both sides, it is clear that there are greater advantages to the traditional work environment. The traditional office space allows for workers to be happier and more productive than those who work at home.

KAPLAN

5. Proofread your work.

Take that last couple of minutes to catch any glaring errors.

BREAKDOWN: ANALYSIS OF AN ARGUMENT

The stimulus and question stem of an Analysis of an Argument topic should look something like this:

> The problem of poorly trained teachers that has plagued the state public school system is bound to become a good deal less serious in the future. The state has initiated comprehensive guidelines that oblige state teachers to complete a number of required credits in education and educational psychology at the graduate level before being certified.
>
> Explain how logically persuasive you find this argument. In discussing your viewpoint, analyze the argument's line of reasoning and its use of evidence. Also explain what, if anything, would make the argument more valid and convincing or help you to better evaluate its conclusion.

The Stimulus

Analysis of an Argument topics that present an argument will probably remind you of those in Critical Reasoning questions. The basic idea is similar. Just as in Critical Reasoning, the writer tries to persuade you of something—her conclusion—by citing some evidence. So look for these two basic components of an argument: a conclusion and supporting evidence. You should read the arguments in the Analysis of an Argument topics in much the same way you read Critical Reasoning questions; be on the lookout for assumptions—the ways the writer makes the leap from evidence to conclusion.

The Question Stem

The question stem above instructs you to decide how convincing you find the argument, explain why, and discuss what might improve the argument. In some topics, the question stem may ask you to decide why the argument is **not** persuasive, explain why, and outline how to further weaken the argument. (It's the flip side of the same assignment.) To perform either task, you'll need to do essentially the same things. First, analyze the argument itself and evaluate its use of evidence; second, explain how a different approach or more information would make the argument better (or worse).

Exactly what are you being asked to do here?

> Explain how logically persuasive you find this argument. In discussing your viewpoint, analyze the argument's line of reasoning and its use of evidence.

Translation: Critique the argument. Discuss whether you think it's convincing or not and explain why.

> Also explain what, if anything, would make the argument more valid and convincing or help you to better evaluate its conclusion.

Translation: Spot weak links in the argument and offer constructive modifications that would strengthen them.

Let's use the 5-Step Method on the Analysis of an Argument topic we saw before:

> The problem of poorly trained teachers that has plagued the state public school system is bound to become a good deal less serious in the future. The state has initiated comprehensive guidelines that oblige state teachers to complete a number of required credits in education and educational psychology at the graduate level before being certified.

> Explain how logically persuasive you find this argument. In discussing your viewpoint, analyze the argument's line of reasoning and its use of evidence. Also explain what, if anything, would make the argument more valid and convincing or help you to better evaluate its conclusion.

1. Digest the argument.

First, identify the conclusion—the point the argument's trying to make. Here, the conclusion is:

> The problem of poorly trained teachers that has plagued the state public school system is bound to become a good deal less serious in the future.

Next, identify the evidence—the basis for the conclusion. Here, the evidence is:

> The state has initiated comprehensive guidelines that oblige state teachers to complete a number of required credits in education and educational psychology at the graduate level before being certified.

Finally, sum up the argument in your own words:

> The problem of badly trained teachers will become less serious because they'll be getting better training.

GO ONLINE

Practice responding to the AWA prompts on your online syllabus. Work on computer, but to mimic test conditions, don't use the automatic spell check or grammar check.

Explain how logically persuasive you find this argument. In explaining your viewpoint, analyze the argument's line of reasoning and its use of evidence. Also explain what, if anything, would make the argument more valid and convincing or would help you to better evaluate its conclusion.

- Credits in education will improve teachers' classroom performance.

- Present bad teachers haven't already met this standard of training.

- Current poor teachers will not still be teaching in the future, or will have to be trained, too.

2. Select the points you will make.

Analyze the use of evidence in the argument. Determine whether there's anything relevant that's not discussed.

- Whether the training will actually address the cause of the problems

- How to either improve or remove the poor teachers now teaching

Also determine what types of evidence would make the argument stronger or more logically sound. In this case, we need some new evidence supporting the assumptions.

- Evidence verifying that this training will make better teachers

- Evidence making it clear that present bad teachers haven't already had this training

- Evidence suggesting why all or many bad teachers won't still be teaching in the future (or why they'll be better trained)

3. Organize.

For an essay on this topic, your opening sentence might look like this:

The writer concludes that the present problem of poorly trained teachers will become less severe in the future because of required course work in education and psychology.

Then use your notes as a working outline. Remember to lead with your best arguments. You might also recommend new evidence you'd like to see and explain why.

The argument says that:

The problem of poorly trained teachers will become less serious with better training.

It assumes that:

- *Course work in education will improve teachers' classroom performance.*

- *Present bad teachers haven't already met this standard of classroom training.*

- *Current poor teachers will not be teaching in the future or will get training, too.*

4. Compose your essay.

Begin typing or writing your essay now. Keep in mind the basic principles of writing that we discussed earlier. And remember the following issues:

What assumptions are made by the author? Are these assumptions valid? Why or why not? What additional information or evidence would make the argument stronger?

Your essay might look something like this:

The writer concludes that the present problem of poorly trained teachers will become less severe in the future because of required credits in education and psychology. However, the conclusion relies on assumptions for which there is no clear evidence.

First, the writer assumes that the required courses will make better teachers. In fact, the courses might be entirely irrelevant to the teachers' failings. If, for example, the prevalent problem is cultural and linguistic gaps between teacher and student, graduate level courses that do not address these specific issues probably won't do much good. The argument that the courses will improve teachers would be strengthened if the writer provided evidence that the training will be relevant to the problems.

In addition, the writer assumes that current poor teachers have not already had this training. In fact, the writer doesn't mention whether or not some or all of the poor teachers have had similar training. The argument would be strengthened considerably if the writer provided evidence that current poor teachers have not had training comparable to the new requirements.

Finally, the writer assumes that poor teachers currently working will either stop teaching in the future or will have received training. The writer provides no evidence, though, to indicate that this is the case. As the argument stands, it's highly possible that only brand-new teachers will receive the training, and the bright future to which the writer refers is decades away. Only if the writer provides evidence that all teachers in the system will receive training—and will then change their teaching methods accordingly—does the argument hold.

5. Proofread.

Save a few minutes to go back over your essay and catch any obvious errors. The best way to improve your writing style is to write, so tackle the sample essay prompts below.

GMAT STYLE CHECKLIST

Cut the fat.

- ☐ Cut out words, phrases, and sentences that don't add any information or serve a purpose.

- ☐ Watch out for repetitive phrases such as refer back or serious crisis.

- ☐ Don't use conjunctions to join sentences that would be more effective as separate sentences.

Be forceful.

- ☐ Avoid jargon and pompous language; it won't impress anybody.

- ☐ Avoid clichés and overused terms or phrases. (For example, beyond the shadow of a doubt.)

- ☐ Don't be vague. Avoid generalizations and abstractions when more specific words would be clearer. (For example, write a waste of time and money instead of pointless temporal and financial expenditure.)

- ☐ Don't use weak sentence openings. Avoid beginning a sentence with there is or there are.

- ☐ Don't refer to yourself needlessly. Avoid pointless phrases like in my personal opinion.

- ☐ Don't be monotonous: Vary sentence length and style.

- ☐ Use transitions to connect sentences and make your essay easy to follow. Paragraphs should clarify the different parts of your essay.

Be correct.

- ☐ Stick to the rules of standard written English.

SUMMARY

The basic principles of Analytical Writing are:

- Your control of language is important.
- Keep things simple.
- Minor grammatical flaws won't harm your score.
- Keep sight of your goal.

Kaplan's 5-Step Method for Analytical Writing is:

Step 1: Digest the Issue/Argument.
Step 2: Select the points you will make.
Step 3: Organize.
Step 4: Write/Type.
Step 5: Proofread.

PRACTICE ESSAYS

Directions: Write an essay on each of the topics below. The writing should be concise, forceful, and grammatically correct. After you have finished, proofread to catch any errors. Allow yourself 30 minutes to complete each essay.

Issue Essay

"The invention of the Internet has created more problems than it has solved. Most people would have a higher quality of life had the Internet never been invented."

From your perspective, is this an accurate observation? Why or why not? Explain, using reasons and/or examples from your experience, observations and reading.

Argument Essay

The following appeared in a memo from the regional manager of Luxe Spa, a chain of high-end salons.

"Over 75% of households in the town of Parksboro have Jacuzzi bathtubs. In addition, the average family income in Parksboro is 50% higher than the national average, and a local store reports record-high sales of the most costly brands of hair and body care products. With so much being spent on the personal care, Parksboro will be a profitable location for a new Luxe Spa—a salon that offers premium services at prices that are above average."

Discuss how well reasoned you find this argument. In your discussion be sure to analyze the line of reasoning and the use of evidence in the argument. For example, you may need to consider what questionable assumptions underlie the thinking and what alternative explanations or counterexamples might weaken the conclusion. You can also discuss what sort of evidence would strengthen or refute the argument, what changes in the argument would make it more logically sound, and what, if anything, would help you better evaluate its conclusion.

After writing out your essays, compare them to the sample responses that follow.

SAMPLE RESPONSES (SCORE 6)

Issue Essay

"The invention of the Internet has created more problems than it has solved. Most people would have a higher quality of life had the Internet never been invented."

From your perspective, is this an accurate observation? Why or why not? Explain, using reasons and/or examples from your experience, observations and reading.

The emergence of the Internet in the 1990's fundamentally changed the way people exchange information. With this dynamic web of technology, people across the world are immediately connected to information—and each other—through the quick click of a button, and normal business operations for major corporations were radically altered. It's true that this industry has had a bumpy beginning—for instance, its spectacular economic meltdown in the late nineties and the advent of file sharing are just a few of the issues raised by the Internet. But while the Internet has created more than its fair share of moral and financial issues for today's consumer, it's unreasonable to assume that the Internet has produced more problems than benefits.

As with any new technology, the Internet opened up infinite avenues allowing businesses to streamline operations. Delivery of information is instantaneous. Communication by email eliminates high phone and paper costs, and contributes to overall efficiency, saving time that would have been spent mailing documents or holding a long conversation on the phone. Web-enabling transactions—whether it be buying products for a major corporation or downloading an application to university—can cut costs in the millions of dollars. In a recent article in the magazine *Fast Company*, Jonathan Ayers, CEO of Carrier Corp (the world's largest manufacturer of air conditioners) used the web to cut costs of over $100 million. In short, the Internet allows companies to execute business quicker and cheaper, which leads to customer satisfaction—and profitability.

Some may say that the speed of the Internet also leads to employee turnover and burnout, or that the web and e-mail are a major distraction for workers. Microsoft is constantly addressing the work-life issue faced by many of its employees; as a part of its retention plan, the company is eliminating vacation caps for top executives and software programmers, and increasing regular salaries rather than depending on shares of stock. While the Internet may promote a fast-paced work environment, it is the company's responsibility to regulate workflow; technology cannot be blamed for bad management.

One of the larger challenges posed by the Internet has to do with intellectual property and copyrighting. Napster was the first to realize a major benefit of the Internet: file sharing. Started in a dorm room, the company's software enabled users to swap digitized music files—for free. Eventually, the software put a significant dent in music sales, becoming a constant worry for music executives and artists alike. However, this isn't the first time the entertainment industry has faced this concern; VHS and audio tape recorders posed the same threat in the seventies and eighties. Companies like Napster and LimeWire simply pushed the entertainment industry to find creative solutions to the copyright issues—and, as the natural ebb and flow of the economy so often proves, creating jobs as they solve the problem. For instance, Apple's iTunes, an online music store where each song costs $0.99, made $70 million in its first year.

From a morality standpoint, the Internet has been fertile ground for pornography as well as a virtual stomping ground for child molesters. Psychologists say that the Internet promotes molesting and porn-viewing habits because of the relative anonymity provided by the medium. But, like everything else, porn and child molesters developed these practices around the advancements of technology and society. They were around long before the Internet. Is it fair to say that the invention of the printing press promoted pornography and sexual abuse?

The economy certainly suffered a great deal in 1999 and 2000, as the world saw the fast-rising dot-com industry implode, causing a depression that was exacerbated by the tragic events of 9/11. The implosion was not due to the technology of the Internet; rather, it was due to distorted, impractical attitudes and unsound business decisions. Wealth was concentrated in shares of stock that were unrealistically inflated, and as long as the stock prices were high, analysts, investors and even federal regulators took a lax attitude towards business models and company practices. Therefore, the dot-com bust can be attributed toward a declining lapse in human judgment rather than the existence of the Internet.

Finally, the consumer benefits of the Internet can't be ignored. Small businesses are better able to promote themselves, and can introduce their products to a far-reaching audience of consumers. The Internet has simplified and improved things like travel reservations, communication, and customer service. For example, customers of shipping companies like FedEx or UPS are now able to track packages online, rather than making a phone call that eventually leads to a ten-minute wait on hold.

The very definition of technology is the application of scientific knowledge in industry or business. A new idea begets other new ideas, and along with that comes a period of adjustment, both for industries and for society. The introduction of the Internet opened up a new world of communication, allowing for business to advance, just like the invention of the car, electricity and the printing press did for past generations. To eschew new technology because of some of its negative characteristics is to deny the progression of society.

Argument Essay

The following appeared in a memo from the regional manager of Luxe Spa, a chain of high-end salons.

"Over 75% of households in the town of Parksboro have Jacuzzi bathtubs. In addition, the average family income in Parksboro is 50% higher than the national average, and a local store reports record-high sales of the most costly brands of hair and body care products. With so much being spent on the personal care, Parksboro will be a profitable location for a new Luxe Spa—a salon that offers premium services at prices that are above average."

Discuss how well reasoned you find this argument. In your discussion be sure to analyze the line of reasoning and the use of evidence in the argument. For example, you may need to consider what questionable assumptions underlie the thinking and what alternative explanations or counterexamples might weaken the conclusion. You can also discuss what sort of evidence would strengthen or refute the argument, what changes in the argument would make it more logically sound, and what, if anything, would help you better evaluate its conclusion.

Though it might seem at first glance that the regional manager of Luxe Spa has good reasons for suggesting that Parksboro would be a profitable place for a new spa, a closer examination of the arguments presented reveals numerous examples of leaps of faith, poor reasoning, and ill-defined terminology. In order to better support her claim, the manager would need to show a correlation between the figures she cites in reference to Parksboro's residents and a willingness to spend money at a spa with high prices.

The manager quotes specific statistics about the percentage of residents with Jacuzzis and the average income in Parksboro. She then uses these figures as evidence to support her argument. However, neither of these statistics as presented really do much to bolster her claim. Just because 75% of homes have Jacuzzis doesn't mean those homeowners are more likely to go to a pricey spa. For instance, the presence of Jacuzzis in their houses may indicate a preference for pampering themselves at home. Parksboro could also be a planned development in the suburbs where all the houses are designed with Jacuzzis. If this is the case, than the mere ownership of a certain kind of bathtub should hardly be taken as a clear indication of a person's inclination to go to a spa. In addition, the fact that Parksboro's average family income is 50% higher than the national average is not enough on its own to predict the success or failure of a spa in the regional. Parksboro may have a very small population, for instance, or a small number of wealthy people counterbalanced by a number of medium to low-income families. We simply cannot tell from the information provided. In addition, the failure of the manager to provide the national average family income for comparison makes it unclear if earning 50% more would allow for a luxurious lifestyle or not.

The mention of a local store's record-high sales of expensive personal care items similarly provides scant evidence to support the manager's assertions. We are given no indication of what constitutes "record-high" sales for this particular store, what "costly" means in terms of real dollar amounts, or how this fact may correlate to a tendency to go to a spa. The manager needs to provide much more specific information about residents' spending habits in order to provide compelling evidence that personal care ranks high amongst their priorities.

In order to make the case that Parksboro would be a profitable location for Luxe Spa, the regional manager should try to show that people there have a surplus of income and a tendency to spend it on indulging in spa treatments. Although an attempt is made to make this very argument, the lack of supporting information provided weakens rather than strengthens the memo. Information such as whether there are other high-end spas in the area and the presence of tourism in the town could also have been introduced as reinforcement. As it stands, Luxe Spa would be ill-advised to open a location in Parksboro based solely on the evidence provided here.

Chapter 12: **Take Control of the Test**

In the earlier parts of this book, we looked at the content covered by the various sections of the GMAT. Then we discussed the test expertise you'll need to move through the sections. Now we turn to the often overlooked topic of test mentality; that is, how to get into peak mental condition for the GMAT.

DEVELOP GOOD MENTAL CONDITIONING

Frame of mind has a lot to do with success. Here's what's involved in developing the best frame of mind for the GMAT.

Test Awareness

To do your best on the GMAT, you must always keep in mind that the test is unlike other tests that you've taken, both in terms of content and in terms of the scoring system. If you took a test in high school or college and got a quarter of the questions wrong, you'd probably receive a pretty lousy grade. But on the GMAT, if you can get the first 10 questions right, you can get lots of later questions wrong and still get a high percentile score!

The test is designed to push test takers to their limits, so people rarely get every question right. In fact, you can get a handful of questions wrong and still score in the top 1 percent.

In other words, don't let what you consider to be a subpar performance on one section ruin your performance on another. A poor performance on a section will not, by itself, spoil your score (unless you literally miss almost every question). But if you allow that subpar section to unnerve you, it can have a cumulative negative effect that can ruin your performance on the other sections. It's that kind of thing that could potentially do serious damage to your score. Missing a few points won't do you in, but losing your head will.

The test is designed to find your limits, so it should be challenging. If you feel you've done poorly on a section, don't sweat it. The point is, you must remain calm and collected. Simply do your best on each section, and once a section is over, forget about it and move on.

Moreover, don't try to guess which questions are unscored (we're referring to the experimental questions we mentioned in Chapter 1). This practice has gotten countless test takers into trouble. They convince themselves that a certain section is the one that doesn't count, and then don't take it seriously. You *cannot know* which questions are experimental, so treat each one as if it counts. That way, you're covered no matter what.

Stamina

The GMAT is a grueling experience, and some test takers simply run out of gas when they reach the final questions. To avoid this, you must prepare by taking several practice tests in the week or two before the test, so that on test day, two 75-minute sections plus two essays will seem like a breeze—at least not a hurricane.

GO ONLINE

Take the timed, full-length practice test on your Online Companion to gauge your test-taking endurance.

One option is to download GMAC's Powerprep software, which contains full-length exams and is available free from **mba.com**. The one drawback to the software is that it recycles questions from the *Official Guide to the GMAT Review*, GMAC's own test-prep book, and these questions come from previously administered "paper-and-pencil" GMATs. The CATs on the software should give you good indication of your score range.

Confidence

Confidence feeds on itself, and unfortunately, so does self-doubt. Confidence in your ability leads to quick, sure answers, and a sense of confidence that translates into more points. If you lack confidence, you end up reading sentences and answer choices two, three, or four times, to the point where you confuse yourself and get off track. This ruins your timing, which only perpetuates a downward spiral.

If you subscribe to a controlled GMAT mindset, however, you'll gear your practice toward taking control of the test. And when you have achieved that goal—armed with the principles, techniques, strategies, and approaches explained in this book—you'll be ready to face the GMAT with supreme confidence.

The Right Attitude

Those who approach the GMAT as an obstacle and who rail against the necessity of taking it usually don't fare as well as those who see the GMAT as an opportunity. Those who look forward to doing battle with the GMAT—or, at least, who enjoy the opportunity to distinguish themselves from the rest of the applicant pack—tend to score better than do those who resent or dread it.

Take our word for it: Attitude adjustment is a proven test-taking technique. Here are a few steps you can take to make sure you develop the right GMAT attitude:

- Look at the GMAT as a challenge, but try not to obsess over it; you certainly don't want to psyche yourself out of the game.

- Remember that, yes, the GMAT is obviously important, but, contrary to popular belief, this one test will not single-handedly determine the outcome of your life.

- Try to have fun with the test. Learning how to match your wits against the test makers can be a very satisfying experience, and the reading and thinking skills you'll acquire will benefit you in business school, as well as in your future career.

- Remember that you're more prepared than most people. You've trained with Kaplan. You have the tools you need, plus the ability to use those tools.

MANAGE STRESS

The countdown has begun. Your date with the test is looming on the horizon. Anxiety is on the rise. The butterflies in your stomach have gone ballistic and your thinking is getting cloudy. Maybe you think you won't be ready. Maybe you already know your stuff, but you're going into panic mode anyway. Don't freak! It's possible to tame that anxiety and stress—before and during the test.

Remember, some stress is normal and good. Anxiety is a motivation to study. The adrenaline that gets pumped into your bloodstream when you're stressed helps you stay alert and think more clearly. But if you feel that the tension is so great that it's preventing you from using your study time effectively, here are some things you can do to get it under control.

KAPLAN

Take Control

Lack of control is a prime cause of stress. Research shows that if you don't have a sense of control over what's happening in your life, you can easily end up feeling helpless and hopeless. Try to identify the sources of the stress you feel. Which ones of these can you do something about? Can you find ways to reduce the stress you're feeling about any of these sources?

Focus on Your Strengths

Make a list of areas of strength you have that will help you do well on the test. We all have strengths and recognizing your own is like having reserves of solid gold at Fort Knox. You'll be able to draw on your reserves as you need them, helping you solve difficult questions, maintain confidence, and keep test stress and anxiety at a distance. And every time you recognize a new area of strength, solve a challenging problem, or score well on a practice test, you'll increase your reserves.

Imagine Yourself Succeeding

Close your eyes and imagine yourself in a relaxing situation. Breathe easily and naturally. Now, think of a real-life situation in which you did well on an assignment. Focus on this success. Now turn your thoughts to the GMAT and keep your thoughts and feelings in line with that successful experience. Don't make comparisons between them; just imagine yourself taking the upcoming test with the same feelings of confidence and relaxed control.

Set Realistic Goals

Facing your problem areas gives you some distinct advantages. What do you want to accomplish in the time remaining? Make a list of realistic goals. You can't help feeling more confident when you know you're actively improving your chances of earning a higher test score.

Exercise Your Frustrations Away

KAPLAN EXCLUSIVE

Never practice for more than about 3 hours at a stretch; take breaks and come back refreshed.

Whether it's jogging, biking, pushups, or a pickup basketball game, physical exercise will stimulate your mind and body, and improve your ability to think and concentrate. A surprising number of students fall out of the habit of regular exercise, ironically because they're spending so much time prepping for exams. A little physical exertion will help you to keep your mind and body in sync and sleep better at night.

Eat Well

Good nutrition will help you focus and think clearly. Eat plenty of fruits and vegetables, low-fat protein such as fish, skinless poultry, beans, and legumes, and whole grains such as brown rice, whole wheat bread, and pastas. Don't eat a lot of sugar and high-fat snacks, or salty foods.

Keep Breathing

Conscious attention to breathing is an excellent way to manage stress while you're taking the test. Most of the people who get into trouble during tests take shallow breaths: They breathe using only their upper chests and shoulder muscles, and may even hold their breath for long periods of time. Conversely, those test takers who breathe deeply in a slow, relaxed manner are likely to be in better control during the session.

Stretch

If you find yourself getting spaced out or burned out as you're studying or taking the test, stop for a brief moment and stretch. Even though you'll be pausing for a moment, it's a moment well spent. Stretching will help to refresh you and refocus your thoughts.

PREPARE THE WEEK BEFORE THE EXAM

Is it starting to feel like your whole life is a buildup to the GMAT? You've known about it for years, worried about it for months, and now spent at least a few weeks in solid preparation for it. As the test gets closer, you may find your anxiety is on the rise. You shouldn't worry. After the preparation you've received from this book, you're in good shape for the day of the test.

To calm any pretest jitters you may have, though, let's go over a few strategies for the couple of days before and after the test.

KAPLAN

The Week before Test Day

In the week or so leading up to Test Day, you should do the following:

- Visit the testing center if you can. Sometimes seeing the actual room where your test will be administered and taking notice of little things—such as the kind of desk you'll be working on, whether the room is likely to be hot or cold, etcetera—may help to calm your nerves. And if you've never been to the test center, visiting beforehand is a good way to ensure that you don't get lost on Test Day. Remember, you must be on time—the computers at the test centers are booked all day long.

- Practice working on test material, preferably a full-length test, at the same time of day that your test is scheduled for, as if it were the real Test Day.

- Time yourself accurately, with the same device and in the same manner in which you plan to keep track of time on Test Day. (The computer has a clock on the screen that you'll see during the test, but it's good to track your own time as well.)

- Evaluate thoroughly where you stand. Use the time remaining before the test to shore up your weak points, rereading the appropriate sections of this book. But make sure not to neglect your strong areas; after all, this is where you'll rack up most of your points.

KAPLAN) EXCLUSIVE

Cramming won't work! It can induce test-taking burnout. On the day before the test, just relax and store energy.

The Day before the Test

Try to avoid doing intensive studying the day before the test. There's little you can do to help yourself at this late date, and you may just wind up exhausting yourself and burning out. Our advice is to review a few key concepts, get together everything you'll need for Test Day, and then take the night off entirely. Go to see a movie, rent a video, or watch some TV. Try not to think too much about the test.

The Day of the Test

Leave early, giving yourself plenty of time. Read something to warm up your brain; you don't want the GMAT to be the first written material your brain tries to assimilate that day.

Dress in layers for maximum comfort. That way, you'll be able to adjust to the testing room's temperature. In traveling to the test center, leave yourself enough time for traffic or mass transit delays.

Be ready for a long day. Total testing time, remember, is three and a half hours. When you add the administrative paperwork before and after, and the two 5-minute breaks, you're looking at an experience of four hours or more.

It's also best to practice using a timing routine that you'll follow during the real test, so that keeping track of time on Test Day is second nature. Of course, the GMAT has a clock on the screen for you.

Here are some other last-minute reminders to help guide your work on Test Day:

- Read each question stem carefully, and reread it before making your final selection.

- Don't get bogged down in the middle of any section. You may find questions that appear later to be more to your liking. So don't freak. Eliminate answer choices, guess, and move on.

- Start strong. The first few questions are important, so spend as much time as necessary on the early ones.

- Don't bother trying to figure out which questions are unscored. It can't help you, and you might very well be wrong. Instead, just determine to do your best on every question.

- Confidence is key. Accentuate the positives, and don't dwell on the negatives! Your attitude and outlook are crucial to your performance on test day.

- During the exam, try not to think about how you're scoring. It's like a baseball player who's thinking about the crowd's cheers and the sportswriters and his contract as he steps up to the plate: There's no surer way to strike out. Instead, focus on the question-by-question task of picking an answer choice. The correct answer is there: You don't have to come up with it; it's sitting right there in front of you!

 GO ONLINE

Download your online Study Sheet and bring it with you for review as you travel to the test center.

CANCELLATION AND MULTIPLE SCORES POLICY

Unlike many things in life, the GMAT allows you a second chance. If you walk out of the test feeling that you've really not done as well as you can, you always have the option to cancel your score—before you see the score, of course. Immediately after you complete the test—but before you view your scores—a message will appear, asking if you want to cancel your scores. You cannot cancel your scores after they are displayed or reported to you.

Canceling a test means that it won't be scored. It will just appear on your score report as a canceled test. No one will know how well or poorly you really did—not even you.

If you cancel your scores:

- They cannot be reinstated.

- You will not receive a refund for the test.

- A score cancellation notice will be sent to you and the schools you selected as score recipients.

- The score cancellation will remain a part of your permanent record and will be reported on all future score reports.

If you do not cancel your scores:

- You can choose to see and print a copy of your unofficial scores for the multiple-choice sections of the GMAT.

- An official score report, including the scores for the AWA, will be mailed to you and your designated schools about 2 weeks after you take the test.

When deciding whether to cancel your score, a good rule of thumb is to make an honest assessment of whether you'll do better on the next test. Wishful thinking doesn't count; you need to have a valid reason to believe that the next time will be different. Remember, no test experience is going to be perfect, and the test is designed to find the limits of your ability.

Two legitimate reasons to cancel your test are illness and personal circumstances that cause you to perform unusually poorly on that particular day. Also, if you feel that you didn't prepare sufficiently, then it may be advisable to cancel your score and approach your test preparation a little more seriously the next time.

KAPLAN) EXCLUSIVE

After all the hard work you've done preparing for and taking the GMAT, make sure you celebrate afterward—and start thinking about all of the great times you'll be having at the business school of your choice!

But keep in mind that test takers historically underestimate their performance, especially immediately following the test. They tend to forget about all of the things that went right and focus on everything that went wrong. So unless your performance is terribly marred by unforeseen circumstances, don't cancel your test. Just remember, cancellations are permanent. Once you hit that button, you can't change your mind.

If you take more than one test without canceling, then the three most recent scores will show up on each score report, so the business schools will see them all. Many business schools either count your highest GMAT score or average your scores. Check with individual schools for their policy on multiple scores.

PART THREE

Full-Length Practice Test

GMAT PRACTICE TEST ANSWER SHEET

Remove (or photocopy) the answer sheet and use it to complete the practice test.

HOW TO TAKE THIS TEST

Before taking this practice test, find a quiet place where you can work uninterrupted for four hours or so. Make sure you have a comfortable desk and several No. 2 pencils.

GO ONLINE

Be sure to add your scores to your syllabus.

This practice test includes two scored multiple-choice sections and two Analytical Writing sections. Use the answer grid that follows to record your multiple-choice answers. Write the essays on the pages provided, or type them into a word processing program for a more testlike experience.

Once you start the practice test, don't stop until you've gone through all four sections. Remember, you can review any question within a section, but you may not go back or forward a section.

You'll find the answer key, scoring information, and explanations following the test.

Good luck!

Quantitative Section

1. Ⓐ Ⓑ Ⓒ Ⓓ Ⓔ   11 Ⓐ Ⓑ Ⓒ Ⓓ Ⓔ   21. Ⓐ Ⓑ Ⓒ Ⓓ Ⓔ   31. Ⓐ Ⓑ Ⓒ Ⓓ Ⓔ
2. Ⓐ Ⓑ Ⓒ Ⓓ Ⓔ   12. Ⓐ Ⓑ Ⓒ Ⓓ Ⓔ   22. Ⓐ Ⓑ Ⓒ Ⓓ Ⓔ   32. Ⓐ Ⓑ Ⓒ Ⓓ Ⓔ
3. Ⓐ Ⓑ Ⓒ Ⓓ Ⓔ   13. Ⓐ Ⓑ Ⓒ Ⓓ Ⓔ   23. Ⓐ Ⓑ Ⓒ Ⓓ Ⓔ   33. Ⓐ Ⓑ Ⓒ Ⓓ Ⓔ   # right in Quantitative Section
4. Ⓐ Ⓑ Ⓒ Ⓓ Ⓔ   14. Ⓐ Ⓑ Ⓒ Ⓓ Ⓔ   24. Ⓐ Ⓑ Ⓒ Ⓓ Ⓔ   34. Ⓐ Ⓑ Ⓒ Ⓓ Ⓔ
5. Ⓐ Ⓑ Ⓒ Ⓓ Ⓔ   15. Ⓐ Ⓑ Ⓒ Ⓓ Ⓔ   25. Ⓐ Ⓑ Ⓒ Ⓓ Ⓔ   35. Ⓐ Ⓑ Ⓒ Ⓓ Ⓔ
6. Ⓐ Ⓑ Ⓒ Ⓓ Ⓔ   16. Ⓐ Ⓑ Ⓒ Ⓓ Ⓔ   26. Ⓐ Ⓑ Ⓒ Ⓓ Ⓔ   36. Ⓐ Ⓑ Ⓒ Ⓓ Ⓔ
7. Ⓐ Ⓑ Ⓒ Ⓓ Ⓔ   17. Ⓐ Ⓑ Ⓒ Ⓓ Ⓔ   27. Ⓐ Ⓑ Ⓒ Ⓓ Ⓔ   37. Ⓐ Ⓑ Ⓒ Ⓓ Ⓔ   # wrong in Quantitative Section
8. Ⓐ Ⓑ Ⓒ Ⓓ Ⓔ   18. Ⓐ Ⓑ Ⓒ Ⓓ Ⓔ   28. Ⓐ Ⓑ Ⓒ Ⓓ Ⓔ
9. Ⓐ Ⓑ Ⓒ Ⓓ Ⓔ   19. Ⓐ Ⓑ Ⓒ Ⓓ Ⓔ   29. Ⓐ Ⓑ Ⓒ Ⓓ Ⓔ
10. Ⓐ Ⓑ Ⓒ Ⓓ Ⓔ   20. Ⓐ Ⓑ Ⓒ Ⓓ Ⓔ   30. Ⓐ Ⓑ Ⓒ Ⓓ Ⓔ

Verbal Section

1. Ⓐ Ⓑ Ⓒ Ⓓ Ⓔ   12 Ⓐ Ⓑ Ⓒ Ⓓ Ⓔ   23. Ⓐ Ⓑ Ⓒ Ⓓ Ⓔ   34. Ⓐ Ⓑ Ⓒ Ⓓ Ⓔ
2. Ⓐ Ⓑ Ⓒ Ⓓ Ⓔ   13. Ⓐ Ⓑ Ⓒ Ⓓ Ⓔ   24. Ⓐ Ⓑ Ⓒ Ⓓ Ⓔ   35. Ⓐ Ⓑ Ⓒ Ⓓ Ⓔ
3. Ⓐ Ⓑ Ⓒ Ⓓ Ⓔ   14. Ⓐ Ⓑ Ⓒ Ⓓ Ⓔ   25. Ⓐ Ⓑ Ⓒ Ⓓ Ⓔ   36. Ⓐ Ⓑ Ⓒ Ⓓ Ⓔ   # right in Verbal Section
4. Ⓐ Ⓑ Ⓒ Ⓓ Ⓔ   15. Ⓐ Ⓑ Ⓒ Ⓓ Ⓔ   26. Ⓐ Ⓑ Ⓒ Ⓓ Ⓔ   37. Ⓐ Ⓑ Ⓒ Ⓓ Ⓔ
5. Ⓐ Ⓑ Ⓒ Ⓓ Ⓔ   16. Ⓐ Ⓑ Ⓒ Ⓓ Ⓔ   27. Ⓐ Ⓑ Ⓒ Ⓓ Ⓔ   38. Ⓐ Ⓑ Ⓒ Ⓓ Ⓔ
6. Ⓐ Ⓑ Ⓒ Ⓓ Ⓔ   17. Ⓐ Ⓑ Ⓒ Ⓓ Ⓔ   28. Ⓐ Ⓑ Ⓒ Ⓓ Ⓔ   39. Ⓐ Ⓑ Ⓒ Ⓓ Ⓔ
7. Ⓐ Ⓑ Ⓒ Ⓓ Ⓔ   18. Ⓐ Ⓑ Ⓒ Ⓓ Ⓔ   29. Ⓐ Ⓑ Ⓒ Ⓓ Ⓔ   40. Ⓐ Ⓑ Ⓒ Ⓓ Ⓔ
8. Ⓐ Ⓑ Ⓒ Ⓓ Ⓔ   19. Ⓐ Ⓑ Ⓒ Ⓓ Ⓔ   30. Ⓐ Ⓑ Ⓒ Ⓓ Ⓔ   41. Ⓐ Ⓑ Ⓒ Ⓓ Ⓔ   # wrong in Verbal Section
9. Ⓐ Ⓑ Ⓒ Ⓓ Ⓔ   20. Ⓐ Ⓑ Ⓒ Ⓓ Ⓔ   31. Ⓐ Ⓑ Ⓒ Ⓓ Ⓔ
10. Ⓐ Ⓑ Ⓒ Ⓓ Ⓔ   21. Ⓐ Ⓑ Ⓒ Ⓓ Ⓔ   32. Ⓐ Ⓑ Ⓒ Ⓓ Ⓔ
11. Ⓐ Ⓑ Ⓒ Ⓓ Ⓔ   22. Ⓐ Ⓑ Ⓒ Ⓓ Ⓔ   33. Ⓐ Ⓑ Ⓒ Ⓓ Ⓔ

KAPLAN

Analysis of Issue Essay
Time—30 minutes

Directions: Analyze and present your point of view on the issue described below. There is no "right" point of view. In developing your point of view, you should consider the issue from a number of different viewpoints. Read the statement below and the directions that follow it. Write your final response on the page provided. Allow yourself 30 minutes to plan and write your response.

"Some people argue that those who do not send their children to public schools should not have to fund these schools through taxes, since neither parents nor children benefit from these schools. They ignore the fact that everyone benefits from the strong economy that a well-educated populace generates."

Which argument do you find more compelling, the case for forcing everyone to fund public schools or the opposing viewpoint? Explain your position using relevant reasons or examples taken from your own experience, observations, or reading.

GO ON TO THE NEXT PAGE

KAPLAN

Use this space to write your essay: (Note: You will have to type your essay on the GMAT CAT.)

_____

_____

_____

_____

_____

_____

_____

_____

_____

_____

_____

_____

_____

_____

_____

_____

_____

_____

_____

IF YOU FINISH BEFORE TIME IS CALLED, YOU MAY CHECK YOUR WORK ON
THIS SECTION ONLY. DO NOT TURN TO ANY OTHER SECTION IN THE TEST. **STOP**

Analysis of Argument Essay
Time—30 minutes

Directions: Provide a critique of the argument below. Focus on one or all of the following, depending upon your considered opinion of the argument: questionable assumptions underlying the reasoning, alternative explanations or evidence that would weaken the reasoning, and/or additional information that would support or weaken the argument. Read the statement below and the directions that follow it. Write your final response on the pages provided. Allow yourself 30 minutes to plan and write your response.

The following appeared in the advertising literature of Travelshack.com, an online travel magazine and vacation resort catalogue.

"Your vacation resort can ill afford not to publicize its offerings on Travelshack.com. Our readership has more than doubled in the past year alone and is dominated by savvy consumers with large disposable incomes. Witness the experience of Snowbert Ski Lodge. Since it began advertising itself on our website a year ago, it is regularly booked to capacity and its annual profits have increased more than threefold from the previous year."

Explain how logically persuasive you find this argument. In discussing your viewpoint, analyze the argument's line of reasoning and its use of evidence. Also explain what, if anything, would make the argument more valid and convincing or help you to better evaluate its conclusion.

GO ON TO THE NEXT PAGE

KAPLAN

Use this space to write your essay: (Note: You will have to type your essay on the GMAT CAT.)

_____

_____

_____

_____

_____

_____

_____

_____

_____

_____

_____

_____

_____

_____

_____

_____

_____

Quantitative Section

Time—75 minutes
37 questions

Problem Solving Directions: Solve the problems and choose the best answer.

Data Sufficiency Directions: In each of the problems, a question is followed by two statements containing certain data. You are to determine whether the data provided by the statements are sufficient to answer the question. Choose the correct answer based upon the statements' data, your knowledge of mathematics, and your familiarity with everyday facts (such as the number of minutes in an hour or cents in a dollar). Choose choice

○ if statement (1) by itself is sufficient to answer the question, but statement (2) by itself is not;

○ if statement (2) by itself is sufficient to answer the question, but statement (1) by itself is not;

○ if statements (1) and (2) taken together are sufficient to answer the question, even though neither statement by itself is sufficient;

○ if either statement by itself is sufficient to answer the question;

○ if statements (1) and (2) taken together are not sufficient to answer the question, requiring more data pertaining to the problem.

Note: Diagrams accompanying problems agree with information given in the questions, but may not agree with additional information given in statements (1) and (2).

Note: Unless otherwise indicated, the figures accompanying questions have been drawn as accurately as possible and may be used as sources of information for answering the questions. All figures lie in a plane except where noted. All numbers used are real numbers.

Example:

$$A \qquad B \qquad C$$

What is the length of segment AC?

(1) B is the midpoint of AC

(2) $AB = 5$

Explanation: Statement (1) tells you that B is the midpoint of AC, so $AB = BC$ and $AC = 2AB = 2BC$. Since statement (1) does not give a value for AB or BC, you cannot answer the question using statement (1) alone. Statement (2) says that $AB = 5$. Since statement (2) does not give you a value for BC, the question cannot be answered by statement (2) alone. Using both statements together you can find a value for both AB and BC; therefore you can find AC, so the answer to the problem is choice (C).

GO ON TO THE NEXT PAGE

KAPLAN

1. The price of copper rose by 25 percent and then fell by 20 percent. The price after these changes was

   ○ 20 percent greater than the original price

   ○ 5 percent greater than the original price

   ○ the same as the original price

   ○ 5 percent less than the original price

   ○ 15 percent less than the original price

2. If Sidney is taller than Roger, Roger is taller than Vernon, and Billy is taller than both Roger and Felix, then which of the following statements must be true?

   ○ Felix is shorter than Roger.

   ○ Sidney is taller than Billy.

   ○ Roger is shorter than Felix.

   ○ Sidney is taller than Felix.

   ○ Billy is taller than Vernon.

3. If $-\frac{3}{4}x + 3y - \frac{1}{2} = \frac{3}{2}y - \frac{1}{4}x$, what is the value of x?

   (1) $y^2 = 4$
   (2) $y = 2$

   ○ Statement (1) by itself is sufficient to answer the question, but statement (2) by itself is not.

   ○ Statement (2) by itself is sufficient to answer the question, but statement (1) by itself is not.

   ○ Statements (1) and (2) taken together are sufficient to answer the question, even though neither statement by itself is sufficient.

   ○ Either statement by itself is sufficient to answer the question.

   ○ Statements (1) and (2) taken together are not sufficient to answer the question, requiring more data pertaining to the problem.

GO ON TO THE NEXT PAGE

4. To meet a government requirement, a bottler must test 5 percent of its spring water and 10 percent of its sparkling water for purity. If a customer ordered 120 cases of spring water and 80 cases of sparkling water, what percent of all the cases must the bottler test before he can send it out?

⬭ 6.5%

⬭ 7.0%

⬭ 7.5%

⬭ 8.0%

⬭ 8.5%

5. If $xy > 0$, which of the following CANNOT be true?

⬭ $x > 0$

⬭ $y < 0$

⬭ $x + y < 0$

⬭ $\dfrac{x}{y} < 0$

⬭ $\dfrac{x}{y} > 0$

6. What is the value of a if $3^{3a + 4} = 9^a$?

⬭ -4

⬭ -2

⬭ -1

⬭ 1

⬭ 4

GO ON TO THE NEXT PAGE

Class	Average Age	No. of Students
A	15 years	6
B	16 years	12

7. Is the standard deviation of ages of students in class A greater than the standard deviation of the age of students in class B ?

(1) The difference between the ages of any two students in class A is always more than 1 year.

(2) No student in class B is more than 6 months older than any other student.

○ Statement (1) by itself is sufficient to answer the question, but statement (2) by itself is not.

○ Statement (2) by itself is sufficient to answer the question, but statement (1) by itself is not.

○ Statements (1) and (2) taken together are sufficient to answer the question, even though neither statement by itself is sufficient.

○ Either statement by itself is sufficient to answer the question.

○ Statements (1) and (2) taken together are not sufficient to answer the question, requiring more data pertaining to the problem.

8. A list contains 11 consecutive integers. What is the greatest integer on the list?

(1) If x is the smallest integer on the list, then $(x + 72)^{\frac{1}{3}} = 4$

(2) If x is the smallest integer on the list, then $\dfrac{1}{64} = x^{-2}$.

○ Statement (1) by itself is sufficient to answer the question, but statement (2) by itself is not.

○ Statement (2) by itself is sufficient to answer the question, but statement (1) by itself is not.

○ Statements (1) and (2) taken together are sufficient to answer the question, even though neither statement by itself is sufficient.

○ Either statement by itself is sufficient to answer the question.

○ Statements (1) and (2) taken together are not sufficient to answer the question, requiring more data pertaining to the problem.

GO ON TO THE NEXT PAGE

KAPLAN

9. The average (arithmetic mean) of $3a + 4$ and another number is $2a$. What is the average of the other number and a ?

   ◯ $2a$

   ◯ $a - 4$

   ◯ $a - 2$

   ◯ $a + 2$

   ◯ $a + 4$

10. Tom reads at an average rate of 30 pages per hour, while Jan reads at an average rate of 40 pages per hour. If Tom starts reading a novel at 4:30, and Jan begins reading an identical copy of the same book at 5:20, at what time will they be reading the same page?

    ◯ 9:30

    ◯ 9:00

    ◯ 8:40

    ◯ 7:50

    ◯ 7:00

11. Todd's construction company is capable of building 40 houses a year. Todd's brother Mike also owns a construction company. How long does it take the two companies together to build 64 houses?

    (1) Mike's construction company is capable of building houses twice as fast as Todd's company does.

    (2) Mike's construction company is capable of building 20 houses every three months.

    ◯ Statement (1) by itself is sufficient to answer the question, but statement (2) by itself is not.

    ◯ Statement (2) by itself is sufficient to answer the question, but statement (1) by itself is not.

    ◯ Statements (1) and (2) taken together are sufficient to answer the question, even though neither statement by itself is sufficient.

    ◯ Either statement by itself is sufficient to answer the question.

    ◯ Statements (1) and (2) taken together are not sufficient to answer the question, requiring more data pertaining to the problem.

GO ON TO THE NEXT PAGE

12. How many multiples of 3 are there among the integers 15 through 105 inclusive?

- ◯ 30
- ◯ 31
- ◯ 32
- ◯ 33
- ◯ 34

13. If x is a prime number, what is the value of x?

(1) $x < 15$

(2) $(x - 2)$ is a multiple of 5.

- ◯ Statement (1) by itself is sufficient to answer the question, but statement (2) by itself is not.
- ◯ Statement (2) by itself is sufficient to answer the question, but statement (1) by itself is not.
- ◯ Statements (1) and (2) taken together are sufficient to answer the question, even though neither statement by itself is sufficient.
- ◯ Either statement by itself is sufficient to answer the question.
- ◯ Statements (1) and (2) taken together are not sufficient to answer the question, requiring more data pertaining to the problem.

14. Steve gets on the elevator at the 11th floor of a building and rides up at a rate of 57 floors per minute. At the same time Joyce gets on an elevator on the 51st floor of the same building and rides down at a rate of 63 floors per minute. If they continue traveling at these rates, at which floor will their paths cross?

- ◯ 19
- ◯ 28
- ◯ 30
- ◯ 32
- ◯ 44

GO ON TO THE NEXT PAGE

KAPLAN

15. George takes 8 hours to copy a 50-page manuscript while Sonya can copy the same manuscript in 6 hours. How many hours would it take them to copy a 100-page manuscript, if they work together?

   ○ $6\frac{6}{7}$

   ○ 9

   ○ $9\frac{5}{7}$

   ○ $10\frac{2}{3}$

   ○ 14

16. For the equation $x^2 + 2x + m = 5$, where m is a constant, 3 is one solution for x. What is the other solution?

   ○ −5

   ○ −2

   ○ −1

   ○ 3

   ○ 5

17. If both 5^2 and 3^3 are factors of $n \times 2^5 \times 6^2 \times 7^3$, what is the smallest possible positive value of n?

   ○ 25

   ○ 27

   ○ 45

   ○ 75

   ○ 125

GO ON TO THE NEXT PAGE

18. If a rectangle has length a and width b, what is its area?

(1) $2a = \dfrac{15}{b}$

(2) $a = 2b - 2$

○ Statement (1) by itself is sufficient to answer the question, but statement (2) by itself is not.

○ Statement (2) by itself is sufficient to answer the question, but statement (1) by itself is not.

○ Statements (1) and (2) taken together are sufficient to answer the question, even though neither statement by itself is sufficient.

○ Either statement by itself is sufficient to answer the question.

○ Statements (1) and (2) taken together are not sufficient to answer the question, requiring more data pertaining to the problem.

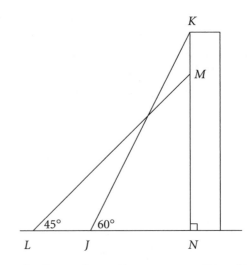

19. In the figure above, line segments JK and LM represent two positions of the same board leaning against the side KN of a wall. The length of KN is how much greater than the length of MN?

(1) The length of LN is $\sqrt{2}$ meters.

(2) The length of JN is 1 meter.

○ Statement (1) by itself is sufficient to answer the question, but statement (2) by itself is not.

○ Statement (2) by itself is sufficient to answer the question, but statement (1) by itself is not.

○ Statements (1) and (2) taken together are sufficient to answer the question, even though neither statement by itself is sufficient.

○ Either statement by itself is sufficient to answer the question.

○ Statements (1) and (2) taken together are not sufficient to answer the question, requiring more data pertaining to the problem.

GO ON TO THE NEXT PAGE ⟶

KAPLAN

20. How many different ways can 2 students be seated in a row of 4 desks, so that there is always at least one empty desk between the students?

- ◯ 2
- ◯ 3
- ◯ 4
- ◯ 6
- ◯ 12

21. What is the ratio of men to women enrolled in a certain class?

(1) The number of women enrolled in the class is 3 less than half the number of men enrolled.

(2) The number of women enrolled in the class is $\frac{2}{5}$ of the number of men enrolled.

- ◯ Statement (1) by itself is sufficient to answer the question, but statement (2) by itself is not.

- ◯ Statement (2) by itself is sufficient to answer the question, but statement (1) by itself is not.

- ◯ Statements (1) and (2) taken together are sufficient to answer the question, even though neither statement by itself is sufficient.

- ◯ Either statement by itself is sufficient to answer the question.

- ◯ Statements (1) and (2) taken together are not sufficient to answer the question, requiring more data pertaining to the problem.

22. A clothing supplier stores 800 coats in a warehouse, of which 15 percent are full-length coats. If 500 of the shorter length coats are removed from the warehouse, what percent of the remaining coats are full length?

- ◯ 5.62%
- ◯ 9.37%
- ◯ 35%
- ◯ 40%
- ◯ 48%

GO ON TO THE NEXT PAGE ▷

23. Are the integers q, r, and s consecutive?

   (1) The average (arithmetic mean) of q, r, and s is r.

   (2) $r - q = s - r$

   ◯ Statement (1) by itself is sufficient to answer the question, but statement (2) by itself is not.

   ◯ Statement (2) by itself is sufficient to answer the question, but statement (1) by itself is not.

   ◯ Statements (1) and (2) taken together are sufficient to answer the question, even though neither statement by itself is sufficient.

   ◯ Either statement by itself is sufficient to answer the question.

   ◯ Statements (1) and (2) taken together are not sufficient to answer the question, requiring more data pertaining to the problem.

24. For a certain performance at a concert hall, a total of 2,350 tickets were sold in the orchestra, first mezzanine, and second mezzanine. How many orchestra tickets were sold?

   (1) The number of first mezzanine tickets sold was one-half the number of second mezzanine tickets sold.

   (2) The total number of first and second mezzanine tickets sold was 50 percent greater than the number of orchestra tickets sold.

   ◯ Statement (1) by itself is sufficient to answer the question, but statement (2) by itself is not.

   ◯ Statement (2) by itself is sufficient to answer the question, but statement (1) by itself is not.

   ◯ Statements (1) and (2) taken together are sufficient to answer the question, even though neither statement by itself is sufficient.

   ◯ Either statement by itself is sufficient to answer the question.

   ◯ Statements (1) and (2) taken together are not sufficient to answer the question, requiring more data pertaining to the problem.

GO ON TO THE NEXT PAGE

KAPLAN

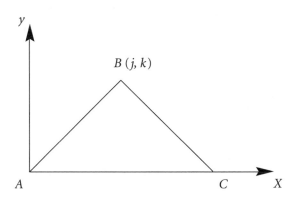

25. If the area of the triangle above is 8, what are the coordinates of point C?

   ○ $(0, 2jk)$

   ○ $(j^2 + k^2, 0)$

   ○ $\left(\dfrac{8}{k}, 0\right)$

   ○ $\left(0, \dfrac{16}{j}\right)$

   ○ $\left(\dfrac{16}{k}, 0\right)$

26. If the probability of rain on any given day in City X is 50 percent, what is the probability that it rains on exactly 3 days in a 5-day period?

   ○ $\dfrac{8}{125}$

   ○ $\dfrac{2}{25}$

   ○ $\dfrac{5}{16}$

   ○ $\dfrac{8}{25}$

   ○ $\dfrac{3}{4}$

27. A recipe for soda requires w liters of water for every liter of syrup. If soda is made according to this recipe using m liters of syrup, and sold for j dollars a liter, what will be the gross profit if syrup costs k dollars a liter and water costs nothing?

   ○ $m(w + j - k)$

   ○ $jm\left(\dfrac{1}{w} + 1\right)$

   ○ $m(jw - k)$

   ○ $(j - k)m$

   ○ $jm(1 + w) - km$

GO ON TO THE NEXT PAGE

28. A certain car dealership has two locations. Last month, an average (arithmetic mean) of 11 cars per salesperson was sold at location *A* and an average of 16 cars per salesperson was sold at location *B*. What was the average number of cars sold per salesperson at this dealership last month?

   (1) Last month, the number of salespeople at location *A* was 3 times the number of salespeople at location *B*.

   (2) Last month, the total number of cars sold at location *A* was 132, and the total number of cars sold at location *B* was 64.

   ⬭ Statement (1) by itself is sufficient to answer the question, but statement (2) by itself is not.

   ⬭ Statement (2) by itself is sufficient to answer the question, but statement (1) by itself is not.

   ⬭ Statements (1) and (2) taken together are sufficient to answer the question, even though neither statement by itself is sufficient.

   ⬭ Either statement by itself is sufficient to answer the question.

   ⬭ Statements (1) and (2) taken together are not sufficient to answer the question, requiring more data pertaining to the problem.

29. If an "anglet" is defined as 1 percent of 1 degree, then how many anglets are there in a circle?

   ⬭   0.36

   ⬭   3.6

   ⬭   360

   ⬭   3,600

   ⬭   36,000

GO ON TO THE NEXT PAGE

KAPLAN

30. In a certain telephone poll, 600 people were asked whether they were in favor of, against, or undecided on a certain bill being debated in the legislature. How many of the people polled were in favor of the bill?

    (1) The number of people who were in favor of the bill was 200 greater than the number of people who were against it.

    (2) Two hundred people were undecided, which was twice as many as the number who were against the bill.

    ◯ Statement (1) by itself is sufficient to answer the question, but statement (2) by itself is not.

    ◯ Statement (2) by itself is sufficient to answer the question, but statement (1) by itself is not.

    ◯ Statements (1) and (2) taken together are sufficient to answer the question, even though neither statement by itself is sufficient.

    ◯ Either statement by itself is sufficient to answer the question.

    ◯ Statements (1) and (2) taken together are not sufficient to answer the question, requiring more data pertaining to the problem.

31. A number of bricks were purchased to build a fireplace at a cost of 40 cents each, but only $\frac{3}{4}$ of them were needed. If the unused 190 bricks were returned and their cost refunded, what was the cost of the bricks used to make the fireplace?

    ◯ $76

    ◯ $228

    ◯ $304

    ◯ $414

    ◯ $570

32. If x is a number such that $-2 \leq x \leq 2$, which of the following has the largest possible absolute value?

    ◯ $3x - 1$

    ◯ $x^2 + 1$

    ◯ $3 - x$

    ◯ $x - 3$

    ◯ $x^2 - x$

GO ON TO THE NEXT PAGE ▷

KAPLAN

33. What is the smallest value of x for which
$$\left(\frac{12}{x} + 36\right)(4 - x^2) = 0?$$

   ○ -3

   ○ -2

   ○ $-\frac{1}{2}$

   ○ $-\frac{1}{4}$

   ○ 2

34. What is the value of b?

   (1) $2a - b = 3$

   (2) $a = b - (1 - a)$

   ○ Statement (1) by itself is sufficient to answer the question, but statement (2) by itself is not.

   ○ Statement (2) by itself is sufficient to answer the question, but statement (1) by itself is not.

   ○ Statements (1) and (2) taken together are sufficient to answer the question, even though neither statement by itself is sufficient.

   ○ Either statement by itself is sufficient to answer the question.

   ○ Statements (1) and (2) taken together are not sufficient to answer the question, requiring more data pertaining to the problem.

35. Which of the following is greater than 1,000.01?

   ○ 0.00001×10^8

   ○ 0.0101×10^4

   ○ 1.1×10^2

   ○ 1.00001×10^3

   ○ 0.00010001×10^7

GO ON TO THE NEXT PAGE

36. If $a \neq b$, what is the value of $a + b$?

   (1) $\dfrac{a^2 - b^2}{a - b} = 6$

   (2) $(a + b)^2 = 36$

   ○ Statement (1) by itself is sufficient to answer the question, but statement (2) by itself is not.

   ○ Statement (2) by itself is sufficient to answer the question, but statement (1) by itself is not.

   ○ Statements (1) and (2) taken together are sufficient to answer the question, even though neither statement by itself is sufficient.

   ○ Either statement by itself is sufficient to answer the question.

   ○ Statements (1) and (2) taken together are not sufficient to answer the question, requiring more data pertaining to the problem.

37. If $2^{2m+1} = 2^{n+2}$, what is the value of $m + n$?

   (1) $2^{3n-1} = 256$

   (2) $2^{m+2n} = 256$

   ○ Statement (1) by itself is sufficient to answer the question, but statement (2) by itself is not.

   ○ Statement (2) by itself is sufficient to answer the question, but statement (1) by itself is not.

   ○ Statements (1) and (2) taken together are sufficient to answer the question, even though neither statement by itself is sufficient.

   ○ Either statement by itself is sufficient to answer the question.

   ○ Statements (1) and (2) taken together are not sufficient to answer the question, requiring more data pertaining to the problem.

IF YOU FINISH BEFORE TIME IS CALLED, YOU MAY CHECK YOUR WORK ON THIS SECTION ONLY. DO NOT TURN TO ANY OTHER SECTION IN THE TEST.   STOP

Verbal Section

Time—75 minutes
41 questions

Reading Comprehension Directions: Each passage will be followed by questions relating to that passage. After reading through the passage, choose the best response to each question and mark it on your answer sheet. Base your answers on information that is either stated or implied in the passage, and not on your own knowledge. You may refer to the passage while answering the questions.

Sentence Correction Directions: These questions consist of sentences that are either partly or entirely underlined. Below each sentence are five versions of the underlined portion of the sentence. The first of these, choice (A), duplicates the original version. The four other versions revise the underlined portion of the sentence. Read the sentence and the five choices carefully, and select the best version. If the original seems better than any of the revisions, select choice (A). If not, choose one of the revisions.

These questions test your recognition of correct grammatical usage and your sense of clear and economical writing. Choose answers according to the norms of standard written English for grammar, word choice, and sentence construction. Your selected answer should express the intended meaning of the original sentence as clearly and precisely as possible, while avoiding ambiguous, awkward, or unnecessarily wordy constructions.

Critical Reasoning Directions: Select the best answer for each question.

GO ON TO THE NEXT PAGE

1. According to a recent study, advertisements in medical journals often contain misleading information about the effectiveness and safety of new prescription drugs. The medical researchers who wrote the study concluded that the advertisements could result in doctors prescribing inappropriate drugs to their patients.

   The researchers' conclusion would be most strengthened if which of the following were true?

   ○ Advertisements for new prescription drugs are an important source of revenue for medical journals.

   ○ Editors of medical journals are often unable to evaluate the claims made in advertisements for new prescription drugs.

   ○ Doctors rely on the advertisements as a source of information about new prescription drugs.

   ○ Advertisements for new prescription drugs are typically less accurate than medical journal articles evaluating those same drugs.

   ○ The Food and Drug Administration, the government agency responsible for drug regulation, reviews advertisements for new drugs before the ads have been printed.

2. Uninformed about students' experience in urban classrooms, critics often condemn schools' performance gauged by <u>an index, such as standardized test scores, that are called objective and can be quantified and overlook less measurable progress, such as that</u> in higher-level reasoning.

   ○ an index, such as standardized test scores, that are called objective and can be quantified and overlook less measurable progress, such as that

   ○ an index, such as standardized test scores, that are called objective and can be quantified and overlook less measurable progress, such as what is made

   ○ an index, such as standardized test scores, that is called objective and can be quantified and overlook less measurable progress, such as what is made

   ○ a so-called objective index, such as standardized test scores, that can be quantified and overlook less measurable progress, such as what is made

   ○ a so-called objective index, such as standardized test scores, that can be quantified and overlook less measurable progress, such as that

GO ON TO THE NEXT PAGE ⇨

3. A common social problem in the workplace occurs <u>when workers accept supervisory positions, and it causes them to lose</u> the trust of their former co-workers.

    ○ when workers accept supervisory positions, and it causes them to lose

    ○ by a worker accepting supervisory positions, which causes him to lose

    ○ when workers accept supervisory positions, and so lose

    ○ when a worker who accepts a supervisory position, thereby losing

    ○ if a worker accepts a supervisory position, he would lose

Questions 4–7 refer to the following passage.

An important feature of the labor market in recent years has been the increasing participation of women, particularly married women. Many analysts suggest, however, that
(5) women comprise a secondary labor market where rates of pay and promotion prospects are inferior to those available to men. The principal reason is that women have, or are assumed to have, domestic responsibilities
(10) which compete with paid employment. Such domestic responsibilities are strongly influenced by social values which require women to give priority to home and family over paid employment.

(15) The difficulties which women face in the labor market and in their ability to reach senior positions in organizations are accentuated with the arrival of children. In order to become full-time employees, women with children must
(20) overcome the problems of finding good, affordable childcare and the psychological barriers of workplace marginality. Some women balance domestic and workplace commitments by working part-time. However,
(25) part-time work is a precarious form of employment. Women part-timers are often the first laid off in a difficult economy. These workers are often referred to as the "reserve army" of female labor.

(30) One researcher has found that approximately 80 percent of women in their twenties who have children remain at home. Such women who later return to work represent another sector of the workforce facing difficulties. When the
(35) typical houseworker returns to the labor market she is unsure of herself in her new environment. This doubt is accentuated by her recent immersion in housework, a very private form of work. Without recent employment experience,
(40) these women confront a restricted range of opportunities and will almost certainly be offered low-status jobs with poor prospects.

Even women professionals who interrupt their careers to have children experience
(45) difficulties. Their technical skills may become rusty or obsolete, important networks of business contacts are broken, and their delayed return to work may mean that they are likely to come up for promotion well after the
(50) age that would be otherwise normal. Consequently, women, even those of high ability, may find themselves blocked in the lower echelons of an organization, overlooked, or even "invisible" to senior management.

4. The author of the passage is primarily concerned with

⭘ advocating changes in employers' practices towards women with children

⭘ examining some of the reasons women rarely reach the higher echelons of paid labor

⭘ describing the psychological consequences for women of working outside the home

⭘ taking issue with those who believe women should not work outside the home

⭘ analyzing the contribution of women to industry and business

GO ON TO THE NEXT PAGE

KAPLAN

5. The passage provides information to support which of the following statements about women workers?

○ It is the responsibility of employers to provide childcare accommodations for women workers with children.

○ Women in high-status positions are easily able to integrate career and children.

○ Conditions for working mothers are much better today than they were twenty years ago.

○ The decision to work outside the home is often the source of considerable anxiety for women with children.

○ With the expense of childcare, it is often not profitable for women with children to work.

6. The author's discussion of women professionals in the last paragraph serves to

○ show that the difficulties of integrating careers and motherhood can be overcome

○ indicate that even women of higher are not exempt from the difficulties of integrating careers and children

○ defend changes in the policies of employers towards working mothers

○ modify a hypothesis regarding the increased labor force participation of women

○ point out the lack of opportunities for women in business

GO ON TO THE NEXT PAGE

KAPLAN

7. According to the passage, men generally receive higher salaries and have a better chance of being promoted because women

   ◯ tend to work in industries that rely almost exclusively on part-time labor

   ◯ lack the technical and managerial experience of their male counterparts

   ◯ have responsibilities outside of the workplace that demand considerable attention

   ◯ are the first to be laid off when the economy grows at a very slow pace

   ◯ suffer discrimination in the male-dominated corporate environment

8. A state legislator argues that her state's ban on casino gambling is inconsistent and impractical, since other forms of gambling such as bingo and the state lottery are legal. She claims that instead of vainly attempting to enforce the ban, the legislature should simply legalize all gambling, and that to do so would also have the positive effect of reducing the crime rate.

   Which of the following, if true, most seriously weakens the legislator's argument above?

   ◯ Since many people enjoy the thrill of participating in illegal practices, legalizing gambling would probably cause a decline rather than an increase in this activity.

   ◯ Because prosecutors rarely seek prison terms for illegal gamblers, legalizing gambling would not result in a significant savings of money.

   ◯ Long-term studies have shown that the number of people who participate in the lottery is higher now than it was when the lottery was prohibited.

   ◯ Legalizing gambling would entice gamblers from states where it is still banned, and many of them are involved in other illegal activities such as drug smuggling.

   ◯ Many people who participate in illegal gambling claim that they would risk their money on the stock market if they had more disposable income.

GO ON TO THE NEXT PAGE ⟩

9. A researcher studying cats discovered that during the dream state of sleep, the cerebral cortex of a cat's brain fires messages to its body as rapidly as it does during wakefulness. In an effort to determine why the sleeping cat's body does not respond to the messages being fired by the brain, the researcher removed a cluster of neurons from a sleeping cat's brain stem, the part of the brain that connects the cerebral cortex to the spinal cord. After he had done so, the still sleeping cat got up, pounced as if it were chasing a mouse, and arched its back.

Which of the following, if true, taken together with the information above, best supports the conclusion that the sleeping cat was acting out its dreams?

○ The neurons that were removed from the brain stem normally serve to trigger the dream state of sleep and the rapid brain activity that accompanies it.

○ The cerebral cortex is able to receive and transmit sensory information even when the brain is in a sleeping state.

○ The neurons that were removed from the brain stem are normally responsible for transmitting messages from the cerebral cortex.

○ The neurons that were removed from the brain stem normally prevent messages fired by the cerebral cortex during sleep from being received by the spinal cord.

○ The types of brain waves produced by the cerebral cortex during sleep have distinctly different properties from those produced during a wakeful state.

10. Glaciologists believe that the frozen corpse recently found in a melting Alpine glacier, <u>apparently that of a shepherd who is thought to have lived</u> about 4,600 years ago, was preserved uncrushed by snow and ice because of the body's unique topographical position.

○ apparently that of a shepherd who is thought to have lived

○ that of a shepherd, apparently, who was thought to live

○ that of an apparent shepherd who was thought to live

○ that of a shepherd who is thought of as apparently living

○ that of a shepherd who was apparently thought to live

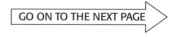
GO ON TO THE NEXT PAGE

KAPLAN)

11. In contrast to Walt Whitman, <u>Ezra Pound considered that late 19th-century American poetry is not a distinct formal repertoire informed by its own ideology, and is</u> essentially an outgrowth of the British poetic tradition.

○ Ezra Pound considered that late 19th-century American poetry is not a distinct formal repertoire informed by its own ideology, and is

○ Ezra Pound considered late 19th-century American poetry not as a distinct formal repertoire informed by its own ideology, but

○ Ezra Pound considered late 19th-century American poetry not a distinct formal repertoire informed by its own ideology, but

○ it was considered by Ezra Pound that late 19th-century American poetry is not a distinct formal repertoire informed by its own ideology, but

○ late 19th-century American poetry was considered by Ezra Pound not to be a distinct formal repertoire informed by its own ideology, and is

GO ON TO THE NEXT PAGE

Questions 12–14 refer to the following passage.

A 1973 Supreme Court decision and related Senate hearings focused Congressional criticism on the 1966 Freedom of Information Act. Its unconditional exemption of any
(5) material stamped "classified"—i.e., containing information considered relevant to national security—forced the Court to uphold non-disclosure in EPA v. Mink. Justice Potter Stewart explained that the Act provided "no
(10) means to question a decision to stamp a document 'secret.'" Senate witnesses testified that the wording of certain articles in the Act permitted bureaucrats to discourage requests for newsworthy documents.

(15) In response, a House committee drafted HR 12471, proposing several amendments to the Act. A provision was reworded to ensure release of documents to any applicant providing a "reasonable description"—exact
(20) titles and numbers were no longer to be mandatory. The courts were empowered to review classified documents and rule on their status. The Senate companion bill, S 2543, included these provisions as well as others:
(25) standardization of search and copy fees, sanctions against non-compliant Federal employees, and a provision for non-exempt portions of a classified document to be released.

(30) The Justice and Defense departments objected to the changes as "costly, burdensome, and inflexible." They argued that the time limits imposed on response "might actually hamper access to information." The
(35) Pentagon asserted that judicial review of exemptions could pose a threat to national security. President Ford, upon taking office in August 1974, concurred.

HR 12471 passed in March 1974; S 2543 was
(40) approved in May after the adoption of further amendments to reduce the number of unconditional exemptions granted in 1966. The Hart Amendment, for instance, mandated disclosure of law enforcement records, unless
(45) their release would interfere with a trial or investigation, invade personal privacy, or disclose an informer's identity. This amendment provoked another presidential objection: Millions of pages of FBI records
(50) would be subject to public scrutiny, unless each individual section were proven exempt.

Before submitting the legislation to Ford, a joint conference of both houses amalgamated the two versions of the bill, while making
(55) further changes to incorporate Ford's criticisms. The administration of disciplinary sanctions was transferred from the courts to the executive branch; provisions were included to accord due weight to
(60) departmental expertise in the evaluation of "classified" exemptions. The identity of confidential sources was in all cases to be protected. Ford nevertheless vetoed the bill, but was overridden by a two-thirds vote in
(65) both houses.

GO ON TO THE NEXT PAGE

12. According to the passage, the Justice and Defense Departments opposed the proposed revision of the Freedom of Information Act on the grounds that it

    ○ was an attempt to block public access to information

    ○ would violate national security agreements

    ○ would pose administrative problems

    ○ was an attempt to curtail their own departmental power

    ○ would weaken the President's authority

13. Which of the following statements, if true, supports the assertion that "judicial review of exemptions could pose a threat to national security" (lines 35–37)?

    ○ Judges lack the expertise to evaluate the significance of military intelligence records.

    ○ Many of the documents which are presently stamped "classified" contain information which is inaccurate or outdated.

    ○ It would be time-consuming and expensive for judges to review millions of pages of classified records.

    ○ Some judges are likely to rule on exemptions in accordance with vested interests of political action groups.

    ○ The practice of judicial review of exemptions will succeed only if it meets with Presidential approval.

14. Which of the following statements is in accordance with President Ford's position on disclosure of FBI records?

    ○ FBI records should be exempt from the provisions of the Freedom of Information Act.

    ○ FBI records should only be withheld from release if such release constitutes a threat to national security.

    ○ It would be too expensive and time-consuming to identify exempt sections of FBI records.

    ○ Protection of the identity of confidential sources is more important than the protection of personal privacy or investigative secrecy.

    ○ FBI records should not be reviewed section by section before being released to the public.

GO ON TO THE NEXT PAGE ⇒

15. Local reporters investigating the labor dispute reported that only half of the workers in the plant were covered by the union health plan; <u>at least as much as a hundred and more others had not any</u> health insurance whatsoever.

   ○ at least as much as a hundred and more others had not any

   ○ at least as much as more than a hundred others had no

   ○ more than a hundred others had not any

   ○ more than a hundred others had no

   ○ there was at least a hundred or more others without any

16. According to a commonly held archaeological theory, the Neanderthals of Europe, an archaic version of *Homo sapiens*, competed with and were eventually replaced by modern humans, with little or no interbreeding between the two populations. A rival theory, developed more recently, suggests that Neanderthals were more similar to modern humans than previously supposed—that, in fact, modern humans evolved from them and from other archaic versions of *Homo sapiens*.

   Evidence that would strongly support the more recent theory concerning the relationship between Neanderthals and modern humans would be

   ○ DNA analyses indicating that modern humans appeared in Africa 200,000 years ago, before migrating to Europe and other continents

   ○ archaeological evidence that Neanderthals and modern humans developed similar cultures, shared stone tools, and performed similar burial rituals

   ○ skulls of early modern humans in central Europe that exhibit a bone near the mandibular nerve that is a typical Neanderthal characteristic

   ○ evidence that the stone tools of Neanderthals remained unchanged for thousands of years, while the tools of modern humans in Europe were more specialized

   ○ biological evidence that Neanderthals had unique physical traits that enabled them to survive ice-age temperatures in Europe

GO ON TO THE NEXT PAGE ⟹

KAPLAN)

17. Archaeologists have shown that ingesting lead in drinking water was a significant health hazard for the ancient Romans, <u>like that of modern Americans</u>.

    ◯ like that of modern Americans

    ◯ as that for modern Americans

    ◯ just as modern Americans do

    ◯ as do modern Americans

    ◯ as it is for modern Americans

18. Born Nathan Weinstein in New York City on October 17, 1903, <u>Nathanael West's first novel, *The Dream Life of Balso Snell* was written during a stay in Paris and published when the author</u> was twenty-eight.

    ◯ Nathanael West's first novel, *The Dream Life of Balso Snell* was written during a stay in Paris and published when the author

    ◯ Nathanael West's first novel, *The Dream Life of Balso Snell*, written while he was staying in Paris, was published when the author

    ◯ Nathanael West's *The Dream Life of Balso Snell*, his first novel, was written while the author was staying in Paris and published when he

    ◯ Nathanael West wrote his first novel, *The Dream Life of Balso Snell*, during a stay in Paris and published it when he

    ◯ when Nathanael West was staying in Paris, he wrote his first novel, *The Dream Life of Balso Snell*, publishing it when he

GO ON TO THE NEXT PAGE ⟶

19. Aggressive fertility treatments are not responsible for the rise in the incidence of twin births. Rather, this increase can be attributed to the fact that women are waiting longer to become mothers. Statistically, women over 35 are more likely to conceive twins, and these women comprise a greater percentage of women giving birth than ever before.

The argument above is flawed in that it ignores the possibility that

- ○ many women over 35 who give birth to twins are not first-time mothers

- ○ women over 35 are not the only women who give birth to twins

- ○ the correlation between fertility treatments and the increased incidence of multiple births may be a coincidence

- ○ on average, women over 35 are no more likely to conceive identical twins than other women are

- ○ women over 35 are more likely to resort to the sorts of fertility treatments that tend to yield twin births

GO ON TO THE NEXT PAGE

Questions 20–23 refer to the following passage.

Modern methods of predicting earthquakes recognize that quakes, far from being geologic anomalies, are part of the periodic accumulation and discharge of seismic energy.
(5) As continents receive the horizontal thrust of seafloor plates, crustal strains develop. Accumulation of strain can take anywhere from 100 years in certain coastal locations to over a millennium in some inland regions
(10) before a critical point is reached and a rupture occurs. In both areas, the buildup of strain is accompanied by long- and short-range precursory phenomena that are crucial to earthquake prediction.
(15) Quakes along active faults—like those along the Pacific coasts—are usually frequent; scientists designate such areas as quake-prone. However, when the time interval between quakes is great, as in inland regions, locating
(20) active faults is only a beginning. Geological scars of past subsidence, cracks, and offsets are useful in determining potential quake locations, as are seismicity gaps, areas where no small quakes have been recorded.
(25) Seismologists may also consult the historical record. Primary sources range from eyewitness accounts of ancient quakes to recent official documentation of quake-related damage.
(30) Once the perimeters of a quake-prone zone are established, a network of base stations can monitor precursory phenomena. Stations must extend over a wide area, yet be placed at measured intervals to obtain precise readings.
(35) Changes in geochemical readings (electric currents, radon concentrations) and in groundwater levels, as well as the occurrence of microearthquakes, are valuable precursors. Crustal movements—tilting, rising, and
(40) expansion or contraction of the ground surface—can be read through triangulation and leveling surveys taken over the course of decades. Theoretically, if an area's critical strain is known—the magnitude of strain
(45) necessary to produce a rupture—subtracting the measured accumulated crustal strain from the critical strain will indicate a time frame for an impending quake.

Violent tilting and foreshocks are among
(50) phenomena classified as short-term precursors. Many are still being identified as new quakes occur. Such precursors are valuable since their appearance can permit prediction of a quake to within hours of the
(55) primary rupture. Here, too, historical documents are useful. Seismologists recognized the liquefaction of sand as a precursor after a 1964 quake in Japan.

20. According to the passage, a major difference between coastal regions and inland regions is that in coastal regions

○ crustal strain does not occur

○ earthquakes are less numerous

○ critical points are reached more quickly

○ precursory phenomena are seldom observed

○ seafloor plate action is less powerful

GO ON TO THE NEXT PAGE

21. The primary purpose of the passage is to

    ○ clarify the way in which earthquakes develop in inland locations

    ○ show that earthquakes are a result of the normal accumulation and discharge of seismic energy

    ○ discuss the accumulation of crustal strain in coastal regions

    ○ argue that precursory phenomena should be disregarded in attempts at quake prediction

    ○ describe methods of earthquake prediction and explain the importance of precursory phenomena

22. The primary function of the third paragraph is to

    ○ explain the relationship between accumulated and critical strain

    ○ describe the use of precise intervals in establishing networks of base stations

    ○ summarize the differences between earthquakes in coastal and inland regions

    ○ outline some of the methods used by seismologists to predict earthquakes

    ○ suggest that critical strain is not spread evenly along most major fault lines

23. According to the passage, knowledge of an area's critical strain can help seismologists

    ○ estimate the date of a future earthquake

    ○ calculate the severity of an initial rupture

    ○ measure the seismic force along a fault

    ○ revise the distances between base stations

    ○ predict the rate of future crustal movement

GO ON TO THE NEXT PAGE

KAPLAN

24. Until the Federal government began providing low-cost flood insurance to coastal property owners, construction along beaches was limited by owners' fears that their property would be washed away. Since the insurance was made available, however, beachfront construction has boomed and land erosion has increased at a dangerous rate.

    Which of the following, if feasible, offers the best prospects for the Federal government to put a stop to the problem of land erosion along beaches?

    ◯ prohibiting beachfront property owners from embellishing or adding to existing buildings

    ◯ utilizing computer science techniques to obtain detailed information on the extent and rapidity of land erosion along beaches

    ◯ enacting building codes requiring new beachfront structures in flood-threatened areas to be elevated above the high water level of a storm

    ◯ compensating beachfront property owners for moving to a new location off the coast while canceling flood insurance benefits for any new or remaining beachfront construction

    ◯ requiring beachfront property owners receiving flood insurance coverage to adopt construction standards that will protect their buildings from inundation

25. In commercial garment construction, one advantage of serging over single-needle sewing is that the seam allowance is overcast as the seam is sewn <u>instead of</u> a separate process requiring deeper seam allowances.

    ◯ instead of

    ◯ rather than in

    ◯ in contrast with

    ◯ as opposed to

    ◯ as against being done in

GO ON TO THE NEXT PAGE ▷

KAPLAN

26. People with Williams syndrome, a rare mental disorder, are often highly articulate and sensitive. Not uncommonly, they are gifted in music and possess rich vocabularies. Yet these same people, because of their lack of ability in basic arithmetic and difficulty distinguishing left from right, are misleadingly labeled mentally retarded. As evaluated by conventional means such as IQ tests, their intelligence is no higher than that of people with Down's syndrome, despite the fact that people with Down's syndrome have uniformly limited cognitive abilities and show no specialized aptitudes.

The author is arguing that

○ conventional methods of measuring intelligence, such as IQ tests, are inadequate for evaluating the capabilities of people with certain mental disorders such as Williams syndrome

○ people with Down's syndrome usually have less verbal and musical ability but more mathematical and spatial ability than do people with Williams syndrome

○ conventional methods of measuring intelligence tend to consider basic mathematical and spatial ability to be more important than verbal and musical skills

○ people with Williams syndrome are only rarely given the opportunity to develop their unique musical and verbal abilities

○ people with Williams syndrome need greater encouragement if they are to develop their mathematical spatial skills

27. When the nineteenth-century German bacteriologist Robert Koch identified a particular bacterium as responsible for cholera, Max von Pettenkoffer, a physician, expressed his skepticism by voluntarily drinking an entire bottle of the allegedly responsible bacteria. Although von Pettenkoffer took his failure to come down with the disease as a refutation of Koch's hypothesis that cholera was caused by bacteria, Koch argued that von Pettenkoffer had been protected by his own stomach acid. The acid secreted by the stomach, Koch explained, kills most ingested bacteria.

Which of the following, if true, provides the most evidence to support Koch's counterargument?

○ Peptic ulcers, often associated with excessive secretions of stomach acid, are common in certain areas characterized by high rates of cholera.

○ As von Pettenkoffer later admitted that he had previously had cholera, it is probable that he had developed antibodies that protected him from a second attack.

○ Cholera is endemic in areas in which poor sanitation results in high concentrations of cholera bacteria in drinking water.

○ Although stomach acid kills most ingested bacteria, large numbers of E. coli bacteria nonetheless manage to make their way to the lower intestine of the digestive tract.

○ Cholera bacteria ingested with bicarbonate of soda, a neutralizer of stomach acid, is more likely to result in cholera than if the bacteria is ingested alone.

GO ON TO THE NEXT PAGE ⇒

KAPLAN

28. The Limón Dance Company believes that, since the death of José Limón in 1972, <u>they have and will continue to perpetuate the shared artistic vision of Limón and his mentor and collaborator Doris Humphrey,</u> who both choreographed works in the company's active repertory.

   ◯ they have and will continue to perpetuate the shared artistic vision of Limón and his mentor and collaborator Doris Humphrey,

   ◯ they have and will continue to perpetuate Limón and his mentor and collaborator Doris Humphrey's shared artistic vision,

   ◯ it has and will continue to perpetuate the shared artistic vision of Limón and his mentor and collaborator Doris Humphrey,

   ◯ it has perpetuated and will continue perpetuating the artistic vision that Limón and his mentor and collaborator Doris Humphrey shared,

   ◯ it has continued to perpetuate the shared artistic vision of Limón and his mentor and collaborator Doris Humphrey,

29. Agencies studying discrimination in housing have experimentally proved that minority clients are often discouraged as prospective buyers of residential real estate and <u>the antidiscrimination legislation of recent decades were only mitigating, rather than abolishing, inequity in housing practices</u>.

   ◯ the antidiscrimination legislation of recent decades were only mitigating, rather than abolishing, inequity in housing practices

   ◯ in recent decades, the antidiscrimination legislation only mitigated, rather than abolishing, inequity in housing practices

   ◯ that antidiscrimination legislation of recent decades has only mitigated, rather than abolished, inequity in housing practices

   ◯ that, in recent decades, antidiscrimination legislation has only mitigated, rather than abolishing, housing practices' inequity

   ◯ that recent decades' antidiscrimination legislation only were mitigating, rather than abolishing, housing practices' inequity

GO ON TO THE NEXT PAGE ⟩

30. Citing the legal precedent set by asbestos exposure cases, a state judge agreed to combine a series of workplace disability cases involving repetitive stress injuries to the hands and wrists. The judge's decision to consolidate hundreds of suits by data entry workers, word processors, newspaper employees, and other workers who use computers into one case is likely to prove detrimental for the computer manufacturing companies being sued, notwithstanding the defense's argument that the cases should not be combined because of the different individuals and workplaces involved.

Which of the following, if true, casts the most serious doubt on the validity of the judge's decision to consolidate the cases?

○ Unlike asbestos exposure cases, in which the allegedly liable product is the same in each situation, the type and quality of the allegedly liable office equipment is different in each case.

○ The fact that consolidation will accelerate the legal process may prove advantageous for the defense, as it limits the number of witnesses who can testify for the plaintiffs.

○ One of the most common causes of repetitive stress injuries is companies' failure to allow its employees adequate rest time from using computer keyboards.

○ Whereas exposure to asbestos often leads to fatal forms of cancer, repetitive stress injury typically results in personal discomfort and only rarely in unemployability.

○ The issue of responsibility for repetitive stress injury cannot be resolved without first addressing the question of its existence as an actual medical condition.

GO ON TO THE NEXT PAGE

31. <u>Each of William Kennedy's novels in the "Albany Trilogy"—*Ironweed, Legs,* and *Billy Phelan's Greatest Game*—are set in the area around Albany, New York,</u> a region whose history also suggested some details of the novels' plots.

    ⃝ Each of William Kennedy's novels in the "Albany Trilogy"—*Ironweed, Legs,* and *Billy Phelan's Greatest Game*—are set in the area around Albany, New York,

    ⃝ *Ironweed, Legs,* and *Billy Phelan's Greatest Game*—each of them novels in William Kennedy's "Albany Trilogy"—are set in the area around Albany, New York,

    ⃝ William Kennedy's "Albany Trilogy" novels—*Ironweed, Legs,* and *Billy Phelan's Greatest Game*—are all set in the area around Albany, New York,

    ⃝ Novels by William Kennedy—*Ironweed, Legs,* and *Billy Phelan's Greatest Game*—each one of the "Albany Trilogy" novels, is set in the area around Albany, New York,

    ⃝ Novels by William Kennedy—*Ironweed, Legs,* and *Billy Phelan's Greatest Game*—every one of the "Albany Trilogy" novels are set in the area around Albany, New York,

32. Between 1977 and 1989, the percentage of income paid to federal taxes by the richest one percent of Americans decreased, from 40 percent to 25 percent. By the end of that same period, however, the richest one percent of Americans were paying a larger proportion of all federal tax revenues, from 12.7 percent in 1977 to 16.2 percent in 1989.

    Which of the following, if true, contributes most to an explanation of the discrepancy described above?

    ⃝ Between 1977 and 1989, the Internal Revenue Service increased the percentage of its staff members responsible for audits and tax collection.

    ⃝ Between 1977 and 1989, the before-tax income of the richest one percent of Americans increased by over 75 percent when adjusted for inflation.

    ⃝ Between 1977 and 1989, many of the richest one percent of Americans shifted their investments from taxable to untaxable assets.

    ⃝ Between 1977 and 1989, the tax rate paid by middle-income Americans was reduced, but several tax loopholes were eliminated.

    ⃝ Between 1977 and 1989, the amount of federal taxes paid by the richest one percent of Americans increased by $45 billion, while the amount paid by all Americans rose by $50 billion.

GO ON TO THE NEXT PAGE ▷

Questions 33–35 refer to the following passage.

Contamination is the unintended presence of harmful substances or organisms in food. While it is true that recent scientific advances have resulted in safer foods, better methods of
(5) preservation, and improved storage practices, it is still necessary to guard against the practices that can increase the likelihood of food contamination. Because foodborne illness poses a potentially serious threat to
(10) public health, preventing contamination of safe food needs to be a prime objective of every foodservice manager. Furthermore, a foodservice manager must possess accurate information on the different hazards
(15) associated with the contamination of food in the event that a foodborne illness crisis does arise. A full understanding of the biological, chemical, and physical hazards allows the foodservice manager to implement the control
(20) measures necessary to minimize the health risks associated with food, and thus to decrease the possibility of contamination.

The most serious risk associated with food is the biological hazard. Biological hazards are
(25) dangers to food from pathogenic (disease-causing) microorganisms, such as bacteria, viruses, parasites, and fungi, and from toxins that occur in certain plants and fish. When biological hazards result in foodborne
(30) illnesses, these illnesses are generally classified as either infections or intoxications. A foodborne infection is a disease that results from eating food containing living harmful microorganisms. One of the most frequently
(35) reported diseases of this type is Salmonellosis, which results from the consumption of food contaminated with live pathogenic Salmonella.

The other major form of biologically induced
(40) foodborne illness is the foodborne intoxication, which results when toxins, or poisons, from bacterial or mold growth are present in ingested food and cause illness in the host (the human body). These toxins are generally
(45) odorless and tasteless, and are capable of causing disease even after the microorganisms have been killed. Staphylococcus food intoxication is one of the most common types of foodborne illness reported in the United
(50) States.

33. Which of the following best expresses the main idea of the passage?

○ Despite recent scientific advances, food-borne illness continues to present a serious risk to public health.

○ Although chemical and physical hazards can cause a foodborne illness, biological hazards pose the most serious risk of food contamination.

○ Knowledge of contamination sources is essential for a foodservice manager to safely operate a food establishment.

○ Biological, chemical, and physical hazards represent the main sources of food contamination.

○ The illnesses caused by the contamination of food by biological hazards take the form of either a foodborne infection or a foodborne intoxication.

GO ON TO THE NEXT PAGE ⟩

34. The author of the passage would most likely agree that a foodservice manager's comprehension of the nature of potential food hazards is

    ○ crucial to the safety of a foodservice operation

    ○ necessarily limited due to the complexity of contamination sources

    ○ the primary factor in an employer's decision to hire that manager

    ○ utilized exclusively for the prevention of foodborne illness

    ○ vitally important but nearly impossible to attain

35. According to the passage, pathogenic micro-organisms

    ○ are the most common form of biological hazard

    ○ can only trigger a foodborne illness when alive

    ○ are toxins that occur in certain plants and fish

    ○ include life forms such as bacteria and parasites

    ○ are difficult to detect because they are odorless and tasteless

36. Still employing the system of binomial nomenclature devised in the 18th century by Linnaeus, <u>new technology enables modern day biological taxonomists to not only classify species, but to sort</u> their evolutionary relationships by an approach that analyzes the sequences of DNA.

    ○ new technology enables modern day biological taxonomists to not only classify species, but to sort

    ○ modern day biological taxonomists using new technology can not only classify species, but also sort

    ○ using new technology enables modern day biological taxonomists to not only classify species, but they also sort

    ○ using new technology not only in classifying species, modern-day biological taxonomists are enabled to also sort them for

    ○ when modern day biological taxonomists are enabled by new technology, not only do they classify species, they also can sort

GO ON TO THE NEXT PAGE ⇨

37. American executives, unlike their Japanese counterparts, <u>have pressure to show</u> high profits in each quarterly report, with little thought given to long-term goals.

   ○ have pressure to show

   ○ are under pressure to show

   ○ are under pressure of showing

   ○ are pressured toward showing

   ○ have pressure that they should show

38. The impact of the 1930s crisis on the different regions of Country *X* varied depending on the relationship of each region's economy to the international marketplace, with Region *A* most drastically affected. Interestingly, demand in foreign markets for Region *A*'s tropical crops was only slightly affected by the drop in income levels after 1929; the same was true of foreign demand for the temperate-zone basic foodstuffs produced by Region *B*. However, Region *B* was better able to survive the crisis because it could adjust the supply of its crops. Since Region *A* could not, its economy was devastated by the slight decrease in foreign demand.

   Which one of the following provides the most reasonable explanation for the fact that Region *A*'s economy was more drastically affected by the slight decrease in demand than was Region *B*'s?

   ○ Tropical crops like those produced by Region *A* usually command higher prices on the world market than do basic foodstuffs like those produced by Region *B*.

   ○ Region *B*'s economy was dependent on annual crops, the supply of which is easily adjusted because the plants are renewed each year, in contrast to the perennial crops grown in Region *A*.

   ○ Because tropical goods are generally bought by more affluent consumers, demand for these products rarely declines even when overall income levels drop.

   ○ The temperate-zone basic foodstuffs produced in Region *B* directly competed with similar crops produced by the countries that imported Region *B*'s goods.

   ○ Because Region *B*'s economy was dependent on the export of basic foodstuffs, there was only a slight decline in demand for its goods even after income levels dropped.

KAPLAN

39. In the late 19th century, <u>when Vassar was a small, recently founded women's college, founding professor and astronomer Maria Mitchell taught as many Astronomy majors in a given year as there are today, when</u> Vassar is a much larger, coeducational college.

   ○ when Vassar was a small, recently founded women's college, founding professor and astronomer Maria Mitchell taught as many Astronomy majors in a given year as there are today, when

   ○ when Vassar was a small, recently founded women's college, in a given year, founding professor and astronomer Maria Mitchell taught just as many Astronomy majors as there are in a given year today, when

   ○ while Vassar was a small, recently founded women's college, founding professor and astronomer Maria Mitchell taught a number of Astronomy majors in a given year such as there are today, when

   ○ while Vassar was a small, recently founded women's college, founding professor and astronomer Maria Mitchell taught such a number of Astronomy majors in a given year as are there today, whereas

   ○ when Vassar was a small, recently founded women's college, founding professor and astronomer Maria Mitchell taught a number of Astronomy majors just as large in a given year as the number that is there today, while

40. The work of short fiction writer Charles Chesnutt reflects characteristic interests of his contemporary "local colorists" <u>as much as the intellectual ferment and historical reassessments of Black American culture during the late 19th century.</u>

   ○ as much as the intellectual ferment and historical reassessments of Black American culture during the late 19th century

   ○ as much as it did the intellectual ferment in, and historical reassessments of, Black American culture in the late 19th century

   ○ as much as it had reflected, during the late 19th century, the intellectual ferment and historical reassessments of Black American culture

   ○ as much as it was reflective and characteristic of the intellectual ferment and historical reassessments of late 19th century Black American culture

   ○ as much as it does the intellectual ferment and historical reassessments of late 19th century Black American culture

GO ON TO THE NEXT PAGE

41. Just as the various languages contributing to English broaden and enrich its expressive range with words as diverse as the Arabic *simoon,* the Greek *zephyr,* and the Native American *chinook,* <u>so the many musical traditions coexisting in U.S. culture create unlimited possibilities for the fusion of musical styles</u>.

   ⬭ so the many musical traditions coexisting in U.S. culture create unlimited possibilities for the fusion of musical styles

   ⬭ similarly, the coexistence of many musical traditions in U.S. culture create unlimited possibilities in the fusing of musical styles

   ⬭ the many musical traditions coexisting in U.S. culture are creating unlimited possibilities in musical styles' fusion

   ⬭ in the same way, possibilities for the fusion of musical styles are unlimited, owing to the many musical traditions that coexist in U.S. culture

   ⬭ so it is in U.S. culture, where the many coexistent musical traditions make it possible that unlimited fusion of musical styles may be created

IF YOU FINISH BEFORE TIME IS CALLED, YOU MAY CHECK YOUR WORK ON THIS SECTION ONLY. DO NOT TURN TO ANY OTHER SECTION IN THE TEST. STOP

PART FOUR

Practice Test
Answers and Explanations

PRACTICE TEST
ANSWER KEY

Quantitative Section

1.	C	20.	D
2.	E	21.	B
3.	B	22.	D
4.	B	23.	E
5.	D	24.	B
6.	A	25.	E
7.	C	26.	C
8.	A	27.	E
9.	C	28.	D
10.	D	29.	E
11.	D	30.	B
12.	B	31.	B
13.	E	32.	A
14.	C	33.	B
15.	A	34.	B
16.	A	35.	E
17.	D	36.	A
18.	A	37.	D
19.	D		

Verbal Section

1.	C	22.	D
2.	E	23.	A
3.	C	24.	D
4.	B	25.	B
5.	D	26.	A
6.	B	27.	E
7.	C	28.	E
8.	D	29.	C
9.	D	30.	A
10.	A	31.	C
11.	C	32.	B
12.	C	33.	C
13.	A	34.	A
14.	A	35.	D
15.	D	36.	B
16.	C	37.	B
17.	E	38.	B
18.	D	39.	A
19.	E	40.	E
20.	C	41.	A
21.	E		

COMPUTE YOUR GMAT PRACTICE TEST SCORE

The steps outlined in the pages that follow will allow you to calculate your GMAT Practice Test score. However, keep in mind that this score should not be taken too literally. Practice test conditions cannot precisely mirror real test conditions. Your actual GMAT scores will almost certainly vary from your practice test scores.

Step 1: Figure out your Quantitative raw score.

Refer to your answer sheet for the number right and the number wrong on the Math sections. Multiply the total number of Math questions you got wrong by .25 and subtract the result from the total number of Math questions you got right. Round the result to the nearest whole number. This is your raw Quantitative score.

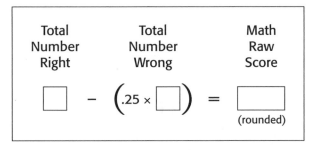

Step 2: Figure out your Verbal raw score.

Refer to your answer sheet for the number right and the number wrong on the Verbal sections. Multiply the total number of Verbal questions you got wrong by .25 and subtract the result from the total number of Verbal questions you got right. Round the result to the nearest whole number. This is your raw Verbal score.

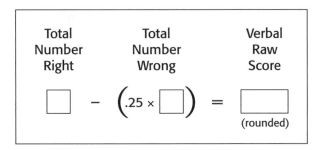

Step 3: Find your Quantitative scaled score and percentile ranking.

Use the chart below to find the scaled score and percentile ranking corresponding to your raw Quantitative score.

Raw Quantitative Score	Scaled Quantitative Score	Quantitative Percentile	Raw Quantitative Score	Scaled Quantitative Score	Quantitative Percentile
37	54	99	18	32	35
36	53	99	17	30	29
35	52	99	16	28	23
34	51	99	15	26	18
33	50	96	14	25	15
32	49	91	13	24	14
31	48	87	12	22	10
30	47	83	11	21	9
29	46	80	10	19	7
28	45	78	9	18	6
27	44	74	8	16	4
26	43	71	7	15	4
25	42	67	6	13	2
24	41	64	5	12	2
23	39	57	4	11	1
22	38	55	3	9	1
21	37	52	2	8	1
20	35	43	1	7	1
19	34	41	< or = 0	5	0

Step 4: Find your Verbal scaled score and percentile ranking.

Use the chart below to find the scaled score and percentile ranking corresponding to your raw Verbal score.

Raw Verbal Score	Scaled Verbal Score	Verbal Percentile	Raw Verbal Score	Scaled Verbal Score	Verbal Percentile
41	50	99	20	27	45
40	49	99	19	26	43
39	48	99	18	25	38
38	47	99	17	23	30
37	46	99	16	22	28
36	45	99	15	20	20
35	44	97	14	19	16
34	43	97	13	18	15
33	42	96	12	17	12
32	41	93	11	16	9
31	40	90	10	15	7
30	39	89	9	14	6
29	38	85	8	12	2
28	37	83	7	11	2
27	36	81	6	10	1
26	35	76	5	9	1
25	33	69	4	8	0
24	32	67	3	6	0
23	31	61	2	5	0
22	30	59	1	4	0
21	28	51	< 0 or = 0	3	0

KAPLAN

Step 5: Find your total scaled score and percentile ranking.

Add your raw Quantitative score and your raw Verbal score from Step 1. This is your total raw score. Use the chart below to find the scaled score and percentile ranking corresponding to your total raw score.

Total Raw Score	Total Scaled Score	Total Percentile	Total Raw Score	Total Scaled Score	Total Percentile
0	200–230	<1	40	560	64
1	240	1	41	560	64
2	250	1	42	570	67
3	260	1	43	570	67
4	270	1	44	580	70
5	280	1	45	580	70
6	290	2	46	590	73
7	300	2	47	590	73
8	310	3	48	600	75
9	320	4	49	600	75
10	330	5	50	610	78
11	340	6	51	610	78
12	350	7	52	620	81
13	360	8	53	620	81
14	370	10	54	630	83
15	380	12	55	630	83
16	390	13	56	640	85
17	400	15	57	640	85
18	410	18	58	650	88
19	420	20	59	650	88
20	430	23	60	660	90
21	440	25	61	660	90
22	450	28	62	670	91
23	460	30	63	670	91
24	470	34	64	680	93
25	480	37	65	680	93
26	490	40	66	690	94
27	490	40	67	690	94
28	500	43	68	700	95
29	500	43	69	710	96
30	510	47	70	720	97
31	510	47	71	730	98
32	520	50	72	740	99
33	520	50	73	750	99
34	530	53	74	760	99
35	530	53	75	770	99
36	540	57	76	780	99
37	540	57	77	790	99
38	550	60	78	800	99
39	550	60			

KAPLAN

Answers and Explanations

QUANTITATIVE SECTION EXPLANATIONS

1. C

Here we have a percent problem with no numbers. One thing you know: *You can't simply subtract the percents to get "25% minus 20% equals a 5% increase," because the percents are of different wholes.* The percent decrease is a percentage of the new, increased amount, not a percentage of the original amount. The best way to solve problems like this is to use a concrete number. *Since we're dealing with percents, the number to start with is 100.* (Don't worry about whether 100 is a "realistic" number in the context of the problem; we just need a convenient number to tell us how big the final amount is relative to the starting amount.) Say the price of copper starts at $100. 25% of $100 is $25, so if the price of copper increases by 25%, it rises by $25 to $125. Now the price decreases by 20%. 20% is just $\frac{1}{5}$, so the price drops by $\frac{125}{5}$ or $25. So the price drops to $100. That's the original price, so the answer is (C).

2. E

This problem is just a matter of keeping the information straight. The easiest way to do this is to make a scratchwork chart, putting one person's initial above another when the first person is known to be taller. *The trick is to make sure you don't unwittingly imply a relationship in heights when none is stated; so draw your chart very carefully.* Sidney is known to be taller than Roger, so Sidney's initial goes above Roger's. Roger is taller than Vernon, so Vernon goes below Roger (and Sidney). Billy is taller than Roger, so he goes above Roger. But who is taller: Sidney or Billy? We have no way of knowing, so we'll put Billy next to Sidney. Billy is also taller than Felix, so we put Felix underneath Billy. However, we have no idea of Felix's height in relation to anyone else's, so we should put Felix off to the side. Your chart might look something like this:

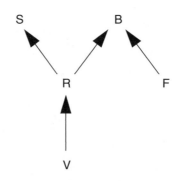

Now try the answer choices. As we just said, we only know Felix's height in relation to Billy, so (A) and (C) are out. (B) isn't necessarily true either: Both Sidney and Billy are taller than Roger, but we don't know which is taller than the other. That kills (D), too: Though Sidney and Billy are both taller than Roger, we can't conclude that Sidney is also taller than Felix simply because Billy is. (E) is left by process of elimination. Just to check, Billy is taller than Roger and Roger is taller than Vernon, so Billy does indeed have to be taller than Vernon.

3. B

We see an equation with two variables, x and y. If we can determine the value of y, we could solve for x. Note that we don't have to do the work.

(1) Insufficient: From statement (1), we know that $y = 2$ or $y = -2$; consequently, x has two values as well. This statement is insufficient, so eliminate choices (A) and (D).

(2) Sufficient: The value of y is given, so the value of x can be determined. The statement is sufficient.

4. B

For the spring water, the bottler must test $0.05(120) = 6$ cases, and for the sparking water, he must test $0.1(80) = 8$ cases. The total number of cases to be tested for the spring and sparkling water combined is $6 + 8 = 14$, which is $\dfrac{14}{200} = \dfrac{7}{100} = 7\%$ of all cases.

5. D

When you're faced with an inequality, make sure you understand what it means—don't deal with it by just manipulating symbols. Here, $xy > 0$ means xy is positive. This means that either x and y are both positive or they're both negative. They can't have different signs. Seeing the question in terms of positives and negatives can make it easy to answer. If x and y are both positive, (A) and (E) are true. If x and y are both negative, (B) and (C) are true. That leaves only (D), which must always be false. A fraction can only be negative if the numerator and denominator (x and y here) have different signs.

6. A

The first thing we know when we see a problem like this is that it doesn't require advanced exponential computation. The GMAT isn't about testing difficult computation; it tests whether we understand the basic rules of manipulating exponents. Indeed, the point is to eliminate the need to work with exponential expressions. We can do that by converting the expressions on either side of the equation into exponents with the same base. The equation can be rewritten: $(3)^{(3a + 4)} = (3^2)^{(a)}$. When we raise a power to an exponent, we multiply the exponents: $(3^2)^{(a)} = (3)^{2a}$. So the equation is $(3)^{(3a + 4)} = (3)^{2a}$. Since both sides of the equation have the same base, 3, we can set the two exponents equal: $3a + 4 = 2a$. The rest is simple algebra. Solving $3a + 4 = 2a$, $a + 4 = 0$, and $a = -4$.

7. C

In order to determine the standard deviation for a set of numbers, you need to know how the numbers are spread out within the set. Since the table (stem) gives us the averages and the number of students, we need information about how spread out the students are in Class A and Class B in order to solve.

(1) Insufficient: This statement gives you information about how spread out Class A is, but offers you no information about Class B.

(2) Insufficient: This statement gives you information about how spread out Class B is, but offers you no information about Class A.

In combination: the statements are sufficient since statement (1) gives information about the standard deviation of Class A and (2) gives information about the standard deviation for Class B. Although you cannot determine the exact standard deviations of either class, you can see that Class B has a much narrower distribution of members than Class A and from this you could determine that Class A would have a greater standard deviation than Class B. Choice (C) is the correct answer.

KAPLAN

8. A

If we can determine the smallest integer on the list or a specific integer on the list when the list is written in increasing order, we can determine the greatest integer on the list.

(1) Sufficient: We're given one variable and one equation for the smallest integer on the list. That means we could solve for the smallest integer and add 10 to find the greatest integer. If you don't see this, consider $(x + 72)^{\frac{1}{3}} = 4$. Cubing both sides, $x + 72 = 4^3$. Then $x + 72 = 64$, and $x = -8$. Adding 10 to -8, the greatest integer is 2. Eliminate choices (B), (C), and (E).

(2) Insufficient: If $\frac{1}{64} = x^{-2}$, then $\frac{1}{64} = \frac{1}{x^2}$ and $x^2 = 64$. So $x = 8$ or $x = -8$. There are two different possibilities for the smallest integer on the list, so there must be two different possibilities for the greatest integer on the list. Statement (2) is insufficient.

9. C

We're told that the average of $3a + 4$ and another number, which we'll call x, is $2a$. That means $\frac{(3a + 4) + x}{2} = 2a$. We can solve for x in terms of a : $(3a + 4) + x = 4a$; $x = 4a - (3a + 4)$; $x = a - 4$. We're asked to find the average of x and a. That's just the average of $(a - 4)$ and a, which is $\frac{(a - 4) + a}{2}$, or $\frac{2a - 4}{2}$, or $a - 2$. The algebra here is simple; the difficult part is remembering what numbers you're taking the average of, and what number we're looking for. First, we're looking for x, but the answer is not x in terms of a; the answer is the average of x (expressed in terms of a) and a. You must also remember that you get the average of two numbers by adding them and dividing by two.

You could also have solved this by picking a number for a, such as 2. Then, $3a + 4$ is 10, and the average of 10 and the unknown number x is $2a$, or 4. So $\frac{10 + x}{2} = 4$, $10 + x = 8$, and $x = -2$. The average of x and a, therefore, is just the average of -2 and 2, which is $\frac{2 + (-2)}{2}$, or 0. So look at the answer choices for the ones that equal 0 when $a = 2$. The only one that fits is (C), $a - 2$.

10. D

We're told to figure out when Jan will catch up with Tom. Jan reads at the rate of 40 pages per hour and Tom reads at the rate of 30 pages per hour. Tom starts reading 50 minutes ahead of Jan. Since 50 minutes is $\frac{5}{6}$ of an hour, by the time Jan starts reading at 5:20, Tom has already read $\frac{5}{6} \times 30 = 25$ pages. You might have saved yourself some work by noticing that Jan gains 10 pages an hour on Tom, since she reads 10 pages an hour faster. Since he's got a head start of 25 pages at 5:20, it should take her $\frac{25(\text{pages})}{10(\text{pages/hour})} = 2.5$ (hours) for her to catch him.

You can also work out the problem algebraically. The number of pages Jan has read at any given time after 5:20 is $40x$, where x is the time in hours from 5:20. At 6:20 she's read 40 pages, at 7:20 she's read 80 pages, etcetera. The number of pages that Tom has read at any time after 5:20 is $25 + 30x$. We want to know when these quantities will be equal, that is, when $25 + 30x = 40x$.

Solving for x, we get $25 = 40x - 30x$, $25 = 10x$, $2\frac{1}{2} = x$.

So it takes $2\frac{1}{2}$ hours for Jan to catch Tom. Since Jan started at 5:20, this means she will catch Tom at precisely 7:50.

11. D

Remember that Work = Rate × Time.

(1) Sufficient: This statement tells us that Mike's construction company builds houses at the rate of $2 \times 40 = 80$ houses per year. The two companies together build houses at the rate of $40 + 80 = 120$ houses per year. So we can determine how long it will take the companies working together to build 64 houses. Eliminate answer choices (B), (C), and (E).

(2) Sufficient: This statement gives us the rate at which Mike's company builds houses. So we can find the rate at which the companies build houses together and we can find how long it will take both companies working together to build 64 houses.

12. B

The multiples of 3 from 15 through 105 inclusive are 15, 18, 21, …102, and 105. Let's write these multiples in a way that makes the solution to this problem clear.

$$15 = 3 \times 5, \ 18 = 3 \times 6, \ 21 = 3 \times 7, \ 24 = 3 \times 8, \ldots$$

$$102 = 3 \times 34, \text{ and } 105 = 3 \times 35.$$

So the multiples of 3 from 15 through 105 inclusive can be obtained by multiplying 3 by each of the integers 5 through 35 inclusive. Therefore the answer to this question is the number of integers from 5 through 35 inclusive. Now $35 - 5 = 30$, but don't make the mistake of forgetting to include 5 as an integer as well. There are $\underline{31}$ integers among the integers 5 through 35 inclusive. Thus, the number of multiples of 3 among the integers 15 through 105 inclusive is 31.

13. E

All we know is that x is a prime number. We want enough information to determine which prime number x is. Our method, then, is to try to find more than one prime that fits with whatever information we're given. If we can, the information is insufficient; if we can't—if we can find only one prime that fits with the information—then the information is sufficient.

(1) Insufficient: If $x < 15$, x could be 2, 3, 5, 7, 11, or 13. Eliminate (A) and (D).

(2) Insufficient: If $(x - 2)$ is a multiple of five, then x is 2 more than a multiple of 5. So the question is: Can we find more than one prime number that is 2 more than a multiple of five? Yes. Multiples of 5 are 0, 5, 10, 15, 20, and so on. Two more than 5 is 7—a prime number. While 2 more than 10 is 12, which isn't a prime number, 2 more than 15 is 17, which is prime. Eliminate (B).

In combination: Statement 1 narrowed down the possible values of x to 2, 3, 5, 7, 11, and 13. Remember that 0 is a multiple of 5 as well. So both 2 and 7 are 2 more than a multiple of 5, so we cannot find a single answer to the question using both statements. Choose (E).

14. C

Both people are traveling at *about* a floor per second. There are 40 floors between them. So it would take one person about 40 seconds to traverse this distance, and it would take two people about 20 seconds when they are traveling towards each other. So each will travel for about 20 seconds. Now, let's plug that in and see just how far off we are. Twenty seconds is one-third of a minute; Steve travels 57 floors a minute; so in 20 seconds Steve travels $57 \times \frac{1}{3} = 57 = 19$ floors. Joyce would, in the same 20 seconds, travel $63 \times \frac{1}{3} = \frac{63}{3} = 21$. That makes exactly 40 stories that the two would travel, which is exactly what we need. Steve moves up 19 stories and Joyce descends 21 stories, both to the 30th floor.

You could also have solved this question by adding the two rates. Steve travels at 57 floors per minute and Joyce at 63 floors per minute. So they are decreasing the number of floors between them at a rate of 57 + 63 or 120 floors per minute. This is 2 floors per second. Since they start out 40 floors apart, it'll take them $\frac{40}{2}$ or 20 seconds to meet. After 20 seconds, which is $\frac{1}{3}$ of a minute, Steve will have moved $57 \times \frac{1}{3}$ or 19 floors and he will be on the 30th floor, the same floor Joyce will be on after 20 seconds.

If you were pressed for time, a third option would be to estimate and guess. Joyce is traveling faster, so she'll go farther. That means they can't have met at the halfway point (floor 31) or any of the floors closer to her. Eliminate (D) and (E). Since they are traveling at nearly the same rate, they would have to meet near the halfway point, floor 31. Eliminate (A). At this point, you can guess between (B) and (C).

15. A

In 8 hours George will have copied 50 pages, and Sonya will have copied more than 50 pages (since she needs only 6 hours to do 50 pages). That means that in 8 hours the two of them together can copy more than 100 pages. But all the answer choices except (A) are longer than 8 hours, so (A) must be correct.

This problem could also be solved using math.

George takes 8 hours to do a 50-page manuscript, so each hour, he copies $\frac{50}{8} = 6\frac{1}{4}$ pages. Each hour, Sonya copies $\frac{50}{6} = 8\frac{1}{3}$ pages. Working together, in one hour they would copy $6\frac{1}{4} + 8\frac{1}{3}$ or $14\frac{7}{12}$ pages. Divide that number into 100 (the number of pages we want copied) and we'll have the number of hours needed. The solution is $6\frac{6}{7}$.

16. A

Because we know that 3 is a solution, we can plug it into the equation. Thus, $3^2 + 2(3) + m = 5$, $9 + 6 + m = 5$, $15 + m = 5$, and $m = -10$. We can now rewrite the equation as $x^2 + 2x - 10 = 5$ or $x^2 + 2x - 15 = 0$. Factoring the left side of this equation, we see that $(x + 5)(x - 3) = 0$, which has the solutions -5 and 3. Therefore, $x = -5$ is the other solution.

17. D

The correct approach here is not to multiply out the numbers, but to factor the large number completely, then compare its factors to 5^2 and 3^3. Any 5s or 3s that can't be factored out of $2^5 \times 6^2 \times 7^3$ will have to be factors of n. So, completing the prime factorization, we get: $n \times 2^5 \times 2^2 \times 3^2 \times 7^3$. We can combine the 2s: $n \times 2^7 \times 3^2 \times 7^3$. The only common factors so far are two 3s. That means that the two 5s and the remaining 3 must all be factors of n, in order for the two 5s and three 3s to be factors of the entire product. The smallest number that has two 5s and one 3 as factors is $5 \times 5 \times 3$, or 75.

18. A

The formula for the area of a rectangle is: area = length × width. So here we have: area = $a \times b$. Since we are only asked for the rectangle's area, rather than its length and width, we can answer the question without actually determining a or b. All we really need is the product of a and b. (After all, a rectangle with area 6 could have sides of 3 and 2 or sides of 6 and 1. Either way, it has an area of 6.)

(1) Sufficient: While we cannot solve the equation for either variable, we can find the product of the two variables. We multiply both sides by b. This gives us $2ab = 15$. Now we can divide both sides by 2 and get a value for ab. Eliminate (B), (C), and (E).

(2) Insufficient: We cannot solve this single equation for either variable, nor can we find the value of ab from it. Choose (A).

19. D

LMN is a 45°–45°–90° triangle, so the lengths of its sides are related by the ratio $x : x : x\sqrt{2}$. Likewise, JKN is a 30°–60°–90° triangle, so the lengths of its sides are related by the ratio $x : x\sqrt{3} : 2x$. For both of these triangles, learning the length of any side enables us to calculate the lengths of the other two sides. In addition, both triangles are formed by leaning the same board against a wall, so $LM = JK$. So learning the length of any side of either triangle enables us to find all the other 5 side lengths for both triangles—the other 2 side lengths of that triangle and also all 3 side lengths of the other triangle. Each statement alone is sufficient since each statement gives a side length of one of the triangles.

20. D

A common mistake is to pick (A). It's a logic task that many people prefer to visualize, using dashes for desks. We'll just refer to the desks as 1, 2, 3, and 4, in that order, and we'll call the students X and Y. In order to keep at least one empty desk between the two, we have to keep either one or two empty desks between them. If we keep only one desk between the two, there are two ways the chairs can be occupied: X can be in 1 with Y in 3, or X can be in 2 with Y in 4. If, on the other hand, we keep two empty chairs between the students, then there's only one way to occupy the desks: X in 1 and Y in 4. Since X and Y can be switched in all three of our orders, the answer is 6.

21. B

We need the ratio of men to women. The only thing to keep in mind is the difference between ratios and actual numbers.

(1) Insufficient: The phrase *3 less than* ruins it. Otherwise we'd have a 1:2 ratio of women to men, giving us a 2:1 ratio of men to women. But with the *3 less than* thrown in, we cannot derive a ratio. *Ratios are comparisons by division or multiplication, using a common divisor or multiple; less than is a comparison by addition or subtraction. We can't get the former from the latter.* To demonstrate by picking numbers, if there are 9 people in the class, we get 8 men and 1 woman—an 8:1 ratio. But if there are 12 people in the class, we get 10 men and 2 women—a 5:1 ratio. Eliminate (A) and (D).

(2) Sufficient: $\frac{2}{5}$ is a comparison by division; it is a ratio. There are 2 women for every 5 men—a 5:2 ratio of men to women. Choose (B).

KAPLAN

22. D

The warehouse has two kinds of coats in it: full-length and shorter coats. Initially 15 percent of the coats are full-length, but then a number of the short coats are removed. We're asked to calculate what percent of the remaining coats are full-length. The key to this question is first to calculate the number of full-length coats. At first, there are 800 coats in the warehouse; if 15 percent of these are full-length, then $\frac{15}{100} \times 800 = 15 \times 8 = 120$ coats are full-length.

Then 500 short coats are removed. So that makes 300 coats in total remaining. There are still 120 full-length coats in the warehouse. What percentage of 300 does 120 represent? $\frac{120}{300} = \frac{40}{100} = 40$ percent.

23. E

We are dealing with three integers, q, r, and s. We need to determine either that they cannot be consecutive or must be consecutive. Anything else is insufficient.

(1) Insufficient: This tells you that q, r, and s are evenly spaced and that r is the middle term, but the terms could be 1, 2, 3; or 0, 5, 10; or myriad other options.

(2) Insufficient: Again, from this statement, all we can determine is that we are dealing with evenly spaced integers, but we do not know whether they are consecutive or spaced further apart.

In combination: Since each statement gave the same information about integers q, r, and s, the statements in combination are insufficient as well. Choice (E).

24. B

This is a typical word problem, which needs to be set up as an equation. We'll use r for orchestra (we don't want the letter o, as it might get confused with the number 0), m for first mezzanine, and s for second mezzanine tickets. The total number of tickets sold is 2,350. Therefore: $r + m + s = 2{,}350$. We need to solve for r. Any information that allows us to solve for r will be sufficient, whether or not it allows us to solve for the other variables.

(1) Insufficient: This equation only relates m to s. We get $m = \frac{1}{2}s$. That tells us nothing about how many orchestra tickets were sold. Eliminate (A) and (D).

(2) Sufficient: By giving us an equation relating r to the sum of the other tickets (the sum of m and s), this statement allows us to replace $m + s$ in the original equation with $1.5r$, leaving only one variable to solve for. We're told that $m + s = 1.5r$. Thus, we can substitute $1.5r$ for $m + s$ and solve: $r + 1.5r = 2{,}350$. Choose (B).

25. E

To solve this, you need to know the formula for the area of a triangle, and you need to understand the basics of coordinate geometry. First, you should notice that point C is on the x-axis. That means C has a y-coordinate of 0, which allows you to eliminate (A) and (D). Even if you couldn't figure out how to do any more, this would considerably improve your odds of guessing. *In general, any time you are told the area of a triangle, you should suspect that the formula for the area ($\frac{1}{2}base \times height = area$) will come into play.* We can use this formula to find the x-coordinate of C. Notice that the segment AC is a base of the triangle. Since this segment lies entirely along the x-axis, and since A is at the origin (with an x-coordinate of 0), the length of the segment is exactly the x-coordinate of C. So if we find the length of the base AC, we'll have C's x-coordinate. The y-coordinate of the apex B is k, so the distance of B above the x-axis is k. Since the base lies along the x-axis, that means the height of the triangle is k. Now we have enough to fill in our equation: $\frac{1}{2}base \times height = area$. $\frac{1}{2}base \times k = 8$, where b, the base, is equal to the x-coordinate of C. We get: $(b)(k) = 16; b = \frac{16}{k}$.

The coordinates of C are $(\frac{16}{k}, 0)$.

26. C

Use the probability formula:

$$\text{Probability} = \frac{\text{Desired \# of outcomes}}{\text{Possible \# of outcomes}}$$

First, determine the number of possible outcomes of rain for City X over a 5 day period. There are two possibilities for each day—rain or no rain—so the total number of possible outcomes would be $2 \times 2 \times 2 \times 2 \times 2 = 32$.

Next, determine the desired outcomes. Your best approach is to list the ways in which you could get rain on exactly 3 days. They are as follows:

RRRNN; RRNRN; RRNNR; RNRRN; RNRNR; RNNRR; NRRRN; NRRNR; NRNRR; NNRRR.

KAPLAN

There are 10 desired outcomes in all, and a systematic run-through of the possibilities should account for them all. So the probability is $\frac{10}{32} = \frac{5}{16}$, and choice (C) is the correct answer.

27. E

The question asks for the gross profit: that's the cost of the soda minus the cost of the syrup used in making the soda. The cost of the syrup is km, the cost per liter times the number of liters of syrup. The cost of the soda is j (the price per liter) times the number of liters of soda. But the number of liters of soda is just the number of liters of syrup, m, plus the number of liters of water, which is mw, since the recipe requires w liters of water for every liter of soda. Therefore, the cost of the soda is $j(m + mw)$. That makes the gross profit $j(m + mw) - km$. The answer is not expressed in exactly this form; finding it depends on your ability to use the distributive law in algebraic expressions. Recognizing (E) as the answer is just a matter of seeing that $jm(1 + w) = j(m + mw)$.

Alternatively, you could do this question by picking numbers. Remember, you still have to figure out how to do the substitution in order to get the right number for the gross profit. Pick small numbers for the variables. Say $w = 2, m = 4, j = 3$, and $k = 5$. Then we have 4 liters of syrup; that costs $4k = 20$ dollars. We have $4w = 8$ liters of water; that makes $8 + 4 = 12$ liters of soda. The total cost of the soda is $12j = 36$ dollars. So the profit is $36 - 20 = 16$ dollars. The correct answer choice should result in 16 if we plug in all the above values for w, m, j, and k. The only choice that works out is (E). *Sometimes when you pick numbers you'll find that more than one choice gives the right answer; in those cases you have to try to narrow it down again with a new set of values.*

28. D

We want the average. Using the average formula, which is $\dfrac{\text{sum of terms}}{\text{number of terms}}$, we can set up the expression for the average number of cars sold per salesperson, $\dfrac{11a + 16b}{a + b}$ where a is the number of salespeople at location A and b is the number of salespeople at location B.

Any information that allows us to evaluate this expression will be sufficient.

(1) Sufficient: Here we get an equation that allows us to express each of a and b in terms of the other. Since a is $3b$, we can substitute $3b$ for a in our original expression and solve for the average. Eliminate (B), (C), and (E).

(2) Sufficient: Here we get the total number of cars sold at each of *A* and *B*. This allows us to determine the number of salespeople at each location, which we've symbolized as *a* and *b*. With values for *a* and *b*, we can find the value of the expression $\frac{11a + 16b}{a + b}$ and thus determine the average. Choose (D).

29. E

If an "anglet" is one percent of a degree, then there are 100 anglets in each degree. Since there are 360 degrees in a circle, there are 100 × 360, or 36,000, anglets in a circle. Never let the introduction of a new term like "anglet" worry you; *questions that introduce new terms are usually easy, involving little more than a simple substitution.*

30. B

You know that 600 people were polled, and you know that they voted either in one of three categories: in favor, against, or undecided. In terms of equations and variables, we have 1 equation and 3 unknowns: $F + A + U = 600$.

(1) Insufficient: Gives you information about those who were in favor and those who were against, but since we are given no information on those undecided, the statement is insufficient.

(2) Sufficient: Gives you the number undecided and an equation from which you can find the number against the bill. Once these two values are determined, you can find the number of those in favor. Choice (B) is the correct answer.

31. B

We're looking for the cost of the bricks that were actually used to make the fireplace. In order to find that, we need to know how many bricks were used, and what each brick costs. Since $\frac{3}{4}$ of the bricks were used, $\frac{1}{4}$ of the bricks weren't used. That unused quarter of the total amounted to 190 bricks. That means that number of bricks that were used, $\frac{3}{4}$ of the total, amounted to 3 × 190, or 570 bricks. Each brick cost 40 cents, so the total cost of the bricks that were used must have been 0.40 × 570 = 228 dollars.

KAPLAN

32. A

This problem asks for the expression with the greatest absolute value, so we have to remember to consider negative values; problems like this are often set up to trip up those who assume the answer must be a positive number. The only way to solve this is to try each choice. Since x can be any number from -2 to 2 inclusive, and we're looking for the greatest possible absolute value, it makes sense to plug these two extreme values of x into each choice. For each choice, then, the largest possible absolute value will result either from giving x the value of 2 or from giving x the value of -2.

In (A), $3x - 1$ is 5 when $x = 2$, and -7 when $x = -2$. In (B), $x^2 + 1$ is 5 when $x = 2$ and also when $x = -2$. In (C), $3 - x$ is 1 when $x = 2$, and 5 when $x = -2$. In (D), $x - 3$ is -1 when $x = 2$, and -5 when $x = -2$. In (E), $x^2 - x$ is 2 when $x = 2$, and 6 when $x = -2$. Out of these possible values for the expressions, -7 has the largest absolute value, so (A) is the answer.

33. B

Don't make the mistake of multiplying out the parentheses—that would be too time consuming and complicated. We're presented with two quantities that have a product of zero. Therefore, at least one of the two quantities must have a value of zero. *So the question is really asking: What's the smallest value of x that will make one of these parenthetical expressions equal zero?*

You can save yourself further time by checking the second expression first (as it is easier to work with). Suppose $x^2 - 4 = 0$. Then $x^2 = 4$, and x can be 2 or -2. That immediately narrows down the choices to (A) and (B), since -2 is already smaller than (C), (D), and (E). You can then check (A) directly by seeing whether $\frac{12}{x} + 36$ is 0 when $x = -3$: $\frac{12}{-3} + 36$ equals $(-4) + 36$, which equals 32, which is definitely not 0. So (A) can't be the answer and we're left with only (B). Alternatively, you could have checked for any other possible values of x by setting $\frac{12}{x} + 36$ equal to 0, and solving: $\frac{12}{x} + 36 = 0$; $\frac{12}{x} = -36$; $-36x = 12$; $x = \frac{12}{-36}$; $x = -\frac{1}{3}$.

You'd still have discovered that -2 is the smallest value of x, but it's a more time consuming method.

34. B

We need b. There's nothing more to it than that.

(1) Insufficient: This is one equation with two variables. We cannot solve for either variable. Eliminate (A) and (D).

(2) Sufficient: *The equation hasn't been simplified, and that should set off alarm bells.* It looks to be insoluble: one equation, two variables. Yet, the variable a occurs twice. When we simplify, by removing the parentheses, we get $a = b - 1 + a$. Subtracting a from each side, we have $0 = b - 1$. This can be solved for b. Choose (B).

35. E

Solving this is just a matter of restating each answer choice as a simple number by multiplying out the powers of 10. *To multiply by a positive power of 10, simply move the decimal point to the right the same number of places as the exponent of 10.* So to simplify (A), take 0.00001 and move the decimal point 8 places to the right. After 5 places we have 1.0; 3 more places gives us 1,000. We want a number greater than 1,000.01, so we move on. Moving the decimal 4 places to the right in (B) only gives us 101. (C) becomes 110. (D) converts to 1,000.01 exactly. Therefore we know (E) is right without figuring it out (as a matter of fact it converts to 1,000.1).

36. A

We want information about the values a and b or about the value of their sum. We keep in mind that neither a nor b is necessarily positive or an integer.

(1) Sufficient: The numerator is *the difference of two squares.* This is a common expression on the GMAT and we know instantly that it factors into $(a + b)$ times $(a - b)$. Canceling the $(a - b)$ from both the numerator and denominator, we're left with the value of $a + b$. Eliminate (B), (C), and (E).

(2) Insufficient: There's a common GMAT trap here. You might have been inclined to remove the exponent from the left side of the equation in order to get a value for $a + b$. We cannot find the value of $a + b$ simply by knowing that $(a + b) = 36$ because both 6 and −6 squared result in 36. Choose (A).

37. D

As with the previous question, we want information about the sum of two variables. Unlike the previous question, though, we get useful information. If the two expressions are equal, and if the bases are equal, then the exponents have to be equal. (2 taken to some power can only equal 2 to that power.) So we start out knowing that $(2m + 1) = (n + 2)$. One equation, two variables.

(1) Sufficient: Approached abstractly, we have another, different equation. Thus, we now have two equations and two variables. We can solve for the variables and add them. Approached less abstractly, this equation allows us to solve for the value of n (hint: 256 is 2^8). Substituting the value of n into the original equation, we can solve for m. Then it's just a matter of adding. Eliminate (B), (C), and (E).

(2) Sufficient: Similar situation here. It's a second, different equation with the same two variables found in the equation in the question stem, so we can solve for the values of the variables. Thus, we can determine their sum. Choose (D).

VERBAL SECTION EXPLANATIONS

1. C

In question 1 we're asked to strengthen the researchers' alarming conclusion that the misinformation they've discovered in journal advertisements could lead doctors into misprescribing drugs. This argument works only if we assume that doctors give credence to the ads. Since *the best way to strengthen an argument is to confirm the truth of an assumption*, we want a choice that says doctors are indeed influenced by the information in the ads. According to (C), doctors use the ads as a serious resource for information about new prescription drugs. So (C) is correct.

(A) indicates the ads are important to publishers as a source of revenue, but does nothing to show that the ads are important to doctors, let alone that they can affect doctors' prescriptions.

(B) and (D) support the notion that the ads are or can be misleading: (B) tells us that journal editors often can't tell whether an ad is deceptive; (D) tells us that ads are usually less accurate than articles evaluating the drugs. But we already know that the ads contain misleading information, so these choices add nothing. (E) weakens the argument by suggesting that a government agency is watching out for potentially harmful, misleading claims.

2. E

The beginning of the underlined part should be "an index ... that is called objective," not "an index ... that are called objective." If you catch an obvious error like this, quickly scan the other choices for versions that repeat it. That knocks out (B). (Remember you don't need to reread (A); it's the same as the original, and we already know that's wrong.) Now, we are left with (C), (D), and (E). The crucial difference here is between the wordy phrase *progress, such as what is made*—in (C) and (D)—and (E)'s *progress such as that*. (E)'s wording is preferable.

3. C

Sometimes the GMAT requires you to recognize grammar you would never use in spoken English. That's true for the use of *and so* here. *And so, to do so,* and similar uses of the word *so* are often featured in GMAT English. Because they're infrequently used even in written English, they sound funny, and the test writers are hoping you'll think they're wrong. Here (C) is best because it replaces (A)'s awkward *it causes them to lose* with the much shorter *so lose.*

Passage 1—Women in the Labor Market

Topic and Scope: Participation of women in the labor market; specifically, the status of women in matters of pay and promotion.

Purpose and Main Idea: The author wants to identify and discuss two to three specific conditions that restrict job opportunities for women, particularly women with children. The main idea is summed up in the second sentence: The author agrees with what "analysts" say—"women comprise a secondary labor market where rates of pay and promotion prospects are inferior to those available to men."

Paragraph Structure: Paragraph 1 lays out the basic viewpoint, explaining that women are disadvantaged by "social values which require women to give priority to home and family over paid employment." Paragraph 2 adds evidence: In order to meet domestic responsibilities, many women work part time, a "precarious" form of employment. Paragraphs 3 and 4 discuss problems faced by women who leave the job market temporarily to have children. Many end up in low-status jobs, and even professional women fail to get promoted.

The Big Picture: The author's viewpoint and the paragraph structure are both clear-cut. And the topic itself is pretty familiar and accessible. So grab onto the small handful of key points, don't linger over the paragraphs, and move confidently to the questions.

4. B

This is the only choice that encompasses the clearly expressed topic, scope, and point of view.

(A) incorrectly broadens the scope to employers' practices in general, whereas the author is concerned only with pay and promotion. Besides, the author restricts himself to discussing the current state of affairs; he doesn't advocate anything.

(C) takes a detail in paragraphs 2 and 3 and wrongly blows it up into the author's primary concern.

(D) and (E) are completely off the topic, and, contrary to what (D) says, the author doesn't take issue with others' views.

- The correct answer to "global" questions has to cover the same topic and scope, and reflect the same tone, as the passage itself.

5. D

Lines 34–36 say that "when the typical houseworker returns to the labor market she is unsure of herself in her new environment." In other word, such women experience anxiety.

Lines 18–21 suggest that it is up to working women themselves, not employers (A), to make child-care arrangements.

(B) is an 180° trap. Paragraph 4 says that women in high-status positions, such as professionals, face problems advancing their careers while caring for their children.

The passage doesn't compare conditions for today's working mothers with those that existed twenty years ago (C). Although lines 16–21 imply that reasonably priced child care can be difficult to find, (E), the passage doesn't go so far as to suggest that the expense of child care often makes it unprofitable for mothers to work.

6. B

The gist of paragraph 4 is that even women of high ability and status—professionals—face career problems if they decide to have children.

(A) is an 180° trap. The point of paragraph 4 is to explain that even the most able women may *not* be able to "overcome" the difficulties "of integrating career and motherhood."

Paragraph 4 does not address labor policies (C) or increasing female participation in the labor force (D). Moreover, the author doesn't ever "defend changes" or "modify a hypothesis."

(E) is too vague. Paragraph 4 draws a definite link between career opportunities and children: It's not about a general lack of career opportunities for women.

7. C

The second sentence of paragraph 1 says that rates of pay and promotion are worse for women than for men. The next sentence attributes this situation to the fact that women have responsibilities at home that interfere with their jobs.

The passage states that some women work part time (lines 23–25), not that women in general tend to get work in industries that rely on part-time labor (A).

KAPLAN

Paragraph 4 indicates that professional women sometimes lack the technical skills of their male counterparts (B) but this isn't the reason the passage gives for their inferior pay and promotion rates.

According to lines 26–27, part-time women, not women in general (as choice (D) says), are likely to be laid off in an economic slowdown. Besides, this fact has nothing to do with inferior pay and promotion rates.

(E) is beyond the scope of the passage: The author doesn't discuss general workplace discrimination against women.

8. D

The legislator in question 8 argues (here's the conclusion) that the state ban on casino gambling should be rescinded because (here's the evidence) one, it's inconsistent with other state policies; two, it's "impractical" because efforts to enforce it are hopeless; and three, legalizing gambling would reduce the crime rate. We're asked for the best weakener, and *in an argument that makes a proposal, we know to look for a choice that shows that the proposal won't achieve its goal (usually for a reason the author hasn't considered) or that it carries unacceptable side effects.* (D) says that legalizing gambling would attract criminals who habitually engage in illegal activities other than gambling. Although their gambling would now be legal, as the author argues, (D) strongly suggests that these hoods would bring other illegal activities to the state. This gravely weakens the legislator's claim that legalizing gambling would reduce crime.

The key to rejecting the incorrect choices lies in accurately remembering the legislator's argument; beware of choices that attack claims she didn't make or undermine a conclusion that she didn't draw. (A) implies that dropping the ban would reduce gambling and (C) implies that it may increase it. Yet the legislator's argument requires neither that gambling remain popular nor that it not become more popular. As for (B), the legislator never gave "significant savings" as a reason for revoking the ban, so the news that there won't be any such savings doesn't hurt her. It's not at all clear what effect, if any, (E) has on her proposal. That alone is good enough reason to discard it. *Remember, in GMAT Critical Reasoning you don't want to make an argument on behalf of an answer choice. If the connection between a choice and an argument is vague or tenuous, look elsewhere.*

9. D

The Kaplan strategy of *looking at the question stem before tackling the stimulus* really pays off with question 9. We're given the conclusion—that the cat in question is acting out its dreams. We'll be looking for the researchers' evidence, and in order to answer the question, we'll be thinking along the lines of adding to this evidence so as to further support the conclusion. Realizing all of this, before we even read the stimulus, makes its story and our lives easier.

Before neuron removal, we're told, the dreaming cat's cortex fires messages but the cat doesn't respond. After neuron removal, the dreaming cat gets up and jumps around. We want to strengthen the conclusion that the cat is acting out its dreams. (D) establishes that the neurons prevented the cerebral cortex's messages from reaching the spinal cord during sleep. Therefore, the removal of the neurons allowed, for the first time, messages to reach the spinal cord while the cat slept. This makes it more plausible that when the cat rose and pounced, it was responding to those messages—acting out its dreams.

(A) is ambiguous and unhelpful. If the cat wasn't already dreaming when the neurons were removed, then their removal would presumably prevent the cat from dreaming (since they trigger the dream state); in that case, it couldn't have been acting out its dreams. If the cat was already in a dream state when the neurons were removed, then we have no idea about the effect of removing the neurons. (B) adds nothing to the information in the stimulus. We already know that the cerebral cortex is busy during sleep. And from the strategic point of view, (B) ignores the experiment with the neurons, and that's precisely what we're interested in; *always be wary of choices that ignore a critical part of the stimulus*. If (C) were true, there would be no messages, therefore no dreams, coming from the cerebral cortex after the neurons were removed, so the cat couldn't be acting out its dreams. Be careful; *on strengthen/weaken questions, the test makers commonly present choices that have the opposite effect of the one they ask for*. (E) is irrelevant, as "brain waves" (*a new term, be wary*) don't matter. We're interested in how brain messages (dreams) travel; specifically, what stops them from being acted on during the sleeping state.

10. A

From a quick scan of the answers, you see the main difference is between choices that use *is* and choices that use *was*. Now, use logic. Pay attention to the time clue *recently*. The shepherd's body was only recently found, so it wouldn't make sense to put the discussion of "How long ago did he live?" in the past. *Is*, in (A) and (D), must be correct. It's also important to be able to recognize and quickly eliminate illogical choices like (D). (D)'s wording doesn't really make sense. If the dead person is "thought of as apparently living," he wouldn't be a corpse.

11. C

Pick up on clues. The sentence begins *In contrast to,* so there has to be some kind of contrast. Problem is, the original version doesn't give you one. It uses the connector *and* to join the sentence halves. Scanning choices, we see that (B), (C), and (D) all end with *but.* This makes sense—American poetry is not distinct but an outgrowth. However, (D) uses the unnecessary *it was considered by.* Avoid the passive when you can. Finally, every time you see a connector like *not … but,* remember you need parallelism between the part of the sentence following *not* and the part following *but.* (C) gives it to you.

Passage 2—Freedom of Information Act

Topic and Scope: Freedom of Information Act; specifically, the amendments to the Act.

Purpose and Main Idea: The author's intent is to describe the positions and roles of the government's legislative, judicial, and executive branches in regard to the Freedom of Information Act's revision. Because the author's purpose is descriptive, not argumentative, the passage has no specific main idea.

Paragraph Structure: Paragraph 1 describes the Freedom of Information Act and provides the historical context for the revision process. Paragraph 2 outlines proposed House and Senate amendments. Paragraph 3 reveals that the executive branch was opposed to these amendments. Paragraph 4 adds more detail about the legislative amendments. Paragraph 5 indicates that the legislative and executive branches unsuccessfully sought compromise; the amendments were adopted despite an executive veto.

12. C

Lines 30–32 say that the Justice and Defense departments objected to revision as "costly, burdensome, and inflexible." They opposed revision, in other words, for administrative reasons.

According to lines 33–35 the Justice and Defense departments argued that changes "might actually hamper access to information." But they did not go so far as to suggest that the revision was an attempt to limit public access to information (A).

Although the Pentagon thought that revision might pose national security problems, it didn't argue that changes violated specific national security agreements (B).

(D) and (E) are beyond the scope: Neither the Justice nor the Defense department protested revision on the grounds that it would weaken either their power or presidential authority.

13. A

The Pentagon voiced this argument, apparently concerned that the judiciary did not have the "departmental expertise" to determine which military records could be released without jeopardizing national security.

(B) and (C) speak of records in general, not military records in particular, so national security isn't necessarily at issue in these choices.

(D) says that some judges may be politically motivated, but that doesn't mean that they'll jeopardize national security.

(E) doesn't connect judicial review to national security. Does the President's approval have any necessary connection to national security? Nothing within the passage would imply this. You will never have to add information or make unwarranted assumptions to justify the correct answer. That kind of creativity isn't rewarded on the GMAT.

14. A

Lines 47–50 indicate that Ford was opposed to the release of FBI records. He didn't want them to be open to public scrutiny.

(B) and (E)—180° choices—wrongly suggest that Ford was open to the idea of a release of FBI records.

Ford might have opposed a release of FBI records for administrative reasons (C), but the passage doesn't say for sure.

There is no hint in the passage that Ford believed it was more important to protect confidential sources than personal privacy or investigative secrecy (D). Paragraph 4 tells us that all three are protected by the Hart amendment, but no distinction like (D)'s is drawn.

15. D

Here's a great example of how concision is rewarded on the GMAT. There's no need to use an awkward construction like "at least as much as a hundred and more" when (D) says the same thing simply and concisely.

16. C

In question 16 you're asked to compare two rival theories; this is a GMAT question type that crops up regularly. *The key is understanding exactly what is under dispute and exactly which theory you're concerned with.* The traditional theory says that Neanderthals were simply superseded by modern humans and there was virtually no interbreeding between the two groups. The new theory says that modern humans evolved from Neanderthals and from other early types of *Homo sapiens*, and are therefore descendants of Neanderthals. So the dispute is whether Neanderthals were supplanted by a rival group of unrelated humans, or by humans who were at least partly descended from them. We're asked to support the new theory. (C) does that by presenting a physical similarity between the early modern humans and the Neanderthals, both of whom lived in central Europe. So we have sort of a "missing link" between the two groups; this doesn't prove the new theory, but we are only asked for support. *On GMAT "strengthen the argument" questions, out and out proof isn't necessary.*

Keep track of the question and the different theories! (A) provides more support for the old theory than for the new one: If modern humans first appeared in Africa and then migrated to Europe, they can't have evolved from "the Neanderthals of Europe." (B) might seem tempting, but these similarities between Neanderthals and modern humans are only cultural; they don't imply a close physical relationship between the groups. (D), like (B), compares the cultures of the two groups, but it points out differences. Since cultural similarities don't provide much support for the theory that the groups are biologically related, cultural differences don't either. (E) refers to "unique physical traits" of Neanderthals, which is the opposite of what we want. We want something that suggests a biological link between Neanderthals and modern humans, whereas (E) sets Neanderthals apart.

17. E

Whenever you see a sentence with the word *like*, remember that it must compare the same type of things, using language that is similar. Ingesting lead "was a significant health hazard for the ancient Romans," just as it "is for modern Americans." What's being compared is the hazard for Romans and Americans, not the hazard to Romans and Americans themselves.

18. D

When an introductory phrase is set off by a comma, make sure it logically refers to what follows. It's not Nathanael West's first novel, or "when Nathanael West staying in Paris," that was "born Nathan Weinstein." It's Nathanael West himself, so (D)'s right.

19. E

Reading the question stem first (always a fine idea) for question 19 warns you to be on the alert for something the author has overlooked. The author argues against the notion that fertility treatments are responsible for the increased incidence of twins by presenting an alternative explanation—that the increase has occurred because more women are having children later in life, and these older women are statistically more likely to bear twins. This sounds plausible, but remember *the key questions in GMAT causal arguments: Is the causality as simple as the author believes? Could another cause have been at work?* If women over 35 are much more likely to use fertility treatments that often result in twin births, then it's possible that the twin births among older women are in fact due to fertility treatments. The problem (E) points out is not that the "alternative explanation" is illogical or impossible, but that it might be dependent on the very explanation it's supposed to replace.

(A) and (D) introduce irrelevant considerations. The author's argument is that fertility drugs aren't responsible for the increase in twins. It doesn't matter that, as (A) says, many of these older women aren't first time mothers. Nor does it matter that, as (D) says, these older women are no more likely to produce *identical* twins. As for (B), the author's point was simply that women over 35 are more likely to have twins than are younger women; her argument doesn't require that only women over 35 bear twins. (C) is wrong: since the author argues that the drugs are not responsible for the increased incidence of twins, she must believe, rather than overlook, the idea that any correlation between drugs and the increase of twin births is coincidental.

Passage 3—Predicting Earthquakes

Topic and Scope: Earthquake prediction; specifically, the passage outlines factors that contribute to earthquakes and that lend themselves to scientific measurement for prediction purposes.

Purpose and Main Idea: The author wants to show that scientists have several methods of monitoring quake-related activity and making predictions.

Paragraph Structure: Paragraph 1 explains that quakes result from identifiable, predictable phenomena. Quake prediction is based on "long- and short-range precursory phenomena." Paragraph 2 differentiates quake-prone regions along active faults near the Pacific from less quake-prone inland regions. Paragraph 3 is about the monitoring of quake-prone zones by networks of "base stations." Various types of precursors are mentioned. Paragraph 4 explains that different types of "short-term" precursors are still being identified.

The Big Picture: The topic and scope are clear from paragraph 1, but the passage goes into a lot of detail. *The way to handle details is to stay keyed to the paragraphs. In other words, don't let details distract you from bigger points.* For instance, paragraph 3 focuses on the use of base stations to monitor precursors—that's the gist there. The detailed facts about precursors should be skimmed. Don't worry about them until a question asks.

20. C

Paragraph 1 contrasts coastal regions, where crustal strains build rapidly, with inland regions, where strains build more slowly. (C) paraphrases that distinction.

(A) flatly contradicts the passage—the first paragraph states that crustal strain is great in coastal regions. (B) contradicts the passage—quakes are less numerous in *inland* areas. (D) also contradicts the passage—you can infer that in coastal areas, which experience frequent quakes, precursory phenomena must be common. (E) contradicts the passage—paragraph 1 indicates that coastal regions confront thrusting sea floor plates.

21. E

Choice (E) encompasses the passage's topic and scope, plus the content of all 4 paragraphs— the importance of precursors.

(A) is too narrow—the passage says little about earthquakes in inland areas. (B) mentions introductory information in paragraph 1. It neglects the passage's topic—methods of earthquake prediction. (C) has the same problem as (A)—it's too narrow. Coastal regions are only part of the picture in this passage. (D) is also too narrow, and it's inconsistent with the passage. Precursory phenomena are key to earthquake prediction.

22. D

This is the best choice. The focus of the paragraph is on "precursory phenomena," which seismologists study in order to predict quakes.

(A) is too narrow—the relationship between accumulated and critical strain only comes up at the end of the paragraph. (B) is also too narrow—the need to space base stations at precise intervals is a minor point made at the beginning of the paragraph. Inland and coastal areas are compared (C) in paragraphs 1 and 2, not in paragraph 3. The paragraph never suggests "that critical strain is not spread evenly along most major fault lines," (E).

23. A

Choice (A) is consistent with the concluding sentence of paragraph 3. Calculations based on an area's critical strain can help in predicting when a quake might occur.

There is nothing anywhere about calculating "the severity of an initial rupture" (B). It's unclear what the term *seismic force* means, so (C) is no good. (D) refers to an unrelated detail from the beginning of the paragraph. (E) is tempting, but (A) captures the idea more precisely. The passage is about earthquakes, not crustal movement in general.

24. D

In question 24, the Federal government provided low-cost flood insurance to coastal property owners. Unfortunately, this caused a new problem—the resulting boom in coastal construction has led to dangerous land erosion. In GMAT Critical Reasoning, *the first task in solving a problem is to correctly identify the cause of the problem*. The cause here is construction, both existing and expected construction. Since beachfront construction caused the erosion, a good solution would be to put an end to this construction. (D) would likely accomplish this. Not only does it discourage new construction by canceling flood insurance benefits, but it may well facilitate removal of some of the existing dwellings by compensating residents to relocate.

(A) may prevent the construction of property additions, but it wouldn't do anything to halt the boom in the construction of new buildings or to get rid of existing buildings. As for (B), we already know that the erosion rate is "dangerous"; that's why we're looking for a choice that suggests a solution. Recommending further study isn't a solution. (C) sounds like a good plan for preventing flood damage to new buildings. We are asked, however, to prevent erosion, and we're given no reason to think that elevating houses will do so. (E) makes the same mistake. (E) would protect the buildings from flood damage, but the problem we're to address is that of protecting the beaches from erosion.

25. B

Think about what the sentence is telling you. The seam "is overcast ... in a separate process." The seam is not "overcast ... instead of a separate process."

KAPLAN

26.A

The author says that conventional methods of measuring intelligence, such as IQ tests, classify people with Williams syndrome as retarded, on a par with Down's syndrome sufferers, because they're poor at math and can't tell left from right. He calls this label "misleading," pointing out that people with Williams syndrome are often gifted in other areas, such as language and music, whereas Down's syndrome sufferers have limited abilities in all areas. His point in telling us this is that the conventional tests don't do a good job of evaluating the people with Williams syndrome, since they miss the gifts that these people have. That's (A): His argument is that conventional intelligence tests can't accurately measure people with disorders like Williams syndrome.

When you're asked for the author's point, be careful not to be misled by choices that simply restate a part of the author's argument. For instance, (B) may or may not be true (it's not stated by the author), but it's not the author's main point. He compares the two syndromes to make another point, about the failure of conventional intelligence tests. (C) is closer: the author seems to imply (C), but this isn't what he's trying to prove. It's merely a piece of his argument, something that he implies on the way to making his point about the failure of intelligence tests to measure people with Williams syndrome. (D) discusses what might happen when people with Williams syndrome are diagnosed as mentally retarded, but the author's focus is on the mislabeling itself, not on its possible results. Like (C), (D) seems reasonably inferable from the argument, but isn't the point of the argument. As for (E), the author never suggests that the mathematical and spatial skills of people with Williams syndrome either can or should be developed.

27. E

After reading the stem for question 27, we go to the stimulus with eyes peeled for Koch's counterargument. Koch, we learn, is unconvinced by von Pettenkoffer's dramatic demonstration. When, after drinking a bottle of bacteria, von Pettenkoffer doesn't develop cholera, he claims to have proved that the bacterium doesn't cause cholera. Koch disagrees, saying that von Pettenkoffer's stomach acid killed the bacteria before it could affect him. Be careful; we don't want to strengthen Koch's original argument—that the bacterium causes cholera, but rather his second argument—that von Pettenkoffer's stomach acid killed the bacteria. (E) says that when the cholera bacteria is ingested with bicarbonate of soda, a stomach acid neutralizer, it's more likely that the person will develop the illness. (E), then, shows that acidity has an inhibiting effect on cholera bacteria, exactly as Koch argued.

(A) sounds intriguing, but according to Koch, the primary way of transmitting cholera can't be through ingestion. So, according to Koch, extra acid shouldn't mean fewer instances of cholera, and (A) can't support his argument. (B) would explain why von Pettenkoffer didn't catch cholera, and leave it possible that the bacterium is indeed cholera-producing, but we want evidence to support the argument that stomach acid prevented von Pettenkoffer from becoming ill. (B) weakens that argument by pointing to antibodies. If (C) is correct, and cholera is endemic in areas where the bacteria is found in the drinking water, then the disease probably is being transmitted by ingestion; this weakens the claim that stomach acid kills the bacteria. (D) is outside the scope of the passage. The existence of *E. coli* bacteria in the lower intestine cannot support Koch's argument that stomach acid kills cholera bacteria.

28. E

GMAT sentences often introduce errors by separating parts of a sentence that must agree, hoping this separation will cause you to miss the fact that these parts don't. "Have" and "will continue to" are both parts of the verb here. Both must go with "perpetuate." But you can't say "they have… perpetuate," as (A) and (B) do. Neither can you say "it has…perpetuate," as (C) does. (D)'s "it has perpetuated and will continue perpetuating" is grammatical but too wordy and awkward. (E) says the same thing concisely using "it has continued to perpetuate."

29. C

You can simplify long sentences like this one by zeroing in on what's being tested. The first thing to do is notice whether you see anything funny when you read the sentence. A key error is that "legislation" is singular, but *were,* its verb, is plural. So (A) can be crossed off. Scan the choices now. How do the choices deal with this one error? (E) repeats it. (D)'s *has only mitigated* isn't parallel to its other verb, *abolishing.* (B)'s *has only mitigated* is not parallel to *abolishing* either. Choice (C), with *only mitigated, rather than abolished,* has two parallel verbs. *Rather than* is a connector that must link grammatically parallel terms.

30. A

We need the choice that suggests most strongly that the judge was wrong to consolidate the cases. Remember, the judge agreed to consolidate the cases based on the precedent set by asbestos exposure cases. So the best way to cast doubt on the judge's decision is to break the link between the asbestos cases (his evidence) and these repetitive stress injury cases (his conclusion). (A) points out a significant difference between the two situations. In the asbestos cases the product in question was the same in each situation, while in the stress injury cases, the type and quality of office equipment is different in each case, suggesting that there may be differences in manufacturer liabilities. So there is less of a reason for combining the individual cases, and the asbestos cases make a poor precedent.

(B) is tricky. It might seem unfair that the judge's decision may benefit the defense by limiting the number of witnesses for the plaintiffs, but (B) doesn't attack the judge's reasoning, which was based on legal precedent. Instead, (B) weakens the author's argument that the decision will hurt the defense. (C) brings up a common cause of repetitive stress injuries, but doesn't tell us that it was actually the problem in these cases. More importantly, it does nothing to show that the judge was wrong to combine the cases. (D) points out a difference between asbestos exposure and repetitive stress injuries, but it's a difference in the severity of the injuries. This doesn't indicate that the judge was wrong to see a legal parallel between the two types of cases. As for (E), the judge's decision to combine the cases doesn't in any way preclude an investigation of the medical condition that the plaintiffs claim. The judge hasn't assigned responsibility or rendered a verdict, only decided on a method of proceeding with the cases.

31. C

In questions like this, temporarily ignore words set off by dashes. Ignoring this material in each version should make it easier for you to "hear" what's wrong. In the original sentence, the actual subject is *each;* this singular noun doesn't agree with the plural verb *are.* (D) reverses the problem: the plural *novels* doesn't agree with the singular verb *is.* (E)'s *every one of the novels* makes the sentence a virtual run-on. (B) has subject/verb agreement but adds the awkward, wordy "each of them novels in William Kennedy's 'Albany Trilogy.' (C) is much less awkward and also features agreement between the plural *novels* and *are,* therefore it is correct.

32. B

We're told that from 1977 to 1989 the percentage of their own income that the richest one percent of Americans paid to federal taxes decreased. At the same time, the proportion (or percentage) of all federal tax revenues that was paid by these same rich Americans increased. We're asked to clear up this apparent discrepancy: A lighter tax burden on the wealthy resulted in their carrying more of the overall tax load. If, as (B) has it, the richest one percent are making much more money than they once did, then the actual amount of money they pay in federal taxes can increase, even though the percentage of their own income that this amount represents decreases. This increased amount of taxes paid could represent an increased proportion of the total federal tax revenues.

(A) suggests that the IRS has increased its tax-collecting efficiency, but this is irrelevant to the question of how one percentage can increase while the other decreases. (C) could explain how taxes on the rich account for more of the total tax revenues (because more of their investments are taxable), but it doesn't explain why these increased taxes account for a smaller percentage of their incomes. (D) raises new questions. If we assume (which we can't) that the elimination of loopholes hurt the rich more than the tax cut helped them, we could see how they might pay more taxes despite the cut in the top tax rate. But that just presents us with the old problem: If they're paying more taxes, how can they be paying less of their income to taxes? On the other hand, if we assume (which we can't) that the tax cut in (D) means they're paying less in taxes, how can they be bearing more of the tax burden? *On a question asking for an explanation, avoid any choice that leaves you wondering.* (E) shows how the richest one percent account for a higher percentage of overall tax revenues. They've paid an additional 45 billion dollars while everyone else has only had to come up with an additional 5 billion—the 5 billion left from the 50 billion after subtracting the 45 billion that the very rich paid. However, this leaves out the other part of the dilemma—it doesn't show how they can be paying less of their income.

Passage 4—Food Contamination

Topic and Scope: Food contamination; specifically, the various hazards that can contaminate food and lead to human illness.

Purpose and Main Idea: The author's purpose is describe, not argue. The passage doesn't have a specific main idea or thesis. Instead, their authors are content to describe and discuss, rather than argue or advocate.

Paragraph Structure: Paragraph 1 is about the definition of food contamination and the three major hazards, and the reminder that it's still important to be on guard against contamination. Paragraph 2 focuses on the hazards; specifically, the most serious risk, biological. It contains a good deal of detail; note it, but it is unnecessary to memorize or even understand it all. Paragraph 3 does more of the same; continuation of biological discussion—more definitions and examples, but nothing that changes the overall idea that we must be on our guard against contamination.

33. C

Choice (C) is the only one that effectively captures the main idea of the entire passage rather than one specific aspect or detail of the passage.

(A) uses some wording from paragraph 1, but leaves out the issue of contamination altogether, and specifically the idea that knowledge of contamination is what's necessary. (B) focuses on a mere detail of paragraph 2—that biological hazards are the most serious. But that's certainly not the main point. (D) and (E) are also statements that may be true, but don't encompass the whole passage. *Wrong choices in Global questions will often be true statements that nonetheless don't rise to level of Main Idea. Here, only (C) is broad enough to cover the passage's topic, scope, and purpose.*

34. A

Not every inference ventures far from the main point or basic gist of the author's argument. (A) fits the bill nicely. Note how closely related this is to the author's overall point.

(B) is a distortion. Although the sources of contamination seem varied and complex, there is nothing here to suggest that a diligent food service manager will be restricted in the amount she can know about contamination.

(C) misses the scope of the passage by focusing on the decision to *hire* a manager. Even if we infer that a manager's understanding of these issues must be a consideration in hiring, since it's so important, we still can't say it's the *primary* consideration. (D) uses the extreme word "exclusively," and consequently is too extreme. In fact, the author states that prevention is only part of the battle—knowledge is also necessary so that a manager knows what to do "in the event that a ... crisis does arise."

(E)'s pessimism is reminiscent of (B). A clear understanding of the author's purpose and tone allows us to eliminate choices like these that don't match with either.

The first few words of (E) are on the right track; in fact, "vitally important" is synonymous with (A)'s "crucial." But the whole choice needs to fit, and the rest of (E) misses the point.

35. D

The striking term "pathogenic organisms" that appears in the question stem is relatively easy to locate in paragraph 2. Correct choice (D) comes right out of lines 24–28, with the keywords "such as" acting as the link between pathogenic microorganisms and bacteria and parasites. Even in a passage with lots of unfamiliar terms, it all boils down to good critical reading. Let's look at the wrong choices. In (A), the passage doesn't tell us what the most common form is. Nothing in paragraph 2 suggests (B), but paragraph 3 actually suggests the opposite—some microorganisms can cause disease even after being killed. A careful reading of the sentence in which "pathogenic organisms" appears shows that choice (C) distorts the meaning of the sentence. Toxins are not the same as pathogenic microorganisms. (E): How hard it is to detect pathogenic organisms is outside the scope— never mentioned or implied.

36. B

It's not the new technology that's "employing the system of binomial nomenclature." Only people can do that. You need the choice that has a group of people as its subject, and that's (B) with "taxonomists." Don't be thrown by technical language. You don't have to understand anything about taxonomy or "binomial nomenclature" to see that the underlined part of this sentence should feature a subject that can be logically modified by the preceding phrase.

37. B

GMAT English is precise. In everyday speech, you can get away with "I have a lot of pressure at work," when you mean "I am under pressure." On the GMAT, you can't. You have to use the correct idiomatic phrase, which is "under pressure to show high profits." Choices (C) and (D) both use "showing;" always be wary of "–ing" verbs. (E) adds needless verbiage.

38. B

Question 38's stimulus describes how two regions of a country were affected differently by the same crisis. Although demand for both the tropical crops of Region A and the basic foodstuffs of Region B was only slightly affected by the drop in income levels after 1929, Region A was much more affected by the decrease in demand. The author gives us a hint when she says that Region B "could adjust the supply of its crops." *Whenever we get a hint on an "explanation" question, we take it.* So what we look for when we go to the choices is the reason why Region B was able to survive the decrease in demand by adjusting the supply of its crops, while Region A could not make these adjustments. The best reason is provided by (B): Since annual crops are renewed each year, the supply can easily be adjusted for the following year. Perennial crops, however, live longer than one year, so adjusting the supply isn't easy. What you plant one year has an impact on the supply of crops for a long time;

small, quick adjustments can't be easily made. So (B) provides information, consistent with the clue we found in the stimulus, that explains why Region A's farmers couldn't follow the example of their colleagues in Region B. Even if you were confused by annual versus perennial, (B) explicitly tackles the question of why Region B's crops were more easily adjusted. That's a tip-off that (B) is correct. Notice that it isn't necessary to understand what economic forces were at play here. *Like Reading Comprehension, Critical Reasoning isn't about understanding every background detail. It's about understanding what the author is interested in telling you.* In this question, that's the information in the last two sentences.

(A) tells us that Region A's crops cost more than Region B's crops, but we've already been told that demand for Region A's crops hasn't dropped much, so we can't take this to mean that the crisis made Region A's crops unaffordable. In general, one would expect the higher prices for Region A's crops to make its economy stronger. (C) says that Region A's tropical goods are less prone to drops in demand. Again, that's not bad news for A's farmers, so it doesn't explain the disaster that befell them; besides, the stimulus already told us that demand for the two regions' crops dropped about the same. (D) tells us about the competition that Region B faced; clearly that doesn't help to explain its success, or Region A's failure. (E) just expands on information we already have. We knew that demand for region B's crops only declined a bit—now we know why. However, demand also dropped only a bit for Region A, so (E) does nothing to explain the differing fortunes of the two regions' economies.

39.A

In a complicated sentence like this, it's probably best to focus on eliminating wrong answers. There are some wrong phrases that are obvious, for instance, the awkward, unidiomatic "such a number of Astronomy majors in a given year as there are today," in (D). There's also the confusing "a number of Astronomy majors such as there are today," in (C). It's unclear what that phrase means, and (C) also begins with the illogical "while." Looking at the other choices, you see that (B) is both awkward and confusing. The meaning of "as many...as there are in a given year today" is unclear, and (B) also makes Mitchell a "founding professor," whatever that is. (E) has the bizarre locution "a number...just as large as the number that is there today." This is both awkward and ungrammatical; "the number that are there" would at least be correct.

Notice how much text is underlined in this sentence. There will only be a few such questions in each section, and they're good ones to take a quick guess on if you're pressed for time.

40.E

You need to be precise and logical to get a question like this right, but you don't need to be a grammar expert. Think about what the sentence is trying to tell you. Chesnutt's fiction reflects the "interests of his contemporary 'local colorists,'" and it also reflects "the intellectual ferment" of the time. In short, his fiction reflects one thing as much as it does another. The word "does" is critical; it's what makes the phrase idiomatic. Choice (E) is correct because it alone contains this logical and idiomatic form of comparison. (E)'s "does" is also the only verb that correctly parallels the verb "reflects" in the first part of the sentence. Choices (B), (C), and (D) all contain verbs—"did," "had," and "was"—that aren't consistent with the present-tense "reflects"; they all add awkwardly wordy phrasing, too.

41.A

Be familiar with idioms likely to appear on the GMAT. The correct idiomatic construction is "just as…, so…" Knowing this, you can narrow the choices down to (A) and (E) here. What follows "just as" must parallel what follows "so." That's why (E) can't be right: "Just as the various languages" isn't parallel to "so it is in U.S. culture." In (A), "the various languages" correctly parallels "the many musical traditions."

PART FIVE

Getting into Business School

Chapter 13: **Where and When to Apply**

When considering where to apply in business school, ask yourself two questions.

- What schools should I consider, regardless of my chances?
- Of those schools, where can I realistically get in?

CONSIDERING WHERE TO APPLY

The decision about where to go to business school should not be taken lightly. It will determine your daily life for the next several years, and will influence your academic and career paths for years to come. Many people let a professor or mentor or rankings in popular magazines influence their choice of school—only to find out that the school was a wrong choice for their personal needs. So by putting in some work today, you'll be ensured a happy business school choice tomorrow. Let's look at some of the factors that you'll need to consider.

Overall Reputation

Each year, several publications release rankings of business schools. You should start with reviewing these rankings because they'll provide a frame of reference for how different schools are regarded in the marketplace.

Don't place too much stock in the rankings, though you should consider a program's overall reputation. The better your school is regarded in the marketplace, the better your job prospects are likely to be upon graduation. You will notice that there is a general correlation between schools' rankings and starting salaries.

Find out which programs are highly regarded in the areas that interest you. Which schools are viewed as responsive to students' changing needs, and which schools are seen as less responsive? What schools are "hot"? How have they earned that designation?

Teaching Methods

Business school professors teach using the case method, lectures, or, in most cases, a combination of both. Everyone learns differently, so select a school with a teaching environment that allows you to thrive.

A lecture-based classroom is, in all likelihood, what you experienced as an undergraduate. The professor provides information, and interaction between the students and the professor, or between the students, is controlled and generally limited. In a case-method environment, on the other hand, the professor doesn't lecture but rather facilitates an open dialogue with the students by asking probing questions and giving students most of the "air time."

Each class revolves around actual business situations, and students are cast in the role of decision maker. You could be given the facts about a struggling business, for instance, and then placed in charge of developing a plan for business improvement. The case method is particularly popular at programs that specialize in teaching general management. Harvard Business School and Virginia's Darden School are two of the better-known schools that use the case method as their principal teaching tool.

Is one teaching method inherently better than the other? That depends on you. Some students prefer the more controlled, structured environment of traditional lectures. Others thrive on the case method, in which a less formal, no-holds-barred, open forum encourages many viewpoints but provides no single answer.

Another issue to keep in mind is that in a case-method classroom, as much as half of your grade will be based on class participation. If you are someone who needs no encouragement to air your views, you'll have no problem. If, however, you think you'd be less than eager to participate in this type of forum, you should seriously consider whether it would be the right environment for you.

Most programs enhance the value of your educational experience by exposing you to real-world situations where possible. For example, many schools will encourage students to undertake a field study in their second year. Business simulations, computer-based programs that enable you to test your decision-making skills, are also a popular teaching tool.

Class and Section Size

Class size and structure are two factors that will have a significant impact on your business school experience. Some students prefer the intimacy of a smaller class and the opportunity to get to know everyone. Others prefer the energy of a larger class and the increased resources and facilities that it can support.

Many programs divide the class into sections, also known as cohorts, and have students take all or most of their first-year classes with that same group. In fact, at some schools, section members actually stay in the same classroom and the professors rotate among rooms.

There are several advantages to the section concept. By working with the same classmates day after day, you build a camaraderie borne out of a shared, often intense, first-year experience. You get to know each other in a way that is not possible in a more traditional classroom structure. More likely than not, you'll forge lasting relationships with your section mates. The downside of the section system is that you have less exposure to classmates who are not in your section. Organized club activities, however, enable you to meet other students outside the classroom who share your interests.

School Location

The two key questions that you should consider regarding a school's location are: How will it affect the overall quality of your business school experience, and how will it affect your employability? Some students prefer an urban setting. Others prefer a more rustic environment. Some want their business school to be part of the overall university campus; others would like a separate campus.

Geography may be an important criterion for you. Perhaps you're constrained by a spouse's job. Or perhaps you know where you want to live after graduation. You won't be limited in where you can find a job if you graduate from a school that has a national reputation, but if you attend a school with more of a regional name, be sure that it is highly regarded in that area.

Curriculum

To maximize the value of your business school experience, be sure that a school's curriculum matches up with your own interests. If your primary interest is general management, then seek out those programs whose strengths include general management.

The top-tier schools tend to be strong in all areas, but even the elite programs are viewed as having particular specialties. For example, Kellogg is thought to be especially strong for marketing, Wharton for finance, and Harvard for general management. Of course, many Harvard M.B.A.'s pursue finance careers; Wharton grads, marketing; and Kellogg grads, general management. You should, nevertheless, familiarize yourself with the general marketplace perceptions about the programs you're considering. It will help you think more clearly about the selection process.

Faculty

The quality of a school's faculty is important and is reflected in each program's reputation. An important question to ask, though, is will you get to take classes with a school's star professors? With the proliferation of executive education programs, top teachers at many highly ranked schools are sometimes assigned to teach executive education students instead of M.B.A.s. If one of your prime motivations in attending a certain program is to take classes from specific professors, make sure that you will have that opportunity.

Competitiveness

By its nature, and by the nature of the students it attracts, business school fosters a competitive environment. But business is also about cooperation—working together towards a common goal. Many schools have addressed this by introducing team-based learning into their curricula.

Some schools have reputations for fostering an intense environment, whereas others are considered more supportive. Try not to base your perceptions about the academic environment at various schools on the schools' reputations alone. Sit in on first-year classes to assess the dynamics. Ask yourself: Do the students work well together? Do they support each other? Do they treat each other with respect, even when they disagree? Does the professor facilitate a positive learning atmosphere? Find out about each school's grading system. When a program grades on a forced curve, some students feel motivated and others feel unwanted pressure. How do you think you'd react to it?

When you visit a school, talk to students to learn how they feel about the environment. You'll probably get a variety of viewpoints, but there's no better way to get a feel for what a school is like, what the students are like, and how you will fit in there.

Placement

When you get right down to it, the main purpose of attending business school is to enhance your career prospects, both short- and long-term. Look into each school's placement records to find out:

- How many companies recruit on campus?

- What kinds of companies recruit on campus?

- What percentage of the class has job offers by graduation?

- What is the breakdown of jobs by industry?

- What is the average starting salary?

Try not to overemphasize the significance of average starting salary when you evaluate programs. Though there is a correlation between the top-ranked schools and starting salaries, other factors, as well, determine your starting salary and your overall attractiveness to prospective employers. Some recruiters place a high value on your pre–business school experience. Others care more about your B-school academic record.

Moreover, some industries—notably management consulting and investment banking—pay at the high end of the spectrum. So the salary statistics of schools that send a high percentage of students into these fields are skewed upward.

If you enroll in a traditional two-year program, learn about summer job opportunities between your first and second year. For one thing, the money will be helpful. For another, your summer position can give you first-hand experience in a new job or industry that you can leverage when you graduate. Many summer jobs ultimately lead to full-time offers. Plus, a substantive summer experience will make you a more attractive job candidate for prospective employers.

Finally, don't just look at the first jobs that a school's graduates take. Where are they in 5, 10, and even 25 years? Your career is more like a marathon than a sprint. So take the long view. A strong indicator of a school's strength is the accomplishments of its alumni.

Class Profile

Because much of your learning will come from your classmates, especially in case-method classes, consider the make-up of your class. A school with a geographically, professionally, and ethnically diverse student body will expose you to far more viewpoints than will a school with a more homogeneous group.

To get a feel for the class profile of a particular school, look at these readily available statistics:

- Undergraduate areas of study

- Percentage of international students

- Percentage of women

- Percentage of minorities

- Percentage of married students

- Average years of work experience

- Types of companies for which students worked

- Average age and age range of entering students

Let's look at average age. Over the past few decades, students attending business school have been getting older. Currently, the average age of the entering student is approximately 27 at many of the top schools. But the average is a little misleading because it consists of many 26-year-olds and significantly fewer 30-, 40-, and 50-year-olds who skew the average upward. So if you're an older applicant, ask yourself how you will fit in with a predominantly younger group of students. For many, the fit is terrific. For others, the transition is tougher.

Networking

Forging relationships—with your section mates, your classmates, and, in a larger sense, all the alumni—is a big part of the business school experience. One of the things that you'll take with you when you graduate, aside from an education, a diploma, and debt, is that network. And whether you thrive on networking or consider it a four-letter word, it's a necessity. At some point it may help you advance your career, land a piece of business, or perhaps even finance a new venture.

Many programs have large, organized networks that you can access. This is a strong selling point for those schools. Like any other single factor, don't make networking potential your sole criterion, but keep it in mind as you evaluate programs.

Workload

Think about how hard you are prepared to work. It's generally true that the more effort you put in the more you'll gain, but some programs really pile it on first-year students. That can limit the amount of time and energy that you'll have left to devote to outside activities.

For students with families, the first year of B-school requires not just a sacrifice of income but of time that you can spend with your spouse or children. Don't underestimate how all-encompassing your first year will be. At some point this can be a strain on even the strongest relationships. Fortunately, the second year tends to be more manageable.

If you enroll in a part-time program, the time constraints may be even more severe because you have to handle the rigors of your course load on top of your job.

Quality of Life

Your business school experience will extend far beyond your classroom learning, particularly for full-time students. Find out as much as you can about the schools that interest you. What kind of city life is available nearby? What kind of recreational facilities are offered? Regardless of your interests, your ability to maintain balance in your life in the face of a rigorous academic challenge will help you keep a healthy outlook.

Housing is another quality-of-life issue to consider. Is campus housing available? Is off-campus housing convenient? Is it affordable? Where do most of the students live?

Quality of life is also an important consideration for spouses and significant others, especially if school requires a move to a new city. When the first year takes over your life, your spouse may feel left out. Find out what kind of groups and activities there are for partners. For example, are there any services to help your spouse find employment?

Full-Time versus Part-Time

In a full-time program, you can focus your energy on your studies to maximize your learning. You're also likely to meet more people and forge closer relationships with your classmates. Many programs are oriented toward the full-time student though they may offer part-time programs. A part-time schedule may also make it difficult for you to take classes with the best professors.

There are, however, many compelling reasons to attend business school part time. The most obvious reason is that you are working full time. Perhaps your employer will help subsidize you if you continue working. Or perhaps you don't want to abandon the career track that you're on.

Though some prospective employers may place more value on an M.B.A. earned full time, others recognize and respect the commitment required to complete an M.B.A. part time. If you decide to attend business school part time, the good news is that there are many fine programs from which to choose.

M.B.A. versus Executive Education

For most applicants with 2, 3, or 4 years of work experience, executive education is not a feasible option because they don't have enough experience. But if you are a middle manager or a small-business owner with a need for functional training, executive education programs may be worth exploring.

Executive education programs, a growing area for many business schools, essentially bring together individuals with similar educational needs and provide a focused, intensive learning experience. For example, middle managers with 10 to 15 years experience may attend a 12-week, full-time program to study such core subjects as marketing, finance, operations, and management accounting. It's sort of a mini-M.B.A.

If the M.B.A. is important for you as a credential, be aware that executive education programs generally do not award M.B.A.'s. But if your organization will be sponsoring you and you plan to stay there, this may be an invaluable career opportunity that you don't want to pass up.

If you are looking for training in very specific areas, then perhaps much of an M.B.A. program's curriculum would not be of interest to you, and executive education would make more sense. So although executive education is not a substitute for an M.B.A., you may find it worth considering.

CONSIDERING WHERE YOU CAN GET IN

Now that you've developed a list of schools that meet your needs, you should take an objective look at your chances of getting into them.

Assess Your Chances

A good way to get a sense of how business schools will perceive you is to make up a fact sheet with your GMAT scores (or projected scores), your GPA, and your work experience. Outside activities will contribute to the overall "score" that admissions officers will use to evaluate you, but let's stick with the raw data for now.

The next step is to find a current source of information about B-school programs. There are several guides published every year that provide data about acceptance rates for given years, median GPA, and GMAT scores. The school of your dreams may not care very much about your GPA, but it might be very interested in your GMAT score. Make sure you find out what your target school prioritizes in its search for worthy applicants.

One of the best ways to gauge whether you're in contention for a certain program is to compare your numbers to theirs. You don't need to hit the nail on the head: Median means average, so some applicants do better or worse than the GMAT score or GPA cited. And remember those other factors—most importantly, your work experience—that add up to make you a desirable applicant. Comparing numbers is merely a good way to get a preliminary estimate of your compatibility with the schools of your choice.

Pick "Safe" Schools

Now that you have some idea of where you fall in the applicant pool, you can begin to make decisions about your application strategy. Some students waste their time and money with a scatter-gun approach, shooting off applications to a host of schools.

No matter what your circumstances, choose at least one school that is likely to accept you. It should be one that fits your academic goals and your economic circumstances. If your GMAT scores and GPA are well above a school's median scores, and you don't anticipate any problems with other parts of your record or application, you've probably found a safe school.

Pick "Wishful Thinking" Schools

Reach high and apply to one or two very competitive programs. You may be surprised! Some people underestimate their potential and apply only to "sure thing" schools. It would be disappointing if you were to end up at one of those schools and discover that it didn't provide the rigorous training you wanted.

DECIDING WHEN TO APPLY

With business school applications on the rise again, the issue of when to apply for admission has become very important. There are perfect times to begin and end the application process. You should begin a year before you plan to enter school. Find out the following essential dates as early as possible and incorporate them into your own personal application schedule:

- Standardized test registration deadlines

- Transcript deadlines (some schools send out transcripts only on particular dates)

- Letters of recommendation

- Application deadlines (submit your application as early as possible to ensure that you get a fair and comprehensive review)

- Financial aid forms (federal/state programs, universities, and independent sources of aid all have definite deadlines)

Setting Up an Application Schedule

The following "seasonal" schedule is organized to help you understand how to proceed through the admissions process.

Summer

- Request applications from schools. If they're not available yet, ask for last year's so you can get a feel for the questions you'll have to answer.

- Write drafts for your essays and talk them over with others.

- Browse through business school catalogs and collect information on different grants and loans. Create your own B-school financial aid library.

- Consider registering for the GMAT in the fall. This will give you plenty of time to submit your scores with your application.

- Research your options for test preparation. Take the test included in this book to give you a good idea of where you stand with regard to the GMAT.

Early Fall

- Ask for recommendations. Make sure that your recommenders know enough about you to write a meaningful letter. Once your recommenders have agreed to write a recommendation, let them know when deadlines will be, so you can avoid any timing conflicts.

Late Fall

- Take the GMAT.

- Request applications from schools, if you haven't already done so.

- Request institutional, state, and federal financial aid materials from school aid offices.

- Request information on independent grants and loans.

- Order transcripts from your undergraduate (and any graduate) institution(s).

Winter

- Fill out applications. Mail them as early as possible.

- Fill out financial aid applications. Mail these early as well.

- Make sure your recommendation writers have the appropriate forms and directions for mailing. Remind them of deadline dates.

Spring

- Sit back and relax. Most schools indicate how long they will take to inform you of their decision. This is also a crucial time to solidify your financial plans as you begin to receive offers of aid (with any luck).

The timing described here is rough, and you needn't follow it exactly. The most important thing is to know the strict deadlines well in advance, so that you'll be able to give your application plenty of quality time.

USEFUL BUSINESS SCHOOL RESOURCES

Here are some resources you should find helpful in your quest for business school information.

M.B.A. Forums

These M.B.A. school fairs, sponsored by the GMAC each year, are a wonderful resource and an excellent way to browse the programs. Representatives of more that 75 graduate management schools from the United States and abroad are on hand to answer questions. The schedule typically includes Forums in New York, Chicago, San Francisco, Los Angeles, and Washington, D.C, among other cities.

Web: mba.com/mba/FindYourProgram

Graduate Management Admission Search Service

A free service, the GMASS makes your name available to schools whose specifications for applicants match your profile, as per your GMAT Registration information. This automatic service will send you mailings from schools about their M.B.A. programs, admissions procedures, and financial aid.

Web: gmass.org

M.B.A. Program Information

The M.B.A. Program Information Site. An international business school site containing a database with details on 2,500 M.B.A. programs from 1,290 business schools and universities in 123 countries, as well as advice pages for the prospective candidate.

Web: mbainfo.com

M.B.A. Explorer

This site includes links to business schools on the web, a school search engine, and information about the GMAT. You can also register online for the GMAT here.

Web: mba.com

M.B.A. Depot

This site provides an open line of communication between students and alumni to share experiences and resources for B-school.

Web: mbadepot.com

E-Student Loan

This free site provides information a student loans. You can instantly compare loans that match your specific needs and provides online applications.

Web: estudentloan.com

FinAid

This site has everything you ever wanted to know about financial aid, including free scholarship and fellowship search services and descriptions of financial-aid sources. Sponsored by the National Association of Student Financial Aid Administrators.

Web: finaid.com

SUMMARY

When considering where to apply, evaluate:

- Overall reputation
- Teaching methods
- Class and Section Size
- School Location
- Curriculum
- Faculty
- Competitiveness
- Placement
- Class Profile
- Networking
- Workload
- Quality of Life
- Full-time versus Part-time
- M.B.A. versus Executive Education

When considering where you can get in, look at:

- Assess your chances
- Pick "Safe" Schools
- Pick "Wishful Thinking" Schools

Chapter 14: **How to Apply**

Your first step is to order the application forms from the various schools that you've selected. You can do it by mail, but the quickest way is to call the admissions offices around July and have them put you on their mailing lists. Once the applications begin arriving you'll notice one thing quickly: No two applications are exactly alike. Some ask you to write one essay or personal statement, and others may ask for three or more. Some have very detailed forms requiring extensive background information; others are satisfied with your name and address and little else.

Despite these differences, most applications follow a general pattern with variations on the same kinds of questions. So read this section with the understanding that, although not all of it is relevant to every application, these guidelines will be valuable for just about any business school application that you'll encounter.

HOW SCHOOLS EVALUATE APPLICANTS

Each business school has its own admissions policies and practices, but all programs evaluate your application on a range of objective and subjective criteria. Regardless of which schools you are pursuing, understanding how admissions officers judge your candidacy can give you a leg up on the competition.

Generally, all admissions officers use the application process to measure your intellectual abilities, management skills, and personal characteristics. When you submit your application, admissions officers will evaluate the total package. Most admissions officers look for reasons to admit candidates, not for reasons to reject them. Your challenge, therefore, is to distinguish yourself positively from the other candidates.

KAPLAN

Intellectual Ability

To assess your intellectual ability, admissions officers look at two key factors: your academic record and your GMAT score.

Academic Record

Your GPA is important, but it's just part of the picture. Admissions officers will consider the reputation of your undergraduate institution and the difficulty of your courses. Admissions officers are well aware that comparing GPAs from different schools and even different majors from the same school is like comparing apples and oranges. So they'll look closely at your transcript. Do your grades show an upward trend? How did you perform in your major? How did you fare in calculus and other quantitative courses?

Admissions officers focus primarily on your undergraduate performance, but they will consider graduate studies and nondegree coursework that you have completed. Be sure to submit those transcripts.

If you have a poor academic record, it will be tougher to get into a top school, but by no means impossible. Your challenge is to find other ways to demonstrate your intellectual horsepower. A high GMAT score, intelligently written essays, and recommendations that highlight your analytical abilities will help. If your record does not show any evidence of quantitative skills, you should consider taking courses in accounting and statistics to demonstrate your aptitude.

GMAT

An integral part of the admissions process at virtually all schools, the GMAT measures general verbal and quantitative skills and is designed to predict academic success in the first year of a graduate business school program.

When admissions officers review your GMAT score, they'll look primarily at your overall score. However, they'll also look at your quantitative and verbal subscores, particularly if they have any questions about your abilities in either area. If you've taken the GMAT more than once, schools will generally credit you with your highest score, though some may average the scores or take the most recent.

Used by itself, the GMAT may not be a great predictor of academic performance, but it is the single best one available. The GMAT does not measure your intelligence, nor does it measure the likelihood of your success in business. As with any standardized test, by preparing properly for the GMAT, you can boost your score significantly.

The GMAT contains two essay sections, dubbed the "Analytical Writing Assessment" (AWA). The essays you type into the computer are graded on a 1 to 6 scale and sent to the schools you designate along with your traditional 200–800 score. The AWA is designed to provide schools with information about your communications skills that is not otherwise captured in the GMAT.

Essentially, the AWA is another tool that schools can use to evaluate you. Although it won't reduce the importance of the essays on your applications, it may alter the number of essays a school asks you to write. Business schools have recognized that the AWA provides you with an opportunity to demonstrate your ability to think critically and communicate complex ideas in a very limited time period. For that reason, admissions officers may be as interested in reading your writing samples as they are in relying solely on your GMAT score.

Even though the AWA is scored separately from the multiple-choice sections, you should prepare for it with the same intensity that you put into preparing for the rest of the GMAT. Outstanding writing samples can help you stand out from the crowd. Conversely, seriously flawed essays can reduce your admissions chances.

Management Skills

To evaluate your management skills, admissions officers look at work experience and other relevant activities. That does not mean that you need to have managed people to be an impressive candidate. Perhaps you've managed projects, resources, or portfolios. Each of these can provide an excellent forum for you to demonstrate evidence of your management aptitude.

You can communicate some of your management abilities through the straightforward "data" part of your application. Be sure to describe your job responsibilities. Don't list your title and assume that an admissions officer knows what you do or the level of your responsibilities. This is especially important if your job is nontraditional for an aspiring M.B.A.

Admissions officers will look at your overall career record. How have you progressed? Have you been an outstanding performer? What do your recommendation writers say about your performance? Have you progressed to increasingly higher levels of responsibility? If you have limited work experience, you will not be expected to match the accomplishments of an applicant with 10 years of experience, but you will be expected to demonstrate your abilities.

The essays also provide an opportunity to demonstrate your management aptitude. Many essay questions specifically ask you to discuss your professional experiences and how you handled different situations. With thoughtful, well-written essays you can highlight your management strengths for admissions officers.

Extracurricular activities and community involvement also present opportunities for you to highlight your skills. For younger applicants, college activities play a more significant role than for more seasoned applicants. Your activities say a lot about who you are and what's important to you. Were you a campus leader? Did your activities require discipline and commitment? Did you work with a team? What did you learn from your involvement?

Active community involvement provides a way for you to demonstrate your management skills and to impress admissions officers with your personal character. In fact, many applications ask directly about community activities. If you are contemplating getting involved in your community, here's a chance to do something worthwhile and enhance your application in the process.

Personal Characteristics

The third, and most subjective, criterion on which schools evaluate you is your personal characteristics. Admissions officers judge you in this area primarily through your essays, recommendations, and personal interview (if applicable). Although different schools emphasize different qualities, most seek candidates who demonstrate leadership, maturity, integrity, responsibility, and teamwork.

The more competitive schools place special emphasis on these criteria because they have many qualified applicants for each available spot in the class. In fact, the top-tier programs generally require numerous essays so that they can get a complete feeling for each applicant's personal qualities.

WHO REVIEWS YOUR APPLICATION?

At most schools, the board includes professional admissions officers. And at some schools, second year students and/or alumni play a role in reviewing applications and interviewing candidates.

Admissions officers are not always representative of the group of students they admit. Many boards contain a high percentage of women and minorities. Board members recognize the importance of diversity in the classroom and in many cases have a mandate to increase it. Although some admissions officers have had management training and business experience, many have not. They tend to be people-oriented and have strong interpersonal skills. They want to get to "know" you through your application, and they are partial to well-written essays.

WHAT DECISIONS ARE MADE

Upon reviewing your application, the admissions board may make any number of decisions, including:

- Admit: Congratulations, you're in. But read the letter carefully. The board may recommend or, in some cases, require you to do some preparatory coursework to ensure that your quantitative or language skills are up to speed.

- Reject: At the top schools, there are far more qualified applicants than there are spaces in the class. Even though you were rejected, you can reapply at a later date. However, if you are considering reapplying, you need to understand why you were rejected and whether you have a reasonable chance of being admitted the next time around. Some schools will speak with you about your application, but they often wait for the end of the admissions season, by which time you may have accepted another offer.

- Deferred admit: This decision is reserved for when the admissions board considers you a strong candidate, but believes you would benefit from an additional year or two of work experience before attending. Because most applicants now have at least two years experience before applying to school, deferred admission is not as common now as it once was.

- Reject with encouragement to reapply: This isn't just a polite rejection. One step down from a deferred admit, it's a way for a school to say, "we like you, and we think with more experience you'd be a strong candidate."

- Hold over until the next decision period: Sometimes the admissions board isn't comfortable making a decision by the scheduled reply date. Perhaps you're right on the borderline, and the board wants to see how you stack up against the next group of applicants. In this case, all you can do is wait, but frequently the result is positive.

- Waiting list: Schools use the waiting list—the educational equivalent of purgatory—to manage class size. The good news is that you wouldn't be on the list if you weren't considered a strong candidate. The bad news is there is no way to know with certainty whether you'll be accepted. Be aware, though, that schools do tend to look kindly upon wait-listed candidates who reapply in a subsequent year.

- Request for an interview: Schools at which an interview is not required may request that you interview prior to making their final decision. Your application may have raised some specific issues that you can address in an interview, or perhaps the board feels your essays did not give them a complete enough picture to render a decision. Look at this as a positive opportunity to strengthen your case.

PREPARING YOUR APPLICATION

There are no magic formulas that automatically admit you to, or reject you from, the school of your choice. Rather, your application is like a jigsaw puzzle. Each component—GPA, GMAT score, professional experience, school activities, recommendations—is a different piece of the puzzle.

Outstanding work experience and personal characteristics may enable you to overcome a mediocre academic record. Conversely, outstanding academic credentials will not ensure your admission to a top-tier school if you do not demonstrate strong management skills and solid personal character. Your challenge in preparing your application is to convince the admissions board that all of the pieces in your background fit together to form a substantial and unique whole.

Your Application as a Marketing Tool

When it comes to applying to business school, you are the product. Your application is your marketing document. Marketing yourself doesn't mean that you should lie or even embellish; it just means that you need to make a tight presentation of the facts. Everything in your application should add up to a coherent whole and underscore the fact that you are not only qualified to be in the class but that you should be in it.

KAPLAN

Many application forms have a certain tone, one that's comforting and accepting. Why would you like to come to our school, they seem to be asking. They do want an answer to that question, but what's even more important—the subtext for the whole application process—is a bigger question: Why should we accept you? This is the question that your application will answer. And with some effective marketing strategies, your answer will be clear, concise, coherent, and strong.

So how do you portray an image? First of all, it should fit; it should be natural. Don't bother to try to sell yourself as something you're not: It'll be uncomfortable to you, and it probably won't work.

Besides, part of what readers do when they evaluate your application is form an image of you from the various parts of your application. Your job is to help them, not hinder them.

MAXIMIZING THE VARIOUS PARTS OF YOUR APPLICATION

Let's look at how you should approach the specific parts of the application.

The Essay

Your essays are a critical part of your application. The situations you choose to write about and the manner in which you present them can have a major bearing on the strength of your candidacy.

Writing an effective essay requires serious self-examination and sound strategic planning. What are the major personal and professional events that have shaped you? What accomplishments best demonstrate your management abilities? Admissions officers are interested in getting to know you as a complete person. The topic and perspective you choose sends a clear signal about what's important to you and what your values are.

Common Essay Questions

Every application is unique, but most will include essay questions that fall into one of several basic types. Here are the kinds of questions you can expect to see:

1. **Describe (1, 2, or 3) significant accomplishments, and discuss why you view them as such.**

Here, the admissions board is looking to get a sense of what you consider important. Throughout the application review process, the board will be gauging not only your management aptitude but also the kind of person you are. The events you choose to write about say a lot about you, as do the reasons you consider them significant.

2. **Why are you pursuing an M.B.A.? Where do you hope to be 5 years from now? 10 years?**

Admissions officers want to see that you've thought through the reasons for going to business school, that you're committed to it, and that you have a clear understanding of what the experience is all about. Although they don't expect you to necessarily map out your entire career path, they will look for you to demonstrate forward thinking.

3. **What are your strengths and weaknesses?**

Answer truthfully. Don't settle for "pat" responses. When discussing your strengths, you may want to include a brief example of an experience that highlights your strengths, if length permits.

Writing about weaknesses can be tricky. The board is looking for evidence of self-awareness and maturity, but be careful about raising red flags. If you apply to a case method school that requires classroom participation, for instance, and you write that you're uncomfortable speaking in front of a group, the board will question whether you can thrive in that environment. Of course, you should be asking yourself the same question, anyway. Describing a weakness that's really a strength ("I'm so honest that . . . " or "I'm so committed to my employees that . . . ") is a common, safe approach, but it doesn't provide much insight and it may turn off some admissions officers.

4. **Describe an ethical dilemma you have faced, and discuss how you handled it.**

With this question, admissions officers will evaluate not just your ethical "compass," but also your thoughtfulness, maturity, and integrity. They want to see how you think through situations in which there are no easy solutions. What's most important is that you demonstrate your ability to exercise responsible judgment and learn from difficult personal circumstances.

5. Is there anything else you would like the admissions board to know about you?

This question is your chance to discuss anything you haven't yet been able to present. If your undergraduate performance is the weak link of your application, this is the place to explain why. Or if there's a gap in your employment record that is likely to raise a red flag, now is the time to discuss it. But don't be defensive. Many people have had to overcome weak grades, unpleasant professional experiences, and difficult personal circumstances. Discussing the hardships you have faced in a straightforward, nondefensive manner can you turn a potential pitfall into a strength on your application.

6. Describe a setback or failure and discuss what you learned from it.

Regardless of the event you choose to discuss, here is an opportunity to demonstrate your thoughtfulness and maturity, as well as your capacity for growth and change.

7. If you could effect one change at your current job, what would it be?

Admissions officers recognize that many (especially younger) applicants have not yet reached levels to make fundamental changes at work. This question lets you flex your brain power in talking about changes you'd like to see. It reveals how knowledgeable you are about business in general and your business in particular. It also provides clues about how you think. For example, do you think about big picture issues, or do you focus on the details?

8. Describe a situation in which you demonstrated…(teamwork, leadership, responsibility).

A question like this will give you insight into the personal qualities that a school considers especially important in its students. Be sure to discuss the specifics of your situation. If the question is about a leadership situation, answer such questions as: How did you demonstrate it? Did you have group meetings? Individual meetings? How did you motivate people? What was the end result? By discussing the details, you'll provide the admissions board with valuable insight into your management style and aptitude.

General Essay Tips

Once you have established your topic, you now need to start writing. Keep the following things in mind:

- **Length:** Schools are pretty specific about how long they want your essays to be. Adhere to their guidelines. If you feel you need to write an extra sentence or two, fine. But don't write three pages when an essay asks for one. If thousands of other applicants can limit their responses to one page, so can you.

- **Spelling/typos/grammar:** Remember, your application is your marketing document. What would you think of a product that's promoted with sloppy materials containing typos, spelling errors, and grammatical mistakes?

- **Write in the active voice:** Candidates who write well have an advantage in the application process because they can state their case in a concise, compelling manner. Less effective writers commonly write "passively." For example:

Passive voice: The essays were written by me.

Active voice: I wrote the essays.

Strong writing will not compensate for a lack of substance, but poor writing can torpedo an otherwise impressive candidate.

- **Tone:** On the one hand, you want to tout your achievements and present yourself as a poised, self-confident applicant. On the other hand, arrogance and self-importance do not go over well with admissions officers. Before you submit your application, be sure that you're comfortable with the tone as well as the content.

- **Creative approach:** If you choose to submit a humorous or creative application, you are employing a high risk, high reward strategy. If you're confident you can pull it off, go for it. Be aware, though, that what may work for one admissions officer may fall flat with another. Admissions officers who review thousands of essays every year may consider your approach gimmicky or simply find it distracting. Remember, your challenge is to stand out in the applicant pool in a positive way. Don't let your creativity obscure the substance of your application.

Making Your Essay Distinctive

Depending on the amount of time you have and the amount of effort you're willing to put in, you can write an essay that will stand out from the crowd. One of the first mistakes that some applicants make is in thinking that "thorough" and "comprehensive" are sufficient qualities for their essays. They try to include as much information as possible, without regard for length limitations or strategic intent. Application readers dread reading these bloated essays. So how do you decide what to include? There are usually clear length guidelines, and admissions officers prefer that you adhere to them. So, get rid of the idea of "comprehensive" and focus more on "distinctive."

Unless they ask for it, don't dwell on your weak points. A strong essay, for example, about how much you learned in your current position and how the experience and knowledge you've gained inspired you to apply to business school will give readers what they want—a quick image of who you are, how you got that way, and why you want to go to their school. One of the best ways to be distinctive is to sell your image briefly and accurately, including real-life examples to back up your points.

"Distinctive" means that your essay should answer the questions that admissions officers think about while reading essays: What's different about this applicant? Why should we pick this applicant over others? Authentic enthusiasm can be a plus, and writing about parts of your life or career that are interesting and relevant help grab a reader's attention.

The Interview

Because communication skills are such an integral part of effective management, many B-schools include personal interviews as part of the admissions process.

- Review your application. If you've submitted your application prior to the interview, your interviewer is likely to use it as a guide and may ask specific questions about it. Be sure you remember what you wrote.

- Be ready to provide examples and specifics. Professionally trained interviewers are more likely to ask you about specific situations than they are to ask broad open-ended questions. They can learn more by asking what you've done in situations than by asking what you think you'd do. Here are a few situations an interviewer may ask you to discuss: "Tell me about a recent accomplishment." "Discuss a recent situation in which you demonstrated leadership." "Give me an example of a situation where you overcame difficult circumstances." As you think about these situations, be prepared to discuss specifics—what you did and why you did it that way. You do not need to "script" or over-rehearse your responses, but you should go into the interview confident that you can field any question.

- Be open and honest. Don't struggle to think of "right" answers. The only right answers are those that are right for you. By responding openly and honestly, you'll find the interview less stressful, and you'll come across as a more genuine, attractive candidate.

- Ask questions. The interview is as much an opportunity for you to learn about the school as for the school to learn about you. Good questions demonstrate your knowledge about a particular program and your thoughtfulness about the entire process.

- Follow proper business decorum. Be on time, dress appropriately, and follow-up with thank you letters. Treat the process as you would a job interview, which in many respects it is.

- Watch your nonverbal cues. Nonverbal communication is much more important than people realize. Maintain eye contact, keep good posture, sustain positive energy, and avoid nervous fidgeting. It will help you come across as confident, poised, and mature.

- Be courteous to the administrative staff. These people are colleagues of the board members, and how you treat them can have an impact, either positive or negative.

- Relax and have fun. Interviews are naturally stressful. But by being well prepared, you can enhance your prospects for admission, learn about the school, and enjoy yourself in the process.

Recommendations

Whether a school requires 1, 2, or 3 recommendations, it will generally look to them as supporting documents that will confirm the substance of your other application materials. Choose recommenders who can write meaningfully about your strengths. One of the more common mistakes is to sacrifice an insightful recommendation from someone who knows you well for a generic recommendation from a celebrity or an alumnus/a. Admissions officers are not impressed by famous names. So unless that individual knows you and can write convincingly on your behalf, it's not a strategy worth pursuing. Good choices for recommenders include current and past supervisors, professors, academic and nonacademic advisers, and people you work with in community activities.

If a school requests an academic recommendation, but you are not able to provide one, try to identify someone who can discuss your intellectual attributes, particularly if your academic record is not your strength. Similarly, if requesting a recommendation from your employer would create an awkward situation, look for someone else who can comment on your management skills. Your recommendations are not likely to make or break your application, but they will confirm your strengths and in some cases help you overcome perceived weaknesses in your application.

If you wish to submit an extra recommendation, it's generally not a problem. Most schools will include the letter in your file, and those that don't will not penalize you for it. You should, however, send a note explaining why you have requested an additional recommendation so it does not appear that you can't follow instructions.

Asking for Recommendations

There are two fundamental rules of requesting recommendations.

Rule 1: Ask early

Rule 2: Ask nicely

As soon as you decide to go to business school, start sizing up potential recommendation writers and let them know that you may ask them for a recommendation. This will give them plenty of time to think about what to say. Once they've agreed, let them know about deadlines well in advance to avoid potential scheduling conflicts. The more time they have, the better the job they'll do recommending you. As for asking nicely, you should let the person know you think highly of their opinion and you'd be happy and honored if they would consider writing you a letter of recommendation.

BEFORE YOU SUBMIT YOUR APPLICATION...

When your essays are complete and you are finalizing your applications, take two more steps to ensure that your applications are as strong as they can be.

1. Reread the essay in the context of your entire application. Does the total package make sense? Does it represent you favorably? Is everything consistent? Have you demonstrated your intellectual ability, management skills, and personal characteristics? Most important, do you feel good about the application? You wouldn't want to be rejected with an application that you don't believe represents the real you.

2. Ask someone whose opinion you respect to review your application. An impartial person is sure to pick up spelling or grammatical errors that you've overlooked. Maybe you have left something important out. In addition, because your application is an intensely personal document that requires significant self-examination, you may not be able to remain objective. Someone who knows you and can be frank will tell you whether your application has "captured" you most favorably.

Some schools prohibit you from using any outside help on your application. A last minute once-over from a friend or family member is probably within reason, but you may want to ask the school directly what is permissible.

SUMMARY

Schools evaluate applicants by the following criteria:

- Intellectual Ability
- Management Skills
- Personal Characteristics

During your interview, do the following:

- Review your application.
- Be ready to provide examples and specifics.
- Be open and honest.
- Ask questions.
- Follow proper business decorum.
- Watch your nonverbal clues.
- Be courteous to the administrative staff.
- Relax and have fun.

A SPECIAL NOTE FOR INTERNATIONAL STUDENTS

The M.B.A. (Master of Business Administration) has become a degree of choice for people around the globe. Variations of U.S.-style M.B.A. programs exist in Asia, Europe, and the Americas. In recent years, hundreds of thousands of international students have studied business and management in the United States.

As the United States participates in the global economy, U.S. business schools are reaching out to attract exceptional international candidates. However, competition for admission to prestigious programs is heavy, and international students need to plan carefully if they wish to enter a top program.

If you are not from the United States, but are considering attending a graduate management program at a university in the United States, here is what you'll need to get started.

- If English is not your first language, start there. You will probably need to take the Test of English as a Foreign Language (TOEFL) or show some other evidence that you are proficient in English prior to gaining admission to a graduate program in business. Some graduate business schools now require a minimum TOEFL score of 550 (213 on the computer-based TOEFL), while others will require a minimum of 600 (250 on the computer-based TOEFL).

- You will need to take the GMAT. Some graduate business programs may require you to take the GRE (Graduate Record Examination) as well.

- Since admission to many graduate business programs is quite competitive, you may wish to apply to 3 or 4 programs.

- Select a program that meets your current or future employment needs, rather than simply a program with a big name. If you hope to work in the hotel and tourism industry, make sure the program you choose specializes in that distinct area.

- Begin the application process at least a year in advance. Be aware that many programs only offer August or September start dates. Find out application deadlines and plan accordingly.

- Finally, you will need to obtain a 1-20 Certificate of Eligibility from the school you plan to attend if you intend to apply for an F-1 Student Visa to study in the United States.

Kaplan English Programs*

If you need more help with the complex process of business school admissions, assistance preparing for the TOEFL or GMAT, or help improving your English skills in general, you may be interested in Kaplan's programs for international students.

Kaplan English Programs were designed to help students and professionals from outside the United States meet their educational and career goals. At locations throughout the United States, Kaplan programs help international students to improve their academic and conversational English skills, raise their scores on the TOEFL, GMAT, and other standardized exams, and gain admission to the schools of their choice. Our staff and instructors provide the individualized instruction that students need to succeed. Here is a brief description of some of our programs:

General Intensive English

This course is designed to help you improve your skills in all areas of English and to increase your fluency in spoken and written English. Classes are available for beginning to advanced students, and the average class size is 12 students.

TOEFL and Academic English

This course provides you with the skills you need to improve your TOEFL score and succeed at a U.S. university or graduate program. It includes advanced reading, writing, listening, grammar, and conversational English. You will also receive training in Kaplan's exclusive computer-based practice materials.

GMAT for International Students

The GMAT is required for admission to many graduate programs in business in the United States.

Hundreds of thousands of American students have taken this course to prepare for the GMAT. This course includes the skills you need to succeed on each section of the GMAT, as well as access to Kaplan's exclusive computer-based practice materials.

*Kaplan is authorized under federal law to enroll nonimmigrant alien students. Kaplan is accredited by ACCET (Accrediting Council for Continuing Education and Training).

KAPLAN)

Other Kaplan Programs

Since 1938, more than 3 million students have come to Kaplan to advance their studies, prepare for entry to American universities, and further their careers. In addition to the above programs, Kaplan offers courses to prepare for the SAT, GMAT, GRE, LSAT, MCAT, DAT, USMLE, NCLEX, and other standardized exams at locations throughout the United States.

Applying to Kaplan English Programs

For more information, contact us at:
Kaplan English Programs
700 South Flower, Suite 2900
Los Angeles, CA 90017
Telephone inside the U.S. and Canada: 1-800-KAPTEST
Telephone outside the U.S. and Canada: 1-212-997-5886
Email: world@kaplan.com
Web: www.kaplanenglish.com

GMAT Resources

Math Reference

The math on the GMAT covers a lot of ground—from basic algebra to symbol problems to geometry. Don't let yourself be intimidated.

We've highlighted the 100 most important concepts that you need to know and divided them into three levels. The GMAT Quantitative section tests your understanding of a relatively limited number of mathematical concepts, all of which you will be able to learn.

Level 1 is the most basic. You can't answer any GMAT math questions if you don't know Level 1 math. Most people preparing to take the GMAT are already pretty good at Level 1 math but look over the Level 1 list just to make sure you're comfortable with the basics.

Level 2 where most people start their review of math. Level 2 skills and formulas come into play quite frequently on the GMAT, especially in the medium and hard questions.

Level 3 is the hardest math you'll find on the GMAT. Don't spend a lot of time on Level 3 if you still have gaps in Level 2; but once you've mastered Level 2, tackling Level 3 can put you over the top.

LEVEL 1 (Math You Probably Already Know)

1. How to add, subtract, multiply, and divide WHOLE NUMBERS

2. How to add, subtract, multiply, and divide FRACTIONS

3. How to add, subtract, multiply, and divide DECIMALS

4. How to convert FRACTIONS TO DECIMALS and DECIMALS TO FRACTIONS

5. How to add, subtract, multiply, and divide POSITIVE AND NEGATIVE NUMBERS

6. How to plot points on the NUMBER LINE

7. How to plug a number into an ALGEBRAIC EXPRESSION

8. How to SOLVE a simple EQUATION

9. How to add and subtract LINE SEGMENTS

10. How to find the THIRD ANGLE of a TRIANGLE, given the other two angles

LEVEL 2 (Math You Might Need to Review)

11. How to use PEMDAS

When you're given an ugly arithmetic expression, it's important to know the order of operations. Just remember PEMDAS (as in "Please excuse my dear Aunt Sally"). What PEMDAS means is this: Clean up **Parentheses** first; then deal with **Exponents**; then do the **Multiplication** and **Division** together, going from left to right; and finally do the **Addition** and **Subtraction** together, again going from left to right.

Example: $9 - 2 \times (5 - 3)^2 + 6 \div 3 =$

Begin with the parentheses:
$9 - 2 \times (2)^2 + 6 \div 3$

Then do the exponent:
$9 - 2 \times 4 + 6 \div 3$

Now do multiplication and division from left to right:
$9 - 8 + 2$

Finally, do addition and subtraction from left to right:
$9 - 8 + 2 = 1 + 2 = 3$

12. How to use the PERCENT FORMULA

Identify the part, the percent, and the whole.

Part = percent × whole

Find the part

Example: What is 12 percent of 25?

Setup: $\text{Part} = \dfrac{12}{100} \times 25 = 3$

Find the percent

Example: 45 is what percent of 9?

Setup: $45 = \text{Percent} \times 9$

$$\text{Percent} = \frac{45}{9} = 5 = 5 \times 100\% = 500\%$$

Find the whole

Example: 15 is $\dfrac{3}{5}$ percent of what number?

Setup: $15 = \dfrac{3}{5}\left(\dfrac{1}{100}\right) \times \text{whole}$

$$15 = \frac{3}{500} \times \text{whole}$$

$$\text{whole} = 15\left(\frac{500}{3}\right) = 5(500) = 2{,}500$$

KAPLAN

13. How to use the PERCENT INCREASE/DECREASE FORMULAS

Identify the original whole and the amount of increase/decrease.

$$Percent\ increase = \frac{amount\ of\ increase}{original\ whole} \times 100\%$$

$$Percent\ decrease = \frac{amount\ of\ decrease}{original\ whole} \times 100\%$$

Example: The price goes up from $80 to $100. What is the percent increase?

Setup: Percent increase $= \frac{20}{80} \times 100\% = 25\%$

14. How to predict whether a sum, difference, or product will be ODD or EVEN

Don't bother memorizing the rules. Just take simple numbers like 1 and 2 and see what happens.

Example: If m is even and n is odd, is the product mn odd or even?

Setup: Say $m = 2$ and $n = 1$.

2×1 is even, so mn is even.

15. How to recognize MULTIPLES OF 2, 3, 4, 5, 6, 9, 10, and 12

2: Last digit is even

3: Sum of digits is a multiple of 3

4: Last two digits are a multiple of 4

5: Last digit is 5 or 0

6: Sum of digits is a multiple of 3 and last digit is even

9: Sum of digits is a multiple of 9

10: Last digit is 0

12: Sum of digits is a multiple of 3 and last two digits are a multiple of 4

16. How to find a COMMON FACTOR

Break both numbers down to their prime factors to see what they have in common. Then multiply the shared prime factors to find all common factors.

Example: What factors greater than 1 do 135 and 225 have in common?

Setup: First find the prime factors of 135 and 225. $135 = 3 \times 3 \times 3 \times 5$, and $225 = 3 \times 3 \times 5 \times 5$. The numbers share $3 \times 3 \times 5$ in common. Thus, aside from 3 and 5, the remaining common factors can be found by multiplying 3, 3, and 5 in every possible combination: $3 \times 3 = 9$, $3 \times 5 = 15$, and $3 \times 3 \times 5 = 45$.

17. How to find a COMMON MULTIPLE

The product is the easiest common multiple to find. If the two numbers have any factors in common, you can divide them out of the product to get a lower common multiple.

Example: What is the least common multiple of 28 and 42?

Setup: The product $28 \times 42 = 1{,}176$ is a common multiple, but not the least. $28 = 2 \times 2 \times 7$, and $42 = 2 \times 3 \times 7$. They share a 2 and a 7, so divide the product by 2 and then by 7. $1{,}176 \div 2 = 588$. $588 \div 7 = 84$. The least common multiple is 84.

18. How to find the AVERAGE

$$Average = \frac{Sum\ of\ terms}{Number\ of\ terms}$$

Example: What is the average of 3, 4, and 8?

Setup: $Average = \dfrac{3 + 4 + 8}{3} = \dfrac{15}{3} = 5$.

19. How to use the AVERAGE to find the SUM

$$Sum = (Average) \times (Number\ of\ terms)$$

Example: 17.5 is the average (arithmetic mean) of 24 numbers. What is the sum?

Setup: $Sum = 17.5 \times 24 = 420$

KAPLAN

20. How to find the AVERAGE of CONSECUTIVE NUMBERS

The average of evenly spaced numbers is simply the average of the smallest number and the largest number. The average of all the integers from 13 to 77, for example, is the same as the average of 13 and 77:

$$\frac{13 + 77}{2} = \frac{90}{2} = 45$$

21. How to COUNT CONSECUTIVE NUMBERS

The number of integers from A to B inclusive is $B - A + 1$.

Example: How many integers are there from 73 through 419, inclusive?
   Setup: $419 - 73 + 1 = 347$

22. How to find the SUM OF CONSECUTIVE NUMBERS

Sum = (Average) × (Number of terms)

Example: What is the sum of the integers from 10 through 50, inclusive?
   Setup: Average = $(10 + 50) \div 2 = 30$
   Number of terms = $50 - 10 + 1 = 41$
   Sum = $30 \times 41 = 1,230$

23. How to find the MEDIAN

Put the numbers in numerical order and take the middle number. (If there's an even number of numbers, the average of the two numbers in the middle is the median.)

Example: What is the median of 88, 86, 57, 94, and 73?
   Setup: Put the numbers in numerical order and take the middle number:

   57, 73, 86, 88, 94

The median is 86. (If there's an even number of numbers, take the average of the two in the middle.)

24. How to find the MODE

Take the number that appears most often. For example, if your test scores were 88, 57, 68, 85, 98, 93, 93, 84, and 81, the mode of the scores is 93 because it appears more often than any other score. (If there's a tie for most often, then there's more than one mode.)

25. How to find the RANGE

Simply take the positive difference between the highest and lowest values. Using the previous example, if your test scores were 88, 57, 68, 85, 98, 93, 93, 84, and 81, the range of the scores is 41, the highest value minus the lowest value (98 − 57 = 41).

26. How to use actual numbers to determine a RATIO

To find a ratio, put the number associated with *of* on the top and the word associated with *to* on the bottom.

$$Ratio = \frac{of}{to}$$

The ratio of 20 oranges to 12 apples is $\frac{20}{12}$, or $\frac{5}{3}$.

27. How to use a ratio to determine an ACTUAL NUMBER

Set up a proportion.

Example: The ratio of boys to girls is 3 to 4. If there are 135 boys, how many girls are there?

Setup: $\frac{3}{4} = \frac{135}{x}$

$3 \times x = 4 \times 135$

$x = 180$

28. How to use actual numbers to determine a RATE

Identify the quantities and the units to be compared. Keep the units straight.

Example: Anders typed 9,450 words in $3\frac{1}{2}$ hours. What was his rate in words per minute?

Setup: First convert $3\frac{1}{2}$ hours to 210 minutes. Then set up the rate with words on top and minutes on bottom:

$$\frac{9,450 \text{ words}}{210 \text{ minutes}} = 45 \text{ words per minute}$$

29. How to deal with TABLES, GRAPHS, AND CHARTS

Read the question and all labels extra carefully. Ignore extraneous information and zero in on what the question asks for. Take advantage of the spread in the answer choices by approximating the answer whenever possible.

30. How to count the NUMBER OF POSSIBILITIES

In most cases, you won't need to apply the combination and permutation formulas on the GMAT. The number of possibilities is generally so small that the best approach is just to write them out systematically and count them.

Example: How many three-digit numbers can be formed with the digits 1, 3, and 5 used only once?

Setup: Write them out. Be systematic so you don't miss any: 135, 153, 315, 351, 513, 531. Count them: six possibilities.

31. How to calculate a simple PROBABILITY

$$Probability = \frac{Number\ of\ favorable\ outcomes}{Total\ number\ of\ possible\ outcomes}$$

Example: What is the probability of throwing a 5 on a fair six-sided die?

Setup: There is one favorable outcome—throwing a 5. There are 6 possible outcomes—one for each side of the die.

$$Probability = \frac{1}{6}$$

32. How to work with new SYMBOLS

If you see a symbol you've never seen before, don't freak out: it's a made-up symbol. Everything you need to know is in the question stem. Just follow the instructions.

33. How to SIMPLIFY POLYNOMIALS

First multiply to eliminate all parentheses. Each term inside one parentheses is multiplied by each term inside the other parentheses. All like terms are then combined.

Example:
$$(3x^2+5x)(x-1) =$$
$$3x^2(x-1) + 5x(x-1) =$$
$$3x^3 - 3x^2 + 5x^2 - 5x =$$
$$3x^3 + 2x^2 - 5$$

34. How to FACTOR certain POLYNOMIALS

Learn to spot these classic factorables:

$$ab + ac = a(b+c)$$
$$a^2 + 2ab + b^2 = (a+b)^2$$
$$a^2 - 2ab + b^2 = (a-b)^2$$
$$a^2 - b^2 = (a-b)(a+b)$$

KAPLAN

35. How to solve for one variable IN TERMS OF ANOTHER

To find x "in terms of" y: isolate x on one side, leaving y as the only variable on the other.

36. How to solve an INEQUALITY

Treat it much like an equation—adding, subtracting, multiplying, and dividing both sides by the same thing. Just remember to reverse the inequality sign if you multiply or divide by a negative quantity.

Example: Rewrite $7 - 3x > 2$ in its simplest form

Setup: $7 - 3x > 2$.
Subtract 7 from both sides:
$7 - 3x - 7 > 2 - 7$
So $-3x > -5$. Now divide both sides by -3, and remember to reverse the inequality sign:
$x < \dfrac{5}{3}$

37. How to handle ABSOLUTE VALUES

The *absolute value* of a number n, denoted by $|n|$, is defined as n if $n \geq 0$ and $-n$ if $n < 0$. The absolute value of a number is the distance from zero to the number on the number line:

$|-5| = 5$

If $|x| = 3$, then x could be 3 or -3.

Example: If $|x - 3| < 2$, what is the range of possible values for x?

Setup: $|x - 3| < 2$, so $(x - 3) < 2$ and $-(x - 3) < 2$
So $x - 3 < 2$ and $x - 3 > -2$
So $x < 2 + 3$ and $x > -2 + 3$
So $x < 5$ and $x > 1$
So $1 < x < 5$

KAPLAN

38. How to TRANSLATE ENGLISH INTO ALGEBRA

Look for the key words and systematically turn phrases into algebraic expressions and sentences into equations.

Here's a table of key words that you may have to translate into mathematical terms:

Operation	Key Words
Addition	sum, plus, and, added to, more than, increased by, combined with, exceeds, total, greater than
Subtraction	difference between, minus, subtracted from, decreased by, diminished by, less than, reduced by
Multiplication	of, product, times, multiplied by, twice, double, triple, half
Division	quotient, divided by, per, out of, ratio of __ to __
Equals	equals, is, was, will be, the result is, adds up to, costs, is the same as

KAPLAN

39. How to find an ANGLE formed by INTERSECTING LINES

Vertical angles are equal. Adjacent angles add up to 180°.

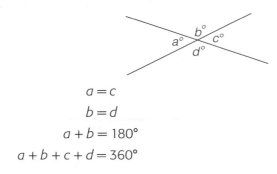

$$a = c$$
$$b = d$$
$$a + b = 180°$$
$$a + b + c + d = 360°$$

40. How to find an angle formed by a TRANSVERSAL across PARALLEL LINES

All the acute angles are equal. All the obtuse angles are equal. An acute plus an obtuse equals 180°.

Example:

ℓ_1 is parallel to ℓ_2
$$e = g = p = r$$
$$f = h = q = s$$
$$e + q = g + s = 180°$$

41. How to find the AREA of a TRIANGLE

$$Area = \frac{1}{2}(base)(height)$$

Example:

Setup: $Area = \frac{1}{2}(8)(5) = 20$

42. How to work with ISOSCELES TRIANGLES

Isosceles triangles have two equal sides and two equal angles. If a GMAT question tells you that a triangle is isoceles, you can bet that you'll need to use that information to find the length of a side or a measure of an angle.

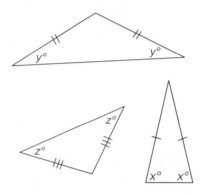

43. How to work with EQUILATERAL TRIANGLES

Equilateral triangles have three equal sides and three 60° angles. If a GMAT question tells you that a triangle is equilateral, you can bet that you'll need to use that information to find the length of a side or a measure of an angle.

44. How to work with SIMILAR TRIANGLES

In similar triangles, corresponding angles are equal and corresponding sides are proportional. If a GMAT question tells you that triangles are similar, you'll probably need that information to find the length of a side or the measure of an angle.

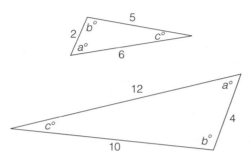

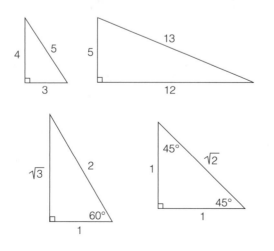

45. How to find the HYPOTENUSE or a LEG of a RIGHT TRIANGLE

Pythagorean theorem: $a^2 + b^2 = c^2$

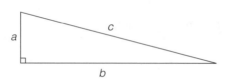

46. How to spot SPECIAL RIGHT TRIANGLES

3-4-5
5-12-13
30-60-90
45-45-90

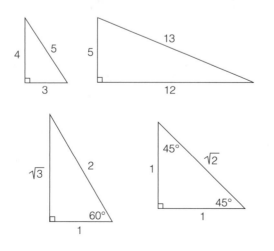

47. How to find the PERIMETER of a RECTANGLE

Perimeter = 2(length + width)

Example:

Setup: Perimeter = 2(2 + 5) = 14

48. How to find the AREA of a RECTANGLE

Area = (length)(width)

Example:

Setup: Area = 2 × 5 = 10

49. How to find the AREA of a SQUARE

Area = (side)²

Example:

Setup: Area = 3^2 = 9

50. How to find the AREA of a PARALLELOGRAM

Area = (base)(height)

Example:

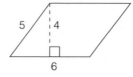

Setup: Area = 6 × 4 = 24

51. How to find the AREA of a TRAPEZOID

A trapezoid is a quadrilateral having only two parallel sides. You can always drop a line or two to break the figure into a rectangle and a triangle or two triangles. Use the area formulas for those familiar shapes. You could also apply the general formula for the area of a trapezoid:

Area = (Average of parallel sides) × (height)

Example:

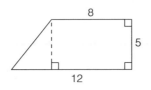

Setup: Area of rectangle = 8 × 5 = 40

Area of triangle = $\frac{1}{2}(4 \times 5) = 10$

Area of trapeziod = 40 + 10 = 50

52. How to find the CIRCUMFERENCE of a CIRCLE

Circumference = 2πr

Example:

Setup: Circumference = 2π(5) = 10π

53. How to find the AREA of a CIRCLE

Area = πr^2

Example:

Setup: Area = π × 5² = 25π

KAPLAN

54. How to find the DISTANCE BETWEEN POINTS on the coordinate plane

If two points have the same x's or the same y's—that is, they make a line segment that is parallel to an axis—all you have to do is subtract the numbers that are different.

Example: What is the distance from (2, 3) to (−7, 3)?

   Setup: The y's are the same, so just subtract the x's.
      $2 - (-7) = 9$

If the points have different x's and different y's, make a right triangle and use the Pythagorean theorem.

Example: What is the distance from (2, 3) to (−1, −1)?

   Setup:

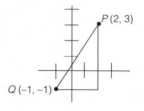

    It's a 3-4-5 triangle!
    $PQ = 5$

55. How to find the SLOPE of a LINE

$$Slope = \frac{rise}{run} = \frac{change\ in\ y}{change\ in\ x}$$

Example: What is the slope of the line that contains the points (1, 2) and (4, −5)?

   Setup: $Slope = \frac{-5-2}{4-1} = \frac{-7}{3}$

LEVEL 3 (Math You Might Find Difficult)

56. How to determine COMBINED PERCENT INCREASE/DECREASE

Start with 100 and see what happens.

Example: A price rises by 10 percent one year and by 20 percent the next. What's the combined percent increase?

Setup: Say the original price is $100.

Year one:
$100 + (10% of 100) = 100 + 10 = 110.

Year two:
110 + (20% of 110) = 110 + 22 = 132.

From 100 to 132—That's a 32 percent increase.

57. How to find the ORIGINAL WHOLE before percent increase/decrease

Think of a 15 percent increase over x as $1.15x$ and set up an equation.

Example: After decreasing by 5 percent, the population is now 57,000. What was the original population?

Setup: $0.95 \times$ (Original Population) $= 57,000$
Original Population $= 57,000 \div 0.95 = 60,000$

58. How to solve a SIMPLE INTEREST problem

With simple interest, the interest is computed on the principal only and is given by:

interest = (principal) × (interest rate*) × (time**)

   * expressed as a decimal

  ** expressed in years

Example: If $12,000 is invested at 6 percent simple annual interest, how much interest is earned after 9 months?

Setup: $(12,000) \times (0.06) \times \left(\dfrac{9}{12}\right) = \$540$

KAPLAN

59. How to solve a COMPOUND INTEREST problem

If interest is compounded, the interest is computed on the principal as well as on any interest earned. To compute compound interest:

$$(\text{final balance}) = (\text{principal}) \times \left(1 + \frac{\text{interest rate}}{C}\right)^{(\text{time})(C)}$$

where C = the number of times compounded annually

Example: If $10,000 is invested at 8 percent annual interest, compounded semiannually, what is the balance after 1 year?

Setup: Final balance

$$= (10,000) \times \left(1 + \frac{0.08}{2}\right)^{(1)(2)}$$
$$= (10,000) \times (1.04)^2$$
$$= \$10,816$$

60. How to solve a REMAINDERS problem

Pick a number that fits the given conditions and see what happens.

Example: When n is divided by 7, the remainder is 5. What is the remainder when $2n$ is divided by 7?

Setup: Find a number that leaves a remainder of 5 when divided by 7. A good choice would be 12. If $n = 12$, then $2n = 24$, which, when divided by 7, leaves a remainder of 3.

61. How to solve a DIGITS problem

Use a little logic—and some trial and error.

Example: If A, B, C, and D represent distinct digits in the addition problem below, what is the value of D ?

$$
\begin{array}{r}
AB \\
+ BA \\
\hline
CDC
\end{array}
$$

Setup: Two 2-digit numbers will add up to at most something in the 100s, so $C = 1$. B plus A in the units' column gives a 1, and since it can't simply be that $B + A = 1$, it must be that $B + A = 11$, and a 1 gets carried. In fact, A and B can be any pair of digits that add up to 11 (3 and 8, 4 and 7, etcetera), but it doesn't matter what they are, they always give you the same thing for D:

$$
\begin{array}{r}
47 \\
+74 \\
\hline
121
\end{array}
\qquad
\begin{array}{r}
83 \\
+38 \\
\hline
121
\end{array}
$$

62. How to find a WEIGHTED AVERAGE

Give each term the appropriate "weight."

Example: The girls' average score is 30. The boys' average score is 24. If there are twice as many boys as girls, what is the overall average?

Setup: Weighted Avg. $= \dfrac{1 \times 30 + 2 \times 24}{3} = \dfrac{78}{3} = 26$

HINT: Don't just average the averages.

63. How to find the NEW AVERAGE when a number is added or deleted

Use the sum of the terms of the old average to help you find the new average.

Example: Michael's average score after four tests is 80. If he scores 100 on the fifth test, what's his new average?

Setup: Find the original sum from the original average:

Original sum $= 4 \times 80 = 320$

Add the fifth score to make the new sum:

New sum $= 320 + 100 = 420$

Find the new average from the new sum:

New average $= \dfrac{420}{5} = 84$

64. How to use the ORIGINAL AVERAGE and NEW AVERAGE to figure out WHAT WAS ADDED OR DELETED

Use the sums.

Number added = (new sum) − (original sum)
Number deleted = (original sum) − (new sum)

Example: The average of five numbers is 2. After one number is deleted, the new average is −3. What number was deleted?

Setup: Find the original sum from the original average:
Original sum $= 5 \times 2 = 10$

Find the new sum from the new average:
New sum $= 4 \times (-3) = -12$

The difference between the original sum and the new sum is the answer.
Number deleted $= 10 - (-12) = 22$

65. How to find an AVERAGE RATE

Convert to totals.

$$Average\ A\ per\ B = \frac{Total\ A}{Total\ B}$$

Example: If the first 500 pages have an average of 150 words per page, and the remaining 100 pages have an average of 450 words per page, what is the average number of words per page for the entire 600 pages?

Setup: Total pages = 500 + 100 = 600
Total words = 500 × 150 + 100 × 450 = 120,000

$$Average\ words\ per\ page = \frac{120,000}{600} = 200$$

To find an average speed, you also convert to totals.

$$Average\ speed = \frac{Total\ distance}{Time}$$

Example: Rosa drove 120 miles one way at an average speed of 40 miles per hour and returned by the same 120-mile route at an average speed of 60 miles per hour. What was Rosa's average speed for the entire 240-mile round trip?

Setup: To drive 120 miles at 40 mph takes 3 hours. To return at 60 mph takes 2 hours. The total time, then, is 5 hours.

$$Average\ speed = \frac{240\ miless}{5\ hours} = 48\ mph$$

66. How to solve a WORK PROBLEM

In a work problem, you are given the rate at which people or machines perform work individually, and asked to compute the rate at which they work together (or vice versa). The work formula states: The inverse of the time it would take everyone working together equals the sum of the inverses of the times it would take each working individually. In other words:

$$\frac{1}{r} + \frac{1}{s} = \frac{1}{t}$$

where r and s are, for example, the number of hours it would take Rebecca and Sam, respectively to complete a job working by themselves, and t is the number of hours it would take the two of them working together.

Example: If it takes Joe 4 hours to paint a room and Pete twice as long to paint the same room, how long would it take the two of them, working together, to paint the same room, if each of them works at his respective individual rate?

Setup: Joe takes 4 hours, so Pete takes 8 hours; thus:

$$\frac{1}{4} + \frac{1}{8} = \frac{1}{t}$$

$$\frac{2}{8} + \frac{1}{8} = \frac{1}{t}$$

$$\frac{3}{8} = \frac{1}{t}$$

$$t = \frac{1}{\left(\frac{3}{8}\right)} = \frac{8}{3}$$

So it would take them $\frac{8}{3}$ hours, or 2 hours 40 minutes, to paint the room together.

67. How to determine a COMBINED RATIO

Multiply one or both ratios by whatever you need to in order to get the terms they have in common to match.

Example: The ratio of a to b is 7:3. The ratio of b to c is 2:5. What is the ratio of a to c?

Setup: Multiply each member of $a:b$ by 2 and multiply each member of $b:c$ by 3 and you get $a:b = 14:6$ and $b:c = 6:15$. Now that the b's match, you can just take a and c and say $a:c = 14:15$.

KAPLAN

68. How to solve a DILUTION or MIXTURE problem

In dilution or mixture problems, you have to determine the characteristics of the resulting mixture when substances with different characteristics are combined. Or, alternatively, you have to determine how to combine substances with different characteristics to produce a desired mixture. There are two approaches to such problems—the straightforward setup and the balancing method.

Example: If 5 pounds of raisins that cost $1.00 per pound are mixed with 2 pounds of almonds that cost $2.40 per pound, what is the cost per pound of the resulting mixture?

Setup: The straightforward setup:
$$(\$1.00)(5) + (\$2.40)(2) = \$9.80$$
The cost per pound is $n = \$\dfrac{9.80}{7} = \$1.40$

Example: How many liters of a solution that is 10 percent alcohol by volume must be added to 2 liters of a solution that is 50 percent alcohol by volume to create a solution that is 15 percent alcohol by volume?

Setup: The balancing method: Make the weaker and stronger (or cheaper and more expensive, etc.) substances balance. That is: (percent/price difference between the weaker solution and the desired solution) × (amount of weaker solution) = (percent/price difference between the stronger solution and the desired solution) × (amount of stronger solution).

In this case: $n(15 - 10) = 2(50 - 15)$
$$n \times 5 = 2(35)$$
$$n = \frac{70}{5} = 14$$

So 14 liters of the 10 percent solution must be added.

69. How to solve a GROUP problem involving BOTH/NEITHER

Some GMAT word problems involve two groups with overlapping members, and possibly elements that belong to neither group. It's easy to identify this type of question because the words "both" and/or "neither" appear in the question. These problems are quite easy if you just memorize the following formula:

Group1 + Group2 + Neither − Both = Total

Example: Of the 120 students at a certain language school, 65 are studying French, 51 are studying Spanish, and 53 are studying neither language. How many are studying both French and Spanish?

Setup: $65 + 51 + 53 - \text{Both} = 120$
$169 - \text{Both} = 120$
$\text{Both} = 49$

70. How to solve a GROUP problem involving EITHER/OR CATEGORIES

Other GMAT word problems involve groups with distinct "either/or" categories (male/female, blue collar/white collar, etc.). The key to solving this type of problem is to organize the information in a grid.

Example: At a certain professional conference with 130 attendees, 94 of the attendees are doctors and the rest are dentists. If 48 of the attendees are women, and $\frac{1}{4}$ of the dentists in attendance are women, how many of the attendees are male doctors?

Setup: To complete the grid, each row and column adds up to the corresponding total:

	Doctors	Dentists	Total
Male	55	27	82
Female		9	48
Total	94	36	130

After you've filled in the information from the question, simply fill in the remaining boxes until you get the number you are looking for—in this case, that 55 of the attendees are male doctors.

71. How to work with FACTORIALS

You may see a problem involving factorial notation. If *n* is an integer greater than 1, then *n* factorial, denoted by *n*!, is defined as the product of all the integers from 1 to *n*. In other words:

$2! = 2 \times 1 = 2$

$3! = 3 \times 2 \times 1 = 6$

$4! = 4 \times 3 \times 2 \times 1 = 24$, etc.

By definition, $0! = 1! = 1$.

Also note: $6! = 6 \times 5! = 6 \times 5 \times 4!$, etc. Most GMAT factorial problems test your ability to factor and/or cancel.

Example: $\dfrac{8!}{6! \times 2!} = \dfrac{\cancel{8}^{4} \times 7 \times \cancel{6!}}{\cancel{6!} \times 2!}$

72. How to solve a PERMUTATION problem

Factorials are useful for solving questions about permutations, i.e., the number of ways to arrange elements sequentially. For instance, to figure out how many ways there are to arrange 7 items along a shelf, you would multiply the number of possibilities for the first position times the number of possibilities remaining for the second position, and so on—in other words: $7 \times 6 \times 5 \times 4 \times 3 \times 2 \times 1$, or 7!.

If you're asked to find the number of ways to arrange a smaller group that's being drawn from a larger group, you can either apply logic or you can use the permutation formula:

$$_nP_k = \frac{n!}{(n-k)!}$$

where $n = $ (# in the larger group) and $k = $ (# you're arranging).

Example: Five runners run in a race. The runners who come in first, second, and third place will win gold, silver, and bronze medals respectively. How many possible outcomes for gold, silver, and bronze medal winners are there?

Setup: Any of the 5 runners could come in first place, leaving 4 runners who could come in second place, leaving 3 runners who could come in third place, for a total of $5 \times 4 \times 3 = 60$ possible outcomes for gold, silver, and bronze medal winners. Or, using the formula:

$$_5P_3 = \frac{5!}{(5-3)!} = \frac{5!}{2!} = 5 \times 4 \times 3 = 60$$

73. How to solve a COMBINATION problem

If the order or arrangement of the smaller group that's being drawn from the larger group does NOT matter, you are looking for the numbers of combinations, and a different formula is called for:

$$_nC_k = \frac{n!}{k!(n-k)!}$$

Where n = (# in the larger group) and k = (# you're choosing)

Example: How many different ways are there to choose 3 delegates from 8 possible candidates?

Setup: $_8C_3 = \dfrac{8!}{3! \times 5!} = \dfrac{8 \times 7 \times 6 \times 5!}{3 \times 2 \times 1 \times 5!} = 56$

So there are 56 different possible combinations.

74. How to solve PROBABILITY problems where probabilities must be multiplied

Suppose that a random process is performed. Then there is a set of possible outcomes that can occur. An event is a set of possible outcomes. We are concerned with the probability of events.

When all the outcomes are all equally likely, the basic probability formula is

$$\text{Probability} = \frac{\text{Number of desired outcomes}}{\text{Number of possible outcomes}}.$$

Many hard probability questions involve finding the probability that several events occur. Let's consider first the case of the probability that two events occur. Call these two events A and B. The probability that both events occur is the probability that event A occurs multiplied by the probability that event B occurs given that event A occurred. The probability that B occurs given that A occurs is called the conditional probability that B occurs given that A occurs. Except when events A and B do not depend on one another, the probability that B occurs given that A occurs is not the same as the probability that B occurs.

The probability that three events A, B, and C occur is the probability that A occurs multiplied by the conditional probability that B occurs given that A occurred multiplied by the conditional probability that C occurs given that both A and B have occurred.

This can be generalized to n events, where n is a positive integer greater than 3.

KAPLAN

Example: If 2 students are chosen at random to run an errand from a class with 5 girls and 5 boys, what is the probability that both students chosen will be girls?

Setup: The probability that the first student chosen will be a girl is $\frac{5}{10} = \frac{1}{2}$, and since there would be girls and 5 boys left out of 9 students, the probability that the second student chosen will be a girl (given that the first student chosen is a girl) is $\frac{4}{9}$. Thus the probability that both students chosen will be girls is $\frac{1}{2} \times \frac{4}{9} = \frac{2}{9}$.

Let's consider another example where a random process is repeated.

Example: If a fair coin is tossed 4 times, what's the probability that at least 3 of the 4 tosses will be heads?

Setup: There are 2 possible outcomes for each toss, so after 4 tosses there are $2 \times 2 \times 2 \times 2 = 16$ possible outcomes.

We can list the different possible sequences where at least 3 of the 4 tosses are heads. These sequences are

HHHT
HHTH
HTHH
THHH
HHHH

Thus, the probability that at least 3 of the 4 tosses will come up heads is

$$\frac{\text{Number of favorable outcomes}}{\text{Number of possible outcomes}} = \frac{5}{16}.$$

We could have also solved this question using the combinations formula. The probability of a head is $\frac{1}{2}$ and the probability of a tail is $\frac{1}{2}$. The probability of any particular sequence of heads and tails resulting from 4 tosses is $\frac{1}{2} \times \frac{1}{2} \times \frac{1}{2} \times \frac{1}{2}$, which is $\frac{1}{16}$.

Suppose that the result each of the four tosses is recorded in each of the four spaces

_____   _____   _____   _____

Thus, we would record an H for head or a T for tails in each of the 4 spaces.

The number of ways of having exactly 3 heads among the 4 tosses is the number of ways of choosing 3 of the 4 spaces above to record an H for heads.

The number of ways of choosing 3 of the 4 spaces is

$$_4C_3 = \frac{4!}{3!(4-3)!} = \frac{4!}{3!(1)!} = \frac{4 \times 3 \times 2 \times 1}{3 \times 2 \times 1 \times 1} = 4.$$

The number of ways of having exactly 4 heads among the 4 tosses is 1.

If we use the combinations formula, using the definition that $0! = 1$, then

$$_4C_4 = \frac{4!}{4!(4-4)!} = \frac{4!}{4!(0)!} = \frac{4!}{4!0!} = \frac{4 \times 3 \times 2 \times 1}{4 \times 3 \times 2 \times 1 \times 1} = 1.$$

Thus, $_4C_3 = 4$ and $_4C_4 = 1$. So the number of different sequences containing at least 3 heads is $4 + 1 = 5$.

The probability of having at least 3 heads is $\frac{5}{16}$.

75. How to deal with STANDARD DEVIATION

Like mean, mode, median, and range, standard deviation is a term used to describe sets of numbers. Standard deviation is a measure of how spread out a set of numbers is (how much the numbers deviate from the mean). The greater the spread, the higher the standard deviation. You'll never actually have to calculate the standard deviation on Test Day, but here's how it's calculated:

- Find the average (arithmetic mean) of the set.

- Find the differences between the mean and each value in the set.

- Square each of the differences.

- Find the average of the squared differences.

- Take the positive square root of the average.

Although you won't have to calculate standard deviation on the GMAT, you may be asked to compare standard deviations between sets of data, or otherwise demonstrate that you understand what standard deviation means.

Example: High temperatures, in degrees Fahrenheit, in 2 cities over 5 days:

September	1	2	3	4	5
City A	54	61	70	49	56
City B	62	56	60	67	65

For the 5-day period listed, which city had the greater standard deviation in high temperatures?

Setup: Even without trying to calculate them out, one can see that City A has the greater spread in temperatures, and therefore the greater standard deviation in high temperatures. If you were to go ahead and calculate the standard deviations following the steps described above, you would find that the standard deviation in high temperatures for City $A = \sqrt{\frac{254}{5}} \approx 7.1$, while the standard deviation for City $B = \sqrt{\frac{74}{5}} \approx 3.8$.

76. How to MULTIPLY/DIVIDE POWERS

Add/subtract the exponents.

Example: $x^a \times x^b = x^{a+b}$
$2^3 \times 2^4 = 2^7$

Example: $\dfrac{x^c}{x^d} = x^{c-d}$
$\dfrac{5^6}{5^2} = 5^4$

77. How to RAISE A POWER TO A POWER TO AN EXPONENT

Multiply the exponents.

Example: $(x^a)^b = x^{ab}$
$(3^4)^5 = 3^{20}$

78. How to handle POWERS with a base of ZERO and POWERS with an EXPONENT of ZERO

Zero raised to any nonzero exponent equals zero.

Example: $0^4 = 0^{12} = 0^1 = 0$
Any nonzero number raised to the exponent 0 equals 1.

Example: $3^0 = 15^0 = (0.34)^0 = -345^0 = \pi^0 = 1$
The lone exception is 0 raised to the 0 power, which is *undefined*.

79. How to handle NEGATIVE POWERS

A number raised to the exponent $-x$ is the reciprocal of that number raised to the exponent x.

Example: $5^{-3} = \dfrac{1}{5^3} = \dfrac{1}{5 \times 5 \times 5} = \dfrac{1}{125}$

$n^{-1} = \dfrac{1}{n}, n^{-2} = \dfrac{1}{n^2}$, and so on.

80. How to handle FRACTIONAL POWERS

Fractional exponents relate to roots. For instance, $x^{\frac{1}{2}} = \sqrt{x}$.
Likewise, $x^{\frac{1}{3}} = \sqrt[3]{x}, x^{\frac{2}{3}} = \sqrt[3]{x^2}$, and so on.

Example: $4^{\frac{1}{2}} = \sqrt{4} = 2$

$(x^{-2})^{\frac{1}{2}} = x^{(-2)\left(\frac{1}{2}\right)} = x^{-1} = \dfrac{1}{x}$

81. How to handle CUBE ROOTS

The cube root of x is just the number that multiplied by itself 3 times (i.e., cubed) gives you x. Both positive and negative numbers have one and only one cube root, denoted by the symbol $\sqrt[3]{}$, and the cube root of a number is always the same sign as the number itself.

Example: $(-5) \times (-5) \times (-5) = -125$, so $\sqrt[3]{-125} = -5$

$$\frac{1}{2} \times \frac{1}{2} \times \frac{1}{2} = \frac{1}{8}, \text{ so } \sqrt[3]{\frac{1}{8}} = \frac{1}{2}$$

82. How to ADD, SUBTRACT, MULTIPLY, and DIVIDE ROOTS

You can add/subtract roots only when the parts inside the $\sqrt{}$ are identical.

Example: $\sqrt{2} + 3\sqrt{2} = 4\sqrt{2}$
$\sqrt{2} - 3\sqrt{2} = -2\sqrt{2}$

$\sqrt{2} + \sqrt{3}$ cannot be combined.

To multiply/divide roots, deal with what's inside the $\sqrt{}$ and outside the $\sqrt{}$ separately.

Example: $(2\sqrt{3})(7\sqrt{5}) = (2 \times 7)(\sqrt{3 \times 5}) = 14\sqrt{15}$

$$\frac{10\sqrt{21}}{5\sqrt{3}} = \frac{10}{5}\sqrt{\frac{21}{3}} = 2\sqrt{7}$$

83. How to SIMPLIFY A RADICAL

Look for perfect squares (4, 9, 16, 25, 36…) inside the $\sqrt{}$. Factor them out and "unsquare" them.

Example: $\sqrt{48} = \sqrt{16} \times \sqrt{3} = 4\sqrt{3}$
$\sqrt{180} = \sqrt{36} \times \sqrt{5} = 6\sqrt{5}$

84. How to solve certain QUADRATIC EQUATIONS

Forget the quadratic formula. Manipulate the equation (if necessary) into the "____ $= 0$" form, factor the left side, and break the quadratic into two simple equations.

Example: $x^2 + 6 = 5x$
$x^2 - 5x + 6 = 0$
$(x - 2)(x - 3) = 0$
$x - 2 = 0$ or $x - 3 = 0$
$x = 2$ or 3

Example: $x^2 = 9$
$x = 3$ or -3

KAPLAN

85. How to solve MULTIPLE EQUATIONS

When you see two equations with two variables on the GMAT, they're probably easy to combine in such a way that you get something closer to what you're looking for.

Example: If $5x - 2y = -9$ and $3y - 4x = 6$, what is the value of $x + y$?

Setup: The question doesn't ask for x and y separately, so don't solve for them separately if you don't have to. Look what happens if you just rearrange a little and "add" the equations:

$$\begin{aligned} 5x - 2y &= -9 \\ -4x + 3y &= -6 \\ \hline x + y &= -3 \end{aligned}$$

86. How to solve a SEQUENCE problem

The notation used in sequence problems scares many test takers, but these problems aren't as bad as they look. In a sequence problem, the nth term in the sequence is generated by performing an operation, which will be defined for you, on either n or on the previous term in the sequence. Familiarize yourself with sequence notation and you should have no problem.

Example: What is the positive difference between the fifth and fourth terms in the sequence 0, 4, 18, … whose nth term is $n^2(n - 1)$?

Setup: Use the operation given to come up with the values for your terms:

$$n_5 = 5^2(5 - 1) = 25(4) = 100$$
$$n_4 = 4^2(4 - 1) = 16(3) = 48$$

So the positive difference between the fifth and fourth terms is $100 - 48 = 52$.

87. How to solve a FUNCTION problem

You may see classic function notation on the GMAT. An algebraic expression of only one variable may be defined as a function, f or g, of that variable.

Example: What is the minimum value of the function $f(x) = x^2 - 1$?

Setup: In the function $f(x) = x^2 - 1$, if x is 1, then $f(1) = 1^2 - 1 = 0$. In other words, by inputting 1 into the function, the output $f(x) = 0$. Every number inputted has one and only one output (although the reverse is not necessarily true). You're asked to find the minimum value, so how would you minimize the expression $f(x) = x^2 - 1$? Since x^2 cannot be negative, in this case $f(x)$ is minimized by making $x = 0$: $f(0) = 0^2 - 1 = -1$, so the minimum value of the function is -1.

88. How to handle GRAPHS of FUNCTIONS

You may see problem that involves a function graphed onto the *xy*-coordinate plane, often called a "rectangular coordinate system" on the GMAT. When graphing a function, the output, *f(x)*, becomes the *y*-coordinate. For example, in the previous example, $f(x) = x^2 - 1$, you've already determined 2 points, (1, 0) and (0, −1). If you were to keep plugging in numbers to determine more points and then plotted those points on the *xy*-coordinate plane, you would come up with something like this:

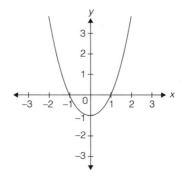

This curved line is called a *parabola*. In the event that you should see a parabola on the GMAT (it could be upside down or more narrow or wider than the one shown), you will most likely be asked to choose which equation the parabola is describing. These questions can be surprisingly easy to answer. Pick out obvious points on the graph, such as (1, 0) and (0, −1) above, plug these values into the answer choices, and eliminate answer choices that don't jibe with those values until only one answer choice is left.

KAPLAN

89. How to handle LINEAR EQUATIONS

You may also encounter linear equations on the GMAT. A linear equation is often expressed in the form

$y = mx + b$, where:

- $m = $ the slope of the line $= \dfrac{rise}{run}$.

   For instance, a slope of 3 means that the line rises 3 steps for every 1 step it makes to the right. A positive slope slopes up from left to right. A negative slope slopes down from left to right. A slope of zero (e.g., $y = 5$) is a flat line.
- $b = $ the y-intercept (where the line passes the y-axis).

Example: The graph of the linear equation $y = -\dfrac{3}{4}x + 3$ is:

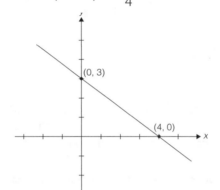

   Note: The equation above could also be written in the form $3x + 4y = 12$.

To get a better handle on an equation written in this form, you can solve for y to write it in its more familiar form. Or, if you're asked to choose which equation the line is describing, you can pick obvious points such as (0, 3) and (4, 0) above, and use these values to eliminate answer choices until only one answer is left.

90. How to find the x- and y-INTERCEPTS of a line

The x-intercept of a line is the value of x where the line crosses the x-axis. In other words, it's the value of x when $y = 0$. Likewise, the y-intercept is the value of y where the line crosses the y-axis, i.e., the value of y when $x = 0$. The y-intercept is also the value b when the equation is in the form: $y = mx + b$. For instance, in the line shown in the previous example, the x-intercept is 4 and the y-intercept is 3.

91. How to find the MAXIMUM and MINIMUM lengths for a SIDE of a TRIANGLE

If you know $n =$ the lengths of two sides of a triangle, you know that the third side is between the positive difference and the sum.

Example: The length of one side of a triangle is 7. The length of another side is 3. What is the range of possible lengths for the third side?

Setup: The third side is greater than the difference ($7 - 3 = 4$) and less than the sum ($7 + 3 = 10$).

92. How to find one angle or the sum of all the ANGLES of a REGULAR POLYGON

Sum of the interior angles in a polygon with n sides =

$(n - 2) \times 180$

Degree measure of one angle in a regular polygon with

n sides $= \dfrac{(n - 2) \times 180}{n}$

Example: What is the measure of one angle of a regular pentagon?

Setup: Plug $n = 5$ into the formula:
Degree measure of one angle =

$$\frac{(5 - 2) \times 180}{5} = \frac{540}{5} = 108$$

93. How to find the LENGTH of an ARC

Think of an arc as a fraction of the circle's circumference.

Length of $arc = \dfrac{n}{360} \times 2\pi r$

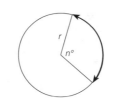

94. How to find the AREA of a SECTOR

Think of a sector as a fraction of the circle's area.

Area of sector $= \dfrac{n}{360} \times \pi r^2$

95. How to find the dimensions or area of an INSCRIBED or CIRCUMSCRIBED FIGURE

Look for the connection. Is the diameter the same as a side or a diagonal?

Example: If the area of the square is 36, what is the circumference of the circle?

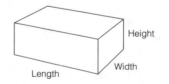

Setup: To get the circumference, you need the diameter or radius. The circle's diameter is also the square's diagonal, which (the diagonal creates two 45-45-90 triangles!) is $6\sqrt{2}$.

Circumference $= \pi(\text{diameter}) = 6\pi\sqrt{2}$

96. How to find the VOLUME of a RECTANGULAR SOLID

Volume = length × width × height

KAPLAN

97. How to find the SURFACE AREA of a RECTANGULAR SOLID

To find the surface area of a rectangular solid, you have to find the area of each face and add them together. Here's the formula:

Surface area = 2(*length* × *width* + *length* × *height* + *width* × *height*)

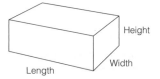

98. How to find the DIAGONAL of a RECTANGULAR SOLID

Use the Pythagorean theorem twice, unless you spot "special" triangles.

Example: What is the length of *AG*?

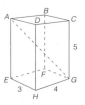

Setup: Draw diagonal AC.

ABC is a 3-4-5 triangle, so *AC* = 5. Now look at triangle *ACG*:

ACG is another special triangle, so you don't need to use the Pythagorean theorem. *ACG* is a 45-45-90, so *AG* = 5√2.

KAPLAN

99. How to find the VOLUME of a CYLINDER

Volume $= \pi r^2 h$

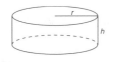

100. How to find the VOLUME of a SPHERE

Volume $= \frac{4}{3}\pi r^3$

NOTES

NOTES

NOTES

NOTES

NOTES

NOTES

KAPLAN) TEST PREP AND ADMISSIONS

Looking for more comprehensive GMAT* prep?

Premium Online	Classroom Course	Private Tutoring
Flexible. On Demand.	Structured. Dynamic.	Exclusive. Personalized.

Ultimate practice test	Only Kaplan students take a computer-adaptive practice test at an actual GMAT testing facility.
Expert instructors	▸ Top scoring and expertly trained ▸ Cover the most frequently tested concepts
Quality study materials	▸ Performance-based study plan for each student ▸ Comprehensive course book and extensive online resources ▸ Advanced content for those targeting 700+
Proven results	We're so confident that our programs will help you score higher, we guarantee it or your money back

Enroll today!

1-800-KAP-TEST | kaptest.com/gmat

Higher test score guaranteed or your money back.

*GMAT is a registered trademark of the Graduate Management Admission Council. Kaplan materials do not contain actual GMAT items and are neither endorsed by nor affiliated in any way with GMAC. **Conditions and restrictions apply. For complete guarantee eligibility requirements, visit kaptest.com/hsg. The Higher Score Guarantee applies only to Kaplan courses taken and completed within the United States, Puerto Rico, Canada, Mexico, the United Kingdom, and France.

TEST PREP AND ADMISSIONS

Submit your business school applications with confidence!

Kaplan's Admissions Consulting team has helped its clients earn acceptance to every top U.S. business school. Our business school clients have received hundreds of thousands of dollars in scholarships.

For more information and to enroll, call today!

1-800-KAP-TEST | **kaptest.com/businessadmissions**

![KAPLAN) TEST PREP AND ADMISSIONS]

Want more practice for the GMAT*?

Build your own quizzes from 1,000+ online questions with Kaplan's GMAT Quiz Bank.

▶ **Target your practice**
Customize by question type, difficulty, and content.

▶ **Test your specific skills**
Take in Timed Mode or in Tutor Mode to see explanations as you work.

▶ **Track your progress**
Receive instant performance reports and get detailed explanations.

▶ **Access at your convenience**
Available 24 hours a day, 7 days a week.

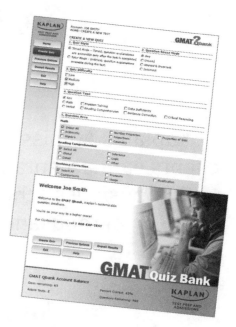

Supplement your prep with Kaplan's GMAT Quiz Bank—
only $199 for 3 months of access!

1-800-KAP-TEST | kaptest.com/gmatquizbank

*GMAT is a registered trademark of the Graduate Management Admission Council®. Kaplan materials do not contain actual GMAT items and are neither endorsed by nor affiliated in any way with GMAC.

It's time
to reach higher.

It's time to change your future.

Earn your MBA online.
Kaplan University makes the journey to the top a lot smoother. Acquire the credentials you need for career advancement, on a flexible schedule that works with, not against, your present job. Kaplan University's MBA classes are taught by real-world experts in a personalized, highly interactive online environment.

Master of Business Administration
- Specialize in finance; marketing; human resources management; information technology; entrepreneurship; or management, communication, and quality.

The Kaplan University/*Newsweek* MBA
- Get a unique global perspective from executives and entrepreneurs making business headlines, and the *Newsweek* journalists probing the stories behind them.
- Specialize in international business or health care management.

Get the Kaplan Advantage:
- Understand your financial options before you enroll
- 24/7 online technical support
- Never have to go to a building or stand in line
- Personal advisors to help decide from over 25 curricula, just a call away
- Kaplan University ranked #1 for quality and value in a survey of online students*

To find out more, visit us at www.ku-mba2.com or call 866.808.7405 (Toll Free)

Kaplan University is regionally accredited by The Higher Learning Commission (HLC) and a member of the North Central Association of Colleges and Schools (NCA). The HLC can be reached at www.ncahlc.org.

*February 2006 Higher Education Survey Report of current and former students of for-profit secondary institutions. For additional information, please go to www.kaplan.edu/ku/surveyresults.

online of course   Building FUTURES   KAPLAN UNIVERSITY